O PIONEER

Eyewitness Accounts of
American Settlers, Pioneers, and Explorers

BY
SUZANNE ALEXANDER

PublishAmerica

Baltimore

First printing

ISBN: 1-4137-2117-6
PUBLISHED BY PUBLISHAMERICA, LLLP
www.publishamerica.com
Baltimore

Printed in the United States of America

FOREWORD

O Pioneer is a collection of eyewitness accounts, narratives and articles of American western exploration and American West observations, originally written prior to the mid-1800s.

This book is divided into three sections: 1] accounts by trappers, explorers and settlers; 2] stories and events of western exploration; and 3] additional letters, articles, and observations that reflect the moral, ethical and physical struggles of American settlement and expansion.

As America grew many, but not all, explorers and settlers moved into territories occupied by other cultures without understanding the people they encountered. Some came with beliefs of inherent sovereignty over the land and its native people; others adopted an attitude of neighbor and partner, forming friendships and regard for the Native American communities that had lived on the land before them. Some Native American tribes embraced the newcomers and attempted peaceful coexistence; others feared them as intruders that threatened their land, possessions and way of life.

This book does not attempt to interpret the meaning of this turbulent time of history for the reader: rather, its intent is to provide "snapshots" – small windows of revelation into the varied feelings, experiences, fears and hopes of individuals who lived during the time.

The stories in *O Pioneer* detail achievements, failures, culture clashes and resulting tragedies, biases and judgments, moments of discovery and peace, instances of conflict and war, and the ability of a few individuals in a few instances to rise above time and circumstance and treat each other with respect.

These narratives and stories have been edited for grammar and style. A few of the selections have also been edited for tone, with every effort being made to preserve the original voice of the author. Every effort was made to provide varied perspectives in order to be true to the confusion, fear, courage, humanity, inhumanity, and hope of the times.

Suzanne Alexander

For Alex

The window of our past provides a vision for our future . . . How that vision is interpreted and applied depends entirely upon the witness:

> Education
> Understanding
> Apology
> Forgiveness
> Acceptance
> Tolerance
> Peace.
>
> —SA

TABLES OF CONTENTS

Tales of The Lost Trappers

Stories of The Great West

Eyewitness Accounts: Treaties, Culture & Wars

TALES OF THE LOST TRAPPERS

PREFACE

During a residence of three years, 1845 to 1847, in the upper part of the State of Missouri, I was occasionally employed in redeeming a promise made to an editor of a newspaper in Virginia, the state from which I emigrated. The promise was to send him, for his paper, such materials of a frontier character as I might be able to pick up, and as would form interesting communications for his columns.

When I took up my residence in Missouri, I found myself among a people much moved and stimulated by western enterprise; a people not only familiar with frontier scenes and events, but deeply interested in things far beyond the limits of their own state. Many of them I observed were engaged in the Santa Fe trade and were making their regular annual trips across the plains to New Mexico.

I frequently sought the company of such gentlemen, whom I found to be intelligent and kind, ready to share with me their experiences. Some of them, indeed all that I met with, would entertain me for hours with interesting accounts of their difficulties in the various expeditions in which they had been engaged. I made it a rule to note down all the important oral information that I was able to gain from our conversations.

Several gentlemen furnished me with a number of very interesting facts on paper, which were of great service to me in the book I now offer to the public. I soon found that the materials accumulated on my hands too fast, and in too great quantity to be published in a newspaper, at so great a distance. I also met with a number of men who had been to Oregon and California, and some who had spent several years in the Rocky Mountains. From these men, I drew a great many interesting facts, which are interwoven in this work.

The most interesting facts, however, that I was able to gather, I found in an old, musty, mutilated journal, kept by Captain Williams, and other papers furnished by Workman and Colonel Cooper, of Howard County, Missouri, giving an account of the expedition, the history of which makes the greater part of this volume. In my opinion, these papers were so badly written, and so defective in many respects that I aimed simply to get the facts, which I always then positioned in my own words.

Many of the most interesting facts that are interspersed throughout this work, I procured in conversation with gentlemen, who, as I have said, had spent years in the Rocky Mountains, and had traveled through Oregon and California. My reason for offering an account of Captain Williams' expedition to the public is that I believe that just at this time {1847} it would be interesting to the great majority of readers.

Indeed, any book detailing the trials and difficulties of those early explorers will be read with avidity. Any publication throwing any light on that vast wilderness between the States and the Pacific, and calculated to open its secrets, will be read with interest. Events are now transpiring, that throw around the regions of the far west an interest, which they never possessed before.

The Oregon question is settled, and our citizens are going there every summer season by the thousands. California is likely to become ours, and who will venture to limit the number of persons emigrating there, if it should be attached to our domain? A mail route from the States across the Rocky Mountains is talked of in high places, and among the great ones of our government; even the idea of a great railway across the Rocky Mountains has entered the minds of some. Our government will, doubtless, soon adopt measures to establish a cordon of military posts between the State of Missouri and the settlements established on the waters of the Columbia. Each one of those posts will be a nucleus around which our adventurous citizens will be sure to collect and form colonies that will expand and cover the whole land.

It may be said that such enterprises will be beset with dangers and trials and hardships, and these things will deter men from such undertakings. But these are the very exciting causes that will prompt men to bold adventure. Those frontier men are fond of excitement, and they desire to be surrounded by exciting circumstances. They are even fond of trials and hardships and dangers, for they stimulate and sustain.

Look at the trapper as he dashes into a wilderness full of danger, to pursue his favorite employment. He is conscious that his undertaking is very hazardous. He is aware that he is liable to be discovered by the Indians every day, and to be cut off. As he paddles about in his little canoe on some nameless stream, he expects every moment to be surprised by the hideous yells of ruthless foes, from whom no mercy can be expected. As he passes along through some solitary and dark ravine of the mountains, he sees the bones and grinning skulls of his brethren, who were waylaid by the Indians and fell by their cruel hand. He is compelled to keep his gun in his hands, night as well as day; nor does he dare for one moment to relax in his vigilance.

If he ventures to close his eyes in sleep, it is only to snatch a morsel of rest, and then to start up, perhaps to witness some new danger in his vicinity. This is a trapper's life—a life of sleepless vigilance and constant toil and danger, yet he prefers it to any other kind of life. A strange infatuation possesses him that makes him passionately fond of the excitement of the wilderness. He despises the dull uniformity and monotony of civilized life, when compared in his mind with the stirring scenes of wild western adventure.

The security and protection of the laws have no attraction for him; he wants no other means of defense than his rifle, which is his daily companion. He is impatient of the formalities and the galling restrictions of well-organized society, and prefers the latitude and liberty of a life in the woods. Seated by his fire in his camp, with a beaver tail spitted before him, or feasting upon his buffalo tongue, or buffalo beef, or buffalo marrow bones, with a piece of dry bark for a plate, he lives better and feels better, and enjoys his repast with a better zest than the citizen who is surrounded with all the comforts and luxuries of a metropolis.

As to the statements that I have made about California, I would mention that men furnished them whose veracity I had no right to mention. I have not seen that country. But if I had, and my account had been made from personal observation, my statements would have been those of one man only. I furnish that kind of representation of California, which speaks the larger portion of a majority of those who have been there. I collected quite a number of items in relation to the climate, fertility, and soil, and productions of that country which I withhold in this book, not that I disbelieve them, but because I was apprehensive that I might be regarded as imposing too heavy a tax on the credulity of my readers.

I know that many descriptions of the far west are too highly colored; that many people have been misled by them and are ready to deplore the hour they read them. But it seems to me that men ought to be able to distinguish those accounts that are extravagant and wild from those which are sober and wear the aspect of truth.

Again, there are many persons who will receive any thing as truth, that may be said about the many and superior advantages in the regions of the west. It is no wonder, then, that they are misled, and do not find things as they expected in those countries. I met with persons in Missouri who had moved to Oregon and California; but while there they became dissatisfied, and returned over a long journey of two thousand miles. I have also been informed that many are moving from Oregon to California, and from California to Oregon. This only proves that as long as there is any country ahead, or to which emigrants can go, there are some persons of unsettled and dissatisfied feelings who will always be traveling. I never ask information from such persons about the countries they may have seen.

As to all the representations then, in this volume, I honestly believe that they may be assumed all true, in which every confidence may be reposed by those who may read them.

David Coyner {1847}

Author of the original collection of narratives, "The Lost Trappers," which follows.

ACROSS THE ROCKY MOUNTAINS

As Lewis and Clark prepared to cross the Rocky mountains, it will be remembered that they endeavored, by all possible means, to assure the many Indian tribes in the far west of the kind feelings and intentions entertained towards them by the government of the United States. The desire of the government was to create and establish upon a permanent basis those friendly relations between the different tribes themselves and the United States, that were preferable to those constant hostilities that then existed. Friendly relations would prove a source of great and almost innumerable blessings and benefits to all parties.

To achieve this the more readily, that party took with them a considerable amount of merchandise, consisting of such articles as were most likely to please those rude and unpolished children of the forest. It was also the design of Lewis and Clark to impress them as far as they could with the number, strength and greatness of our people, that they might see the importance and advantage of always being at peace with such a people. To this end, on their return, they were anxious to bring with them to the States as many of the Chiefs of the different tribes as could be persuaded to accompany them. But in this they almost entirely failed, as the Indians generally were very suspicious and expressed their fears that those that might go would never return to their tribes.

Having wintered among the Mandan tribe on their way across the Rocky Mountains, (whose villages are high up the Missouri river,) the Lewis and Clark expedition to some extent had gained the confidence of that tribe. On their way home, they prevailed on one of the Mandan Chiefs, Big White, to go with them and take his wife and son to see our people and the President.

The Mandan nation at that time were at war with the Sioux, a numerous, war-like and formidable tribe, whose villages were below on the Missouri and who would intercept, if they could, any of the Mandan people going down the river and prevent them from going farther. This fact was a matter of much dread and anxiety to the Chief, Big White, and promised to be an insuperable barrier in the way, but Captain Lewis placed himself under every obligation to protect him and gave a pledge on behalf of his government that a company of armed men should guard the chief on his return to his tribe.

As this pledge was redeemed by the government of the United States, it is our purpose in this volume to give the history of the return expedition, the object of which was not only to guard the Mandan Chief to his home in the far west, but to explore the country on the waters of the Missouri, to trap for beaver, and even to penetrate and cross the Rocky Mountains.

It was in the spring of 1807 that this expedition set out from St. Louis. The party consisted of twenty men under the direction of Captain Ezekiel Williams, a man of great perseverance, patience and with an unflinching determination of character. His men were citizens of Missouri, which was at that early day an almost unbroken wilderness. They were all accustomed to the privations and hardships of a frontier life. Like most frontier men, they were fond of adventures and daring enterprises, were well skilled in the use of the rifle, and entertained a strong partiality for those hazards and exploits that are peculiar to a frontier and Indian life.

The outfit of each man was a rifle, together with as much powder and lead as it was supposed would last for two years. Each one took six traps, which were packed upon an extra horse which was furnished to each man. Pistols, awls, axes, knives, camp kettles, blankets and various other essential little articles also made a part of the equipage. Captain Williams provided himself with an assortment of light portable little notions intended as presents for the Indians. To the expedition also belonged four dogs—great favorites of their masters—one of which was a very superior greyhound taken along by his owner to catch deer on the plains.

On the 25th of April, the party started on their way, exhibiting all the glee, excitement and laughter of men enjoying the wild freedom of frontier life. They were expecting to pass through scenes of adventure and danger that would fully test their patience and courage and perhaps be marked by the effusion of blood.

At that season of the year, there was sufficient grass for their horses. As for the men, they intended to depend on their rifles for provisions. Captain Williams planned to reach Fort Mandan as early in the trapping season as practical, so the party abandoned the meanderings of the Missouri and launched forth into the seas of prairie south of that river. They had no other guide than that very imperfect knowledge which was then known of the country.

The expedition of Lewis and Clark was confined to the Missouri, as they went up and came down. The party headed by Captain Williams was the first overland expedition ever undertaken to and across the Rocky Mountains from the United States. Some of the party had been up the Missouri River some distance previously, trading with the Indians for furs, but none of the company had any personal knowledge of the country through which they were to pass on this particular expedition.

The difficulties they encountered were numerous and trying. However, they found the Mandan Chief, Big White, to be of great value to them as an observer. His timely suggestions and counsel often prevented the party from being entirely cut off. He always urged upon Captain Williams the great importance of constant vigilance day and night, the strictest attention to the position of their encampments and the situation of their horses. The Captain learned from him that the Indian, although generally inclined to surprise and assault, was not given to rash and careless adventure. The Indian would never attack a party that was prepared and on the alert.

They traveled about twenty-five miles each day. When night approached, they selected a position to camp where wood, water and grass were convenient. Large fires for the first eight or ten nights were kindled up, around which they gathered and roasted their fat venison, ate, laughed, talked and passed their rough jokes until they sank into the embraces of sleep. This unguarded and careless way of encamping, however, was abandoned when they entered the region of country home to the Indian and hostile bands of Indians, against whose assaults they found it necessary to guard at all times. For the first two hundred miles, game was not very abundant, although they killed enough to supply them with provisions.

About the twelfth day, the prairies seemed to enlarge and approach nearer the river. Timber was not so abundant. The face of the country improved and was much more interesting and the soil was evidently richer as they traveled westward. On the evening of the twelfth day, the party was encamped at the edge of a beautiful prairie about two hundred and forty miles from St. Louis, having crossed the Gasconade, the Osage, and several tributaries to the Missouri. Two very fine deer were killed by some of the company near the encampment, the blood and entrails of which attracted a band of hungry, saucy wolves nearby.

There were not less than twenty wolves of different sizes and color. There were also some of the smaller kind and they were crowded out of the feast, keeping up a very plaintive whine and howl. The dogs belonging to the company began to bark very fiercely, rushed out after them and pursued them around a point of timber; but as soon as they were out of sight, the wolves turned upon their pursuers and chased them back within a short distance of the camp. One of the dogs, the most resolute of the pack, in a bold attempt to stand his ground, was seized by as many as could get at him and was torn to pieces almost instantly.

That evening, one of the men set one of his traps. He baited it with a piece of venison hung on a bush immediately above the trap. In the morning, the venison and the trap were gone, much to the surprise and mortification of the inexperienced trapper, who, knowing little about the business, had not observed the precaution of fastening the trap to something permanent.

While breakfast was being prepared and horses were filling themselves with grass, the unlucky trapper went in quest of his trap. A wolf had been caught and as he dragged the trap along he left a very distinct trace in the grass, by which he was easily followed. The wolf had crept into a very thick patch of brush, which was made almost impenetrable by a rank growth of hazel. How was the trap to be recovered? The wolf was undoubtedly alive and it would be very hazardous to attempt to enter his place of refuge.

An effort was made to encourage the dogs to go in, but they recollected the rough fare they experienced the previous evening and would not go beyond the edge of the thicket. In the midst of his perplexities, the young trapper was relieved by the arrival of two of the company, one of whom climbed a pin-oak tree that stood in the edge of the brush. From the top of this tree, he had a fair view of the formidable occupant of the brush-patch. In this position, he shot the wolf with his rifle.

All danger being now removed, the dead wolf was dragged from his fastness, with one of his forefeet in the trap. He was of the largest kind and almost black. As there were no wolves to be seen on the prairie in the morning, it was feared that the one in the trap had led off the wolf pack—and that trap and wolf would not be seen again.

On the frontier, where wolves are very troublesome, the following expedient is sometimes resorted to, to drive them out of the country. Several fishhooks are tied together by their shanks with a silk thread and put in a piece of fresh meat, which is dropped where it is likely to be found by them. The hooks are buried completely in the meat and made very fast to prevent the wolf from shaking them off. Those acquainted with the habits of wolves state that this animal never eats a morsel of anything without first picking it up very cautiously and giving it a shake. When a piece of meat, baited so, is swallowed, the hooks generally stick fast in the throat, inflicting the most excruciating pain.

The unlucky wolf immediately begins to scratch and tear his neck and howl most piteously. In this condition he hurries away from the place of his great mishap, running, raving, scratching, and howling. Curiosity and sympathy, or some other feeling, equally active, prompts every other wolf in sight and in hearing, to follow the one injured. Away the pack goes, increasing its numbers, until every wolf in the vicinity follows. The pack can end up perhaps fifty miles from the place where the matter began.

On the evening of the fourteenth day of the expedition, which was the ninth of May, another little mishap took place creating some anxiety of mind and loss of time. Five of the horses were missing. The party at first believed the Indians had taken the horses, but they had not encountered any tribes, having not yet reached the country beset with danger. The horses, perhaps, had broken their fetters and straggled off.

Big White told them that their horses were not stolen; that Indians could have stolen all the horses as easily, if not more easily than five. If they had taken five, they would have taken all. This very reasonable suggestion of one well acquainted with the practices and customs of Indians prompted the men to make an effort to find them. Their trail was soon found in the grass and was made very plain by the dew. It led back the way the party came. The horses had, by some means, cleared themselves of their shackles and were now striking for home and it was not until evening that they were overtaken and brought back.

A day was lost, but the company was taught the importance of being more cautious, particularly at night. The Mandan Chief also took the occasion to raise concerns of his own. He told them that so far they had been on safe ground and that no harm had resulted from the absence of vigilance and caution, but that elsewhere, precautionary measures would be indispensable for their safety.

An Indian by birth and education, he knew the habits and practices of the different tribes in the far west much better than any of the party. Their journey was long, very long, and led through a country occupied by tribes that would waylay them in every ravine and watch their movements from the top of every hill in order to surprise them and take their equipage, horses, and perhaps scalps.

The counsel of the venerable warrior, delivered with great earnestness and Indian gravity, had its effect. The company adopted the plan of journeying until about an hour before sunset, when they came to a halt, relieved their horses of their burdens, and turned them out to grass. In the mean time, a fire was started, and food for the men prepared.

About dark the horses were brought in, and saddles and baggage placed upon them. The fires were renewed, the company would then spring into their saddles and push on some eight or ten miles further, where they would come to a second stop, relieve their horses of their burdens, tether them, and station their guards. They divided the night into four watches, with three men on each watch, while the others, wrapped up in their blankets, were resting upon the ground. Fires were not kept burning, as the light could be seen at a great distance on those extensive prairies, and might betray them into the hands of some lurking foe.

In the morning, some of the men moved the horses to fresh grass, that they might the more easily fill themselves, while others were expediting their morning routines and attending to the other concerns belonging to an encampment. By sunrise, they were generally going ahead.

Captain Williams In Kansas

In the journal before me, nothing noted is of much importance until they reached the Kansas River, a tributary of the Missouri River. This river rises in the plains west, and runs east into the Missouri. It is about three hundred and thirty yards wide. The party was able to ford it. When they were about ten miles from this river, they thought they saw several Indians, but soon lost sight of them.

As they approached the Kansas River they observed a great many horse tracks, some of which were very fresh, and several places where the Indians had killed buffalo. They were evidently in the neighborhood of Indian villages. Big White said they were the Kansas tribe, a fierce and warlike nation. They had lived higher up the Missouri, where they were involved in a number of unfortunate wars with some of the neighboring tribes, which almost resulted in their extinction. They had been negatively impacted and had lost quite a number of their braves. They were driven down toward the Kansas, about one hundred miles.

There were signs of buffalo and the men were anxious to engage in a buffalo hunt. Two antelope were seen on the prairies, wheeling and prancing about, and gazing upon the party with much curiosity. As the men had heard a great deal about the speed of this animal, a general desire was expressed to test the relative speed of the greyhound and the antelope, as an opportunity now presented itself. Accordingly, the dog was started, and the antelope allowed him to get within fifty yards of them. They then wheeled and put off with the space between them and the dog widening so fast that the latter stopped suddenly, apparently abashed and disappointed and returned to the company.

All descriptions of this beautiful animal represent its speed as not only very great, but equal, if not superior, to that of any other animal in the world. Its motions are very graceful and easy and made without any visible effort. It runs very level and as it moves over the plains, it seems to fly rather than run.

The company encamped about a mile and a half from the west side of the Kansas River, on the border of a prairie. They had not been there long before they saw a small party of Kansas Indians, passing not very far from the company. Some of the men approached them, making signs of friendship and induced them to come to the camp. They cast very inquisitive looks upon the white men and at first seemed rather alarmed, but the kindness of the party towards them soon dispelled their fears. With the aid of the Mandan Chief, who partially understood their language and acted as a kind of interpreter, Captain Williams learned that they belonged to the Kansas nation and had been out on a hunt to procure buffalo meat. They represented one of their villages as being about six miles down the Kansas River.

With a view of securing their friendship, Captain Williams gave them several little presents, with which they were greatly pleased. In return, they gave Captain Williams some buffalo meat, upon which his men feasted very heartily that night. Big White, acting on behalf of the company, sent word to the Chiefs that the party would visit their village the next day. It was deemed advisable by the men to take every pain to secure the horses and to be prepared for any emergency.

A very amusing circumstance occurred during the night. One of the men, who in all probability had overloaded his stomach with buffalo meat and whose mind, perhaps, had been haunted in day time by frightful visions of Indians, suddenly started up shouting, "Indians, Indians, Indians! Yonder they are! Shoot, shoot!" At the same time, he was running back and forth, making the most violent gestures. In a moment, all were wide-awake and in another moment all were in possession of their arms. The guard rushed in to see what was wrong. The very dogs partook of the excitement and barked fiercely. The frantic vociferations of the frightened man continued. "Indians! Indians! Indians!" "And where are they?" was asked everywhere.

It was soon discovered, however, that the fellow was asleep and dreaming; a camp-kettle full of water was thrown into his face, which brought him to his right mind. It was some time before quietude and sleep resumed their reign in the camp. The next morning, the frightened dreamer and his dream were quite a laughing stock and a matter of much amusement. As he was compelled to tell his dream, he said that he thought the company had come in contact with a band of hostile Indians, with whom they were about to have a difficulty, but his unpleasant dream was interrupted by the cold water that was thrown in his face.

After breakfast, the principal Chiefs and several of the warriors of the Kansas tribe came to the camp on horseback. Captain Williams received them with very marked respect and kindness. The pipe of peace was passed around. The object of the expedition was explained and Captain Williams gave several gifts to them. As they had heard of Big White going down with Lewis and Clark, they very much admired the conduct of the whites in being true to their promise by taking the Mandan Chief back to his people.

This circumstance induced them to have great confidence in the party and to place the most implicit faith in all their statements. The party agreed to accompany the Kansas to their village, as the men were generally anxious to join them in a buffalo hunt.

As they went to their village, the Kansas braves asked Big White a thousand questions about the country he had recently visited and seemed greatly interested with his answers. They gathered around him and received the information with a great deal of avidity. Captain Williams expressed a desire to salute the village with a round or two from their rifles. As the Kansas had a few firearms, they expressed a wish to return the salutes, but they had nothing to "make their arms talk," by this meaning they had no ammunition. Captain Williams therefore gave them some powder, with which one of their warriors hurried off to the village to make the necessary arrangements. When the party came in view of the village, all the women and children were out of their wigwams and looked wild and much affrighted.

Their men had advanced a little, out from the village, and from their few firearms answered to the salutes of Captain Williams' men. When this ceremony was over, by which the Chiefs and warriors seemed to feel themselves much honored, the party, including Big White and his wife and son, were conducted to lodges fitted up expressly for their reception. The pipe was passed around, according to a uniform practice among the tribes in the far west. Captain Williams renewed his efforts to secure their good will by distributing a few articles most likely to please them.

The kind feelings of the Kansas were manifested by serving the company with the best food they had and in great profusion, such as the meat of buffalo, deer and the antelope, beside several kinds of roots. Big White made a speech in which he alluded to the kindness with which he was received by his white brothers, and their riches, number and strength.

He advised the Kansas to cultivate the most friendly relations with his white brothers and their father, the President of the United States, as they would furnish his poor red brothers with everything they wanted; such as knives, guns, powder, lead, blankets, and whisky. He advised them to go and see their white brothers. Nearly the whole of the night was spent by the Kansas in putting questions to the Mandan people, particularly the Chief, about his trip to the land of the pale-faces.

Captain Williams and his party resolved to spend two or three days with this tribe, to take a buffalo hunt. Arrangements were made with the Kansas to take the hunt the next day. It had been reported that the plains were darkened with thousands and thousands of buffalo, not more than twenty miles from their village. The animals had not been frightened and were in all probability in the same neighborhood yet. Accordingly, early the next morning, ten Kansas hunters on horseback with spears and bows and arrows, with the same number of Captain Williams' men, set out for the buffalo ground. The Indians were not only good hunters they were very superior horsemen. Their horses too were familiarized to buffalo hunts and buffalo baits and well trained in all those dexterous movements to be practiced in a buffalo battle.

Not so with Captain Williams' men. Most of them had never seen a buffalo and their horses were as inexperienced as their riders. Horses are generally very much frightened the first time they are ridden into a hunt of this kind. Additionally, the men had to use rifles, which are a kind of arms too unwieldy and ponderous for such business. Inexperienced men, too, are very apt to become excited and run themselves into dangers from which it is difficult, if not impossible, to escape. Untried men upon untried horses, with unhandy arms and greatly excited in the bargain, are very apt to fail in their first attempts to kill buffalo, if they do not share a worse fate than simply a failure. For it often happens that horse and rider are killed.

After sweeping over the prairie for twelve miles, the hunting party came to a halt, to hold a conference about their future movements. They believed they were in the vicinity of the buffalo. Two of the Kansas hunters were sent ahead to scout the plains, and report by signs when they saw the buffalo. They set off at a brisk hard gallop upon their ponies, while the company moved along more at their leisure. In less than an hour, the two Kansas braves were seen on a hill, making signs that the buffalo were in view. The party rushed up and they saw thousands of buffalo within a mile, all quiet and feeding on the plains.

The men dismounted and girthed their saddles more securely, adjusted their arms for the attack, sprang again into their saddles, and in a few minutes were on the outskirts of the multitudinous herd. Each man selected his prey and dashed after it. The Indians picked out the males, as they were fatter than the cows, which at that season, had their calves.

26

In a moment the innumerable multitude were in motion, frightened by the horrible yelling of the Kansas Indians, men and horses, and buffalo were seen scattering in every direction. The very plains seemed to tremble; the rumbling sound created by the running of the buffalo resembled distant thunder and could be heard for many miles.

The Indians seemed to be perfectly at home when mounted on horseback and dashing among the buffalo, shooting their sharp-pointed arrows, and launching their spears. Their horses too seemed to understand the business. They would advance close up to the buffalo, and when they heard the twang of the bow that sped the arrow, they would wheel and bound off. When they perceived that they had shot an arrow and launched a spear in a fatal place, the Kansas would abandon the bleeding victim to die, and dash after another. In this way they continued for an hour, when men and horses were overcome by labor and fatigue. Some ten or twelve bulls lay bleeding on the plains, some dead and others badly wounded.

Captain Williams' men, not being able to manage their rifles and horses, failed to accomplish anything. Indeed, one of their horses took fright and ran away, a mile or two from the scene of action, before the rider was able to stop him. Another hurled his rider with violence from his saddle, upon the ground. A third one rushed upon an infuriated bull that one of the Kansas had wounded, and had his entrails torn out by the bull's horns, and was left dead on the ground, his chagrined and deeply mortified rider being left to foot it back to the camp.

The chase being ended, the party went to work to dispatch those that were wounded, which, by the way, was accompanied with no little danger. Some of the bulls were very furious, and made deliberate bounds at the horses, even pursuing them. Captain Williams observed that the Indians exercised a great deal of coolness and judgment. They reserved their arrows until they were able to make a sure and effective shot.

They always aimed to launch their spears and arrows behind the ribs, so as to range forward and in this way penetrate the vitals. A single arrow, in several instances, would dispatch a large bull, and when the carcasses were opened by the Indians to get their arrows, they were found to have passed from the flank obliquely through the body, and lodged against some of the bones on the opposite side.

It is very common for an arrow to pass completely through the body when it does not strike a bone. The points of their arrows and spears are made of iron and steel, procured from the whites, and made very sharp. Their bows are sometimes made of wood, but their strongest and most efficient weapons of this kind are made of pieces of bone and horn, spliced and glued together, and strung with sinews of buffalo. Their spears are generally eight or ten feet long, including the handle, which is made of light elastic wood, and wrapped with the sinews of buffalo.

Having taken as much of the choicest portions of the meat as they could carry, the party turned their faces toward the Kansas village. But as it was late in the afternoon before they set off, they raised a fire, around which they prepared their hunter's meal, the horses at the same time being permitted to graze upon the grass. They traveled about eight miles from their grand scamper that evening, and then stopped until the next morning, when very early they reached the Kansas village. The party was richly laden with fat buffalo meat, but was minus a very fine horse.

LIFE AMONG THE KANSAS

While among the Kansas, Captain Williams' men were informed that a large black bear had been frequently seen on an island in the river about a mile from the village, and that several efforts made by the Indians to take him had been unsuccessful. There was a dense thicket of plum bushes and hazel, to which he always took himself when assailed, and into which his pursuers thought it unsafe to follow him. As the dogs belonging to the expedition were trained to hunt such game, they were taken across the river to the island by some of the men.

A number of the Kansas went with them to witness the performance of the dogs, which the Indians admired very much for their superior size. Within a very short time, the bear was started from the thickets, and being pursued closely, and now and then nipped by the dogs, took to a tree. One of the men shot him. He was uncommonly large and very fat, and furnished a fine meal for the company that night

The Kansas were delighted with the courage of the dogs, and the principal Chief of the village expressed a desire to purchase one of them. He offered Captain Williams a fine young horse in exchange for a large mastiff, for which he took a particular fancy. Captain Williams' men were beginning to consider the mastiff a useless part of the expedition calculated by its barking to betray them into the hands of lurking parties of Indians. The offer was timely and a bargain was soon struck.

The Chief took his dog, and Captain Williams his horse, both alike well pleased with their trade. The village generally seemed delighted with the new acquisition of an animal so much superior, in every way, to the small, half-starved, half-wolf, roguish-looking breed which they had in their village. Indian dogs seem to be wolves of the smaller kind domesticated, and are of no value except to those tribes who have no horses. The smaller dog common to the Indian village is often used to convey baggage.

Having passed three days with this tribe, Captain Williams resumed his journey with his men, greeted with the best wishes of these unsophisticated children of nature, for their future good luck. He was advised by Big White to bear more to the west, to avoid the broken, hilly country near the Missouri, and to avoid the difficulty sometimes experienced in crossing its tributaries near their mouths. The hostile parties of Indians, too, with whom they might fall in, would not be very large, and of course less formidable, as their villages generally were near the Missouri River.

Captain Williams, therefore, determined to cross the Platte a short distance below the junction of the north and south forks of the river, and pursued his course accordingly. The company traveled over a dry, elevated, rich prairie country. Buffalo were seen in great numbers. Elk, deer, and the antelope were frequently to be seen, scampering and curveting, and sometimes gazing with wild curiosity upon the company as they passed along. Frequent signs of Indians were seen through the day, but the fears of the party were not excited, as in all probability they were made by the hunting parties of the Kansas.

An hour before sunset the company came to a halt to refresh themselves and their horses. This evening the dog that had been exchanged for a horse overtook them, and seemed much pleased with rejoining his old acquaintances. There was a piece of rawhide attached to his neck, by which he had been tied, and which he had cut, and in this way made his escape. How he passed, without being attacked by wolves and torn to pieces, was a matter of surprise to the party, who had observed that wolves were very numerous.

At dark, a light was observed across the prairie, which was most likely that of an Indian camp. The company put out their fires, mounted their horses, and traveled eight or ten miles further, then unpacked and fettered their horses, and turned them out to graze, while they wrapped themselves up in their blankets and laid themselves down to sleep. The light of the ensuing morning revealed to the men the most extensive and beautiful prospect they had ever seen.

They found themselves on the most elevated point in a grand prairie that spread almost immeasurably in every direction. In every way they looked a beautiful sea green surface spread onward and onward, until it united with the utmost verge of the sky, bearing a striking resemblance to the undulating surface of the ocean.

The prairie was dotted, here and there, with bands of the different kinds of animals, which at that early day were very numerous in the far west. Far away, in the distance, was to be seen a herd of buffalo, some quietly grazing, and others reposing upon the grass. Near at hand was a band of hungry and roguish-looking wolves, curiously eyeing the company, and patiently licking their lips in anticipation of the sweet morsels and bones they expected to pick up about the camp when the party were gone.

In this beautiful, exciting panorama of nature were the elk and the antelope, the one crowned with his stately, wide-spreading antlers; the other sweeping and curveting around with so much grace and ease, as scarcely to appear to make a single muscular effort. Nearby was a little village of prairie dogs, the industrious inhabitants of which were up at the first break of day, yelping, and skipping about, darting into their holes, and as quickly coming out again, and in this way expressing the surprise and curiosity created by the presence of these intruders. We promise the reader, in another part of this volume, a fuller account of this curious, antic little inhabitant of the prairie.

Although the company was delighted with the scene, they did not think it safe policy to occupy so conspicuous a place very long, as they might be espied many miles in every direction, by any roving bands of Indians that might be in that region. Without, therefore enjoying their usual morning repast, they hurried off, and traveled until noon, when they came to timber, in which they passed several hours of rest both to themselves and their horses. In the afternoon of this day they met a small hunting party of Kansas, belonging to the village the party had visited. They held a short parley with them, in which they learned of the trade made by Captain Williams and the Chief of the Kansas village. They seemed to place confidence in the statements of Captain Williams, confirmed as they were by the testimony of the Mandans and took possession of the renegade dog for the purpose of conveying him back to his legitimate owner.

In the latter part of this day, a rumbling, rolling noise from the south was heard, resembling distant thunder. Big White, who was an experienced buffalo hunter, said that it was made by the running of a very large herd of frightened buffalo and as the sound became more and more distinct, he stated that in all probability they were coming toward the company, a circumstance that would be attended with danger if the herd was as numerous as the noise indicated.

For one hour, the thundering continued, becoming more and more audible until the dark rolling mass of living, moving animals was seen on the verge of the horizon, coming directly towards the company, and apparently covering the whole earth. Under such circumstances there is no retreating, and a party of men in such a situation are reduced to the desperate expedient of standing their ground and facing the danger.

A part of the men secured the horses by tethering them, at the same time ridding them of their burdens; the others rushed forward with their arms to meet the herd two or three hundred yards in advance of the horses. The only thing that could be done to prevent being overrun and trampled to death was to divide the crowd of charging buffalo. The company was able to accomplish this by firing their guns as fast as they could load, and by shouting and waving their hats.

As the vast throng came up, they divided to the right and the left, leaving a passage about forty or fifty yards wide, which was occupied by the men and horses. But the shouting, and shooting, and waving of hats had to be kept up while the denser part of the throng was passing by, which consumed at least one entire hour. Big White and his son, who understood the disposition of the buffalo better than any present, aided in the matter, and rendered most efficient help by their tremendous yells, which seemed to frighten the buffalo more than anything else. The greyhound dog belonging to the company, frightened and confused, darted into the crowd of buffalo and was trampled to death.

To some, these statements about the vast number of buffalo may seem to invite incredulity, and may be classed among those extravagant stories that are frequently associated with the excitement belonging to frontier adventure. They may be thought to be true only in part, but it should be remembered that they are confirmed by the observation of all men who have traveled through buffalo country, some of whom are certainly entitled to credit for what they say. The same statements are made about their vast number even at the present day and if they are correct now, how much more true were these numbers forty years ago?

That the number of buffalo has been diminished very fast is certainly true and in another part of this book there will be found some interesting data to this effect, which we gathered from the expeditions of Captain Fremont. When buffalo are seen frightened and running, it is regarded as evidence they are pursued by Indians. It was not the case, however, in the present instance. As the company expected the buffalo to be followed by Indians, they did not once think of securing a supply of meat, but allowed the opportunity to pass. Captain Williams thought it wise to be on the alert, as this was a season for hunting, and the prairies were doubtless covered with hunting parties which could surprise them. They therefore traveled hard and late before they came to a halt. Three men left the main body of the company to kill some game, as provisions were somewhat scarce. They were to join the company at a point of timber that was visible at that time, and seemed to be about six miles off, but the distance proved much greater.

The men were strictly ordered by Captain Williams not to separate from each other, as they were now on very dangerous ground, and their safety required the strictest vigilance. The party reached the point of timber about sunset, and dined upon a very scanty supply of meat. About dark, two of the hunters came in, bringing a fine deer. They reported that the other hunter had left them to get a shot at some elk that were about a half-mile off, while they wound around and about to kill their deer. In this way, they lost sight of him. They further stated that they had seen three men on horses going in the direction the absent man had gone. This circumstance awakened the most painful apprehensions in the camp as to his safety.

It was now too late to go in search of him, and if alive he was doomed to spend the night on the prairie entirely unprotected. Captain Williams thought at one time of kindling up a large fire, hoping that the lost man might see the light and find his way to the camp, but then this plan might betray the whole company into the hands of hostile Indians and on that account was abandoned. The fires were extinguished and the guard was required to be very cautious.

If the missing man had fallen into the hands of the Indians, these Indians would most likely meditate an attack upon the main body. The night passed without anything to disturb their slumbers except their concern for the lost hunter, and at the earliest dawn of day, ten men, including the two that had acted as hunters the evening before, set off to find the one that was absent. They went to the place where Carson, (for that was his name) was represented as being last seen, but no signs of his being there could be found.

The surface of the ground was such that if he had been there, he would have left some impression that would still be perceptible. No tracks made by his horse could be found. It could not be the place where he had been last seen, for he could not have been there at all. The men frequently fired their guns, rode about and shouted at the top of their voices, and waved their hats, but no answer was received. Nothing like a man could be seen anywhere on the wide expanse of prairie that spread around.

As they swept around, however, they saw a horse standing in a patch of brush. When they approached the animal, he recognized the company and neighed. This brought the men to a halt, uncertain as to what it meant. They called and shouted, but no one answered. This tended to confirm their unfavorable apprehension as to the fate of Carson. He was in all probability killed, and his horse and equipage were in the possession of Indians. They could be concealed in the thicket just before them. They were determined to know for themselves and approached the horse very cautiously, with their fingers upon the triggers of their guns ready to fire, and expecting at any moment to be fired upon.

When they were sufficiently near, they discovered the horse was carefully tied and a short distance off lay Carson under a tree, with his head upon his saddle. The men thought he was dead, but they soon found out that he was in a sound sleep, and indeed enjoying a very pleasant dream at the same time. When they aroused him, he at first seemed bewildered and wild. He gave a doleful account of himself as he passed the night lost and alone. In his eagerness to shoot an elk, he lost his course and wandered about long after dark, perhaps until midnight, hoping that he might see the light of the encampment.

Failing in this, fatigued and hungry, he laid himself down to sleep if he could, but his mind was so much impressed with the dangers by which he was beset, that he lay wide awake until about the break of day, which was the cause of his being asleep when they found him. He saw the Indians seen by the other men. They passed within a hundred yards from him, but did not see him, as he was hid, as he thought, in the same thicket in which he spent the night.

As his horse was very impatient to join the company again, and frequently neighed, Carson was very much afraid that it would betray him into the hands of those three Indians that passed so near. To prevent this, he blindfolded the horse by binding his handkerchief over its eyes, an expedient that had the effect of entirely subduing the horse's restiveness and ill-timed impatience. He thought the Indians were traveling in a southern direction, and their horses seemed very much fatigued. They were well armed with bows and arrows, and long spears, and Carson thought each one had several scalps dangling to their bridle bits. They were evidently returning home, perhaps from some adventurous tramp, in which they may have sought revenge on some rival party.

From the description of these Indians, Big White thought they were of the Kite Indian tribe, who were aggressive in the extreme and who would have shown no mercy whatsoever to Carson, if they had seen him. He spoke of them as being very much reduced in number by their constant wars with other tribes and yet perfectly indomitable. They were great horsemen and very swift. Captain Williams embraced the opportunity this occurrence furnished to urge upon his men the most scrupulous observance of the regulations belonging to the company, as very necessary for their safety.

Journey West

The lost man being found, the party resumed their journey, exercising renewed caution as they saw abundant signs of Indians. The tracks of their horses and their vacated camps were frequently observed, while the game along the route seemed alarmed and easily frightened. About noon, some Indian scouts were seen by the aid of a glass on an eminence a long way off, evidently reconnoitering the movements of the company.

Toward the latter part of the day, the same scouts were again following along at a distance on their trail. They were supposed to be spies belonging to some hostile tribe, perhaps large, in that neighborhood who intended if an opportunity offered that night to steal their horses and perhaps attack the company. Late in the afternoon, they came to a small stream of very pure water, where they decided to take a little refreshment and to permit their horses to graze.

The Mandan Chief told Captain Williams that the scouting party was dogging them and may have bad designs towards his company. The Chief felt they would not attempt to execute those designs until a late hour in the night, perhaps a short time before day, when the party would be asleep, and that it was good policy on his part to act as though he suspected nothing of the kind and to be perfectly at ease.

At dark, they renewed their fires to deceive the lurking foe and then quietly and silently started off into the night. Turning their course to the north, they traveled about ten miles and then stretched their weary limbs on the green grass until the light of another morning.

Immediately after daybreak, the company was underway, exulting in the present security and in having outwitted as well as out-traveled the enemy. They did not in the least relax their speedy gait until noon, at which time they reached a ravine where wood and water were abundant. There they remained for two hours. A scout or out-sentinel was stationed on an eminence in the prairie to scan the country around, and report by signs anything and everything that looked in any degree suspicious.

We now pass on to that part of the journal that details the events of the expedition when they arrived on the Platte River. They reached the waters of this river about the first of June. One of the men, whose name was William Hamilton, had taken sick the day before and not being able to travel, the party were compelled to encamp. He had a very high fever and was frequently wild and flighty. Captain Williams made several efforts to bleed him, but without success. He also gave him a dose of calomel, which likewise was not accompanied with any beneficial effect. Poor fellow! In his lucid moments, he frequently expressed an earnest wish to see once more his native home and his friends, but he had bid them adieu for the last time and it was his fate to end his days in the wilderness.

As they would in all probability be compelled by the situation of Hamilton to remain there, perhaps for several days, the men on the first day were engaged in constructing a sort of breast-work for the greater safety of the party.

The next morning, five men swept around a mile or two from the camp and returned with part of the meat of a fine young buffalo and the carcass of an antelope, which was the first that had been killed by any of the party. Its meat was thought to be very fine and much like venison. Indeed, the antelope exactly resembles the common deer in every respect except as to its horns, which differ from those of the deer being straight, slender, erect and without any branches.

The man who killed it said that it would not permit him to approach within the range of his rifle. He therefore threw himself upon the ground and elevated his handkerchief on the end of his gun-stick and as it waved in the wind the curiosity of the animal seemed to gain the better of its normal caution and shyness. It wheeled about and returned, running around and around, drawing still nearer every circuit it made, until it actually came within thirty steps of him. He then shot it as he lay in a horizontal position.

During this day a party of Indians on horseback and bearing a warlike aspect made their appearance near the camp and gazed with much curiosity upon the company. Captain Williams, accompanied by Big White, advanced towards them making signs of friendship. With some little difficulty, they were brought to a conversation in which he learned that they were a war party of Pawnees who had been out in pursuit of some Osages who had stolen some of their horses. They had overtaken and killed most of them. They were in possession of a number of scalps, as so many trophies and had regained the stolen horses. There were thirty Pawnees, well armed with bows and arrows, shields, and spears.

They seemed very friendly, especially when they learned that the object of the expedition was to take the Mandan Chief home to his tribe. They had received presents from Lewis and Clark the year before, which laid the foundation of partiality for the whites, a feeling which Captain Williams strengthened very much by giving them tobacco and several other articles. Having been conducted to the camp, they received every kindness that the party could bestow upon them. They seemed to feel very much for Hamilton, who continued to be very sick and were greatly surprised to witness Captain William's' effort to extract blood. It was not possible to make them understand how it could benefit the sufferer.

They brought in a number of roots and weeds, which they eloquently affirmed by sign, would be an infallible remedy. They also urged sweating and bathing, to which the Indians east and west of the mountains always resort as a remedy not only for fever, but almost every kind of disease.

As the reader may not understand their *modus operandi* in the use of this remedy, it may be important to describe it. A vapor bath, or sweating house, is "a hollow tub six or eight feet deep, formed against the river bank by damming the other three sides up with mud and covering the top completely, except for an aperture of about two feet wide. The bather descends by this hole, taking with him a number of heated stones and jugs of water. After seating himself, he throws water on the stones until the steam becomes sufficiently hot for his purpose.

The baths of the Indians in the Rocky Mountains are of different sizes, the most common being made of mud and sticks like an oven, but the mode of raising the steam is exactly the same. Among those nations, when a man bathes for pleasure, he is generally accompanied by one and sometimes by several of his acquaintances. Indeed, it is so essentially a social amusement that to decline going in the bath when invited by a friend is one of the highest insults offered.

The Indians on the frontier generally use a bath that will accommodate only one person and which is formed of a wicker-work of willows, about four feet high, arched at the top and covered with skins. In this, the bather sits until by means of the steam from the heated stones, he has perspired sufficiently. These baths are almost universally in the neighborhood of running water, into which the bather plunges immediately on coming out and sometimes he returns again and subjects himself to a second perspiration. The bath is employed for pleasure, as well as health, and is used indiscriminately for all kinds of diseases.

It is also used for another purpose. When an Indian trapper is unsuccessful in trapping for beaver, he enters the sweating house where he remains for some time sweating most profusely. In this condition, he immediately plunges into the cold stream fancying that by this means he rids himself of some peculiar odor or impurity of body that kept the keen-scented beaver from his traps. Having passed through this purification and cleansing, he returns to his work with renewed confidence and hopes of success.

Two of the men went with the Pawnee warriors to their village, which was about fifteen miles northeast. They took with them some presents for their chiefs, as they had learned that the various tribes were very receptive to gifts and always expect the white men to confirm their professions of friendship by things that are visible as well as tangible.

The latter part of this day the sick man died, a melancholy event that was not expected so soon. His body was immediately wrapped in a blanket and deposited in a grave. In the bark of a tree standing at the head of his grave, his name was cut by one of the men with his pocketknife. His death cast a deep gloom over the camp, as he was greatly beloved by the company and esteemed and admired for his great fortitude and prudence.

The Mandan Chief, who sympathized very much with the party in their great loss and affliction, expected that the burial of a white brave would have been accompanied with more parade and ceremony and was particularly surprised that he was not furnished with horses and arms to use when he should reach those happy hunting grounds, to which the braves are conducted after death.

It is the custom of the various tribes to furnish their heroes with horses that are slain on their graves and with moccasins and arms of every description, to be used in that Elysium to which they pass in death. On the grave of a very distinguished brave, fifteen or twenty horses are sometimes sacrificed, together with a corresponding outfit for hunting in the other world.

Early the next morning after the death of Hamilton, mingled feelings of sadness and indignation were created in the camp by seeing a band of wolves on his grave, most industriously digging out the loose earth to get at his body. The men suddenly and simultaneously grasped their rifles to revenge the indignity offered to the dead by a general fire upon the pack, but Captain Williams checked them, suggesting that their enemies might hear the report of their rifles and bring them into a difficulty. They therefore quietly drove them away and covered the grave with long heavy pieces of timber, which the wolves would not be able to remove.

Captain Williams learned from Big White that the wolves would always dig up the dead, if not buried so as to prevent it, and that they always most greedily devour the slain on the field of battle, if left on the surface of the ground. Their scent is so very acute, they can smell a dead body three or four feet under ground and having dug it up, feed upon it with the greedy rapacity of the hyena.

The two men sent to the Pawnee village returned about noon, stating that there were none but women, children and very old men at the village. The Chiefs and the young men had gone to hold a council with the Otto and Missouri tribes. That afternoon the party was again under way, traveling due west, as it was the most direct route to the Mandan country.

AWAY IN THE WILDERNESS

It may be remarked, as the general character of the country between the State of Missouri and the Rocky Mountains, that the greater part of it is undulating prairie, almost as vast and trackless as the ocean and at the time, a *terra incognita* to the white man. Some geologists suppose the prairies to have formed the ancient floor of the Ocean countless ages since, when its primeval waves beat against the granite bases of the Rocky Mountains. But the opinion most generally entertained by those persons who reside in the great prairies of the West is that the prairies are formed by the fires that nearly destroy them every autumn.

In favor of this opinion, quite a number of facts can be brought up. Where the fires still prevail, they encroach upon the timber that exists and diminish its quantity every year. It is not difficult to see that in the process of time these regular autumnal fires would destroy all the timber on the surface of the earth, where it may be unprotected. Again, it is to be remarked that in all low places such as ravines, hollows, river bottoms and small valleys, where the dampness of the soil and vegetation is such as to check the progress of these great fires, there and there only, is timber to be found. It may be further stated that where the fire has been kept out twenty-five or thirty years, the face of the country becomes covered again with a growth of young timber, thirty and forty feet high.

The trunks of trees are sometimes found in those prairies in a state of petrifaction, which is evidence that those vast plains were once clothed with timber. Although in many parts of the prairie country timber is scarce, the supply is sufficient for present purposes and its growth is very rapid in consequence of the great fertility of the soil. Therefore, the production of timber in this region is believed to be amply sufficient for all future demands.

These great fires are sometimes very beautiful and even grand when seen in a dark night. As the light of the sun is withdrawn and nightfall comes on, the light of those fires becomes more and more distinct and bright until a beautiful long and luminous line is to be seen stretching afar to the right and the left across the plains. The flames generally rise to the height of five or six feet, but when the consuming element reaches those places where the growth of vegetation is luxuriant, it blazes up thirty or forty feet high. The reflection of the light on the distant horizon may be seen for fifty miles and looks like the approach of the great luminary of day.

It sometimes happens that a solitary tree, from some peculiar locality, remains unscathed and is permitted to grow and attain considerable dimensions, while not a shrub or twig of any description is to be seen in any direction for many miles. Alone and isolated, it stands as a beacon to the traveler over a sea of prairie and constitutes a pleasant and permanent object on which he may rest his eyes, wearied with the monotony around him.

On the afternoon of June 5th, something in motion was discovered on the prairie ahead of the company, but so far off they were not able to determine what it was. As they approached it, Captain Williams, by the aid of a glass, ascertained that it was a band of wolves in full chase after a buffalo coming directly towards the party. All were anxious to see the race and how it would terminate, so they placed themselves in a position not to be noticed very readily by the wolves. In a few minutes, they had a fair view of the whole affair.

The buffalo proved to be a well-grown young bull in fine condition. There were about twelve wolves of the largest kind and they must have had a long, tight race, as they seemed {both wolves and buffalo} very much fatigued. As they ran, the wolves were close around the buffalo snapping and snatching all the time, but they were observed not to seize and hold on like a dog. Their method of killing a buffalo is to run the animal down. When it is completely out of breath, by a constant worrying and snatching kept up by all members of the pack, they drag the buffalo to the ground and then fill themselves with his flesh, sometimes before he is entirely dead.

Indeed in this case they seemed to feed upon their victim as they ran, for every thrust they made at him they took away a mouthful of his flesh, which they gulped as they ran and by the time they had brought him to the ground, the flesh of his hindquarters was taken away to the bone. So eager were they in the chase, and so fierce was the contest, that they did not observe the company until they rode up within ten steps from them. Even then they did not appear to be much frightened, but scampered off a short distance and sat down and licked their lips and waited with much impatience to be permitted to return to their hard-earned feast. The buffalo had suffered violence in every part. The tendons of his hind legs were cut asunder, the tuft of hair at the end of the tail was taken away, with part of the tail, pieces of hide and flesh, as large as a man's hand, were jerked out of his sides in several places, his ears were much torn and in the battle he had lost one of his eyes.

Just before they succeeded in bringing him to full ground, one of the pack, a very large gray wolf, was seen to spring upon his back, tear out a mouthful of his hump, and then bound off. Having gratified their curiosity, the men withdrew and the hungry pack in a moment set in with fresh rapacity, tearing away and gulping the bloody flesh of their victim that still faintly struggled for life.

Captain Williams represents the wolves as being very numerous and always to be seen hanging about the outskirts of a buffalo herd. They kill a great many calves and any that are unable, from any untoward circumstances, to resist successfully their attacks are sure to fall victims to their rapacity.

This particular evening, when the company had gone into camp and were enjoying their usual routines, two young Indians, a young man and a squaw, rode up and alighted in the midst of the men, apparently much fatigued and way-worn. Their presence filled the company with amazement, and the safety of the party required of them a very prompt explanation. The newcomers might belong to some marauders in that vicinity who might give some trouble. The young Indian, under the pretext of friendship, might be the spy of a hostile band, which was meditating an attack upon them. But what about this pretty young girl who is with him? War parties are never encumbered with women. The jaded condition of their horses also to some extent allayed their fears, as it was evident that they were on a long and severe journey.

The Mandan Chief interrogated him as to his object and destination and learned that Doranto (the young man) was a Pawnee who had been taken captive about a year before by the Sioux. He had been conveyed up the Missouri to one of their villages in which he remained until an opportunity to make his escape to his own tribe presented itself. The young girl with him, Niargua, was a Sioux with whom he had fallen in love while among that tribe. The attachment was mutual and they hoped to consummate their bliss, finding it necessary to elope. They were now fleeing to his native village, to which another night's ride, he thought, would bring them. As they seemed very fatigued and were without any provisions, the party very promptly tendered them the best they had, which was consumed with all good relish by the two lovers. After this, they enjoyed a little repose.

Captain Williams, through the interpretation skills of Big White, drew from the young Pawnee the following details that shall furnish matter for a short chapter.

DORANTO AND NIARGUA

Doranto belonged to the Pawnee Loups, who dwelt (if said to dwell anywhere) on the Wolf fork of the Platte River. In company with several of his young brethren, he had sauntered some distance from their village. The young men were bathing and swimming about in a small stream of water when some marauders belonging to the "Tetons of the Burnt Woods," a tribe of Sioux, suddenly came upon them and made a prisoner of him. The other men in his party were able to make their escape.

He was instantly snatched up, tied on a horse, and hurried away. The horse that he rode was led by one of the Sioux and goaded on by another that followed immediately behind. They traveled night and day, hard, until they had reached a point entirely out of the reach of danger. The Tetons of the Burnt Woods have their main village in the Grand Detour or Great Bend of the Missouri River, the circuit of which is thirty miles, while the distance across it is a little over a mile.

Doranto proved to be a son of a grand Chief of the Pawnee Loups, so he was greatly prized as a captive, and on that account was placed in the family of a principal Chief of the Tetons. There was something very interesting in the person of the young captive which no doubt secured to him more consideration and a kinder and more respectful treatment than captives generally experience in the hands of their captors. Although, according to his own statement, he had seen but sixteen winters, he was about five-feet-nine or five-feet-ten inches high, and in the view of Captain Williams, one of the handsomest and best proportioned men he had ever seen.

The expression of his countenance, which was very fine, was very different from that which human nature usually bears in its elementary state. He certainly possessed, to a remarkable degree, that daring intrepidity of character so much admired by Indians and which, of itself, and unassociated with other excellencies, in their view constitute a great man and a brave.

It is frequently the lot of captives and prisoners, to some extent, to occupy the relation of servants and have assigned those menial and domestic offices that are never performed by men, but constitute the employment of women. To be compelled to occupy this position in society was very mortifying to the Indian pride of Doranto, but he was somewhat reconciled to it as it threw him in the company of a beautiful daughter of the Chief, whose name was Niargua. He was not permitted to go to war or to hunt the buffalo, the elk, and the antelope. It was a mode of life too tame and inactive for his restless and mettlesome spirit, but then it gave him frequent opportunities of walking, talking, and laughing with the Teton maiden over whose heart it was his good fortune to gain a complete victory.

It would not do for the daughter of a distinguished Chief to be the wife of a captive slave belonging to a tribe against which the Chief had entertained a deep-seated hostility for past insults and injuries. This would be a flagrant violation of every notion of Indian aristocracy. By the way, the mother of the young princess, who had noticed the growing familiarity of the two lovers, reported the matter to the Chief, whose duties had kept him generally from home. As the intelligence was very unexpected and by no means agreeable to his feelings, his daughter was very roughly reproved, and a severe flagellation was inflicted to appease his wrath.

He threatened to shoot an arrow through Doranto for his bold pretensions. The result of this effort "to break the match," in this, as in similar cases in civilized life, was not only unsuccessful, but served to increase the flame it was intended to extinguish and to strengthen, instead of dissolving, the attachment between the parties. If their partiality for each other was not so visible and open, they were not the less determined to carry out their designs.

When Doranto perceived that difficulties were in the way, that would ever be insuperable while he remained among the Tetons, he immediately conceived the bold design of eloping to his own people and embraced the first opportunity to apprize his betrothed of his thoughts. The proposition met with a prompt and a hearty response on her part. She was ready to go with him wherever he went and to die where he died.

But there was a young warrior among the Tetons who also desired the hand of the Sioux beauty and greatly envied the position Doranto occupied in the eyes of Niargua. Indeed he entertained the most deadly hate toward the Pawnee captive and suffered no opportunity to show it, to pass unimproved. Doranto was by no means ignorant of the young warrior's feelings of jealousy and hate, but he sensibly felt his disabilities as an alien in the tribe and pursued a course of forbearance as most likely to ensure the accomplishment of his designs. Still there were bounds beyond which his code of honor would not suffer his enemy to pass. On one occasion, the young brave offered Doranto the greatest and the most intolerable insult, which in the estimation of the western tribes one man can give to another: "you stink," were the offensive words of the Teton warrior, embracing the great indignity.

The person who is offended, by a law among those tribes, may take away the life of the offender, if he can, but it is customary and thought more honorable to settle the difficulty by a single combat in which the parties may use the kind of weapons on which they may mutually agree. Public sentiment will allow no compromise. If no resistance is offered to the insult, the person insulted is thenceforth a disgraced wretch, a dog, and universally despised.

Doranto forthwith demanded satisfaction of the young Sioux, who by the way, was "cut and dry" to give it, being full of game and mettle, as well as sanguine as to the victory he would gain over the young Pawnee. They agreed to settle their difficulty by single combat and the weapons to be used were war clubs and short knives.

A suitable place was selected. The whole village of the Tetons emptied itself to witness the combat. Men, women and children swarmed about the arena. The two youthful combatants made their appearance, stark naked, and took their positions about thirty yards apart. Just when the signal was given, Doranto caught the eye of Niargua in the crowd. Then, he said, "my heart was big and my arm strong; no fear, then, in Doranto."

As the champions advanced towards each other, the Sioux warrior was too precipitate and by the impulse of his charge, was carried beyond Doranto, who being more cool and deliberate, gave him a blow with his war club as he passed on the back of his neck. That action perfectly stunned him and brought him to the ground. Doranto then sprang upon him and dispatched him by a single thrust of his blade. The relatives of the unfortunate Sioux raised a loud lament and with that piteous kind of howling peculiar to Indians, bore him away.

Doranto was now regarded as a young brave and was greatly advanced in the general esteem of the village. He must now be an adopted son and no longer a woman, but go to war and hunt the buffalo, the elk, and the antelope.

The father of Niargua, however, in this matter was not appeased. In the general excitement on behalf of the lucky captive, he lagged behind and was reserved and sullen. Having conceived a dislike for Doranto, he was not inclined to confer upon him the honors he had so fairly won. And then, it would not do to appear delighted with the valor of the young Pawnee. Niargua was his favorite child and she must be the wife of some distinguished personage.

But the Chief was doomed, as many a father is, to be out-witted by his daughter in matters of this kind.

At a time when he was absent, holding a council with a neighboring tribe of the Sioux upon great national affairs, Doranto picked out two of the Chief's best horses, on which to escape with his girl to his own tribe. Niargua was ready. When the village was in a profound sleep, she met him in a sequestered place bringing a supply of provisions for the trip. In a moment they were in their saddles and away. They were not less than three long sleeps from his own people and would be followed by some of the Tetons as long as there was any hope of overtaking them. By morning, however, there would be such a wide space between them and their pursuers as to make their escape entirely practicable.

If no mishap should befall them on the way, they "had good horses," said Doranto, "good hearts, good moon, good weather, good country to travel over and above all a good cause, and why not good luck." They traveled day and night, never stopping any longer than was absolutely necessary to rest their horses.

Captain Williams represented the Teton maiden as very pretty, but very young for an undertaking requiring so much self-denial, patience, and fortitude and in which she was exposed to great fatigue and very severe toil. Her resolution was, however, quite commensurate to her difficulties and trials.

The company tried to prevail upon the young Pawnee to stay with them until morning and enjoy that rest and refreshment which he and his girl so much needed, but he replied that they had not slept any since they set out on their flight, nor did they even dare to think of closing their eyes before they should reach the village of the Pawnees. He knew that he would be pursued as long as there was the faintest hope of overtaking him and he also knew what his doom would be if he again fell into the hands of the Sioux.

Having remained, therefore, in the camp scarcely an hour, the two fugitive lovers were again on the wing, flying over the green prairie, guided by the light of a full and beautiful moon and animated and sustained by the purity of their motives and the hope of soon reaching a place of safety and protection. The party could not help but admire the courage of the Teton beauty and the cheerfulness and even hilarity that she manifested while in their camp. When about to set off, she leaped from the ground unassisted into her Indian saddle, reined up her horse, and was instantly beside him with whom she was now ready to share any trial and to brave any danger.

What an exhibition this is of female fortitude that brings forth this kind of heroism, peculiar to the sex, which elevates woman to a summit perfectly inaccessible to sublunary difficulties and enables her to view with undisturbed complacency of soul all that occurs beneath her feet. What an auxiliary to man is woman in bearing his quota of life's trials and difficulties and how does she light up his dark hours of adversity with her sunny smiles of cheer, and prompt him to make another effort, when and where, unassisted and un-encouraged, he would have yielded to despair.

LAND OF THE SIOUX

Having reached the Platte country, Captain Williams was aware of the fact that increasing dangers beset their route, and that he was now in a region full of hazard, and in which the utmost caution was necessary to prevent his company from being cut off. The greater part of the country, at that day, between the Platte River and the Mandan nation, was infested with a variety of tribes of Sioux, whose predatory habits had justly secured to them the title of "land pirates." They were a terror to all other tribes on account of their superior numbers and their ferocious disposition.

Lewis and Clark represent them as being subdivided into ten tribes: Yanktons, Tetons, Minnake-nozzo, Tetons Saone, Yanktons of the Plains, or 'Big Devils', Wapatone, Mindawarcarton, Wahpatoota, or 'Leaf Beds', and Sistasoona. By means of different interpreters, while in the Sioux country, they learned that their men of war numbered about two thousand, five hundred.

In 1836, the Sioux were represented as numbering about 27,000 men, women, and children. A subsequent account speaks of these bands as probably numbering from 40,000 to 60,000. We are disposed to receive these accounts, as we receive all statements about the numerical strength of the tribes of the far west, as very uncertain. Correctness no doubt has been aimed at, but correctness in a great majority of cases cannot be attained. One thing is certain: the Sioux have been diminishing very fast. Many of the tribes have been broken down and lost their names, and the nation now is not such a formidable body as they were in earlier days.

The ten tribes, whose names we have furnished, were scattered up and down the Missouri river and were constantly on the prowl, scouring the country from the waters of the Platte River to the Black Hills and the Mandan region. They were very hostile to the Mandans, who dwelt above them on the Missouri and as they had seen Big White on his way to the states in company with Lewis and Clark, they expected his return and were on the alert to prevent his going

49

back to his nation. They entertained the idea that the whites would furnish the Mandans with arms and make them more formidable than they were at that time.

For this reason, the Sioux aimed to intercept all communication between our people and the tribes above them. For a number of years subsequent to 1807 they resisted all efforts made by various expeditions to push their way to those upper tribes. Captain Williams was fully impressed with the fact that the difficulties before him were much greater than those his party had already encountered, and that their vigilance must be increased and every expedient adopted to elude the observation of those "land pirates," whose country they were now passing through.

It was some consolation to the party that the Sioux expected them to ascend the Missouri river, and in all probability the greater part of their warriors would be collected on that river to drive them back. For this reason, and another, stated in another place, Captain Williams left the Missouri not less than one hundred miles on his right and thereby avoided all the large Indian towns on that river. If he should fall in with any of the Sioux on the route he was pursuing, they would be dispersed hunting parties with whom he would be able to cope, if it should be his misfortune to be involved in a difficulty. Game, too, would be more abundant in that region, and the more easily and safely procured, which was an important consideration, as the safety of the party required that they should push their way through this dangerous country with all possible speed.

On the day after leaving the main Platte River, a band of buffalo were observed feeding very quietly about a fourth of a mile from the party, offering an opportunity for those who desired it to show their horsemanship and skill in a buffalo hunt. Although they had a supply of meat, and Captain Williams had requested there be no more shooting than was necessary, the impetuous youth, Carson, begged permission to try his hand.

The Captain granted his request, as it was near sunset and the company had come to a halt to take their usual repast and to witness the exploits of the young Nimrod. The more experienced men of the company urged Carson not to venture too near the object of his pursuit, nor too far from the company, as both steps would be accompanied with much danger. The young man felt it to be the safer plan to undertake the matter on horseback and as the rifle is not easily handled when horse and buffalo are at full speed, he armed himself with two braces of pistols. The buffalo very soon observed his approach, looked frightened and put off at quite a fast gait. This made it necessary for him to increase the speed of his horse, and immediately hunter, horse and buffalo were out of sight.

Having refreshed themselves and their horses, the party would have resumed their journey, but Carson had not returned. Nightfall came on, and still he did not make his appearance. Many unhappy fears now pervaded the camp as to his safety and the suspicious circumstances of his absence prevented many men from sleeping that night. Early the next morning, some of the men went to hunt Carson and without much difficulty found him. He was sitting on a rock near a small stream, perfectly lost. Some of the men, when looking for him, had seen him when about a mile off and supposed that he was an Indian, as he had no horse.

They were very near leaving him to his fate, but the thought that they might be mistaken prompted them to approach him and they recognized him. He had a doleful history to give of his buffalo hunt. According to Carson, he pursued the buffalo four or five miles before he could overtake them. At first, and for some time, he could not get his horse near enough to use his pistols with any effect. After repeated unsuccessful efforts to ride up by the side of a very large bull, he fell immediately behind him, firing as the animal ran.

His repeated shots threw the animal into the greatest rage and as bull, horse and rider were in full drive down the side of a declivity, the infuriated buffalo stopped suddenly and wheeled about for battle. Carson's horse, not trained to such dangerous exercises, following immediately behind and at the moment perfectly unmanageable, rushed upon the horns of his antagonist and was thrown headlong to the ground with his rider.

When he had recovered from the confusion of the moment, and gained his feet again, Carson was glad to see his buffalo moving off as fast as his legs could carry him, but his horse was so badly wounded that he could be of no service to him. When he recalled his party, and would have returned, he knew not the way to go. In the great excitement of the chase, he paid no attention to the direction he was going. And what was worse, he was now on foot and several miles from the company.

To be lost in a prairie country is worse than being lost in woodlands. His horse was so badly injured that he abandoned him and wandered about until he crept into a hazel patch, where he slept until morning without anything to disturb his rest except several bruises he received in the fall from his horse.

At the earliest dawn of day, he crawled out of his hiding place and very cautiously examined the sea of prairie around him to determine whether any Indians were to be seen. Observing nothing that indicated danger, he set out in search for his party and tramped about and around, until hunger and fatigue compelled him to sit down where he had been found.

As they returned to the camp, they passed his unfortunate horse. He was dead and a band of hungry wolves had already found his carcass and were greedily snatching and gulping his flesh. In fact, the men thought the wounded horse had been killed by the wolves, as they were very numerous and fierce and would attack a horse as soon as anything else, especially if they were incited by the smell of blood.

They had even committed violence upon Carson's saddle, which he had removed from his horse and left on the prairie for want of a tree in which to secure it. Frequently, the wolves get together in considerable gangs, and when emboldened by numbers, and especially when infuriated by hunger, dreadful is the fate of anything that crosses their path. The unlucky and now crest-fallen hunter had a hundred questions to answer when he returned to camp, nor did he feel like being taunted in this way as he had fasted for the last twelve to fifteen hours, had undergone great fatigue, and had received several severe bruises in the bargain.

The horse was a favorite animal, but he had learned a lesson (though dearly) that was worth a number of horses to him and to the company. A party of raw and inexperienced men in these kinds of expeditions generally learn their lessons at this dear cost. In a majority of cases, they cannot be prevailed upon to practice the necessary caution until by the want of it they are betrayed into a few and sometimes very serious difficulties. It is very rash and extremely hazardous for a single man to engage in a buffalo chase in a country known to have bands of hostile Indians. It was viewed as a mere accident that Carson was not killed by the buffalo he had wounded or that he had not fallen into the hands of hostile Indians.

When he set off on the chase, Big White shook his head by way of disapprobation and as prognostic of some mishap that was likely to befall him and the party always found that the suggestions of the old Mandan Chief could not be neglected with safety, as he was a veteran warrior, habituated to all that kind of unremitting watchfulness that an Indian begins to practice from his infancy.

We have said that it was very dangerous for an inexperienced hand to engage in a buffalo hunt on a horse that has not been trained to the business. A well trained horse will always bound off to one side or the other out of the way of the buffalo when he stops to fight and it frequently happens, if the rider is not "up to" the quick and sudden movements of his horse, he is thrown into the midst of danger. The buffalo stops to make battle only when he is wounded or finds escape impossible. He then wields his great strength and activity in self-defense.

We have read of a number of incidents said to have occurred in buffalo hunts, the correctness of which we are disposed to doubt as we think they are unauthorized from what we have been able to gather from men who have spent half of their lives in buffalo country. We have alluded to their great strength and remarkable activity and quickness of motion. The horse that overtakes them must be very fast. Buffalo run for many miles over the plains without seeming to fail. When broke to work (a thing very easily done) one buffalo will break down three or four of our cattle. This has been fairly frequently tried on the frontier. A gentleman living in Missouri informed me that he had a buffalo bull that would work all day on an inclined plane, while he was obliged to change his tame cattle every three hours. Another gentleman in the same region of country had a buffalo bull that would leap over an enclosure eight and ten rails high without touching it. This bull, in a contest with one of our domestic animals, would always prove himself victor in a very few moments. The males frequently attain an enormous size and it is no uncommon thing to see on the plains those that will weigh three thousand pounds, gross.

As they were favored with moonlight and very fine weather, the company thought it a safer plan to travel during the night when circumstances were favorable, and to remain the greater part of the day in a state of inactivity, at least when it would be accompanied with much danger to move. They procured their meat during the day and enjoyed their repast at the same time, as they never kindled fires after dark, for light in a prairie country is seen a great distance and more than anything else, would lead to their discovery.

During their passage through this region of danger, their usual way was to travel all night until about eight o'clock the next morning, when they would seek some sequestered place to refresh themselves and their horses. They always occupied an attitude of defense and everyone lay with his firearms beside him, while they never failed to position scouts to keep watch for Indians. They slept by turns and never more than half the men slept at a time. In this way, they traveled for twenty days performing a greater part of their travel after night.

Game was very abundant, but they killed no more than was necessary to furnish themselves with meat. Their nocturnal movements were not, however, without interest, nor were they barren in interesting events. In those regions, the atmosphere is very pure and elastic, and the sky is a delightful blue in which anything like vapor or clouds cannot be seen for weeks and even months.

When the moon shone, it was with an effusion almost equal to that of a vertical sun. When the moon did not favor them with her light, the starry firmament appeared with brilliance and glory unlike anything they had ever witnessed in any other country.

This dryness, purity, and elasticity of atmosphere, this delicious transparent blue, said to belong also to Italian skies, increase as the traveler approaches the Rocky Mountains. The usual dry season that prevails in that country had already commenced, waterways were very low, and there were few obstructions in their way. Vast prairies generally spread around them, covered with a luxuriant growth of grass and wild flowers. But the face of the country was frequently cut up by deep, dry, ravines or gullies, which being impassable made the route sometimes very circuitous.

Along the rich bottoms of the rivers and ravines were groves of trees with thick entangled undergrowth, in which our little party generally sought to hide themselves from the observations of the prowling Sioux. From one of those fastnesses, in the latter part of the day, they would secretly and silently emerge and travel all night. The next day, they would turn aside into another of these hiding places.

They dispensed with fire as often as they could, for the smoke ascending very high was apt to attract the notice of Indians. They frequently saw bands of Indians that invariably hovered about their route, but by making sham encampments and deceptive fires and then traveling all night, they succeeded in escaping the clutches of the hostile tribes of the west.

One night about an hour after dark, they saw before them a light that indicated, as they thought, an Indian encampment. As they approached it, they found that they were not mistaken. Captain Williams thought it the safer plan for his party not to pass very near their camp and when within a mile of it, he directed his men to come to a halt and to remain where they were until he, in company with the Mandan Chief, would approach the camp near enough to make some observations.

Accordingly, accompanied by Big White, he crept up within a few hundred yards and reconnoitered their camp for a half-hour. They had twelve or fifteen fires and there must have been not less than one hundred Indians. Some were lying down and some were passing to and fro, while others were standing around the fires. A portion of them were squaws, who seemed to be very busy, for Captain Williams discovered they were a hunting party procuring meat in that region and the squaws were drying it for winter. He observed their long poles, on which they exposed their meat to the sun. A great number of horses were grazing around the camp.

Having gratified their curiosity, the Captain and the Chief quietly made their way back to their company, fully convinced of the expediency of getting out of that region as fast as their horses could carry them. They were apprehensive that these Indians might observe their trail and endeavor to overtake them. They therefore pushed ahead all that night and the greater part of the next day before they made camp.

Without troubling the reader with all the incidents of this part of the expedition, we will state that on the first day of July, Captain Williams, with his party, arrived safely at Fort Mandan in the territory of the Mandan Nation.

THE MANDAN NATION

Nothing could exceed, says Captain Williams, the enthusiastic joy of the Mandan people upon the arrival of their old and much loved Chief. It was something they had not expected as they had heard (a thing very likely to occur) he had been killed on the Missouri River by the Sioux, together with the party that were conducting him home. As they had believed the report, knowing as they did the hostile character of the Sioux, they had mourned for their lost Chief and had gone through the usual forms intended to express their sorrow and regard for the dead. Their surprise was equaled only by their joy when they had the unexpected pleasure of again looking upon the face of their venerated and long-absent hero. They received him as directly from the spirit land and as one from the grave. For several days, the excitement produced by his arrival was kept up and kept everything in motion.

There was feasting and there was dancing throughout the village. They sang their wild chants and while they extolled the faith of the whites in bringing back their Chief and his family, they made their thanksgiving sacrifices to the Great Spirit, for that protection that had overshadowed their old warrior. Runners were sent to other villages in several directions to spread the news and for several days hundreds of curious visitors, consisting of men, women and children, came to see the party of white men and especially Big White, who now in their eyes was something superhuman.

The reader may be ready to suppose that the old acquaintances of Big White would tease him almost to death with innumerable questions about the country of the white man, from which he had just returned, but it may be stated, as something peculiar to Indians generally, that they always repress a curiosity of this kind and conduct themselves with great dignity, gravity and silence when one of their company may be detailing important information. This seems to be a part of their education and a rule into the violation of which they are seldom betrayed by any kind of excitement.

Indians, generally, are prone to be taciturn and grave yet their natural sensibilities are very deep and strong. A mutual and ardent attachment pervades the whole tribe, however numerous, and binds them all together as closely as brothers and although a tribe may number several hundred, if anyone dies or is killed by a foe, all alike give themselves up to most wild and extravagant grief – nor does the greatest victory over their enemies in battle atone for the loss of a single warrior. The lamentations of grief about an Indian village after a battle are to be heard in every direction, although they generally aim to retire to some sequestered spot to empty the heart of its abounding sorrow.

Irving, in his Astoria, alludes to this practice among the western tribes in the following beautiful language: "But sounds of another kind were heard on the surrounding hills; piteous wailings of the women, who had retired thither to mourn in darkness and solitude for those who had fallen in battle. There the poor mother of the youthful warrior, who had returned home in triumph but to die, gave full vent to the anguish of a mother's heart. How much does this custom of the Indian women, of repairing to the hilltops in the night and pouring forth their wailings for the dead, call to mind the beautiful and affecting passage of scripture, 'In Rama was there a voice heard, lamentation, and weeping, and great mourning; Rachel weeping for her children, and would not be comforted, because they are not.'"

Big White made a long speech to his people, in which he spoke in eloquent terms of the kindness with which he was received by the whites. He also alluded to the riches, number, and great strength of our people, urging upon them not only the necessity of maintaining a constant peace with us, but the advantages that they would experience from the existence of friendly relations between them and the whites.

"Brothers," said he, "do you see yon prairie (pointing at the same time to a prairie several miles wide), the white man has a gun that will kill Indians across that prairie." He referenced the cannon that he had seen when in the states.

An important point in the expedition being attained and a long and perilous journey having brought our little party to the Mandan country, they once more felt themselves in a land of comparative safety and among friends, not the less friendly because they were Indians. They were now at liberty to relax from that intense vigilance necessary to be practiced in a country full of danger and to give to themselves and their worn out horses that rest which they so much needed.

A week, however, had not passed away before Captain Williams' men manifested a restless spirit and were anxious again to launch into the boundless wilderness, the great *terra incognita* that was before them. A recollection of their past good fortune greatly animated them, while they were stimulated by the prospects that were before them. They fancied that all danger was behind them, in the land of the Sioux, through which they had passed without difficulty.

But it was only fancy, delusive fancy. Little did they know of the dangers before them, or of the unexpected and formidable foes inhabiting the country they would be exploring. Little did they dream of the unhappy fate that awaited the greater part of their party. When they left the Mandan country, a few day's travel brought them to the country over which roved and prowled the ferocious Black-feet Indians, then as well as now, one of the most cruel and relentless tribes of the far west. The Blackfoot Indian is an embodiment of every quality that is worrisome to the feelings of civilized man.

Lewis and Clark, in passing through their country, killed one of their tribe. This act created an implacable hatred for the whites from that day until the present. Of the hostility of this tribe to the whites, on this account, Captain Williams' men were not apprised and were not expecting to meet with a foe writhing under the recollection of past injuries and who had sworn destruction to every white man that should venture to put his foot upon their territory.

We would state that it was the object of Captain Williams and his party to spend the approaching fall and winter on those upper rivers, trapping for beaver, until spring, when they intended to push their way into the Rocky Mountains and carry on their trapping operations on the head waters of the Columbia.

It was also a very praiseworthy object of the expedition to find a more practicable pass through the Rocky Mountains than the route of Lewis and Clark. Such a pass, it was believed, could be found south of the sources of the Missouri. When, therefore, they reached the mouth of the Yellow Stone River, they turned in a southwest direction, following its meanderings. Up the Yellow Stone they journeyed for several days, looking for a region where beaver were very abundant. Such a region they soon found and the traps of the company were soon scattered up and down every little mountain brook and branch for several miles around.

In the meantime, while some were constructing a temporary camp and fortress, others were beating up and down the adjacent hills and hollows in the pursuit of game. They were now in a perfect Elysium. Buffalo, elk, antelope, white and black-tail deer, *ah-sah-tu,* or Big Horn, could be seen every day and the innumerable little rills around abounded with fish of the finest flavor.

In the way of trapping, the men had a great run of good luck, for every morning nearly every trap in the neighborhood was found holding in its iron jaws a fine beaver. These employments and enjoyments the party had long craved and they now had them in the greatest exuberance. From day to day, the men were variously engaged in trapping and skinning beaver, fishing and hunting, eating, laughing and jesting.

Their horses also were recovering very fast from the effects of the long journey they had performed and were fattening. Their feet and backs were getting well and sound again and they were soon in fine plight. The party had seen no signs of Indians to excite any apprehensions of danger, until one morning one of the men discovered that an Indian had been caught in a trap. The Indian had succeeded in extricating himself, as the trap was found near the place where it had been set.

It would seem that the Indian was not disposed to carry it off, but was satisfied to be rid of a thing that, for a short time, at least, had held him in painful custody. He no doubt was of the Black-foot tribe and had been sent as a scout to pry into the condition of Captain Williams' camp and report the same to his people, as another and very melancholy event which we will record, will prove.

A day or two after this Indian was taken in a trap about ten of the men left the camp on a buffalo hunt. At the commencement of the chase, the buffalo were not more than a mile from the camp, but they were pursued for three or four miles which led the men into danger. A company of Black-feet, numbering at least one hundred, suddenly appeared on horses from behind a cover of trees and undergrowth and dashed toward the men as they were scattered over a plain pursuing and shooting the buffalo.

Five of the men on fast horses flying at top speed were able to escape, but the rest of the party was intercepted and their escape to camp was cut off. They fell an easy prey into the Indians' hands and were in all probability the first whites that were killed by that tribe, and killed, too, to appease the vengeance awakened against the whites by the act of Lewis and Clark.

The five men who made their escape were pursued within a half mile from the camp by several Black-feet. One of these Indians manifested a disposition to follow the men into the very camp of our little party, after the others had wheeled their horses and were returning to the main body of their party. But he paid dearly for his rashness. One of the men, whose gun happened to be loaded, stopped his horse and sent a ball whizzing through his body and tumbled him from his horse dead.

The loss of five men sustained by a party which numbered only twenty to start, the killing of one of the attacking Indians which would rouse feelings of vengeance in those Indians to a still greater pitch, and the presence of hostilities in their immediate vicinity, made the situation of Captain Williams and his now reduced party very critical and hazardous indeed. A consultation was immediately held and they determined to leave that night, as it would be very unsafe to remain there. Indeed, they expected every moment to see the whole body of the Black-feet party coming upon them, especially if they had any knowledge of the size of their little party. If they did not know the strength of Captain Williams' party they would be more cautious, as Indians rarely run dangerous risks.

The exploration party was, however, now certain of one thing and that was that Black-feet scouts had watched them for several days. They had observed movement among the rocks several times on the summit of an adjacent mountain. They had assumed that the peering eyes were wolves, but now it seemed more likely it was the actions of Indians examining their location and endeavoring to ascertain their strength.

The melancholy event that we have just detailed took place in the latter part of the day; it was not long before the party of Captain Williams was under the cover of night. All the horses were brought in when the alarm was given. When night came on, all hands were busy collecting their traps and making ready for their departure that night as soon as possible.

Large and numerous fires were made to deceive the enemy, from which the men withdrew at least a mile where they remained until they were ready to set off. About midnight they leaped into their saddles and set out south. They traveled as fast as they could for twenty-four hours without giving rest to themselves or horses.

Their journal states that they soon reached the country of the Crow Indians, who were very friendly to the whites at that time. At one of the Crow villages they remained about a week, during which time they took a buffalo hunt; but as they desired to reach a country where beaver were more abundant than in that of the Crows, they continued to travel south under the east side of the Rocky Mountains until they came to the sources of the Platte River. This route, the Crows informed them, was greatly to be preferred if they wished to penetrate the Rocky Mountains and beaver were very abundant along its course.

We will conclude this chapter by stating that one of Captain Williams' men, whose name was Rose, expressed his intention to abandon his party and remain among the Crows. It appears that while the men were in the Crow village, Rose was not able to resist the charms of a certain Crow beauty, whom he afterwards selected as his wife, and with whom he lived for several years. We will give some account of this man Rose in the next chapter, as he was an egregious character in the history of those times.

ROSE AMONG THE CROW

The character of the man, "Rose," was not known to Captain Williams when Rose joined his party. This fellow, it appears, was one of those desperados of the frontiers, outlawed by their crimes, who combine the vices of civilized and Indian life and who are ten times as bad as the Indians, with whom they consort. Rose had formerly belonged to one of the gangs of pirates who infested the islands of the Mississippi plundering boats as they went up and down the river. These pirates sometimes shifted the scene of their robberies to the shore, waylaying travelers as they returned by land from New Orleans, with the proceeds of their downward voyage, plundering them of their money and effects and often perpetrating the most atrocious murders.

These hordes of villains being broken up and dispersed, Rose betook himself to the upper wilderness, and when Captain Williams was forming his company at St. Louis, this fellow came forward and offered his services. Captain Williams observed that he had a sinister look and suspected that his character was not too fair, but it was difficult to get men to join an expedition so risky and full of danger.

He was dropped among the Crow (or Upsarokas, as they are sometimes called)—a race of Indians whose habitudes of life were much more congenial to the feelings of such a man as Rose than the restraints of civilized life. He took several of their women as wives, by whom he had children and became a great man among them. As he lived among the Crows several years, he could speak their language very fluently and had a very general knowledge of the extensive country ranged by these Indians.

In the year 1810 or 1811, he was picked up somewhere on the Missouri by Mr. Hunt, who was at that time on an expedition across the Rocky Mountains. From his knowledge of the Crow country and the Crow language and from the fact of his affiliation with that tribe, Mr. Hunt thought he might be of great service to him while passing through their country and in any intercourse he might have with them. Rose was therefore engaged as guide and interpreter when Hunt's party should reach the country of the Crows.

He had been attached to this party but a few days before he began to exhibit his dark and perfidious spirit by tampering with the fidelity of certain of the men and suggesting to them a design he had been concocting in his own mind, in which he wished them to cooperate with him. The plan of this treacherous scoundrel was that several of the men should join with him, when in the Crow country, in deserting to those Indians, taking with them as many horses and goods as they could. He assured the men of the kindest reception among the Crows, with whose principal Chief he was well acquainted, and tempted them by artful stories of the honors and privileges they would enjoy.

They could have the handsomest women and the daughters of the Chiefs for wives, and as many as they pleased. This plan, too, would set them up for life. When the treachery of this vagabond became generally known, it created much anxiety in the breasts of Mr. Hunt and his friends, as they were sensible that he might do them much mischief, as he could succeed in carrying out his nefarious designs if he could seduce some of the men to cooperate with him. An affair of this kind might be ruinous to the expedition.

To divert the mind of Rose from his wicked thoughts and to tempt him to give up his perfidious purposes, Mr. Hunt treated him with great attention and kindness. He told him that in parting with him in the Crow country, he would pay him half a year's wages in consideration of his past services and would give him a horse, three beaver traps, and sundry other articles calculated to set him up in the world.

This liberal proposition had the desired effect and from that time the whole deportment of Rose underwent a change. He was no longer that surly, sullen, silent, designing fellow. Ever after he was cheerful and seemed honestly to desire the success of the expedition. Still, it was the fixed purpose of some of Hunt's party, that if Rose showed the least inclination to carry out his knavish designs, to shoot the desperado on the spot.

While among the Crows, however, Rose exhibited no bad feelings toward the party and when they took their leave of those Indians, Mr. Hunt consigned him to their cherishing friendship and fraternal adoption as their worthy and old confederate.

Rose was powerful in frame and fearless in spirit, and very soon by his daring deeds took his rank among the first braves of the tribe. Nothing but daring deeds and desperate exploits in the estimation of an Indian will make a brave. In repeated actions of the Crows with the Black-feet, Rose won many laurels.

On one occasion, it is said, a band of Black-feet Indians had fortified themselves within a breastwork and could not be harmed. Rose proposed to storm the work. "Who will take the lead?" was the demand. "I!" cried he, and at their head, he rushed forward. The first Black-foot that opposed him was shot down with his rifle and snatching up the war-club of his victim, he killed four others within the fort.

This victory was complete and Rose returned to the Crow village covered with glory and bearing five Black-foot scalps to be erected as a trophy before his lodge. From this time forward, he was known among the Crows by the name of Che-ku-kaats, or "the man who killed five."

The Crows and Black-feet have always been the most implacable and deadly foes; this daring deed of Rose, therefore, would naturally make him a popular idol of the village. But Indians, like white people, are invidious beings. The popularity of Rose awakened the envy of the native braves. He was a white man, and interloper. Two rival parties sprung up, between whom there were feuds and civil wars that lasted for two or three years until Rose, having contrived to set his adopted brethren by the ears, left them and went down the Missouri, in 1823.

He afterwards enlisted as guide and interpreter for Fitzpatrick and Sublette, who conducted a trapping expedition sent by General Ashly across the mountains. When they got among the Crows, he was able to some extent to revive his popularity, by being very liberal and kind among his old acquaintances, at the expense, however, of the expedition. This company was robbed of their horses when in the Green river valley and it was believed that this man Rose had a hand in the matter.

When General Atkinson went up the Missouri in 1825, he met with Rose among the Crows who, as usual, was a personage of much consequence among them. He is represented as suppressing a chance medley fight that was on the point of taking place between the military of General Atkinson and those Indians. It appears the Crows contrived to stop the touchholes of the field pieces of the expedition with dirt and then became very insolent. A tumult arose and blows began to be dealt out.

As the Crows were evidently in the fault, Rose grasped his gun and broke the stock of it over the head of a brave and laid so vigorously about with the barrel that he soon put the whole throng to flight. Here the affair ended.

Of the subsequent history of this voluntary exile from civilized life, little is certainly known. Some reports say that he died of a disease brought on by his licentious life and others state that he was killed by some of his adopted brethren, the Crows. He is said to have taught the Crows the policy of cultivating the friendship of the white men. This is a policy they still observe to some extent, since the death of Rose.

"If we keep friends with the white men," said one of their Chiefs, "we have nothing to fear from the Black-feet, and can rule the mountains." That is the story of Rose, the heroic vagabond and renegade.

While we are with Captain Williams, among the Crows, we will state a few things about those Indians and the country over which they range. The Crows are to be found on the west of the Missouri and along the east side of the Rocky Mountains, although they often cross the mountains on their predatory excursions, which they are constantly making. They perhaps excel all tribes of the west in their roving, wandering habits and horse-stealing propensities. They not only scour the country east of the Rocky Mountains for several hundred miles, but they are often on the wing along the headwaters of the Columbia, carrying on their plundering and horse-stealing operations.

The horse is the idol of the Crow Indians and their skill and audacity in stealing this animal is said to be astonishing. It is the business of their lives and their glory and delight. An accomplished horse-stealer fills up their idea of a hero. They are called Crows, because they are always on the scamper and the foray and like the bird of the same name, winging their roguish flight from one region to another.

A Rocky Mountain trapper, with whom I met on the frontier of Missouri and who had spent several years as a trapper in the Black Hills and Rocky Mountains, told me that he once accompanied a party of Crows across the mountains, whose object was to steal horses. It was at a time of the year when trapping is suspended. (June, July and August.) He had nothing to do and therefore accompanied this party merely for the purpose of seeing the country and witnessing their mode of operating in their favorite employment.

They were gone about eight weeks and returned with eighty horses. My informant thought they were generally taken from the lower Nez Pierces and also the white settlers on the waters of theColumbia. They performed this trip, stole this number of horses and returned, and such was their adroitness and skill that they did not meet with a single difficulty.

The Crows were once a numerous and powerful tribe of Indians, but their constant wars with the Black-feet and their roving and predatory habits are wearing them away very fast. They seem doomed to that tendency to extinction, which is to be seen among the western tribes.

I will take the privilege of giving a very interesting account of the Crow country, which is to be found in Captain Bonneville's notes prepared for publication by Irving. It is a description of the Crow country given by a Crow Chief, Arapooish, to Mr. Robert Campbell of the Rocky Mountain Fur Company:

"The Crow country," he said, "is a good country. The Great Spirit has put it exactly in the right place—while you are in it you fare well, whenever you go out of it, whichever way you travel, you will fare worse. If you go to the south, there you have to wander over great barren plains, the water is warm and bad and you meet the fever and ague.

To the north it is cold. The winters are long and bitter, with no grass. You cannot keep horses there, but must travel with dogs. What is a country without horses! On the Columbia they are poor and dirty, paddle about in canoes, and eat fish. Their teeth are worn out; they are always taking fish-bones out of their mouths. Fish is poor food.

To the east they dwell in villages, they live well, but they drink the muddy water of the Missouri that is bad. A Crow's dog would not drink such water. About the fork of the Missouri is a fine country, good water, and good grass, plenty of buffalo. In summer it is almost as good as the Crow country, but in winter it is cold, the grass is gone, and there is no salt weed for the horses.

The Crow country is exactly in the right place. It has snowy mountains and sunny plains, all kinds of climate and good things for every season. When the summer heats scorch the prairies, you can draw up under the mountains where the air is sweet and cool, the grass fresh and the bright streams come tumbling out of the snow banks. There you can hunt the elk, the deer, and the antelope and when their skins are fit for dressing, there too you will find plenty of white bears and mountain sheep.

In the autumn, when your horses are fat and strong from the mountain pastures, you can go down into the plains and hunt the buffalo, or trap beaver on the streams. And when winter comes on, you can take shelter in the woody bottoms along the rivers. There you will find buffalo meat for yourselves and cotton-wood bark for your horses, or you may winter in the Wind River Valley where there is salt weed in abundance.

The Crow country is exactly in the right place. Everything good is to be found there. There is no country like the Crow country."

Such is the eulogium on his country by Arapooish.

A Confrontation

While journeying on the headwaters of the Platte River, Captain Williams' party met with another disaster. One morning seven of the men, including Captain Williams, went to bring in the horses, which had been turned out to graze the previous evening. As they were still in the country of the Crows, whom they regarded as their friends, they had not exercised the usual precaution of bringing in their horses and carefully securing them for the night. They simply fastened two of their feet together to prevent them from wandering too far and then turned them out, while they retired a short distance into the edge of some timber and stretched themselves out upon their buffalo skins for the night. The next morning the horses were missing, but their trace in the deep, dewy grass was soon discovered, very fresh, and leading across a low ridge in the prairie.

The men in pursuit of the horses soon found some of the cords by which they had been tied. They were not broken by the horses, but had evidently been taken off, a circumstance that filled their minds with painful anxiety, but they continued to follow the trace to the top of the ridge. There they were suddenly struck with the sight of about sixty Indians at the base of the hill, in possession of their horses. They seemed very busy, preparing, no doubt, to make an attack upon the party, for when they observed the men at the top of the hill, they sprang upon their horses and dashed up the hill toward them, at the same time making everything ring with their terrific and hideous yells.

Captain Williams urged his men to escape to the timber, but before they could reach it, five of them were overtaken and killed. Captain Williams and another of the seven succeeded, though very closely pursued, in gaining the timber. The other men that had remained in camp, seeing the Indians coming, had snatched up their rifles and each one taking a tree, they opened fire upon them, which caused the Indians to wheel and withdraw a short distance leaving several of their men upon the ground dead and wounded.

In a few minutes the Indians dashed up again, shouting and yelling, and launching their arrows in the timber. There was dense undergrowth that not only prevented them from riding into the timber, but also prevented them from seeing Captain Williams' men. This was a lucky circumstance and but for it they would all have been cut off.

Captain Williams told his men to take good aim and not to fire until they were certain of making an effectual shot. By observing this plan, and by reserving their shots until the Indians would come to the very edge of the timber the sharp report of a rifle was always followed by the tumbling of an Indian from a horse. Four successive times these Indians dashed up to the timber, launched their arrows, and then wheeled and withdrew out of the reach of the rifles of Captain Williams' men. Being unable to dislodge our little band and having sustained a great loss of men, the Indians abandoned the field of battle and rode off.

As a scalp is a great and favorite trophy with an Indian, these Indians did not neglect to carry off with them the scalps of the five men they had killed. They also took with them two or three (it was thought) of those Indians wounded in the fray, but left nineteen on the ground. The party remained behind their fortress of trees and thick undergrowth while one of the men went out to evaluate the motions of the Indians. He returned, reporting that he had seen them at least three miles off going at a brisk gait.

Captain Williams saw his party now reduced to ten, without a single horse to carry their accoutrements, and what could they do in a country full of Indians on foot? It was probable that these same Indians, knowing the almost helpless condition of the little party and infuriated by the slaughter of so many of their men, would hurry off to the main body of their tribe and return with increased forces to do a work of total destruction.

There was therefore no time to be lost. The company gathered up their furs and as many traps as the ten could carry and traveled about ten miles, keeping close to the timber. They avoided as well as they could making any tracks by which they might be pursued. When night came, they crept into a very dense thicket where they spent the greater part of the night erecting a scaffold upon which they cached their furs and traps and any items they deemed inconvenient to carry.

Captain Williams did not know to what tribe of Indians the band belonged that attacked his party. They were in all probability Crows, and perhaps from the very village in which our little party had spent several days, although they professed great friendship for the whites. This conjecture is the more plausible when we remember that the friendship of those Indians is about as uncertain as their locality and the consciences of these notorious horse-thieves would not let them rest very easy if they should suffer such a cavalcade to pass through their country without, at least, an effort on their part to steal their horses. The party, however, did not suspect the Crows as they supposed they were out of the Crow country and on the Arkansas River. This supposition, however, proved to be erroneous, for they were still in the country of those treacherous, crafty, roving Indians and on the upper waters of the Platte River.

As the prospects of the company were now gloomy in the extreme, the spirits of the men drooped and their hearts became sad. They were many hundred miles from the abodes of civilized life in the heart of a wilderness almost boundless, where they found themselves beset on every side with Indians ready, at a suitable opportunity, to pounce upon them and make them their easy prey.

They were now without horses and their number was so reduced they could scarcely indulge a hope of escaping the cruel hands of the natives. It is hardly necessary to state that they were compelled to abandon their intentions of crossing the Rocky Mountains and trapping on the waters of the Columbia. But Captain Williams, who is represented by one who knew him well, "as brave and cautious and the best and most feeling companion in the world," in all his difficulties wore a serene and cheerful countenance and encouraged his men not to give up the hope of yet succeeding in their trapping enterprise. Should they succeed, they would not only be independent, but rich for life.

They left this region of danger, and the following spring found them on the sources of the Arkansas River, where they encamped. Beaver were very abundant here and there was a prospect of their gathering in a large harvest of rich peltries.

The very succinct and imperfect and much mutilated journal before me states that the party scattered about on the various little streams that put into the Arkansas and that one after another was cut off by a fierce tribe of Indians called the Comanche, until but three of the party remained: Captain Williams and two others, whose names were James Workman and Samuel Spencer. These three were all that were left of those early adventurers in the fur trade, a melancholy fate indeed, that verifies the assertion "that of the hardy bands of trappers that first entered those regions, three-fifths have fallen by the hands of Indian foes."

Williams, Workman and Spencer now determined to return, if they could, to St. Louis, but what route should they take to reach there and where were they? These were troubling questions that sprung up in the anxious minds of the lost trappers. Captain Williams thought, based on the distance they had traveled, that they were on the Red River and proposed descending it in canoes. Williams, Workman and Spencer thought they were not far from Santa Fe, in New Mexico and proposed going there as the only way they could adopt to avoid being killed by the Indians. Strange as it may appear, and dangerous as their situation was, the three lost trappers separated. Workman and Spencer struck out towards the Spanish country and Captain Williams descended, as he supposed, the Red River. Before they separated, however, they cached all their peltries and whatever traps they could not take with them.

As it is our object to give a faithful and full account of these three wandering trappers, subsequent to the time when they parted in a region of great danger, we will furnish the reader with the account of Captain Williams' first.

Encounters On The Plains

We have already alluded, with great surprise, to the fact that these three lost trappers should have separated, when all hope of regaining their homes depended upon their remaining together. When their party was now reduced to three, by the ferocity of the Indians of the West, how could they expect to escape the clutches of these wild bands? How could two men expect to escape—let alone how could one? Yet startling as the fact may be, they separated—and separated in a region where several of their party had been killed, a region full of danger and lurking foes. We would state that at that early day, our men were not as well acquainted as they are now with the modes of warfare practiced by the western tribes, nor were those tribes as well apprised as they are now of the efficiency of our rifles.

The melancholy consequence has been, as already stated, the loss of three-fifths at least of those early adventurers into those regions and the killing of a great many Indians. Since, however, our men have gained a knowledge of the way in which the Indians practice their hostilities and especially since the various tribes have ascertained the distance and accuracy with which our rifles shoot, those Indians are much more cautious and the consequence is the loss of life on either side has not been so great for a number of years.

Our men, too, have found it to be good policy to take with them into that country, guns that carry very heavy balls. These are better for killing buffalo and they keep off hostile Indians at a greater distance. In a prairie country, men engaged in shooting at anything are apt to mistake the distance, always supposing the object nearer than it really is. Hence the advantage in having guns that will carry up for several hundred yards.

Indians will never rush upon a party of white men unless they know their guns are empty or when they may have some other advantage. "They know," said a free trapper of great intrepidity, "that the crack of a rifle is always followed by the loss of one of their men." They therefore regard the rifles of our men as very dangerous things. A handful of men behind a fortification of some kind may keep off a hundred Indians. Their guns, (all of them), should not be empty at the same time. It is the custom of experienced men to reserve several shots to always keep some of their rifles charged.

The same free trapper informed the author, "that in several difficulties with the Black-feet tribes, two other trappers and himself, snugly entrenched behind some logs, had compelled a large body of those Indians to leave the field of battle, howling and whining most mournfully for their losses. They will not rush upon a loaded rifle." It was the misfortune of Captain Williams' men that they did not understand the most successful and the safest way of fighting hostile tribes, and the results were the melancholy events we have detailed.

Before Williams, Workman and Spencer separated, they cached the skins they had procured, expecting, if they should be fortunate enough to reach the abodes of civilization, to form another company and return for the purpose of conveying their peltries to St. Louis. They also cached all their traps, except as many as they could conveniently carry. Workman and Spencer could take none, as they intended to strike across the watercourses for the Spanish country. Captain Williams was able to take six or eight traps, as he constructed a canoe in which he conveyed them.

We have said that we would follow Captain Williams throughout his subsequent history and then return to that of Workman and Spencer, whom we now leave on the head waters of a strange river, entangled in a labyrinth of wild and unexplored region, scarcely knowing which way to go. Captain Williams, although a great woodsman, very cool and brave, and holding on with great tenacity to his original purpose of making himself rich by the traffic in the rich peltries of those nameless and unknown rivers, was no less perplexed in his own mind about his locality.

As the country was an unexplored region, he might be on a river that flowed into the Pacific or he might be drifting down a stream that was an affluent to the Gulf of Mexico. He was, however, inclined to believe that he was on the sources of the Red River. He therefore resolved to launch his canoe and go wherever the stream might convey him, trapping on his descent when beaver might be plenty.

The first canoe that he used he made of buffalo skins. As these kinds of water conveyances soon begin to leak and rot, he made another canoe of cottonwood as soon as he came to timber sufficiently large to construct it.

Completing the cottonwood canoe, he again embarked for a port unknown. For most of his travel, Captain Williams performed during the hours of night, except when he felt it perfectly safe to travel in daylight. His usual plan was to glide along down the stream, until he came to a place where beaver signs were abundant. There he would push his little canoe to the shore, into some eddy among the willows where he remained concealed, except when he was setting his traps or visiting them in the morning.

He always set his traps between sunset and dark and visited them at the earliest break of day. When he had taken all the beaver in one neighborhood, he would untie his little conveyance and glide onward and downward to try his luck in another place. Thus, for hundreds of miles did this solitary trapper float down this unknown river, through an unknown country, here and there lashing his canoe to the willows and planting his traps in the little tributaries around it. The upper part of the Arkansas River (for this proved to be the river upon which he was trapping) is very destitute of timber and the prairie frequently begins at the bank of the river and expands on either side as far as the eye can see.

Captain Williams saw vast herds of buffalo, and as it was running season, the bulls were making a wonderful ado, making the plains roll with their low, deep grunting or bellowing, tearing up the earth with their feet and horns, whisking their tails, and defying their rivals to battle. Often they would come together in fierce battle, with a fury and force that reminded the spectator of the collision of two steamboats. Smaller game were also seen by Captain Williams in great abundance

Large gangs of wild horses could be frequently seen grazing on the plains and hillsides. As it was the spring of the year, the neighing and squealing of the stallions might be heard at all times of a still night. Captain Williams never used his rifle to procure meat, except when it was absolutely necessary, and when it could be done with perfect safety. On one occasion, when he had no beaver flesh, upon which he generally subsisted, he killed a deer, and after refreshing an empty stomach with a portion of it, he placed the carcass, which he had cut up, in one end of his canoe. As it was his invariable custom to sleep in his canoe, the night after he had laid in a supply of venison he was startled in his sleep by the trampling of something in the bushes on the bank.

Tramp, tramp, tramp went the footstep, as it approached the canoe. Captain Williams first thought it might be an Indian that had found out his locality, but an Indian would not approach him in that careless manner. Although there was beautiful starlight, the shade of the trees and dense undergrowth made it very dark on the bank of the river. Captain Williams always adopted the precaution of tying his canoe to shore with a piece of rawhide about twenty feet long, which let it swing from the bank about that distance. This precaution he adopted at night, that in an emergency he might cut the cord that bound him to the shore and glide off without any noise.

During the day he hid his canoe in the willows. As the sound of the footsteps grew more and more distinct, the Captain observed a huge grizzly bear approach the edge of the water and hold up its head as if scenting something. He then let his huge body into the water and made for the canoe.

Captain Williams snatched up his axe as the most suitable means of defending himself in such a scrape and stood with it uplifted and ready to drive it into the head of the huge aggressor. The bear reached the canoe and immediately placed his forepaws upon the hind end of it and nearly turned it over. Captain Williams struck one of his feet with the edge of his axe, which caused him to relax his hold with that foot. He, however, held on with the other foot and Captain Williams inflicted another blow upon his head, which caused him to let the canoe go entirely.

Captain Williams thought the bear sunk in the water from the stunning effects of the blow and was drowned. He saw nothing more of him, nor did he hear anything. The presumption was that he went under the water. His aim was to get at the fresh meat in the Captain's canoe. The next morning there were two of the bear's claws in the canoe that had been severed from one of his feet by Captain Williams' axe. The resolute Captain carefully preserved the claws for a number of years as a trophy, which he was fond of exhibiting and the history of which he delighted to detail.

We have said that Captain Williams subsisted principally upon the flesh of the beaver, which he caught in his traps. When the hide is taken off and dressed, this animal weighs about twelve pounds and its flesh, although a little musky, is very fine. Its tail, which is eight or ten inches long, is flat and oval in its form and is covered with scales about the size of those of a salmon fish.

The beaver tail is a great delicacy in the estimation of the mountain trapper. He separates it from the body of the beaver, thrusts a stick in one end of it and places it before the fire with the scales on it. When the heat of the fire strikes through so as to roast it, large blisters rise on the surface, which are very easily removed. The tail is then perfectly white and very delicious. Next to the tail is the liver. This is another favorite dainty with the trapper and when properly cooked, constitutes a delightful repast in the eye of these mountain epicures.

This animal is exceedingly wily and is sometimes too cunning for the most experienced trapper. If, by scent, or sound or sight, he has any intimation of the presence of a trapper, he puts at defiance all his traps. The trapper, therefore, finds it necessary to practice great caution when in the neighborhood of a beaver lodge. He avoids riding over the ground, lest the sound created by the feet of his horse strike dismay among the furry inhabitants beneath the surface.

Instead of walking on the ground he wades in the water, lest he might leave a scent behind by which he might be discovered. He also plants his traps under the surface of the water, where they can be neither seen nor smelled. But one kind of bait is used, because no other kinds are needed and this kind is the best. The beaver has two pair of testicles, one containing the semen, by which he propagates his race and the other containing the matter that gives to his body the musky smell that is peculiar to it. These testicles are opened and their contents are put in separate horns, which the trapper carries by his side. When he uses it for bait, he thrusts a small stick in both of his horns, about an inch deep in the matter and then plants it upright in the water, between the jaws of the trap, leaving the baited end of it several inches above the surface of the water.

A natural propensity prompts the beaver to seek the place from where the scent issues and he is taken. In this respect the beaver resembles the dog that always seeks to smell the place where one of his kind may have spent his urine. It is worthy of notice that the beaver feed exclusively on the bark of trees and shrubs, while the otter lives on fish and reptiles. The consequence is that the flesh of the former is very fine, while that of the latter is very offensive to the taste.

An experienced trapper always aims so to set his traps as to drown the beaver when they are taken. This is accomplished by sinking the trap several inches underwater, and by driving a stake through a ring on the end of the chain into the bottom. When a beaver discovers he is fastened in a trap, he pitches and plunges about until his strength is exhausted, he then sinks down and is drowned. If a beaver succeeds in getting to shore, he always extricates himself by cutting off the leg that is in the trap.

This animal is furnished with several large front teeth that are curved, by which he is enabled to cut down trees that are from six to twelve inches in diameter. Armed with these formidable tusks, he will cut a dog that happens upon him immediately into pieces. They bestow a great deal of labor and pains in the construction of their dams and generally make them so firm that a man may pass over them on horseback with perfect safety.

The last thing that I shall state, at present, by way of description of the beaver is that his fur, which is of the finest quality and remarkably thick on the hide, very much resembles in color the fur of our common wild rabbit.

But let us return to our solitary trapper, as we find him gliding about in his cottonwood canoe on the bosom of an unknown river, upon the banks of which no white man had ever been present to leave his footprints behind him. We confess that we never contemplate this part of Captain Williams' history but with a feeling of astonishment, as well as unrestrained curiosity.

What contempt of danger, or rather superiority to it! What zealous perseverance in the prosecution of his purposes and at the same time, what caution and constant vigilance he must have practiced to avoid being discovered by Indians.

For several months, he was certain that no eye saw him but that of his God, nor did he see the face of a fellow being, civilized or Indian. He communed with none but his own heart, nor did his eyes gaze upon the face of any mortal except that of himself, as it was reflected back from the surface of those wild waters. Day after day did he add to his stock of rich peltries, but day after day passed away without bringing any light as to the destiny before him. Week after week had he descended this river and no frontier cabin greeted his return.

Wilderness and solitude still reigned everywhere, but Captain Williams was a man of as much patience as fortitude and possessed a cheerful disposition that made him look upon the "sunny side" of everything and "always hoped for the best." Solitary as he was and exposed to danger all the time, he frequently spoke of this kind of life as having its peculiar attractions. But it would have been a miracle if he had entirely escaped the observation of the Indians. Circumstances occurred that led to his discovery and threw him into their clutches.

As he was descending the river with his peltries, which consisted of one hundred and twenty-five beaver-skins, besides some skins of otter and other smaller animals of the fur-bearing race, all of which he had procured since he parted with Workman and Spencer, he overtook three Kansas Indians who were also in a canoe descending the river, as he learned from them, to some post to trade with the whites. They manifested a very friendly disposition toward Captain Williams and expressed a wish to accompany him down the river. He learned from them, to his great gratification, that he was on the Big Arkansas River and not more than five hundred miles from the whites.

By this time Captain Williams had learned how much confidence he could repose in Indians and their professions of friendship. He had learned enough to know that they would not let a solitary trapper pass through their country with a valuable collection of furs without, at least, making an effort to rob him. The plan of these Kansas would be to decoy him into a friendly intercourse with them and then seize the first suitable opportunity to strip him of everything he had. He resolved, therefore, to get rid of them as soon as possible and to accomplish this, he plied his oars with all diligence. The Indians had no disposition to belabor themselves in this way, but managed their route more leisurely, being content to be carried along by the current of the water.

Captain Williams soon left them, as he supposed, far behind him and when night came on, as he had labored hard all day and slept none the night before, he resolved to turn aside into the willows to take a few hours of sleep. But he had stopped scarcely thirty minutes before he heard some Indians pull to shore just above him on the same side of the river. He immediately renewed his fire, loosed his canoe from shore and glided smoothly and silently off and away, rowing hard and faithfully for two or three hours, until he again put to shore and tied up.

But again, a short time after he had landed, he heard some Indians going in to shore on the same side and just above him. A second time the vigilant Captain slipped out from the willows and glided stealthily away from that dangerous ground, pulling ahead with great industry until sometime after midnight when he supposed he could, with safety, stop traveling to snatch a morsel of sleep.

Captain Williams was apprehensive that he was in a dangerous region. The anxiety of his mind therefore kept him awake, and it was a lucky circumstance, for as he lay in his canoe invoking sleep, he heard for a third time the canoe land as before. He was now satisfied that he was being dogged by the Kansas whom he had passed the day before. In no very good humor, therefore, Captain Williams snatched up his rifle and walked up the bank to the place where he had heard the canoe land. As he suspected, they were indeed the three Kansas, and when they saw the Captain, they renewed their expressions of friendship and wished him to partake of their hospitality.

Captain Williams stood aloof from them and shook his head in anger and charged them with their villainous purposes. In the short sententious manner of the Indians, he said to them "you now follow me three times—if you follow me again, I will kill you," and wheeled about abruptly and returned to his canoe. A third time our solitary trapper pushed his little craft from land and set off downstream, to get away from a region where to sleep would be extremely hazardous.

Captain Williams faithfully plied his oars the balance of the night and solaced himself with the thought that he was very lucky, when no evil had befallen him, except the loss of a few hours of sleep. But while he was escaping from the villainous pursuers behind him, he was running into new dangers and difficulties.

The following day he overtook a large company of the same tribe (Kansas), headed by a Chief who was also descending the river. Into the hands of these Indians he fell a prisoner and was conducted to one of their villages. The principal Chief took all of his furs and traps and all his chattels.

A very short time after this, the Kansas went to war with the Pawnees and took Captain Williams with them. In a battle in which the Kansas gained a most decided victory, Captain Williams acted a distinguished part by killing a number of Pawnees and indeed, by his very efficient services, caused the affair to terminate in favor of the Kansas.

When they returned to the Kansas village, the Captain, who had always been treated with kindness, was now thought to be a great brave and could have been advanced to all their honors and been made one of their principal Chiefs. But, as the Kansas had set him at liberty for the services he had rendered them, in their late difficulty with a formidable and inveterate foe, he determined to return to the white settlement on the Missouri.

However, they retained his furs and indeed all his chattels except his rifle, with as many rounds of ammunition as would be necessary to secure him provisions along his route. Captain Williams was the more reconciled to the loss of his furs as he believed the Indians would preserve them with a view of taking them to a trading post. He formed the purpose of being present there to secure them again.

As to the furs that were cached before he parted with Workman and Spencer, he intended to return for them as soon as he could get a sufficient number of men to accompany him. As Captain Williams knew not where he was at the time he cached his furs, while he was with the Kansas, he was able to procure some facts in relation to the country that were of value to him.

When he left the Platte River, which he supposed to be the Arkansas River, he descended a stream that interlocked with the main branch of the Platte River and is an affluent to the Big Arkansas River. They cached their furs near the mouth of this stream. Here, and indeed for a long distance below, the Rocky mountains are to be distinctly seen covered with perpetual snow. When he separated from Workman and Spencer, they set off up a stream emptying also into the Arkansas, (supposing it to be the main stream), and coming from the south. This proved to be what, in those days, was called the third fork of the Arkansas River, on the west side.

The Captain also learned, while with the Kansas, that they expected to repair the following spring to Fort Osage on the Missouri River to receive some annuities due them from the United States and he knew that his furs would be found there at that time.

There was a fort of white men, which at that time was called Cooper's Fort, somewhere on the side of the Missouri River opposite the post of trade where the Kansas expected to assemble. He therefore set off for that point on the Missouri to be ready the following spring, to regain if he could his peltries that were now in the hands of the Kansas.

WHEN CULTURES CLASH

On the frontiers of the West, the outskirts of civilized society then as now, there has always been a certain motley class of men, trappers, traders, renegades, and refugees from justice who seem to have become disgusted with the tameness and monotony of civilized life and made exiles of themselves by going where the restraints and the security of laws are not felt. For these men, who by the way are very numerous, Indian life seems to have its peculiar charms.

They take to themselves wives and domesticate themselves among the different tribes in the west and live and die among them. If one of these men should happen to return to the abodes of his white brethren, he feels like a fish out of water and is impatient and restless, and seeks the earliest opportunity to get back to the country of his choice.

The result of this intermixing and marrying has been the springing up of numerous hybrid beings that constitute a medium through which, it is hoped, at no distant day the laws, arts, and habitude of civilized life may be successfully introduced. This would be the means of reclaiming them from the ignorance and barbarities in which they have been so long enthralled.

These half-breeds are already very numerous and it is difficult to distinguish them from white men for they seem just as intelligent and just as decent as to their exterior, and speak our language just as fluently as our own citizens and really vary but little from them in the color of the skin. As Captain Williams was journeying from the Arkansas to the Missouri, he met with one of those white men that had taken up his residence among the Osages and who was, to some extent, engaged in an effort to teach that tribe how to cultivate the soil.

He had married quite a good-looking squaw with whom he was living and by whom he had several black-eyed little children. He had erected two or three comfortable cabins around which he had several acres of ground under cultivation. Captain Williams came upon his residence late in the evening and was received by him with backwoods hospitality.

As the Captain was much fatigued, he stayed with him that night. It was now late in the fall and the cold winds had already begun to sweep over those extensive prairies. He was not only fatigued, but also hungry, and after enjoying a very abundant meal, he became very sleepy and stupid and expressed a wish to lie down. The landlord accordingly conducted him to one of the cabins in which there were two beds standing in opposite corners of the room. Captain Williams threw himself upon one of the beds and was soon in a very deep sleep.

About midnight, his slumber was disturbed by a singular and very frightful kind of noise accompanied by struggling on the other bed, in the opposite corner of the room. What it was, the Captain was entirely at a loss to understand. There were no windows in the cabin to furnish any light, the door was shut, and it was as dark as Egypt. A fierce contest seemed to be going on. There were deep groans and hard breathings, the snapping and gritting of teeth was constantly going on. Occasional struggling took place, in which great muscular power seemed to be employed. For a moment the noise would subside, with drawing the breath at long intervals as if death was taking place. Then again the struggling and scuffling would be renewed, accompanied as before with groaning and deep sighing and grinding of the teeth and the exercise, it would seem, of great physical power.

The bedclothes, that consisted of a blanket or two and a buffalo robe, were pulled about and very much torn. At last slam-bang the whole mysterious affair fell upon the floor and carried on in the same frightful and unearthly way. Captain Williams stated that in all his difficulties with the Indians, his fortitude had never been so fairly tested, as on this night. "To be able to see danger," he said, " takes away at least one half of its terror."

But here was a mysterious, formidable, invisible something, which he could not see. He did not know where to find the door, as he had forgotten where it was. As for his rifle that had often saved his life, he now recollected that he had left it in the cabin occupied by the family. He had a knife but it was attached to his hunting coat, which he had hung on the corner of the other bedstead. The danger was between him and his knife.

For a moment, the sounds would subside as if death had succeeded, and then again every power seemed to be wakened up and the same unseen and mysterious and dreadful tragedy repeated. All over the floor it shifted about, until it got under the bed of Captain Williams. Here, as by convulsive efforts, it raised the bed with the perplexed Captain on it off the floor several times and after belaboring itself dreadfully for several minutes, it moved rather to the side of the bed.

Captain Williams then raised himself to a sitting position on the bed and threw around him a buffalo skin to protect himself, if an effort should be made to injure him, but in an instant the skin was snatched and pulled off and the Captain left uncovered and unprotected, at least so far as a buffalo robe might prove a shield. Another violent snatch took away a blanket upon which the Captain was seated and nearly took him with it. As the next thing might be a blow in the dark, he felt, as he jocularly remarked (if he could not see), that it was high time to shift his quarters.

So he made a desperate leap from his bed and alighted on the opposite side of the room and called for the landlord, who came immediately to his relief by opening the door. The Captain told him the devil, or something as bad, he believed, was in the room and he wanted a light. The accommodating host hurried back and in a moment returned with a light that soon revealed the awful mystery.

It was an Indian who at the time was struggling in convulsions, which he, it appears, was in the habit of having. He was an old Chief who the Captain ascertained to be a relative of the wife of the landlord and generally made his home there. Being absent when the Captain arrived, he came in at a late hour when all were asleep and repaired to the bed he usually occupied. It was not known to anyone that he was on the premises, until he was found in the above miserable condition. The poor fellow had dreadfully mangled himself by tearing his flesh, particularly his arms, with his teeth. His nose, which was uncommonly large, was much bruised and skinned. He was removed out of the cabin and our guest, who was not to be frightened out of a night's rest, soon again sunk into a profound repose.

Captain Williams reached Cooper's fort in the beginning of winter, which was at that time occupied by a few white men, having now been absent one year and eight months. When Captain Williams reached Cooper's fort, he learned that a United States factor (trader) named Mr. C. Cibley was expected from St. Louis that winter. Mr. Cibley was to go up to Fort Osage to meet the Osages and the Kansas and pay them their annuities. Mr. Cibley came up the Missouri as far as Cooper's Fort, but was not able to get to Fort Osage, due to the ice and the severity of the winter.

The Indians were therefore compelled to come down the river to a place now called Arrow Rock, where Mr. Cibley met them. Captain Williams was present and there met the very Indian Chief that had robbed him of his furs on the Arkansas. The agent of the United States had already been apprised of the whole affair and informed the Kansas Chief that as Mr. Williams was a citizen of the government for which he was acting, he would not pay them their annuities unless they returned the furs properly belonging to Mr. Williams.

They at first were unwilling to admit their villainy, but Mr. Cibley was very positive and determined and finally succeeded in bringing them to an acknowledgement of the deed. In compliance with the orders of the agent, the guilty-looking fellow sneaked off to their lodges to bring out the furs and returned with four packages, which Captain Williams proved were his by the initials of his name, E. W., which were on them. The agent inquired if that was all. Captain Williams replied there were eight more. The fraudulent Chief said there were no more. Mr. Cibley peremptorily demanded the whole of the furs. Three more packages were then brought out, which the Chief affirmed made up the number he had taken.

Mr. Cibley gave them every assurance that he would not pay them their annuities if they did not comply with his orders. One after another, three of the bales of skins were reluctantly brought forward until they numbered eleven. Mr. Cibley demanded the twelfth, but "it could not be found," said the Indian Chief. "But it must be found," said Cibley. The old Kansas Chief went away and after an absence of an hour, during which time he was busy searching among the lodges for the last pack, returned and told Mr. Cibley that "he could not find it, and he believed that God Almighty could not find it," by which he meant to be understood that such a bale of fur did not exist.

Captain Williams, who was much amused with the answer of the Chief, suggested to Mr. Cibley that it was possible that one of the packages might have been lost and stated, furthermore, that he would not insist upon their returning it. Here the matter ended and to the great advantage of Mr. Williams, as he got rid of the very difficult job of conveying his peltries to the Missouri river.

The following spring Captain Williams took his furs down the Missouri and sold them in St. Louis and then returned to Cooper's Fort for the purpose of raising a body of men to go with him for the furs he had cached on an upper tributary of the Great Arkansas River.

COOPERS AND COMANCHE

The gloomy and melancholy account that Captain Williams had to give of his expedition and the horrible representations that he was compelled to make of the great majority of the western tribes, was by no means favorable to Captain Williams' purpose of raising a body of men to accompany him back to the mountains, for his furs were still cached at the point the Great Arkansas River issues from the Rocky Mountains. Nor did his accounts as to the great abundance of valuable furs in those regions seem to have much effect. The most dreadful stories had been told about the Indian cruelty of the piratical Sioux, the ferocity of the ruthless Black-feet, and the treachery of the thieving and dishonest Crows, and they were most abundantly confirmed by the fate of Captain Williams' party.

His furs, too, were in a country infested by bands of wandering Comanche, a tribe that was not behind any other tribe in the far west in point of strength and ferocity. They were represented as the best horsemen in the world and as having the fleetest horses. Their mode of fighting was always on horseback. They would hang by one leg on the withers of their horses, throw themselves on one side so as to make a breastwork of the animal and shoot their arrows from under the horses' necks while at full speed. They could shoot an arrow completely through a man, horse, or buffalo, with all ease. Again, a body of men should be large to go through those regions of danger and such a body could not be raised anywhere near St. Louis, as there were very few white people at that day near said town.

These difficulties met Captain Williams whenever he made an effort to collect men to go with him. The summer passed away and autumn came on and not a single man as yet had agreed to go. It was not until the latter part of December that two young men informed Captain Williams they would join him. They were very young and as there was a strong probability that their friends would interfere and persuade them to abandon a trip so very dangerous, the

Captain found it to be good policy to start within two or three days after they consented to go.

On the 25th of December, the old veteran trapper and his two youthful companions, Joseph and William Cooper, left Cooper's Fort to brave the perils of the wilderness. They set out on horses with ten days of provisions and traveled up the Missouri River to Fort Osage, where they left the river and went a southwest course until they struck the Osage River.

Here they found fine grass for their horses. In the prairies, there was a deep snow and the wind blew very cold. Leaving the Osage River, they journeyed westward until they came to the Neasho River, which is an affluent to the Great Arkansas River, and interlocks with the tributaries of the Kansas River.

Two days before they reached the Neasho River, their provisions failed and not a living thing was to be seen on the face of the earth. If there had been any game, they probably could not have secured it as there was a thick, hard crust on a deep snow that covered the prairie. When they walked on it, it created a cracking sound that could have been heard a great distance. They encamped before night in a walnut grove on the bottom of the river, wearied, cold, and weak from hunger. For two days, traveling over bleak prairies pierced with merciless winds, they had had nothing to eat.

The thought presented itself that there might be walnuts under the trees composing the grove where they were encamped. They therefore immediately began to remove the crusted snow and found this fruit very abundant. While they were busily cracking nuts, the sun came out from behind some dark winter clouds and shone warm and beautiful. The sight of some squirrels coming out into the sunlight provided hope that the party would not go hungry for long.

They succeeded in killing eight squirrels and ate three of them that night. The next day they resumed their journey and trudged along for three days, having nothing on which to subsist but five of the eight squirrels they had killed. On the fourth day, they came to the Verdigris River, another tributary of the Great Arkansas River, and found two Indian camps. They were members of the Osage tribe, who had been out on a buffalo hunt, but their supply of provisions was scanty. The Indians, however, manifested a very friendly disposition and very promptly furnished the men with something to eat. Men as hungry as they were are not disposed to be very fastidious as to what they eat, or the manner in which it may be prepared and served up.

A squaw, for the purpose of cleaning a wooden bowl, set it out of the lodge that the dogs might lick it and when this was done by the canine part of the household, it was filled with a kind of porridge, in which there was meat and

Indian corn. To season this, an old squaw added some small pieces of buffalo tallow. As she labored under the disadvantage of not having a knife to cut it, she resorted to the expedient of gnawing off piece after piece and spitting it into the bowl.

On the next day, Captain Williams and his two men left the lodges of the Osages, taking with them five quarts of corn, which they parched, to eat along the way. After traveling two or three days, William Cooper fainted on the prairie from hunger and fatigue, but Captain Williams and Joseph Cooper carried him to a point of timber where they raised a fire.

Here fresh buffalo signs were abundant and Captain Williams and Joseph Cooper went out and killed two bulls. They took as much meat as they could carry to camp and when they had all eaten of it, their faces as well as their prospects seemed to brighten up, and they felt ready as well as renewed for the resumption of their journey.

For seven or eight days they continued to go westward, being favored with good weather, except one day the wind blew so hard from the west that they were compelled to stop as they could not get along against it. About the fifth of February, another snow fell and the weather turned intensely cold. The little party had been traveling on the north side of the Arkansas River and now crossed that river to reach a warmer climate.

They report the cold as being so great that it was with difficulty that they saved their horses from being frozen to death. Continuing a southwest course, within a day or two, they came to a region where there was no snow and grass was very abundant. A great many wild horses were to be seen on the prairies, elevating their heads and tails when the men would approach them, and snorting, wheeling, and curveting around.

The horses were of all colors. Large gangs, also, of buffalo and elk were feeding about and on the outskirts of the buffalo herds there were the usual appendages, that is, bands of hungry wolves sitting about watching the buffalo. Encouraged by numbers and mad from hunger, they frequently make the most desperate assaults upon the buffalo and even ran down a deer.

While in this region of good weather, grass and game, the party lived well and all were in good cheer. When they wanted meat, they would kill the buffalo cows, which were very fat and fine. But the weather turned cold as they approached the mountains, and the buffalo disappeared. There was nothing to be seen but wild horses and restless packs of wolves gadding about, pinched with cold and hunger.

It is an old saying, *"Canis non est canem,"* (dog does not eat dog). The same may be said of wolves. *"Lupus non est lupum"* (wolf does not eat wolf). Yet their ravenous propensity is so great as to prompt them to attack everything else but their own race.

Captain Williams and his men again found themselves destitute of provisions in the midst of winter and suffering from hunger. When they looked out upon an ocean of prairie, they could see nothing but a little half-starved wolf that frequently came to gnaw some buffalo bones. Hunger constrained them to shoot it. "Within ten minutes," say the notes in their journal, "his hide was taken off and some of the meat was cooked and ready to be eaten." They speak of his flesh as having a good flavor and being very refreshing to their hungry stomachs.

They also cleaned his entrails and carefully preserved them for future necessities. Such are the means to which the early adventurers in that country were compelled to resort to keep from starving to death. The party also procured a fat raccoon, which made a fine repast. One day an old wild stud was seen by the men, pawing at the ice to get to water, at a considerable distance from the party in the prairie.

Joseph Cooper took the advantage of some sand hills and got within one hundred and forty yards, (as he supposed) when the horse trotted up within eighty yards and received a shot in the bulge of the ribs, which only caused him to snort and prance about for the moment. Cooper then shot him the second time in the point of one of his shoulders, which made him run off a short distance and lie down. Cooper was so weak from hunger that he was compelled to make a rest of his gun stick and wiping stick, before he could hold up his gun with sufficient firmness to shoot with any degree of accuracy.

Captain Williams observing the inefficiency of Cooper's shots came up and shot the horse in the head. They skinned him and supped upon his flesh. His hide they preserved for tugs to bind up their furs, as they were now only a short distance from the caches. This flesh, to some extent, satisfied the cravings of their hungry appetites, but it was very coarse and strong and as they expressed themselves, "not fit for a white man to eat."

It would remain in the stomach for a long time, in a state of indigestion and for several days, (eight or ten they said), "they belched up the old stud as strong as ever."

They reached the caches about the 10th of March. They found them undiscovered by wolves or Indians and, of course, undisturbed. Up to this time they had lost none of their horses and now that they had reached the point, both of place and time, beyond which they would not have much need of their services, they were not much concerned about their preservation. Indeed, as they intended to take their furs down the river and as their horses might betray them into the hands of Indians, the safety of the party required that they should get rid of them some way.

It would not be safe to turn them loose. They would wander about, be picked up by the Indians and lead to their discovery. They, therefore, determined to shoot them and preserve them by drying some of their flesh and throw the rest into the river.

Within a day or two, after they reached the caches, a herd of buffalo made their appearance, but on the opposite, (north), side of the river. They were moving toward their camp. The men crossed the river and met them about eight miles from camp and killed six of them. They skinned three of them and took as much meat as they could carry with the three hides back to their camp. By the time they had finished the work of skinning and cutting however, night came on and they were compelled to spend the night in the prairie without fire.

They broke some of the bones of the buffalo and procured a supply of marrow, upon which they supped in its raw state. They thought it a great luxury. Their bedding was at their camp and they could get no wood to make a fire as the timber on that side of the river seemed at least twenty miles off. In this emergency, they spread one of the raw hides on the ground, upon which they stretched themselves while they used another of the hides for a covering. The cold weather froze the covering very hard and it would not fit down and around them.

The consequence was that the cold wind blew under their coverings and they suffered greatly from cold during the night. Very early the next morning they returned, crossing the river to the south side to their encampment. They then went to work to construct what are called bullboats. These boats would be used to convey their fur down the river when the spring rise came, caused by the melting of the snow in the Rocky Mountains. A bullboat is made by stretching a "green" buffalo hide over a light frame of willows or some other type of wood. It is then turned up to the sun to dry before it is launched. It is a very convenient kind of watercraft and answers a good purpose, where timber cannot be had to make canoes.

In crossing streams that cannot be forded, bullboats are generally used as they are very easily constructed and can be made in a very short time. However, they also soon begin to leak and it is necessary to take them out of the water and dry them. In a few days, they begin to rot and are of no further use. Williams and the two Coopers made three boats of this kind, and after drying them, concealed them so as to have them ready for the spring thaw and rising water levels.

As there was no rise in the Arkansas River that spring, our little party, for the sake of greater security, went down the river to a large plum thicket, into which they crept. In the center of this fastness they cut away the brush so as to open a place spacious enough to allow them to lodge there at night. They also opened a narrow path from the center to the outside for ease of passing in and out. At the same time, they cut a small hackberry bush, which they made to answer the purpose of a gate. At night it was placed in this narrow path and made it perfectly impassable. In the morning, it was rolled out of the path upon the thicket. Here they took up their residence until the river should rise or some marauding band of Indians should find them.

While here and at a time when they were almost destitute of anything to eat, as they were lounging about the border of the plum thicket peering over the prairies, they saw at a great distance a large bull attacked by two wolves. He was coming toward the thicket and as he passed the men the number of the wolves had increased to about fifty. He betook himself to the river, which was but a few steps from the camp. The wolves dashed into the water after him. As the river was very low and the water shallow, no part of him was covered but his legs, although sometimes he was covered with the wolves gnawing him in every part. At last they cut his hamstrings, which caused him to sink down. The men then shot the buffalo and drove away the wolves and took possession of his carcass.

During their imprisonment in this thicket, one day seemed as long as four, as they had no way to amuse themselves. They were compelled to spend day after day, and night after night, in and about their sequestered lodge. They were in a region full of danger, as they frequently saw Indians on the prairie. Joseph Cooper had a small prayer book that he read every day to his two companions and in the evening he was in the habit of sticking it up in the fork of a little hackberry tree. It would appear that the lessons read from the prayer book were not very acceptable to the company as one morning the book was found in the ashes and burnt. Joseph Cooper seemed not to miss his book, but occasionally recited from his memory, an exercise equally as dry and tasteless as the book.

After being there about twenty long days, the monotony of the place was interrupted by three Comanche braves, who discovered the men and shot several arrows at them before they got into their place of security.

Two of the Indians remained to watch the men, while the other one put off to communicate the news to their party.

During the absence of the one, Captain Williams spoke to the two that stood as guard about sixty yards from the thicket, and from the information he received he went to them and succeeded in getting them to the camp. The men gave them the best they had to eat and got them in a very pleasant and talkative mood. About three hours later, they saw a great fog or dust and after a little time they discovered that it was created by a great many Indians on horseback. They came ready for battle, naked, except a flap and furnished with bows and arrows and arrow-fenders or shields.

When the Indians came within forty yards of the camp, they were met by the two braves who had remained behind. After a talk among them that lasted about five minutes, they dismounted and stripped their horses to remain there all night. Having regulated matters about their camp, they went to that of Captain Williams.

They had a great curiosity to know something about the white man's gun, which they had never seen before. They expressed a wish to see it used and made a small circle, which they drew with a piece of charcoal on a piece of cottonwood. Captain Williams shot at this target to show them the dexterity of the white man in the use of the rifle. The Captain shot and nearly drove the center of the circle. They were delighted with the performance and expressed a wish to see the other men shoot. Captain Williams told them that these two men would put their balls just there, pointing at the same time to the center.

The party was certainly very fortunate in getting on the right side of these Indians. The Comanche are one of the most ferocious and barbarous tribes in the far west and notorious for their cruelty to those who fall into their hands and for many years subsequent to that day for being the implacable foes of the white man. The Comanche Indians may be justly called "the terror of the Santa Fe trade." Captain Williams found it necessary, for their escape, to practice some deception upon them.

The Comanche were very shortly going to war against the Pawnees and were actively engaged in preparing for it. This fact the sagacious Captain learned from the two that had remained to watch their lodge. He professed to have sustained injuries from that tribe and to entertain designs of revenging them and offered to join the Comanche against them.

This plan acted like a charm. They treated the three men with much friendship, and informed our men that they were going to one of their villages and that they would return in four days and when they returned it was with a mutual understanding that the three white men were to accompany them against the Pawnees. The Indians, after spending the night with them, left them the next morning.

Early the following night, our little party hurried away from the place where they had made so narrow an escape. They took the trace made by the Indians down the river, and followed it for several miles. Their policy in doing this was to prevent their own trace from being perceived. They traveled hard that night and waded the river three or four times and about sunrise they reached another large plum thicket on an island in the Arkansas River, in the heart of which they opened room for another lodge. Here they laid themselves down to take that rest they so much needed and a snow fell upon them about three inches deep.

Although it was the latter part of April, the proximity of this region to the Rocky Mountains made the weather at that time of the year quite cold. They were afraid to move, as there was a snow on the ground and therefore remained not only that day, but that night also, wrapped up in their buffalo robes under the snow, without fire or anything to eat.

They remained on this island until the middle of June, during which they found plenty of game on the island for their purposes. They then started back up the river, which was then rising, went to their caches, raised their fur, and set off with it with all haste down the river in their bullboats. They glided along smoothly and quietly for ten days when they were compelled to stop and dry their boats. After starting for the second time and traveling a few miles, they saw a large company of Indians who had been encamped a short distance from the bank of the river and were taking up their lodges to leave.

The men glided along under a bluff bank, which prevented them from being discovered. Their boats lasted only four days longer, when they began to leak and the party was compelled to stop and kill buffalo and make new boats of this kind, as they had not yet come to timber of which canoes could be made. These boats proved to have less durability than the first they made, as they lasted but nine days, when they were abandoned as useless. By this time, however, they had come to timber and they went to work with two axes and made two canoes, which they lashed together and in which they put their furs.

In these they resumed their journey and floated down with the current, without anything occurring to excite unusual apprehensions of danger until the fourth day, when they heard below them the report of guns and the sound of that which seemed to be bells. They therefore pushed their canoes to shore and concealed them by hacking down bushes over them and remained there until about ten o'clock in the night.

They then very cautiously pushed their canoes into the current and as the night was dark and rain was falling, they passed without being seen by the Indians. When they were passing the Indians, through the flashes of lightning, they unexpectedly found themselves traveling the considerable falls in the Arkansas, of which they had no knowledge. They passed over without any unfavorable accident.

Two days journey from these falls they overtook eight Cherokee Indians going down to one of their villages. At first they were very shy and alarmed, but the party laid down their guns and made signs of friendship. They then met Captain Williams and talked with him. He procured from them some salt and tobacco, luxuries which they had not tasted for the last six months. When the interview ended between the Captain and the Indians, they both moved on in their canoes.

The Indians showed a disposition to keep with the Captain, but the Captain, knowing the treacherous character of the Indians, was as anxious to get rid of them. For two or three days they hung about the little party in spite of all that they could do to prevent it, landing when they would land and traveling when and only when they would travel.

When they drew near a Cherokee village, these fellows went ahead, as it afterwards appeared, to communicate to their people the fact of these men being on the river and to prepare to rob them. For when they approached the village, the river was absolutely covered with canoes, playing about on the surface of the water and a drum and fife were making music. When Captain Williams' canoes came opposite to their village, the Indians rowed up by the side of them, sprung into them, seized the rifles, claimed the three men as prisoners and tumbled all the furs out on shore and carried them off.

In the meantime, Captain Williams and the two Coopers were ordered to follow a large Indian, while they were guarded by about fifty with guns. They were conducted about ten miles to an agent for the United States, a Mr. Lovely, for trial as they were suspected for being three men who had robbed the Osages and whom Lovely had authorized to be apprehended. They were detained about three days when, having satisfied the agent that they were not the men being sought by the authorities, they were discharged and their furs were restored to them.

Down the Arkansas River our three adventurers continued to float in their cottonwood craft, delighted with their success in escaping all the dangers behind them, and with the prospect of soon being within the limits of the country inhabited by the white man. After passing the Cherokee village, they soon reached a trading post not far above what is now the seat of government of Arkansas. Here they disposed of their furs to a white trader whose name was Mr. Murray for the snug sum of about five thousand dollars. Those furs would now bring double that amount. From this point, they crossed to St. Louis and from there up the Missouri back again to Cooper's fort, after an absence of about one year.

COLORADO RIVER TO CALIFORNIA

Before we return to the narrative of the events that attended the wanderings of Workman and Spencer, we will furnish a few facts in relation to the Arkansas River and the country through which it passes. This great affluent to the Mississippi, from its mouth to its source, is upwards of two thousand miles in length and is navigable to the mountains during the spring freshet; at any other time of the year its navigation is extremely uncertain that high up.

It has one peculiarity noticed by all who have seen it. About two hundred miles from its source it has a deep, navigable stream any season of the year, while for an extent of four or five hundred miles below the mountains, the bed of the river is wide and a perfect sandbar which, in the summer season, is so near dry that the water does not run, but stands about in ponds. The water, no doubt, stinks.

"The borders of the Arkansas River," says one who explored that country in 1807, "may be termed the terrestrial paradise of our territories" for the wandering Indian tribes. Of all countries visited by the footsteps of civilized man, there never was one, probably, that produced game in greater abundance and we know that the manners and morals of those erratic nations are such as never to give them a numerous population. I believe that there are buffalo, elk and deer sufficient on the banks of the Arkansas alone, if used without waste, to feed all the Indians in the United States territory one century."

The above extract is from Pike's journal and although it may seem extravagant, it is most abundantly confirmed by the observation of all men who traveled through those regions at that early day. A gentleman now living in Missouri, whose word is as good as that of any living man and who was among the first traders to Santa Fe, informed me that his wagons were stopped for two hours by a frightened herd of buffalo that threatened to overrun their caravan.

They succeeded in dividing the multitude by firing their guns and shouting at the top of their voices and they passed on both sides. As far as they could see, in every direction from the point they occupied, the face of the country seemed to be densely covered with the moving mass of living animals. How immensely great must the herd have been, for their passing of the caravan consumed about two hours.

We could give many other similar statements, if it were necessary, made by a gentleman of veracity, going to prove the abundance of buffalo at that time on all the western and southwestern waters. The earliest adventurers were under the impression that game could not become scarce and that it would be abundant for the Indians for many ages to come.

Let us compare these statements with those found in Captain Fremont's expedition in the years 1843 to 1844. "A great portion of the region inhabited by this nation (the Shoshone) formerly abounded in game, the buffalo ranging about in herds as we found them on the eastern waters, and the plains dotted with scattering bands of antelope, but so rapidly have they disappeared within a few years, that now, as we journeyed along, an occasional buffalo and a few wild antelope were all that remained of the abundance which had covered the country with animal life.

The extraordinary rapidity with which the buffalo is disappearing from our territory will not appear surprising when we remember the great scale on which their destruction is yearly carried on. With inconsiderable exceptions, the business of the American trading posts is carried on in their skins. Every year, the Indian villages make new lodges for which the skin of the buffalo furnishes the material and in that portion of the country where they are still found, the Indians derive their entire support from them, and slaughter them with thoughtless and abominable extravagance. Like the Indians themselves, they have been a characteristic of the west, and like them, they are visibly diminishing."

About twenty-five years ago, near the sources of the Colorado and Bear River, buffalo existed in great abundance and seemed to be an inexhaustible source of subsistence upon which the Indians might safely depend for a century to come. But the buffalo are gone from that region and the poor destitute natives are frequently exposed to starvation.

There is reason to believe that buffalo were never so abundant in, and west of, the Rocky Mountains as they were on the eastern waters. Throughout all the country east of the mountains are found what are called buffalo paths or routes that continue for hundreds of miles, from several inches to several feet in depth. These ancient vestiges are not met with west of the mountains.

The time was when expeditions crossing the plains from Missouri to Santa Fe, and from Missouri to the Rocky Mountains, could almost at any time see bands of buffalo ranging about and could safely depend upon them for subsistence. Now an expedition does not think of depending upon the game of the country to sustain them on their journey, but are always supplied with provisions to take them through. A company going either to Oregon or Santa Fe would have to travel several hundred miles from Independence, a frontier town of Missouri, before they would see buffalo and when they see them, they may look out for Indians as they now, like the wolves, follow the buffalo.

To give the reader some idea of the extent of the trade in buffalo skins, as carried on by the different companies, we would state that Captain Fremont gives a statement furnished him by a partner of the American Fur Company, which fixes the total amount of robes annually traded to the different companies at ninety thousand. But we are to remember that there are a number of tribes of Indians who depend upon the buffalo for subsistence, which furnish no skins for trade.

The Indians, too, generally kill the greatest number of buffalo in the summer and fall seasons to avail themselves of a hot sun to dry the meat for winter provisions and yet at this time the skins are not fit for purposes of trade. The skins that are good for dressing are only those that are procured in the winter when the wool and hair is long. To this is to be added the fact that the hides of bulls are not taken off and dressed at any season. And then again, wolves kill a large number of calves.

Immense, therefore, as the herds of buffalo may have been, it will not be difficult to see that the day is not far distant when the race of that animal will be almost, if not quite extinct on the plains and prairies of the far west. The question may be asked, what will be the means of subsistence left the different tribes when this takes place? We answer: those tribes are diminishing and disappearing as fast, if not faster, than their means of subsistence.

Such are the dreadful conflicts that are constantly taking place between the different tribes, such the massacres and burning of each other's towns and villages besides acts of cruelty perpetrated by individuals, that scarcely the name remains of tribes that were once very numerous and formidable. And if these Indian customs are kept up, as they in all probability will be, the race of the red man will diminish so fast that they will not furnish any obstruction to the expansion of our population and the occupation of their territory.

When their country may be needed to receive the surplus of our rapidly increasing population, there will be no necessity to prompt us to get it by conquest or by purchase. The original proprietors will not be there to vindicate their claims to it or to waylay the white man and take his scalp.

Captain Williams speaks of the country near the Arkansas as generally beautiful and rich, as admirably adapted to the raising of stock of every kind. Any number of horses, cattle and sheep could be kept there, as the earth, both winter and summer, furnishes spontaneously an abundance of food. The difficulty in the way of that country being densely populated is the total want of timber in many parts. But it has been satisfactorily demonstrated that timber can be raised with success in the rich soil of the west. The discovery of coal, no doubt, will make the country habitable. In many places in the prairie states, coal has been found in abundance, supplying the absence of timber.

We have said that Williams, Workman and Spencer supposed they were on the Red River and the little knowledge they had of the country led Workman and Spencer to think that if they ascended the Red River to its source and crossed a mountain range of the Rocky Mountains, they would be in the Spanish country and somewhere near Santa Fe, the seat of government. And they would have reached Santa Fe by this route, if they had really been on Red River, but they were on the great Arkansas River. Laboring under this mistake, our two trappers set off up the river, resolved to follow the main branch to its source, from which they must have been at that time not less than three or four hundred miles.

Fortunately, they were but a few days' travel from the Rocky Mountains and passed over that part of their journey by the exercise of a great deal of caution, without being detected by the Indians. When they reached the mountains, they observed game was diminishing in quantity, which was a circumstance in their favor as the country was not likely to be overrun with prowling bands of Indians.

Indeed they saw very few signs of Indians and what they saw were very old. When they entered the mountains, they traveled on the south side of the river for two or three days and then crossed to the north side. They speak of a very high peak that was visible nearly all the time they were on that river. Its top was covered with snow and glistened in the sun. It seemed so very high, to use their own words: "that a cloud could not pass between its top and the sky." It was most probably the peak, the altitude of which was taken by Lieutenant Pike, the year before in 1807 and found to be about eighteen or nineteen thousand feet above the level of the ocean.

This peak is so very remarkable as to be known to all the Indian nations for hundreds of miles around and to be spoken of with admiration by the Spaniards of New Mexico and was the bounds of their travel northwest. Pike speaks of it not being out of sight for twenty-five or thirty days.

It is characteristic of the very high peaks in the Rocky Mountains, that they can be seen a very great distance, although they may appear to be within a day's ride. The tops of some of these peaks are inaccessible from obstructions that are in the way and from the fact that they are covered with deep snows. Workman and Spencer, while on the Arkansas River, observed an old trace of a party ascending the river which proved to be that of Pike's party in 1807, as they saw the names of the men occasionally engraved on rocks and trees, and the name Red River also, a circumstance that confirmed their notion that they were on that river.

This fact was calculated to encourage them, as they were not aware that Lieutenant Pike himself was laboring at the time that he was on the Arkansas River under the same mistake and found himself on the Rio Del Norte in the Spanish country, to his great regret and contrary to his intentions. They, therefore, aimed to follow the trail of Pike's company, as it would lead them to the source of the Red River, where they would cross into New Mexico.

As it was summer season, Workman and Spencer fared much better than they would have done if it had been winter. They traveled all day when they thought it safe to do so and killed no more game than was necessary to supply them with provisions. As they approached the source of the Arkansas, the altitude of the country seemed to be very great and there were a number of peaks of vast elevation that were nearly all the time to be seen, distinctly covered with snow. The country was generally destitute of timber, except scattered clumps of trees that were a variety of pines. Some cedar was also to be seen.

In giving an account of the ramblings of these two trappers in this *terra incognita*, it is proper to state that they ceased to make notes of the events of their wanderings. They found it inconvenient and it consumed time. Indeed, they had not paper nor the disposition. As they were anxious to extricate themselves from those labyrinths in which they had been entangled so long, they thought but little about enlightening the minds of others, especially as they thought it very doubtful whether they would ever again reach the abodes of civilization.

All the facts, therefore, which they were enabled to furnish connected with this part of their expedition, were drawn from memory and although interesting, they must constitute but a small amount of that kind of valuable information which a journal faithfully kept would have furnished about a region and its inhabitants, of which, even yet, but little is known.

They represent beaver, as they ascended this river, as very abundant, frequently furnishing their principal food. As they had no traps, they used their rifles to procure them. Another article of food they survived on is commonly called "mountain mutton," which is very delicate and sweet. It is the flesh of the mountain sheep, which is variously called the "Bighorn" by the trappers, the "Asahto" by the Mandans and the "Argali" and "Ibex" by others.

These animals go in flocks and generally frequent the cliffs of the mountains. If they are alarmed while in the valleys, into which they sometimes descend, they will escape to the highest precipices, where they indulge their curiosity by gazing on all below them. They generally seek the places among the rocks that are the most inaccessible to man. They are said not to be very wild and to fall far behind the antelope in the grace, ease and fleetness with which the latter animal moves over the ground.

A little caution on the part of the hunter enables him to get within a shot of it when it is on the ground. It is called the Bighorn from its horns, which are very large and twisted like those of a ram. They are very long also and a gentleman now living in Missouri informed me that he had seen them used by the Upper Nez Pierces for the purpose of blowing.

The Bighorn has short hair like a deer and resembles it in shape, except as to its head and horns, which resemble those of a sheep. It abounds in the Rocky Mountains, from the sources of the Missouri River and the Columbia River to California. It is of the size of a large deer and the horns of a full-grown, large male are frequently three-feet-six-inches long and one foot and three inches at the base.

North of the country ranged by the Bighorn is found the woolly sheep, which is sometimes confused with the Bighorn. It is, however, a very different animal and in its habits and appearance resembles the goat and more properly belongs to that genus. Its covering is a growth of long white wool, interspersed with long hair.

Like a goat, it has a beard, short legs, a deep belly and is not very active. Its horns, which are from four to six inches long, have a polished surface and are very black. They are by no means very abundant and not much can be said in favor of their flesh as an article of diet. The trappers represent the fleece of this animal as exceedingly fine and would be very valuable if it could be procured in sufficient quantities.

The Flat-head Indians are said to use the skins of these animals for purposes of clothing. The flocks of the Bighorn seen by Workman and Spencer increased as they approached the head of the Arkansas River and could be seen on the brow of mountains, and often standing on the edge of very high and shelving rocks. They seemed to enjoy a great deal of security when they had reached some extreme height and added much to the wild and imposing character of mountain scenery. When they killed a young one, which was sometimes the case, they had a fine meal, as its flesh was very tender as well as fat.

It was when Spencer was making an effort to shoot a "mountain mutton" that he sustained an injury in one of his feet that caused them to suspend their wanderings for two weeks. It was in the neighborhood, as they believed, of the headwaters of the river whose courses they had been following so long and so faithfully. This interruption caused them to select a clump of pines, in which they fixed up a lodge on such a plan as to defend themselves with more success if approached by hostile Indians.

Here, they whiled away the slow revolving hours of twelve or fifteen long summer days, devising every plan "to kill time" of which they could think and which they could safely adopt. Every circumstance seemed to combine to make time irksome and tedious. They were lost in their own minds as to their precise locality. They had abandoned all hope of seeing the country from which they had set out. They were seeking safety from the Indians by betaking themselves to a country, the inhabitants of which could not boast of a very great degree of civilization, and were at that time not very favorably disposed towards our citizens. And then they had lost the trail of Pike's party and might not be on the right route, or even any route, to the Spanish country.

The sacred Scriptures tell us that we shall have grace given us according to our day and trials. It would seem that there are latent energies in man, which are wakened up whenever, and only when, their exercise is necessary to raise us above our trials and hardships or to enable us to combat our difficulties with success. These energies or capabilities of buffeting difficulties in the case of some men may never be developed, because they may never be surrounded by circumstances that make their exercise necessary. We are not, therefore, to suppose that they did not exist and that such men, under certain circumstances, would not also be patient in enduring hardships and trials, and brave in the hour of danger.

In the midst of their perplexing difficulties these men avow they kept in good cheer. Now and then Workman killed some game, as they needed it, and it was his daily business to scout the country around to ascertain whether there was anything to be seen calculated to awaken apprehensions of danger. By means of nooses on the end of long, light poles, they caught several birds (magpies). These, after cropping one of their wings to prevent them from flying off, they would throw into the branches of the trees and then they would practice with bows and arrows which they made, trying to bring them down in Indian style.

While Workman was beating about one day in the vicinity of their camp, he saw a huge grizzly bear about a fourth of a mile off jogging along down a small stream going (he was pleased to observe) directly from their camp. They had had no thoughts about such unwelcome predators, as they had observed no signs of their presence in that neighborhood.

These men were now in a region, they believed, that gives rise to the Platte River, the Yellow Stone River, the great south-western tributary of the Missouri, the Arkansas River, the Rio del Norte and the Rio Colorado of California. Speaking in reference to this particular region, Lieutenant Pike says: "I have no hesitation in saying that I can take a position in the mountains, from whence I can visit the source of any of these rivers in one day." This assertion may be true, and we do not know that any discoveries that have been made prove it untrue.

There is one thing, however, certainly true and that is that the region to this day remains to a great extent unexplored and the statements Pike received and which he seemed to credit about some of these rivers, were incorrect, as subsequent discoveries will show. "By the route of the Arkansas and the Rio Colorado of California, I am confident," says Pike, "in asserting (if my information from Spanish gentlemen of intelligence is correct), there can be established the best communication on this side of the Isthmus of Darien, between the Atlantic and Pacific oceans, as admitting the utmost, the land carriage would not be more than two hundred miles and the route may be made quite as eligible as our public highways over the Allegheny Mountains. The Rio Colorado River is to the Gulf of California what the Mississippi River is to the Gulf of Mexico and is navigable for ships of considerable burden opposite to the upper part of Sonora."

This information furnished Lieutenant Pike about the Colorado, or Green River, as it is now sometimes called, has been proved by subsequent discoveries to be entirely incorrect. Its length is about twelve hundred miles, eight hundred of which are broken into falls and rapids, so numerous and dangerous as to defy navigation in any way whatsoever. Approximately one to two hundred miles of its lower part is in all probability navigable for vessels of the larger class. But we'll learn more about the Rio Colorado River in another place.

We have said that Workman and Spencer gave it as their opinion that there is a region (in the opinion of Pike of no great extent) which constitutes the great fountainhead of the great rivers we mentioned. This region is the most remarkable and highest of the Rocky Mountains and is a bed of lofty mountains covered with eternal snow! It is said to be about one hundred miles long and about thirty miles wide, and is now called the Wind River Mountains.

Although Workman and Spencer may have wandered about in the south extremity of what is now understood to be the Wind River Sierra, we think the Arkansas River and the Rio Del Norte River perhaps have their fountainheads further south. It is now well known that the Columbia, Colorado, and the main tributaries to the Missouri Rivers can be traced to this grand treasury of waters.

One of the highest peaks in the Rocky Mountains is in the Wind River Range and is probably fifteen thousand feet above the level of the sea. Various estimates have been made of the height of the Rocky Mountains and it is believed that when justice is done to their real altitude, they will be only second to the highest mountains on the globe.

Their height has been diminished to the eye by the great elevations from which they rise. They consist, according to Long, of ridges, knobs, and peaks, variously disposed. They were called by some of the first discoverers the Shining Mountains, from the fact that the higher parts are covered with perpetual snows, which give them a luminous and brilliant appearance. By the joint means of the barometer and trigonometric measurement, one of the peaks has been ascertained to be twenty-five thousand feet and there are others of nearly the same height in the vicinity.

Workman and Spencer relate a phenomenon that at first gave them much anxiety of mind. It was that there were reports of singular explosions among these mountains resembling heavy distant thunder. They could be heard at all times of the day and night and more particularly in clear, calm weather. At first, they had various conjectures about the cause. They thought at one time it was distant thunder and again they supposed it to be the report of artillery. A third explanation was that the mysterious sounds were produced by volcanic eruptions.

Lewis and Clark and others who have been in those regions mention the existence of this phenomenon in the Rocky Mountains. It is a mystery that excites the admiration and awe of the various tribes and some of them regard it as the voice of the great Wauconda (Supreme Being), who holds his residence, as they believe, in those mountains.

When Spencer was able to walk, the two solitary trappers with their rifles in their hands struck out for the sources of the Del Norte, traveling a westerly course. They state that the country through which they passed was generally mountainous prairie, abounding in fountains, lakes and vast beds of snow that are the sources of those mighty rivers, east and west of the Rocky Mountains. A few days of faithful journeying brought them to an elevation in the mountains where there was a delightful spring of water, remarkably pure and cold.

This spring ran a westerly course and this, in their view, must be the source of the Del Norte River. Now their hearts were glad, as they fancied they had struck a stream which would lead them out of the extensive wilderness in which they had been lost for so long a time. Here I would remark, the subsequent history of these two wanderers will show that they were again mistaken. The bubbling fountain, which they supposed to be the source of the Del Norte, was one of the many fountains of the Colorado.

They followed a small streamlet until it swelled into a mighty river that dashed its waters against rocks and precipices, rolled on and widened, deepened, for more than a thousand miles. When the stream acquired a magnitude that they thought would justify it, they went to work with a light axe, which they had retained, and constructed a small canoe. They hoped the craft would save them many a long and weary tramp in those Alpine regions.

While Spencer was making the canoe, Workman consumed a day in examining the river to ascertain if it was navigable. He reported that he had reached a very high point near the river, from which he had a most delightful view of its banks and course, and that its surface seemed to be remarkably placid and free from falls. Its banks were also very low and destitute of timber.

This discovery seemed almost, in their minds, to put an end to their difficulties. In a few days they would glide on the beautiful surface of this peaceful river into some of the Spanish settlements, which would be home to them when compared with their present forlorn situation. But they were doomed to more disappointments. New and fresh difficulties and mazes were before them.

When they had procured a supply of meat that would last them several days and had put it into their little boat, they committed themselves to the current. They glided along in fine style for the first fifty miles. Through this distance, a beautiful undulating prairie without a stick of timber for many miles stretched out from the banks of the river in every direction. Towards sunset, however, the aspect of the country before them began to assume a wild, romantic, and forbidding character. A frowning mountain enclosed their prospect and seemed to hem in the river.

As they approached this unexpected obstruction, the surface of the water began to be irregular and rough. They did not think it safe to travel after nightfall. Therefore, they pulled to shore to await the disclosures that might be furnished by the light of another day.

The next morning very early, with rifles in hand, they left their canoe and walked ahead to gain some point from which they might be able to examine the country and the channel of the river, and learn something about both. After several hours of toil and ascent, they reached an elevation where they had a view of the scenery before them. It was wilder and more imposing than anything they had ever seen before.

The bed of the river, which had generally been from three to four hundred yards in breadth, was now contracted to a passage not more than forty yards wide and walled up several hundred feet high by tremendous battlements of basaltic rock. Through this narrow defile, the river flowed almost with the velocity of an arrow. Beyond these rapids there were evidently falls, as their tumultuous roar could be distinctly heard, and clouds of spray could be seen suspended in the air.

For an hour or two, our trappers remained seated upon the ground, gazing with mingled feelings of disappointment and astonishment at this magnificent scene. At one time, the roaring of the distant cataract would rise and swell with the breeze that bore the lulling sound to their ears. Again, as the gentle gale would sink, the tumult of angry waters would, for a while, die away in the distance. The feeling of disappointment, for a time, was lost in those moments of wonder and awe, and the trappers seemed to forget their situation as they mused upon the beauty and romance of this exhibition of nature.

Seeing satisfactorily that quick destruction awaited them if they should attempt to pass the narrow defile, they returned to their camp to get a few articles they had left in their canoe, as well as some provisions. But when they came in view of the place where they had left their canoe, they saw three Indians in the act of pushing it from shore.

The trappers made signs to them, which seemed only to frighten them and to cause them to make the greater effort to cross the river. Understanding how to manage such a watercraft, the Indians soon reached the opposite shore. As they now felt secure, they paused on the bank to gaze with curiosity and surprise at the two white men, when Workman raised his rifle and fired it towards them. The report of his gun and the sight of the fire struck a panic into them that caused them to break and run. The trappers were particularly concerned about their axe, which they supposed was in the canoe and was, of course, taken away. However, fortunately they had left it on the land and the Indians had not seen it.

The trappers were unsure who these Indians were or what tribe they were from, as they could not be approached for a parley. Their bodies were nearly naked and they presented a most degraded appearance. They perhaps belonged to a tribe of *"les dignes de pitie"* (objects of pity) as such Indians are sometimes called who represent the lowest, most neglected of the tribes.

Workman and Spencer now resumed their travel overland aiming to follow the river as near as they could. When they had passed the narrow passage, the Colorado expanded again to its usual breadth and poured over falls about forty feet high. The river in the falls was full of large rocks, many of which projected above the surface of the water. Against these, the waters of this great river dashed and rebounded, and boiled up, until the whole surface seemed to be in a perfect rage.

After spending the day in clambering the sides of very rough mountains and winding around and around to avoid obstructions and to find ground on which they could travel, they succeeded in getting below the falls where the river again assumed a tranquil and placid surface. Here, a beautiful and delightful prairie country came to the very banks.

These men would have made another canoe and tried it again, but there was no suitable timber and they thought it the better policy to ascertain something more about the navigation before they should again commit themselves to its uncertain current. They therefore followed it from day to day, as near as they could get to its banks, until they were satisfied that it was filled with rapids, rocks, and other obstructions that not only rendered the navigation unsafe, but utterly impossible. Necessity, therefore, reconciled them to the toil of traveling on foot.

They kept near the river, resolved to follow it, letting it take them where it might. The country was sometimes very broken and mountainous. Often, they would have to turn back and retrace their steps, making a circuit of several miles to find a way through which they could pass. They frequently passed places where for several miles the banks rose up into precipices of an awful height, from the tops of which they sometimes took a view of the river below, as it whirled, dashed about, foamed and struck the basaltic rock, impatient, furious and wild.

These men give it as their opinion that the scenery of the Rio Colorado River is equal, perhaps, to that of any other part of North America. Their statements are very applicable to the Snake River scenery, which is also represented as being wild and grand beyond description. Indeed it may be noticed as a characteristic of the rivers west of the Rocky Mountains, that they are marked by a wild majesty, produced by the frequent recurrence of rocks and rapids, that place them in striking contrast to the smoothness and placidity of the streams east of said mountains.

This distinction in favor of the eastern rivers will operate against the navigation of the western waters and, of course, against the interests of the country through which they pass, if those countries should ever be settled by a civilized people.

Having descended this river for several hundred miles, still believing it to be the Rio del Norte and wondering why they had not reached Santa Fe, they came to a place apparently used frequently as a crossing. There were a great many signs of horses and mules, but they were old and all pointing an east course. Indeed, the tracks were so plentiful that Workman and Spencer conjectured there must have been several thousand.

Without the least hesitation, the trappers resolved to follow this great trail and to take the way the signs indicated the last caravan had gone. They felt confident that this trail had been made by the Spaniards and not by Indians. They traveled it two days, when they met a caravan of Spaniards (forty or fifty) on the trail, but going an opposite direction.

They were at first fearful they were Indians, but when they found out they were Spaniards, their joy was too great to be described. Neither of the trappers could speak the Spanish language, but there was an Englishman in the caravan and one or two Spaniards who could speak the English language with some fluency. They therefore found no difficulty in communicating to the company what had been their history in the mountains, and the fact that they were now seeking security in their country.

The caravan then selected a suitable place for encampment, for the purpose of adopting some plan for the protection of the two men who had thrown themselves upon their mercy, for these Spaniards were, by no means, insensible as to their situation. Until midnight, they listened with thrilling interest to the details, as the trappers gave them, of their trials and hardships since they had left the United States.

They informed Workman and Spencer that the river they descended was the Rio Colorado and they were about five hundred miles from Santa Fe. In passing over that distance they had met with a good deal of trouble from the Indians and they gave it as their opinion that the two trappers could not pass through to Santa Fe without being cut off by the Indians.

The caravan was going towards Pueblo de Los Angelos, a town in Upper California near the coast of the Pacific. This was the region of country they expected to be engaged in trading until the following spring, when they were to return to Santa Fe with horses and mules. Part of the company was men who lived in Upper California, but they had accompanied a caravan last spring to Santa Fe and were now returning home. Workman and Spencer determined to join the company and go to California, where they would spend the approaching winter, and in the spring continue with them to New Mexico. From New Mexico, they hoped some opportunity would present itself of getting back to the United States. They were therefore regularly taken into the service of the company, which was under the direction of a Captain and furnished with mules and any supplies they needed.

The next morning, the company set out and was about twenty days' travel from San Gabriel, on the Bay of San Pedro. In passing over this distance, a great deal of the road was very rocky and rough. The season was dry (a circumstance by no means unusual in that country) and the company had often to perform long and toilsome treks before they could reach water. In one or two cases, the distance from one watering place to another was not less than one hundred miles and very often from thirty, to fifty miles.

The surface of the country was also often a bed of sand, which furnished nothing to sustain their mules. It will therefore be seen that there are through this country regular jornadas (as the Spaniards call them) and stages where grass and water can be had for caravans, while the country intervening is almost as desolate as the Sahara of Africa.

By making these regular jornadas, or day's journeys, and reaching those regular stages, caravans are able to make their way through from California to Santa Fe. If a caravan breaks this regular chain of stages, their toils and suffering are often quite severe. These caravans are often very great, numbering sometimes several thousand horses and mules, which sweep away all the grass near their route and leave the earth very bare.

As they journeyed along, Workman and Spencer observed the bones of animals scattered about in great profusion in some places and upon asking for an explanation, they were informed that they were the bones of horses and mules that were lost by caravans from a disease very common in that region called the "foot evil," which sometimes causes the loss of whole bands of horses and mules. It seems to be aggravated, if not really created, by traveling over hot, sandy plains and deserts and suffering from want of water.

After crossing the Colorado and traveling northwest several days, the company turned and traveled a southwest course until they reached the Spanish towns on the Pacific. On the right of their route, very high mountains were visible all the time, the peaks of which were white with snow.

This range of mountains (no doubt what is now called the Wahsatch Mountains) seemed to be infested with predatory bands of Indians whose regular business was to beset the route of these caravans for the purpose of plunder. As this company passed, they could be frequently seen on the tops of the mountains peering over the plains and reconnoitering their movements. We would briefly state that our two trappers spent the winter of 1809 in Upper California, which time Workman spent in examining the country and traveling from place to place to gather all the information he could of a country about which our citizens at that time knew little or nothing.

As it is our object in another part of this volume, to give a short, faithful account of California, it is our intention to interweave all the statements of Workman in that account. We will, therefore, suspend for the present, his descriptions of California, that they may appear in a more proper place and we will ask the reader to go with us to Santa Fe, where in the summer of 1810, we find our two mountaineers and trappers safely landed with a large caravan of mules and horses, both in fine health and good cheer.

SEVERAL YEARS IN SANTA FE

Workman and Spencer, being men without families in the States and being foiled thus far in their efforts to make fortunes, resolved to try their luck in Santa Fe, as gold and silver seemed to be very abundant. They, therefore, took up their abode at the seat of government (Santa Fe) with the purpose of remaining there for several years if their success should justify it. When and if they amassed a sufficiency of precious metals, they thought of returning to the United States, if a safe opportunity should present itself.

This shows how men become weaned from the habitudes of civilized and cultivated society and are so charmed with the wild adventure connected with Indian life, that they are seldom satisfied unless they are braving the toils and difficulties of the wilderness, not realizing the excitement belonging to such a life.

Workman and Spencer remained in and about Santa Fe for fifteen years and had abandoned all thought of regaining the place of their nativity. But the Santa Fe trade was opened up and large companies every spring crossed the plains from Missouri to New Mexico with goods, which they exchanged at a great profit for gold and silver. One of the first of these large companies was under the direction of Captain Means, who with part of his men were killed by the Comanche, while the others barely escaped with their lives, leaving everything they had to be carried off by these ruthless Indians.

In consequence of this disaster, the General Government sent a company headed by Captain Riley to escort the next trading expedition the following spring, over all the dangerous ground to the Big Arkansas River, where Captain Riley was ordered to remain until a specified time, awaiting the return of the trading company to conduct them back to the States.

This company reached Santa Fe in safety and after disposing of their goods in that market, turned their faces towards the States. They were fortunate enough to meet with an opportunity to go under the protection of the Spanish government, a circumstance that was brought about in the following way. Some half a dozen of wealthy Spaniards residing in Santa Fe had been found guilty of some treasonable designs against that government and had the privilege of leaving the country in so many days, or being hung.

They, of course, preferred the former kind of punishment and determined to go with their families and fortunes to the States. The governor of Santa Fe therefore ordered a Captain Viscarro with sixty men, ten of whom were brave Purbulo Indians living near Santa Fe, to conduct these exiles and the company until they should meet Captain Riley on the Big Arkansas River, from which point Captain Viscarro was to return to New Mexico.

Workman and Spencer, when they saw this very safe opportunity of getting back to the States, felt the love of their native land, which had been almost extinct, revive in their hearts and they determined to join the party on their homeward route.

They had been quite successful while in New Mexico in advancing their fortunes, and now they would make an effort to return to renew their acquaintance with those whom they once knew, but from whose memory all recollection of them had now perhaps passed away, as of those long ago dead and gone. At that time, a trip from Santa Fe was very dangerous and the Indians had been very successful in frightening the mules of caravans and causing them to break loose and run off. But the company got along very smoothly until they were within sixty miles of the Arkansas River.

When near the Semirone river and just when the company was driving up to a spring around which they intended to encamp that night, a large party of Indians on foot, perhaps one hundred and fifty, emerged from cover and arrayed themselves on open ground, in a right line facing the traders. "What tribe are they?" was a question that was quickly asked and as quickly passed around the camp. "Comanche," was the answer from one who knew. And that was enough, for the company knew what they were to expect.

In the Comanche Indian is embodied every trait of a warrior whose hand is raised against every man and who is even more aggressive than the gangs of hungry wolves that roam over those extensive plains. They made known their hostile feelings and challenged the traders by brandishing and flourishing their arms, and by acting the mad buffalo, which consists in gathering the dust in one hand and then in the other, and throwing it into the air, after the manner of that animal when he is provoking one of his peers to combat. So menacing was their appearance that the traders hesitated as to holding a parley with them, and indeed few, if any, were willing to undertake it.

Finally, one of the company members went out and was met half way by one of the Comanche, with arms in one hand and his cross in the other. But they had scarcely met before two other Comanche broke the line and dashed up to the party. This movement being not understood by the traders, two of them, Barnes and Wallace, ran up to protect their man, if it should be necessary. A momentary and fearful pause ensued. The parties stood for the half of a minute in perfect silence, keenly eyeing each other, with their fingers upon the triggers of their guns.

The Indians seemed eager to begin the work and but for one circumstance the combatants, the next moment, would have been thrown into dreadful conflict. That circumstance was this: the ten Purbuloes who, under the Spanish Captain, Viscarro, were accompanying the traders to Big Arkansas River and who had gone out on a hunt that afternoon, were at that time near at hand upon a ridge, skinning and cutting up a buffalo which they had killed. They had a full and fair view of all that was taking place below them and abruptly leaving the carcass of the buffalo, they raised a dreadful war shout, and came bounding down the hill, charging and pitching like mad horses, and rushed up into the very faces of the Comanche.

The sudden and unexpected sight of these braves perfectly electrified the Comanche, not that they dreaded ten Purbulo, but because they conjectured that a party (perhaps large) of that warlike tribe were concealed behind the adjacent ridge. One of the Purbuloes, a game youth of about sixteen, observing a very gaudy pair of socks under the belt of a Comanche, laid violent hands upon them and gave the owner of them a tremendous kick in the posterior that nearly lifted him off the ground. The crestfallen Comanche received the insult without resistance.

Balked in their designs, the Comanche began to make professions of friendship, in which some of the traders were foolish enough to confide. Indeed the whole company, with a few honorable exceptions, was over-awed by the Indian appearance and disposition of the Comanche. This the Purbuloes perceived with surprise and great indignation. They assured their party that the Comanche intended to attack them and that the only alternative was to fight.

The Spaniards under Captain Viscarro excused themselves by stating that they had recently entered into a treaty of peace with the Comanche and did not wish to violate their faith. The Purbuloes knew this was only an excuse and therefore charged them with cowardice. They told Captain Viscarro that they would no longer submit to him as an officer, for he had not the bravery of a squaw.

Becoming furious, they threw their shields upon the ground by way of appeal to the courage of the company and proclaimed themselves ready to fight without anything to defend them against the darts of the enemy. All this, however, had no effect upon their quailing, faltering spirits. They did not intend to strike the first blow.

This was discovered by the Comanche and prompted them to come nearer the company and to be more impudent. In fact, in their reprehensible timidity, the company had permitted the daring Comanche to mix among them to some extent. The Purbuloes kept their eyes constantly upon them and only grew the more impatient as they observed that the Comanche were waiting for a favorable opportunity to make an assault.

One of them, a tall, stalwart and distinguished warrior, perceiving something among the enemy very suspicious, sprang to his feet and seemed to look wild. Seizing a moment when the eyes of the company were generally turned away from them, the Comanche fired and in a kind of headlong hurry ran across a creek that was near the camp to reload. The worst predictions of the heroic Purbuloes were realized. Four of their greatest warriors fell dead and so did a number of the tame and spiritless Spaniards.

A great uproar now prevailed. Some flew to their frightened mules to prevent them from breaking loose, some flew to their arms, and some, there is reason to believe, flew to the wagons for safety. As the Comanche crossed the creek, one of their men received a ball from the rifle of Workman, who pulled the Indian to the ground by his long hair and then pushed past him.

Although mortally wounded and unable to get upon his feet, the indomitable Comanche reloaded his gun as he lay upon the ground and as one of Captain Viscarro's sergeants rode up with sword in hand to dispatch him, shot him between the eyes. The Spaniard instantly fell lifeless from his horse. The six surviving Purbuloes, deeply mortified at the miserable management of the company, would not join in the fight but remained near their dead brothers, chagrined, disgusted, and filled with sullen rage.

The Comanches had but two or three rounds of balls and powder, which they speedily used and then betook themselves to flight. Sixteen of the traders followed them. A few of the traders, however, had the presence of mind to get their horses when they found that the Indians could out-leg them.

Away they went on foot and on horseback, shooting as they went. Among those in the chase was a Spaniard on horseback, but he had no firearms and he did not appear to desire any, his aim and business being to rob the slain and to get the spoils. He had collected a sufficient number of bows and arrows, buffalo robes and blankets, and trinkets and trumpery of all sorts, to completely cover and conceal the horse and his rider.

Barnes and Wallace, (old Wallace as he was often called) of whose bravery we have sufficient proofs, of course, were in the number of traders following the Comanche. The former was well mounted. Wallace was in his glory, but he was on foot and an old man in the bargain. He asked the Spaniard for the use of his steed, but the Spaniard thought too much of his plunder to part with the means of conveying it to the camp.

Barnes thought the emergency should justify Wallace in taking the horse, *vi et armis*. The suggestion was scarcely made before it was carried into effect. In a moment, the venal Spaniard came heels over head upon the ground with his bows and arrows, dry buffalo skins, trinkets, and trumpery of all sorts rattling around his ears and in another moment, Wallace was on the Spaniard's horse and away. As the encounter began between sunset and dark, nightfall soon came on and all the pursuers turned back to the camp but Wallace and Barnes. They held on until nine or ten o'clock, shooting and pursuing, pursuing and shooting, until their guns became so hot by frequent firing and so dirty they were compelled to desist.

The moon shone as bright as day and an open and extensive plain spread around. Barnes and Wallace thought they had followed the Indians for seven or eight miles and they stated that the Indians retreated all that distance in a right line, nor was there at any time any confusion or breaking of ranks. They farther reported that they saw at some distance off what they believed to be another party of Indians that seemed to be very large. On the part of the Comanche, this was a very unsuccessful adventure and dearly did they pay for their impudence. They were most sadly drubbed and lost many of their greatest warriors, as was ascertained the following year. The night did not pass, however, with its usual rest and repose.

The company had had a sample of Indian fighting, treachery and cruelty, which was by no means calculated to invite sleep. They were at that time in a country populated with Indian tribes who might dog them for hundreds of miles. They had just had a fight with a party of them and other parties, perhaps very large, were in the neighborhood. The company of men sent by the governor of Santa Fe under Captain Viscarro to protect them to the Big Arkansas had proved timid and cowardly in the affray that had taken place. They therefore could not safely depend upon them for aid in a difficulty.

Captain Riley by this time had, in all probability, left Big Arkansas River and turned his forces towards the United States. They had many and strong reasons to fear that they would be unprotected throughout the whole of the dangerous route that lay before them. The next day they expected the Comanche to return with renewed and multiplied forces, to slay and rob. Under these circumstances, and with these gloomy prospects and feelings, the light of the next day dawned upon them.

After the fight on the previous evening, two of the Comanche that were badly wounded were seen scrambling along on the ground to a ledge of rocks, in which they hid themselves during the night. The Purbuloes, being apprised of that fact, hurried to the spot and found them. One of them was dead. The other was living and the partial opportunity to sate their thirst for blood was embraced with Indian greediness. He was dragged out by the infuriated Purbuloes and cut to pieces. Their scalps, of course, were taken. As these crown their original owners, they crown and complete the victories of those who take them. But the dead were to be buried this morning and the company had to prepare for the anticipated difficulties of the day and these they were afraid would be many and trying.

Every arrangement would be made to meet them. Accordingly, after an early and hurried breakfast, graves were dug and the slain were put in the ground as decently as circumstances would admit.

In the meantime, the mules and horses were permitted to fill themselves with grass and then brought within a circular fortification made of the wagons and baggage. Their firearms were put in a state of readiness and sentinels were placed out on elevated points to scout the surrounding country and to report everything that appeared above the verge of the horizon. However, the day passed and contrary to their calculations, they saw no Indians, but the slain that lay here and there, who, as they were now objects of no real terror, were still less in the estimation of the company, entitled to the rite of sepulture, but were doomed to lie on their native plains, to feed the hungry wolf attracted that way by the scent of their putrescent bodies.

Although they had not been molested that day, still the company knew that they were on very dangerous ground, as large bands of hostile Indians were believed to be hovering about their route, seeking a suitable opportunity to make an attack. Their location was about sixty miles from Big Arkansas River, where it was hoped Captain Riley might still be awaiting their return, although it was a week past the time to which he was limited and when he had expected to set out on his return to the United States.

As this distance could be ridden on good horses in a night, it was proposed to send an express to Captain Riley, (if he should still be there), to apprise him of their dangerous situation and to request him to wait until they should be able to reach him. But who would undertake it? If the company were in danger, the express would certainly be much more so.

The route lay through the most dangerous part of the country, between Santa Fe and Independence. The moon was full and shone very bright, but if this circumstance would facilitate the undertaking, it would at the same time expose the party to the danger of being more easily discovered by Indians. The wealthy Spanish exiles seemed to be very much alarmed, offered large rewards in gold and silver to any party that would undertake to carry the message to Captain Riley that night.

The danger was great, it was true, but the reward was too tempting to be withstood. Remember, reader, it was gold and silver and everyone knows what gold and silver has done and can do. A small party agreed to go and mounting their horses, set out. But in less than an hour they came back at the top of their speed, dreadfully frightened and stating that they had seen a great many Indians.

"Where did you see them? What number did you see? What were they doing? Were they encamped or moving?" These questions and many others were put to them, first by one member of the party and then by another. But as the answers returned were not very satisfactory, and the statements of the party somewhat conflicting, the company doubted whether they had seen any Indians at all. They finally said they thought they had seen Indians. The wealthy Spaniards increased the reward and another party set out. But they returned also in a short time, frightened half to death and telling the same story. They, too, gave the company reason to believe that the Indians seen were only imaginary.

This second failure aroused the game spirits of Wallace and Barnes. They had no time to lose, so they told the company that if they were furnished with the best men and best horses belonging to the expedition, they would undertake it. The proposition was immediately accepted. The selection of men was easily and soon made. The rich exiles furnished the horses, as their animals were very superior. Wallace, Workman, Barnes, the six Purbuloes and seven other members of the party constituted the band that was not to be so easily deterred.

They took a full supply of arms, leaped into their saddles, which they had cinched very tight upon their horses and put off. Away they went, silently and swiftly careening over the plains and keeping a most vigilant lookout in every direction. The moon shone with brightness inferior only to the light of a vertical sun. The deep and sepulchral silence that prevailed was sometimes broken by the shrill neighing of the elk and by the howling of hungry, saucy gangs of wolves that sometimes whipped across their route.

They had traveled more than half the distance before they saw anything that was calculated to excite apprehensions of danger or to interrupt their nocturnal purpose. As they were approaching the edge of a bluff that overlooked an extensive plain, a horse came up the bluff towards them and when he noticed the party neighed and seemed to be perfectly tame. Here was a mysterious circumstance, a mysterious horse that needed to be understood before they could venture any further in safety.

"How came he there?" As he was tame, he must belong to some Indian encampment that might be very near. After holding a consultation and interchanging opinions for a few minutes, it was determined to secretly scout the plain that lay beneath the bluff, particularly as the mysterious horse came from that direction. Wallace, (Colonel Wallace I will call him, for he ought to have been a colonel), who was always the first to dash into danger and upon dangerous ground, gave the reins of his horse to Barnes and crept along to the edge of the bluff.

After making a thorough examination, he returned cautiously to his party, reporting that the plain that lay beneath the bluff was covered with thousands and thousands of animals that might be Indians and Indian horses, but he saw no fires—a circumstance, however, that he said did not signify anything, as Indians always put out their fires after eating, or leave them and go somewhere else to encamp.

Barnes, who was always the right hand man of Colonel Wallace, next crept up to the edge of the bluff and after making a careful examination returned stating the same thing: that the plain below was covered with thousands and thousands of something, but he could not say what it meant. Workman then went and after an absence of a few minutes returned, reporting the same thing, to wit, that thousands and thousands of animals covered the plain, which he took to be Indians and Indian horses.

The six Purbulo braves must next go and see for themselves and satisfy their curiosity. After prying and peeping most cautiously for some time over the bluff, they brought back the same account, that animals lay by thousands and thousands over the plain, which they conjectured were Indians.

"Well, under the circumstances, what are we to do?" was the problem, the solution of which was not very easy. The present party was prompted not so much by the prospect of a great reward in gold and silver, as by a nobler impulse that made them insensible to danger and raised them superior to it.

They determined to dash through any and all obstructions that might be in their route, or sacrifice their lives in the attempt. To turn back, therefore, was not to be recognized by them at any time as a way of avoiding or getting rid of a difficulty. A free interchange of views and notions resulted in that of adopting the following purpose and plan: they resolved to surprise and stampede the mysterious things, though they might prove to be thousands and thousands of Indians and Indian horses.

To accomplish this, they were to go down to the plain and approach the encampment, or whatever it might be, as secretly and as silently as possible, with the six Purbuloes going before. Their aim would be to strike a panic among the horses of the Indians by a general yell and frighten them off. "And what can an Indian do on foot?" said they, with feelings of anticipated triumph.

Accordingly, every one adjusted his saddle and arms and down they went, creeping along in breathless silence, the Purbuloes leading the way. When they were sufficiently near, they raised a tremendous shout and dashed ahead. In a moment, the whole plain was alive and moving. The mystery was solved. Thousands and thousands of wild buffalo and wild horses darkened the plain and fled in headlong confusion. This vast assemblage of wild animals was easily explained. The season was very dry and they had come and congregated there for water. The mysterious horse had saddle marks on him and was really tame. He was most probably a stray from some Indian encampment, perhaps not far off.

The headlong and continued running of the buffalo and horses created a rumbling sound that was heard for more than an hour and resembled distant and prolonged thunder. The party then, in fine cheer, pushed on, and without anything to interrupt their course, arrived at the Big Arkansas River the next day sometime in the afternoon, at the place where Captain Riley had encamped. But Captain Riley had gone.

They knew, however, from fresh signs, particularly the remains of buffalo killed but a few hours before that he had been there the previous night, and following on they overtook him the same day. Captain Riley, after hearing of the exposed condition of the expedition, agreed to await their arrival.

The company followed the express the next day, and traveled very hard to get away from a country so full of danger. For two days, the Purbuloes kept up a constant howling and lamenting that was very annoying to the company. On the third day, they ceased their wailings, wiped away their tears, and were in fine cheer. Two days' travel brought the company into Captain Riley's camp. Captain Viscarro here turned his face back to New Mexico, while the company going to the States continued their journey under the protection of Captain Riley's forces and finally reached Independence.

PEOPLE OF CALIFORNIA

Workman and Spencer remained about six months in Upper California, during which time Workman was generally engaged in traveling about, collecting information by personal observation of the climate, face of the country, its productions, and the customs of the people who inhabit that country. We will give a short account of that country, as furnished by Workman, which we believe to be strictly true because it harmonizes exactly with the accounts of several other gentlemen who have been there, and who are regarded as incapable of intentionally misrepresenting anything.

California is divided into Upper and Lower areas. Lower California is a peninsula about seven hundred miles in length and about sixty wide, with the Pacific on one side, and the Vermillion sea, (or as it is now called, the Gulf of California), on the other. A part of Lower California is in the torrid-zone and the climate is therefore very hot. A great deal of this peninsula consists of sandy fertile plains and mountains that give to it an aspect that is rather stern, rather than inviting.

Frequently for many miles, deserts of hot sand spread in every direction, on the face of which not a single sign of vegetable life can be seen. And then again, the face of the country swells into barren mountains that are equally as destitute of any kind of vegetation. In some parts of Lower California, however, there are valleys of great fertility in which are to be found all the productions of the tropics, such as olives, oranges, dates, figs, citrons, pomegranates, sugarcane and indigo.

Jesuits, an order of the Roman church, settled this part of California in 1678. They were successful in gaining the affections of the natives and acquired a powerful and extensive influence over their minds. A number of missionary establishments were built in different parts of Lower California, to which the natives gathered from different portions of the country to be initiated in the principles of the Catholic faith.

It cannot be denied that the efforts of these Jesuit priests effected a complete change in the habitudes and customs of these Indians and they succeeded in persuading them to abandon their barbarous practices and to adopt, to some extent, the arts and habits of civilized life. But the Spanish government, fearing the growth of the power and influence of the Jesuits, caused them to be banished from the country.

The Jesuits were succeeded by the Franciscans. The Franciscans were succeeded by the Dominicans. After the expulsion of the Jesuits, to whom the natives were affectionately devoted, the aspect of the various missions became worse and worse and now all of the missionary establishments are in ruins, except one that continues a monument of the former power and prosperity of the order. This establishment is situated in a beautiful valley and was once the residence of the principal of the Jesuits in that country.

Although a monument of the strength of a very powerful order, it now is silent as the grave, nor is a human being living at this time within thirty miles of the place. The edifice is of hewn stone, one story high, two hundred and ten feet in front and about fifty-five feet deep. The walls are six feet thick and sixteen feet high, with a vaulted roof of stone about two and a half feet in thickness.

There is but little in Lower California to invite immigration. Barren mountains and sandy plains traverse the largest portion of land, and make a very unfavorable impression upon the minds of those who visit that region. A few settlements of whites have been attempted, but they have nearly all failed. The population of the peninsula is supposed to be about 12,000. This includes Indians, converted Indians, and whites. So much is said for Lower California.

We come now to Upper California, the hunter's dream, the wilderness paradise, land of milk and honey, to which so many thousands and thousands are now turning their eyes as their future home and which, by the way, constitutes a *ne plus ultra* beyond which the restless, roving emigrant cannot go.

Workman represents the Spaniards as a people who devote the greater portion of their time to sporting and various kinds of amusements. This is owing to the fact that very little exertion is necessary to secure a competency of food and raiment. The peculiarity with which he was very much struck was their superior horsemanship and their equestrian exercises, in which they are constantly engaged.

The vast number of horses both wild and tame in California makes everyone a cavalier who is nearly always in the saddle and there is no country, perhaps, in the world with better riders. They begin riding when they are very small and many of their children are killed in this manner. When they have strength to manage a horse, it is no uncommon thing for them to noose a horse perfectly wild and then mount him in the open prairie and let him go.

The frightened animal darts off with great and desperate speed, rearing and plunging to rid himself of his terror until he worries himself down by his violent exertions and submits to the government of his rider. It is remarkable that the wildest horse, sometimes in two hours, will become perfectly passive and tractable. A boy of ten or twelve years old is generally a good horseman and it is difficult to get him to do anything on foot. Any Californian would think less hard of riding one hundred miles than he would of walking four hours on foot.

They do the most of their labor on horseback, such as taking care of cattle and horses, and catching wild cattle and horses with the lasso. On horseback, with the lasso, they noose bear and it is very common to draw their wood to their houses by means of this cord, which they, without dismounting, will throw around the end of a log.

The California horses are of a hardy nature, as may be seen by the inhuman way the natives, in general, treat the animals. If a man has to travel from thirty to forty miles from his residence, he saddles his horse and mounts him. On his arrival at the destination, he ties the horse to a post. He may, in some cases, give him a drink of water and should he remain away from home four or five days, his horse gets nothing but water, without food, all that time. If he is a horse of the middling class of California horses, he will travel those thirty or forty miles back again with the same free gait at which he started on a full belly and in good condition. Of course this is only in summer season, when the grass has substance and the horse is in good order.

It is customary with the Indians, as well as the Californians, when they wish to perform a long, hard, and perhaps a dangerous ride, to tie up their horses for several days, and give them nothing to eat. When a horse is equipped for a journey in that country, he generally carries, besides his rider, a weight of from fifty to sixty pounds of saddle gear, and should the weather be rainy and the saddle get wet, the weight is doubled. It requires two large tanned ox hides to fit out a California saddle, add to this a pair of wooden stirrups three inches thick, the saddle-tree, heavy iron rings and buckles, with a pair of spurs weighing from four to six pounds, a pair of goat skins laid across the pommel of the saddle, with large pockets in them which reach below the stirrups, and a pair of heavy holsters, with the largest kind of horse pistols. Notwithstanding this burden, their horses are active and travel very freely.

In California the inhabitants are not only said to be almost born on horseback, but to be almost married in the saddle. Workman's statements correspond with those furnished by one now living in that country about the marriage ceremonies. When the marriage contract is agreed on by the parties, the first business and care of the bridegroom is to get, by buying, begging, or even stealing, (if necessary), the best horse that can be found in his district. At the same time, by some of the above means, he must get a saddle with silver mountings about the bridle and the over-leathers of the saddle must be embroidered. It matters not how poor the parties may be, the articles above mentioned are indispensable to the wedding.

The saddle the woman rides has a kind of leather apron, which hangs over the horse's rump and completely covers his hinder parts as far as halfway down the legs. This, likewise, to be complete, must be embroidered with silks of different colors and gold and silver thread. From the lower part upwards, it opens in six or eight places, each of which is furnished with a number of small pieces of copper or iron, so as to make a noise like so many cracked bells. One of these leather coverings will sometimes have not less than three hundred of these small jingles hanging to it.

The bridegroom must also furnish the bride with no less than six articles of each kind of women's clothing and buy up everything necessary to feast his friends for one, two, or three days, as the inclination of the attendants may dictate. The day for the celebration of the wedding having arrived, the two fine horses are saddled and the bridegroom takes up before him, on the horse he rides, his future godmother and the future godfather takes before him, on his horse, the bride and away they gallop to church. I say gallop, for you will never see a Californian going at any other gait than a brisk hand-gallop.

As soon as the ceremony is over, the new married couple mount one horse and the godfather and godmother mount the other and in a hand-gallop gait they return to the house of the parents of the bride, where they are received with squibs and the firing of muskets. Before the bridegroom has time to dismount, two persons who are stationed at some convenient place near the house, seize him and take off his spurs, which they retain until the owner redeems them with a bottle of brandy or money.

The married couple enters the house, where the near relations are all waiting in tears to receive them. They kneel down before the parents and ask a blessing, which is immediately bestowed by the parents. All persons, at this moment, are excluded from the presence of the parties and the moment the blessings are bestowed, the bridegroom makes a sign or speaks to some person near him and the guitar and violins are struck up and dancing and drinking is the order of the day.

The moment a child is born on a farm in California, and the midwife has had time to clothe it, the baby is given to a man on horseback, who rides posthaste to some Mission with the newborn infant in his arms and presents it to a priest for baptism. This sacrament having been administered, the party returns and the child may rest sometimes for a whole month without taking an excursion on horseback, but after the lapse of that time (one month) it hardly escapes one day without being on horseback until the day of sickness or death. The above statements will show how much truth there is in the assertion that the Californians are almost born and married in their saddles.

Workman represents the whole of California as given up to pleasurable amusements, some of which are very cruel but suited to the minds of these people. These are bear and bull fighting, cock fighting, fandangos— amusements in which they generally indulge on the Sabbath and to which they generally repair after divine service. These fights are allowed by a priesthood more frequently seen in cockpits and amphitheaters, or at card tables, than in the sanctuary of the Most High. These amphitheaters vary as to their area, according to the size of the towns, in the vicinity of which they are always made.

Mr. Workman was frequently present at these exhibitions and witnessed their performances in amphitheater of very great size. He states the assemblage was always immense and the excitement and noise very great. A bullfight always draws forth the greatest concourse, a real, old-fashioned, old Spain bullfight. Thousands and thousands come and cram the seats that are fixed up, one rising above the other, around the amphitheater and make a multitude that would seem to be the whole population of California.

A wild bull of the fiercest kind, which has been taken with their lassos and exasperated until he is in a tremendous rage, is turned loose upon the arena and is followed by the bullfighters, some of whom are on foot and some on horses armed with spears and swords. And now the contest begins, for the moment the bull sees his adversaries, he makes a desperate spring at them and all the equestrian skill and tact of these distinguished horsemen are put into practical exercise to keep beyond the reach of his horns and at the same time to dispatch him.

No horse is taken into an amphitheater that is not well trained to bull baiting and it is therefore generally the case that the horses, which are used on these occasions, show as much tact as their riders. Yet it sometimes happens that both horse and rider are killed in the contest and it often happens that men and horses are badly gored.

During the contest, as the enraged animal variously attacks the footmen and horses, he is pierced and goaded with spears and lances which make him the more furious. Finally, exhausted from rage, violent exertions, and the wounds he has received, he lolls out his tongue and bellows, which being an omen of victory on the part of his assailants, elicits one tremendous burst of applause after another from the excited multitude. In the meantime, the goading and piercing is kept up until the bull is dispatched, amid the shouts of thousands and thousands.

The dead bull is then removed from the amphitheater and another bull is brought in and the same scene is acted over again. Sometimes a bear is turned in with the bull, and then the amphitheater is smaller, so as to bring the combatants more immediately together. A contest between a bear and a bull is generally soon terminated, as one of the combatants or the other, by acquiring some advantage at the outset, very soon dispatches his adversary.

The constant indulgence in such cruel and inhuman amusements and exhibitions as the above will lead the reader to see that the inhabitants of California are not a very refined and enlightened people. It is true, there are a number of missions that are occupied by Catholic priests, whose ostensible object is to propagate the principles of the Christian religion, but what can a set of men do in an undertaking of this kind when in their own mode of living, they daily violate and trample under their feet every principle of that faith, in the spread of which they profess to be engaged! What importance can the Indians of that country attach to the Christian religion when they are told that such priests are its divinely authorized representatives?

If it is true that abominations of the priesthood in that garden spot of the globe occur as alluded to, that order must be a perfect embodiment of every wicked attribute that darkens the character of corrupt human nature. Mr. Hastings, who was in that country in 1843 and who is now residing there, gives a very well delineated account of the religious condition of California and when I read his statements about the missions, and those who occupy them, I confess that I viewed them as the exaggerated and distorted representations of a mind laboring under some strong prejudice. But when these statements were fully supported by the testimony of Workman and several other citizens of this country who have visited California, I am constrained to believe them to be entirely correct.

These missionary establishments are the residences of the priests, to each of which are attached fifteen square miles of land, which is divided into lots to suit the native converts belonging to the establishment. On these lots the converts, (or I should rather call them, poor humbugged vassals and dupes) dwell in their miserable huts, in the most degrading submission to a sacerdotal domination.

As the produce of the lands and all the stock about these establishments, as well as the proceeds resulting from sales, are entirely at the disposal of the priests, the wealth of these religious dignitaries is sometimes very great. Over these fifteen square miles allotted to each mission by the government, vast droves of horses numbering several thousands and herds of cattle even more numerous, and sheep, and hogs, may be seen watched by servile Indians, who like the stock, are the property of the priests.

Appertaining to these establishments are also extensive vineyards that yield an abundance of wine for the use of the priesthood. In the midst of this domain sits enthroned a fat, pursy, pompous, wine drinking, debauched priest, who is lord of all the country and consciences within the above named limits {fifteen miles square}.

We have said that the Californians are a very ignorant and degraded people. Indeed they are but little above the Indians with whom they have intermarried and are in all respect assimilated. It is the policy of their religious rulers to keep them in this condition, to perpetuate their wealth, power, and influence. But it is gratifying to be able to say that this deplorable state of things seems to be destined very shortly to mutation.

The great fertility of the soil, the remarkable aspects of the climate, its various valuable productions and its vast resources of every other kind are now acting as a charm, and inducing many of our intelligent citizens and the citizens of other countries, to seek their fortunes in that land of great promise. The people hail them as benefactors, although the priests and those in authority may view them with suspicion. The principles of civil and religious liberty are being introduced to a strong partiality and expressed by the people to our forms of government and religion and unless measures are adopted by that government to prevent our people from immigrating into that country, a revolution in favor of our institutions must take place and who would not be delighted to see such a happy change?

Who does not desire to see the twenty thousand semi-barbarians of Upper California, now in a state of wretched vassalage, elevated to the condition of a people enjoying the blessings of education, and the liberty of a free and enlightened conscience? Will the government of Mexico venture to say that our citizens and those of any other civilized and Christian country, shall not take up their residence in California, because, perchance, her duped, downtrodden, priest-ridden people may get a little too much light, and see and feel their own situation and the tyranny by which they are now oppressed?

The juxtaposition of the two governments, (ours and that of Mexico), the constant intermingling of their citizens, the opportunity which the natives of New Mexico and California have of becoming acquainted with our citizens and trading with them and of learning something of the excellency of our various institutions, all have the effect of prepossessing them in favor of our principles and have already caused thousands of anxious eyes to be turned to the United States as their friends and future benefactors.

In writing on this subject, I derive my information from gentlemen who have been engaged for a number of years in the Santa Fe trade and those who have traveled through all of California have heard these gentlemen frequently assert that when our forces in the present war with Mexico shall march into Santa Fe and Monterey, the Capitol of Upper California, instead of meeting with resistance, they would be hailed as their deliverers.

In fulfillment of these prophecies, look at Colonel Kearney as he enters Santa Fe and lifts and unfurls the flag of our country, greeted by the united voices of a people who feel that deliverance has at last come. Look also at our flag at Monterey, the Capitol of Upper California, as it waves in the breezes of the Pacific and infuses joy into thousands of hearts. And look at our little exploring party of sixty men only, led on by Captain Fremont, as they put to flight and pursue without the loss of a single man, Castro, the Mexican governor of California, with all his forces and tell me what these things mean, if they do not clearly show that the majority of the people are with us.

In support of what has been stated above, we will give an extract from a letter written by a gentleman, one of our own citizens, who is at this time, Chief Magistrate of Monterey in Upper California.

"I was elected," says he, "by the suffrages of the people. The vote polled was a very large one, though no officer or seaman connected with our squadron went to the polls. I mention these facts as an evidence of the good feeling that prevails here toward our flag. Any hostility must have defeated my election. The office is one which (many) do not covet; it is full of labor and responsibility.

"It covers every question of civil policy in Monterey and reaches to the lives and fortunes of the inhabitants through an immense jurisdiction. General Castro's officers and men have returned to their homes and signed a parole not to take up arms against the authority of the United States, or say or do anything to disturb the tranquility of the present government. This puts an end to all further war in California; indeed, there is no disposition here among the people to offer resistance. The masses are thoroughly with us and right glad to get rid of Mexican rule.

"Had it been otherwise, they would never have elected me to the Chief Magistracy of Monterey. We are all regarded more in the light of benefactors than victors. Their friendship and confidence must never be betrayed. California must never be surrendered to Mexico. If that country has still good claims to her, let those claims be liquidated by an equivalent in money. But it would be treason to the lives and fortunes of the best inhabitants to surrender the province itself. Let Congress at once annex her to the Union as a territory and establish a civil government. We require a new judicial system; the present one throws all the responsibility on the Alcades {justices of the peace}.

"I broke through the trammels of usage a few days since and impaneled the first jury that ever sat in California. The first men in Monterey were on it; the case involved a large amount of property and the allegation of a high crime. No one man should decide such a case. The verdict of the jury was submitted to without a murmur from either of the parties. The community seemed much gratified with this new form of trial; they think, and very rightly too, that twelve men are less liable to partiality, prejudice and corruption than one.

"It was the establishment of trials by jury here that probably led to my election as Magistrate. Mr. Semple, an emigrant printer and myself have established a small paper here, the first published in California. It is issued every Saturday; its appearance made not a little sensation. We found the type in the forsaken cell of a monk and the paper is such as is used here for cigar wrappers and was imported for that purpose. It is printed in English and Spanish. We are going to send, at once, to the United States for larger paper and a fresh font of type. With this new engine of power, we are going to sustain the genius of American institutions here. "Three thousand emigrants from the United States, it is understood, have just arrived at San Francisco in two companies, one commanded by Captain Hastings and the other by Captain Russell and ten thousand more on the way."

So much information is given for the people of California and their present condition and future prospects. In our next chapter, we will give the reader a description of the country as to climate, health, productions, soil, and local advantages.

UPPER CALIFORNIA

As there are many in the United States who are now thinking of going to California and no doubt many more will remove there if that country should be attached to our territory, I would state that Upper California is west of the Rocky Mountains and between latitude 310 and 420 on the Pacific and about two thousand miles from the frontier of the State of Missouri, and the route, the greater part of the way, is the way to Oregon.

Emigrants going to the two countries travel together to Fort Hall, at which place they are about twenty days' journey from their destination. The climate of California is a point upon which every man who thinks of going there will aim at obtaining all that correct information that can be had. The journey is very long and tedious and the advantages gained ought to be many and valuable.

When an emigrant goes to the western frontier of our states and finds a climate that is destructive to his health, it is very easy for him to find a very healthy region to which he may repair and rebuild a broken down constitution. Persons, however, who go to Oregon, or California, will in all probability bury their bones there, whatever the country may prove to be. For but few families would have perseverance enough to retrace their steps for two thousand miles through a country not inhabited except by Indians. Although I did meet with persons during my residence in the State of Missouri who had moved with their families to Oregon, and staying there for a time, returned to the States much dissatisfied, and of course, disposed to give the country a very bad name.

That California is healthy must be evident from the fact that it is a country of valleys and mountains. For it is generally the case that the face of a country determines its character, as it regards health. A country of valleys and very high mountains is always blessed with a pure elastic atmosphere and an abundance of fine water, which everyone knows is essential to good health.

The mountains of California are much higher than the Rocky Mountains themselves. The remarkable phenomenon has been made known that near the coast of the Pacific and at the extremity of the continent there is a range of mountains (the Sierra Nevada), one of the highest on the face of the globe. Its lofty peaks in all parts of California and along the shores and far on the waters of the Pacific may be seen covered with perpetual snow and glistening in the sun. My authority for these statements is Captain Fremont, who recently traveled through Oregon and Upper California, exploring the country and taking the altitude of the highest peaks and ranges of mountains.

He represents a pass in the Sierra Nevada, or Snowy Mountains, as 2,000 feet higher than the South Pass in the Rocky Mountains, and several peaks in view that were several thousand feet still higher. Those who have read Mr. Hastings' account of the Sierra Nevada, or as he calls them, "the California Mountains," will remember that he speaks of this range as "much less elevated than the Rocky Mountains."

We consider Captain Fremont as the best authority, as he did what Mr. Hastings did not, that is, he ascertained the altitude of those mountains by the use of proper instruments, while Mr. Hastings most probably was guided in his calculation by the unassisted eye, and information derived from others. It is easy, however, to conceive how two men, both of whom may be aiming to state nothing but that which is correct, may differ in opinions about a country, of which so much yet remains to be known.

Trappers who have been in the Rocky Mountains from six to ten years have informed me that they have frequently come upon large rivers in those mountains, of the name and even the existence of which they had no knowledge whatever, and the course of which are not to be found laid down in any map of that country. Such is the great extent of that country lying between the States and the Pacific, a great deal of which is now, and is likely to continue to be, unexplored regions.

But let us return to the climate of California, as this is a matter in which every emigrant to that country takes a deep interest and about which he wants nothing but facts. The united testimony of all men who have been in California make it not only healthy, but also equal in this advantage, to any part of the world. It is not subject to the extremes of heat and cold peculiar to the climate of all the States. In any part of Upper California snow seldom falls and it soon and always disappears at the rising of the sun. This applies to the lowlands, or the valleys and tablelands, which are the parts of the country that are destined to be settled and improved.

The remarkable uniformity of temperature peculiar to California and the mildness of its climate is owing to the fact that during the summer, the winds almost constantly prevail from the north or northwest, and sweep over vast bodies of perpetual snow, making them very cool and refreshing. And during the winter there are regular warm sea breezes, which tend to diminish the cold. The heated and rarified air of the valleys and lowlands ascends and gives place to the exhilarating and refreshing streams of pure air that come from the adjacent snow-capped mountains.

As there is very little cold weather during the winter, and no snow or frost to do any harm, there is perpetual life in the vegetable kingdom. This must be the case, otherwise there would be no adequate means of subsistence for the thousands, and ten, and twenty, and fifty thousands of wild horses and cattle that are in California.

In the winter, (if they can be said to have a winter season), that is, during the months of our winter, all the productions of the earth are growing, some of them rapidly, refreshed as they are by frequent warm rains and in the spring, at any rate in the beginning of summer, crops of all kinds are fully matured. This seems to be a wise provision of Providence, for in the latter part of summer, there is generally not only a want of rain, but frequently severe droughts, which has made water and food to be so scarce as to cause the loss of thousands of stock. This is the only objection that I have ever heard urged against that country and it must be acknowledged that it is, to some extent, an unfavorable trait in its character.

It seems that the success of the crops depends upon the quantity of rain that falls in the rainy season, which is in the winter months. If a great abundance of rain falls during the winter, the crops that ensuing summer are said to be very abundant and on the contrary, if there be a lack of rain during the rainy season, the crops are not so abundant. But even in a dry season, so great is the fertility of the soil that the crops, compared with those in the states, are immense. The uniformity then of temperature, the dry summer and autumn seasons, the pure streams of water, an atmosphere remarkable for its elasticity and purity, the presence of very high mountains, whose peaks are always white with snow, must convince any man that Upper California cannot be anything but a very healthy part of the world.

All descriptions of this country, as it regards the climate, whether written or oral, with which we have met speak of California in the same unmeasured terms of praise. Should it be attached to our domain, thousands of our enterprising citizens will be seen every spring taking up their line of march from the frontier of Missouri for that country. Then again, during all seasons of the year, the population is in the most perfect health and none of those diseases that make the happiness and lives of people so precarious are seen that are so common in our new and western states.

We will state another fact (lest we may forget to do so elsewhere) connected with emigrating to California or Oregon. A trip to either of those countries or to Santa Fe is sure to make a great improvement on the health of invalids who may undertake the journey. I have known many who were completely broken down by the diseases of Missouri that took trips of this kind in search of health and have always returned, not only completely restored, but even more fleshy than they had been at any period of their lives.

If there be a certain cure for diseased lungs in the world, I believe it to be a trip to one of those countries. Let no invalid be afraid to try it. If he thinks the trip too long to California or Oregon, let him go to Santa Fe, which is but about nine hundred miles from Missouri and the strength to ride, his health will improve from the start. I have met with many gentlemen in the state of Missouri who were of the opinion that from ten to twenty years had been added to their lives by a trip to Santa Fe.

An impression exists that California is not well supplied with timber, which is certainly very erroneous. It is true timber is not as abundant in some parts of that country as it is in the old states and it is one of the advantages that it is not so abundant. There seems to be a great mistake in the minds of the majority of people as to the quantity of timber necessary for the various purposes to which it is usually applied. When there is more than a sufficiency for said purposes, the surplus must be an expensive obstruction in farming operations. Too much timber must be cut down and removed off the ground, and this often costs more than the land is worth. If the whole face of the country in California were covered with timber, so exuberant is the growth it would be next to a physical impossibility to settle the country.

One of the greatest facilities experienced by emigrants in settling the prairie states is the absence to a great extent of timber. When they have made the rails and enclosed the land, their farms are made and these farms are rich and beautiful in the bargain, made in a few weeks. By the time they may want a new supply of rails to enclose their farms a second time, timber will have grown up to sufficient size to make them. How different is the case with regard to the lands in some of the old states that are covered with a dense and heavy growth of timber.

It is the lot of many a "young beginner in the world" to have to go into the forest, alone, and without any assistance, to open a farm. By the time the trees and stumps are moved off his tract of land and he has things fixed to his notion and taste, he is an old, worn-out man, if not in years, at least in feeling. And what is worse, he has nothing to show for his time, labor, and expended energies, but a farm that will not bring as much per acre as it would have cost to remove the timber. I have known farmers in Illinois and Missouri to make their rails ten miles from their prairie lands and haul them that distance. They can make a prairie farm infinitely easier than they could have opened a farm in the woods.

The timber in California is abundant in the mountains, along the rivers, and coast, growing to an extraordinary size and height. Workman affirms that he saw trees on the coast that were not less than two hundred feet high, without a limb the first hundred feet, and being about thirty feet in circumference.

The principal varieties of trees are oak, ash, fir, pine, spruce, cedar of great size, (called red wood), cherry, and willow. The prickly pear and wormwood are also to be found, constituting the only vegetation in some parts of California as well as Oregon and the Rocky Mountains. The forests abound in wild grapes, which connected with the fact that there are extensive vineyards belonging to the Missions, shows that California is admirably adapted to the cultivation of the grape. There are orchards attached to those missions that furnish every variety of fruit, northern and southern, which settles another important question in regard to the fruits of the country.

Vegetables of all kinds are produced in the greatest abundance; wheat, corn, rye, oats, hemp, and tobacco are cultivated with as much success as in any part of the world. In the southern part of Upper and Lower California, cotton, rice, coffee, cane, and the tropical fruits, such as oranges, pomegranates, citrons, lemons, et cetera, are cultivated and come to perfect maturity. Clover, flax, and oats are in many areas spontaneous productions of the earth and may be seen in vast fields. The wild flax in California is the same as our variety and is to be seen in Oregon and the Rocky Mountains. The wild oats and clover, in almost every respect, resemble those of the states.

Wheat may be sown any time between fall and spring, and the time of cutting depends on the time it is sown. If it is sown in the fall, it will mature in the spring. The quality and quantity of tobacco cultivated is said to be equal to that of any portion of the world. Indeed, all the experiments that have been made in cultivating the different kinds of grains and fruits have resulted in the most satisfactory and flattering developments. Every variety of spontaneous fruit found in the States is found in California, luxurious and abundant.

One of the most interesting characteristics of this country is the immense herds of partially wild cattle and horses that may be seen grazing on the prairies and plains. The almost endless number of cattle and horses, their rapid increase, and the ease with which they are raised in California, makes it perhaps the greatest stock country in the world. Indeed, for many years cattle were raised (if they can be raised) for their hides and were slaughtered by thousands while their flesh was left on the ground as food for wild beasts. Recently, there has been an increasing demand for their tallow and beef and, indeed, a great many cattle are driven to Oregon to supply the emigrants.

It would appear that the cattle of California are of an inferior quality, as the people of Oregon greatly prefer the cattle taken from the state of Missouri. Hence, several droves of cattle (cows principally) have been taken to Oregon by speculators from Missouri and sold at a very high price, four times as much, perhaps, as the price of a cow from California. The preference for our cattle may arise from the fact that they are tamer and easily managed. The California cattle are said to be very wild and ferocious, and from the fact that no pains are taken to cross and improve the race, they are in all probability very rough. They are certainly very large and generally weigh more than our domesticated race, which excels them in neatness and gentleness of disposition.

The country is also very favorable to the raising of hogs and sheep, of which any number may be raised with little or no trouble. Horses are the favorite stock with the Californians. A Californian well mounted is in his glory. His equipments, in our idea, are awkward and clumsy. His saddle, which is after the Moorish mode, is high behind and before. The front part, called the pommel, is made very strong, as the Californians are in the habit of fastening their lasso to it when they have noosed a wild horse, cow, or bear.

Indeed, the lasso is always hanging coiled up on the pommel of the saddle and it is astonishing to what a variety of uses they apply it and with what dexterity they throw it. The tree of a California saddle is covered with two or three covers of rawhide, which is sometimes carved and embroidered. The stirrups, which are of wood and very clumsy, are also sometimes carved. A tremendous pair of spurs, as large as pitchforks and fastened by chains jingles at the heels of the equestrian. As to the bridle, it often has such mechanical force that it is perfectly easy for the rider to break the jaws of his horse. The seat of the saddle is so deep that when the rider occupies it, it is almost impossible for the most vicious horse to dismount him.

In no part of the world are horses so numerous as they are in California. One man will frequently own from ten to twenty thousand, some of which are distinguished from those belonging to other men by being branded. These horses are slightly smaller than our horses, but they are very clean-limbed, active and capable of enduring great fatigue. It is said to be very common for a Californian to ride one hundred miles in a day, or one hundred miles in ten hours, on the same horse. It is to be remembered, however, that the face of the country is very level and the roads very fine, circumstances that very much determine the distance a horse will travel in a day. Their horses, no doubt, are of the pony kind and from the fact that no pains are taken to improve the race, they must be very degenerate. As numerous as horses are in California and Oregon, and as cheap as they are, there is a demand for our horses there and one good horse from the States is worth twenty of those trifling little ponies.

SANTA FE TRADE

We have stated that our two lost trappers, Workman and Spencer, returned to the States with a company of Santa Fe traders. We have also alluded to the beneficial effect a trip to Santa Fe always has on the health of invalids and we have recommended persons laboring under pulmonary diseases to take a trip of this kind as an almost certain cure.

It may not be improper to give the reader a short account of the Santa Fe trade, which is now a regular business, in which a number of our citizens are regularly engaged, and in which an immense amount of capital is invested. I am not able to state the year when this trade assumed its present weight and importance, but it was not long before 1824 or 1825. Before that time, now and then, a few adventurous individuals would venture through the immense wilds of Louisiana with a few light articles.

This trade differs in one respect from the fur trade—the fur trade is carried on by companies with very heavy capital, whereas the Santa Fe trade is carried on by individuals. A man engaged in this trade buys his goods in the eastern market and has them taken to the frontier of Missouri. There he hires a sufficient number of hands to drive his teams across the plains to Santa Fe and as many more as may be needed for other purposes. His goods are conveyed in wagons usually drawn by mules. Oxen are now substituted.

A Santa Fe company generally numbers about one hundred men and it was customary to depend upon game for provisions, but now every company takes a supply to carry them through. The buffalo have become wild and it takes too much time to hunt and kill them. Moreover, serious disasters have befallen several companies by permitting the men to leave their wagon teams to engage in buffalo hunts, as Indians have sometimes seized such times as a suitable opportunity to rush in upon a company and run off their mules and perhaps cut off that party.

The Indians along that route have learned that it is very easy to frighten a caravan of mules and their policy is always to strike a panic among them and a mule frightened is a mule frantic. They cannot be restrained, but break loose and dash off, pursued by the Indians, who keep up the panic by a constant yell. Formerly, the traders were in the habit of buying mules in Santa Fe and bringing them to the States, but the Spanish mules are very small and since our own citizens have engaged in the raising of mules, that kind of stock is not at this time ever brought to the States from New Spain.

When mules were the purpose of a trade, the traders met with many mishaps. Whole droves of mules numbering from three to five hundred were sometimes lost. Cattle are preferred to mules for another reason. They are stronger than mules, and can stand the heat as well. A duty of one hundred dollars is to be paid in Santa Fe on every wagon, without any reference to the size and the amount of goods. To take advantage of this regulation, the traders have wagons made that will contain seventy or eighty hundred weight, with very wide tires.

Oxen are better adapted than mules, by superior strength, to draw such heavy wagons. When the expedition approaches Santa Fe, the freight of three wagons is put into one and the empty wagons are destroyed by fire to prevent them from falling into the hands of Indians. In this way, the traders manage to avoid paying a great deal of duty.

When they have sold their goods, they also sell their teams at a very fair price. One of these Santa Fe traders will buy up from eighty to one hundred pair of oxen every spring for his trip. From this, it will be very readily inferred that there is quite a demand for oxen in Missouri, at least once a year.

Gold and silver being the articles for which the traders exchange their goods, our citizens are required by the authorities of Santa Fe to pay a heavy duty on the precious metals they take out of that country. To avoid paying this tax, they have large false axle-trees on the wagons, in which they convey their money back to the States. These axle-trees are excavated and the precious metals are concealed inside them. When the proper officer examines the contents of the wagons, he is perfectly unaware of the artifice.

A great deal of capital is invested in this trade. Some expeditions return to the State with fifty, and sometimes, as much as one hundred thousand dollars. By this means {false axels} a great deal of Mexican coin is brought to this country.

During the first few years of this trade, indeed until very recently, the Indians between Missouri and Santa Fe were very troublesome, particularly the Comanche. The companies generally keep some cannon buried on the Big Arkansas River, where the danger begins and when they reach there, they take the cannon up and convey them through the dangerous country, and then bury them again until they return.

The caravans leave Independence in the spring and if they go no farther than Santa Fe, they return the following autumn; but, if they go on to Chihuahua, which is five hundred miles beyond Santa Fe, they are absent a year. Heavy capitalists now generally go on to Chihuahua.

As there is nothing else to induce our citizens to go to that country, but its precious metals, very few of them take up their residence there for life. The regular traders who have families leave them in Missouri and it is rare to see one of our female citizens in a company going to Santa Fe. A German who was going to Santa Fe to become a resident in that country is said to have had a great deal of trouble in consequence of his having a wife with him. She was perhaps the first white woman that ever passed through that country (and for any thing that I know, she was the last) and when she was seen by the Indians curiosity could scarcely be repressed. They gazed upon her beautiful white face with astonishment.

They wanted the privilege (that is, some of the principal Chiefs) of riding with her in the conveyance in which she was seated and some even followed the train of wagons for two or three days, simply to enjoy the pleasure of gazing upon her. One of the Indians, a Comanche Chief, expressed a wish to buy her and offered her husband two buffalo skins, which the Indian thought a very fair price for a wife. It is hardly necessary to state that the German had a very different notion about the value of a wife and declined the offer of the Comanche Chief. It is said that his mind experienced many anxious fears, lest he might lose his " better half," and he declared that if he succeeded in getting to Santa Fe with his wife, he never would again run the like risk of losing her, or put himself in a situation where he would again be taunted with two buffalo skins.

The Santa Fe trade is not now as sure a road to wealth as it was some years ago. There are too many engaged in it. Competition has reduced the price of goods and the Spaniards themselves have recently engaged in it, so that it is now somewhat overdone. Such is a brief account of a trade that has made many of our enterprising citizens very wealthy and caused the precious metals to circulate in great abundance in this country.

THE TONQUIN FUR TRADERS

The traffic in furs has taken many of our citizens beyond the boundaries of the States and prompted them to penetrate the vast wilderness between the States and the Pacific, to explore regions that, but for the efforts of these early adventurers, would have remained perhaps until this day a *terra incognita.* None but the Indian admired the land's beauty, grandeur and fertility. As these adventurers acted the part of precursors as well as trappers, and went in advance of civilization, and discovered countries now occupied by the agriculturalists and mechanics, we propose giving the reader a succinct account of the fur trade and some interesting facts connected with it.

The French, who settled on the banks of the St. Lawrence, were among the first who engaged in this trade on a plan somewhat extensive and they seem to have been the first to discover the vast sources of wealth that were to be found in the rich peltries of the western wilderness. They procured large quantities of the most valuable furs from the natives by giving them in exchange little trinkets that were of very little value and in this way realized vast profits.

When the French lost possession of Canada, the trade fell into the hands of British subjects, where it contracted to very narrow limits and seemed to labor with difficulties. About four years afterwards, it seemed to expand again and was pushed on by an additional number of enterprising merchants who enlarged the field of their operations, and penetrated deeper into the wilderness.

The field of adventure in this trade continued to enlarge over the course of time, until it covered the great chain of Lakes, the sources of the Mississippi, the Missouri, Columbia and Colorado, and eventually reached within the Arctic Circle, a field of enterprise so wide and abounding in such vast treasures of hidden wealth, that it naturally called into existence a great many companies.

The first company that was formed was the Hudson Bay company, which was chartered in 1669 or 1670 by Charles II, who granted to said company the exclusive privilege of establishing trading posts on the shores and the tributary waters of that bay.

After enjoying almost uninterrupted control of the trade for several years, this company found a rival in an association of several wealthy Scottish gentlemen (merchants) who had established a trading post at Michilimackinac, which became the center of the trade extending from Lake Superior to the upper Mississippi and to Lake Winnipeg. The evils arising from the competition of trade brought the two companies together, under the name of the Northwest Company.

After this, as the trade increased, one company after another sprang up until at different times there have been eight or ten different companies, the names of which we will give here. We have mentioned the Hudson Bay Company, afterwards called the Northwest Company; the Mackinaw Company; the American Fur Company; the Pacific Fur Company; the Missouri Fur Company; the Rocky Mountain Fur Company, and several others. It is not our purpose to furnish a history of each one of those companies, but simply to state some facts in relation to that trade which we think will be interesting.

The Rocky Mountains embrace the region in which this trade at this time is more particularly going on. It is about the streams and lakes in that vast wilderness, more than anywhere else, that the adventurous trapper is to be seen passing away his solitary days, and intensely engaged in his efforts to take the beaver. The first company that attempted to establish a trading post on the waters of the Columbia was the Missouri Fur Company, formed at St. Louis in 1808, at the head of which was Manuel Lisa, a Spaniard. He established posts on the Upper Missouri and one on Lewis River, the south branch of the Columbia. This appears to have been the first post established by white men in the country drained by the Columbia, but the enmity of the Indians and scarcity of food caused it to be abandoned by Mr. Henry in 1810.

In this same year (1810), Mr. Astor of New York engaged in the bold scheme of establishing a number of trading posts on the Columbia and its tributaries, along the shores of the Pacific and the headwaters of the Missouri, with a factory at the mouth of the Columbia. His plan was to send goods from New York by sea to this factory to be exchanged for furs, which he intended to have conveyed to China. He would then bring back the silks and teas of that country to New York.

In this magnificent scheme, Mr. Astor had associated with him four gentlemen, under the firm of the Pacific Fur Company. Another part of his plan was to send an expedition overland up the Missouri destined also for the mouth of the Columbia. The object of the land expedition was to open a communication through the Rocky Mountains to gather all necessary information about the country and to plant trading posts along the route.

We have said that Mr. Astor's plan was to forward all necessary supplies by sea to the mouth of the Columbia. In the execution of this plan, he fitted out a large vessel called the Tonquin with men, guns, and everything that might be needed at his posts on the Pacific and the Columbia. This vessel was committed to the hands of a Captain Thorn, a man who may have known how to manage a ship, but who did not know how to manage Indians to the best advantage, or at least for his own good.

It has always been good policy to treat them kindly and not to regard them as civilized beings expected in all instances to do what is right. The observance of this kind of policy has often prevented difficulties that would, in all probability, have resulted in very serious consequences. It seems to have been the misfortune of the Captain of the Tonquin that he was of a petulant disposition and rough and stern in his manners. He was very impatient under any provocation, and it would seem conceived an unfavorable opinion and a sovereign contempt for his crew, which were not of the kind of materials that he admired or would himself have selected for the voyage.

Entertaining this opinion, his suspicious disposition made everything foster it. The relationship between the splenetic Captain and his men, being of a very unpleasant character, their trip was by no means a pleasant one. After a voyage of five months, Mr. Astor's ship reached the mouth of the Columbia. If the Captain experienced trials before he reached that point, his little stock of patience was now doomed to be exhausted. The mouth of the Columbia, according to all accounts, must bear a very frightful aspect and is said to have extensive sandbars. Its entrance was very difficult and dangerous, a fact that will always diminish the value of that river from a commercial point of view. There seems to be vast bodies of sand about the mouth of the Columbia, that are carried by its current and which accumulate at its communication with the ocean.

The constant swelling of the sea tends to throw the sand back, and thus it becomes an obstruction that must ever be in the way of vessels that would enter that river. The Tonquin met with delays, difficulties, and disasters when she reached the mouth of the Columbia. From shore to shore there was a wild confusion of angry waves lashed, by their collision, into a tumultuous uproar that spread fear through the hearts of all the crew. The Tonquin stood out aloof from the danger that was before her for several nights and days.

In the meantime, the authoritative Captain sent out a boat, under circumstances that seemed almost to insure its loss. His conduct seems to have been not only very reprehensible, but also even cruel. Four of his men were ordered out in a whaleboat to ascertain the channel, and to examine the bar.

The poor fellows submissively entered the boat, but they cast a look upon the Tonquin, accompanied with tears in their eyes as they left her, that showed that they felt they were going to a watery grave. The mouth of this river is upwards of four miles wide, and at that time, an angry sea lashed into rage by a strong northwest wind was throwing its white foam and surges against the shore and across the mouth of the river.

It was not long before the Tonquin lost sight of the doomed boat in the tumult of angry waters. A dark, tempestuous night ensued and this authorized the men in the Tonquin to indulge in the most painful anxiety and fears about the fate of the whaleboat. The next day another small boat was sent to hunt the channel as well as to look for the missing boat. The fate of this boat was nearly as sad as that of the first, as it was capsized near the shore and but two of the crew made their escape.

The whaleboat was no doubt lost, for no account could be had of it. Thus, eight or ten of the crew of the Touquin were lost before she found shelter from the storm. It is due to Captain Thorn to say that when he landed, he caused a diligent search to be made along the shore for the men that were absent, but they could not be found.

As this account of Mr. Astor's enterprise in the fur trade is only intended to be a hasty sketch, we would state that the crew selected a site for a trading post and that all hands went to work to erect the necessary buildings. When these were put up, the Tonquin was relieved of her cargo and Captain Thorn, in compliance with his orders, put out into the Pacific to sail to the north.

By the way, an Indian interpreter was picked up by the Tonquin to aid them in their interactions with the Indians along the coast. This interpreter was well acquainted with the various tribes the ship was likely to meet and when they reached Vancouver's Island, he informed Captain Thorn that this part of the coast was populated with a very treacherous and uncertain tribe, whose professions of friendship could not be safely trusted.

But the Captain was a man of his own head and did things in his own way. He landed at the island where the Indians received him with apparent friendship, and manifested an interest in trading by bringing their peltries.

Captain Thorn, expecting a prompt and ready sale, soon made quite a display of that variety of notions and trinkets that he hoped would catch the eye of the Indian. He seems to have calculated, too, upon getting their peltries at a very reduced price, but the natives had dealt with other vessels trading along the coast and had gained some tolerably correct idea of the value of their furs.

When Captain Thorn learned their prices, he treated them and their skins with contempt and withdrew from them, much fretted and vexed. But he could not escape the importunities of the Indians, who perhaps had not as yet conceived any bad designs against the crew and the ship. It is said that among the Indians there was an old Chief who followed the Captain to and fro, taunting him with his mean offers, holding out at the same time a sample of his skins to tempt him to buy. This was more than the patience of the vexed Captain could stand.

He snatched the skin from the hands of the Chief, rubbed it in his face and then kicked him overboard. He then in a very rash manner cleared the deck of skins and Indians. The badly treated old Chief, who by his fall in the water had been completely submerged, came again to the surface and paddled his way in a dreadful rage to the shore, from which, as he cast his eyes upon the Tonquin, he seemed to say, "I'll have revenge." And revenge he secured, as the account will show.

Some of the crew who were better acquainted with Indian character than the Captain, assured him that the natives would resent the indignity offered their Chief and that it would be very unsafe to remain there. The Indian interpreter also added his testimony to confirm the above opinion. But a parcel of naked Indians were no terror to the Captain's mind, nor was he a man to confess that any difficulty could be brought about by indiscretion on his part, for he was not willing to acknowledge any indiscretion. On the next day, some of the Indians very early in the morning made their appearance, and came along side of the Tonquin in a canoe making signs of friendship and manifesting a desire to trade.

As punctilious to a fault as the Captain was in strictly observing the instructions of Mr. Astor in other things, here he failed to do as his employer had advised him and that was to treat the natives kindly and not to suffer too many at a time to go aboard of his ship. This precaution seems to have escaped the mind of the very scrupulous Captain, as these Indians, notwithstanding the previous occurrence, were permitted to mount the deck.

Indeed, there seems to have been no restraint of this kind practiced, as one company after another they came in their canoes, enjoyed the same unsafe privilege and in the space of an hour, the Tonquin was completely surrounded with canoes full of Indians and the deck was crowded. The interpreter, who being an Indian himself and knowing the perfidy of this tribe, manifested great anxiety for the welfare of the ship and informed the Captain that the greater part of the Indians wore short mantles of skins, under which it was customary to conceal their arms. This suggestion met with no better reception from the Captain than the advice that was given at other times

But the crowd of canoes and Indians became so dense that he, at last, when it was too late, became alarmed and gave orders to push out from shore. The Indians, as the ship was about to depart, now intimated that they would let the Captain have their furs at his own price and a brisk trade commenced. But they all wanted knives for their skins, and as fast as one party was supplied, another came forward. Everything that occurred on this occasion, in the view of men at all acquainted with Indian character, was calculated to prove that these Indians had some hostile scheme on foot.

And yet, *mirabile dictu,* it seems, nothing of this kind entered the mind of the Captain until he was completely in their clutches. In the space of an hour's trading, almost every Indian had supplied himself with a knife. The number of the crew did not exceed twenty-five or thirty, while the Indians numbered several hundred on the ship and on the shore. Having thus successfully armed themselves, the Indians had in this action accomplished one important part of their plan and were ready for the work of vengeance.

In a moment, a yell was raised in one part of the deck and was in an instant responded to in every other part. Knives and war clubs were now seen in the hands of the Indians, who rushed upon the crew. This melancholy affair is graphically described in Irving's *Astoria*, in the following language:

> The first that fell was Mr. Lewis, the ship's clerk. He was leaning with folded arms over a bale of blankets engaged in bargaining when he received a deadly stab in the back and fell down the companion way. Mr. Mc Kay who was seated on the taff-rail, sprang on his feet, but was instantly knocked down with a war club and fell backwards into the sea, where the women in the canoes killed him.
>
> In the meantime, Captain Thorn made a desperate fight against fearful odds. He was a powerful as well as resolute man, but he had come upon deck without weapons. Shewish, a young Chief, singled him out as his peculiar prey and rushed

upon him at the first outbreak. The Captain had barely time to draw a clasp-knife and with one blow he laid the young Indian dead at his feet. Several of the stoutest followers of Shewish now set upon him. He defended himself vigorously, dealing crippling blows to the right and left and strewing the quarter deck with the slain and wounded. His object was to fight his way to the cabin where there were firearms, but he was hemmed in with foes, covered with wounds and faint with loss of blood. For an instant, he leaned on the tiller wheel, when a blow from behind with a war club felled him to the deck, where he was dispatched with knives and thrown overboard.

While this was transacting upon the quarterdeck, a chance, medley fight was going on throughout the ship. The crew fought desperately with knives, handspikes and whatever weapon they could seize upon in the moment of surprise. They were soon, however, overpowered by numbers and mercilessly butchered. As to the seven who had been sent aloft to make sail, they contemplated with horror the carnage that was going on below.

Being destitute of weapons, they let themselves down by the running rigging in hopes of getting between decks. One fell in the attempt and was instantly dispatched, another received a deathblow in his back as he was descending, and a third, Stephen Weekes, the armorer, was mortally wounded as he was getting down the hatchway.

The remaining four made good their retreat into the cabin, where they found Mr. Lewis still alive, though mortally wounded. Barricading the cabin door, they broke holes through the companionway and with the muskets and ammunition, which were at hand, they opened a brisk fire that soon cleared the deck. Thus far, the Indian interpreter, from whom these particulars are derived, had been an eyewitness of the deadly conflict. He had taken no part in it and had been spared by the natives, as being of their race. In the confusion of the moment, he took refuge with the rest in the canoes. The survivors of the crew now sallied forth and discharged some of the deck guns, which did great execution among the canoes and drove all the Indians to shore.

For the remainder of the day, no one ventured to put off to the ship, deterred by the effects of the firearms. The night passed away without any further attempt on the part of the natives. When the day dawned, the Tonquin still lay at anchor in the bay, her sails all loose and flapping in the wind and no one apparently on board of her. After a time, some of the canoes ventured forth to reconnoiter, taking with them the interpreter. They paddled about, keeping cautiously at a distance, but growing more and more emboldened at seeing her quiet and lifeless.

One man, at length, made his appearance on deck and was recognized by the interpreter as Lewis. He made friendly signs and invited them on board. It was long before they ventured to comply. Those who mounted the deck met with no opposition; no one was to be seen aboard, for Mr. Lewis, after inviting them, had disappeared. Other canoes now pressed forward to board the prize; the deck was soon crowded and the sides covered with clambering Indians, all intent on plunder.

In the midst of their eagerness and exultation, the ship blew up with a tremendous explosion. Arms, legs and mutilated bodies were blown into the air and dreadful havoc was made in the surrounding canoes. The interpreter was in the main chain at the time of the explosion and was thrown unhurt into the water, where he succeeded in getting into one of the canoes. According to his statement, the bay presented an awful spectacle after the catastrophe. The ship had disappeared, but the bay was covered with the fragments of the wreck, with shattered canoes and Indians swimming for their lives, or struggling in the agonies of death, while those who had escaped the danger remained aghast and stupefied, or made with frantic panic for the shore.

Greater than one hundred Indians were destroyed by the explosion, many more were shockingly mutilated and for days afterwards the limbs and bodies of the slain were thrown upon the beach. The inhabitants were overwhelmed with consternation at the astounding calamity, which had burst upon them in the very moment of triumph. The warriors sat mute and mournful, while the women filled the air with loud lamentations. Their weeping and wailing, however, was suddenly turned into yells of fury at the sight of four unfortunate white men brought captive into their village. They had been driven on shore in one of the ship's boats and taken at some distance along the coast.

The interpreter was permitted to converse with them. They proved to be the four brave fellows who had made such defense from the cabin. The interpreter gathered from them some of the particulars already related. They told him further that after they had beaten off the enemy and cleared the ship, Lewis advised that they should slip the cable and endeavor to get to sea. They declined to take his advice, alleging that the wind set too strongly in the bay and would drive them on shore. They resolved as soon as it was dark to put off quietly in the ship's boat, which they would be able to do unperceived, and to coast along back to Astoria. They put their resolution into effect, but Lewis refused to accompany them, being disabled by his wound, hopeless of escape and determined on a terrible revenge.

On the voyage out, he had repeatedly expressed a presentiment that he should die by his own hands, thinking it highly probable that he should be engaged in some contest with the natives and being resolved, in case of extremity, to commit suicide rather than be made a prisoner. He now declared his intention to remain on board of the ship until daylight, to decoy as many of the Indians on board as possible, then to set fire to the powder magazine and terminate his life by a signal act of vengeance. How well he succeeded has been shown. His companions bade him a melancholy adieu and set off on their precarious expedition.

They strove with might and main to get out of the bay, but found it impossible to weather a point of land and were at length compelled to take shelter in a small cove, where they hoped to remain concealed until the wind should be more favorable. Exhausted by fatigue and watching, they fell into a sound sleep and in that state were surprised by the natives.

Better had it been for those unfortunate men had they remained with Lewis and shared his heroic death. As it was, they perished in a more painful and protracted manner, being sacrificed by the natives to the manes of their friends with all the lingering tortures of Indian cruelty. Sometime after their death, the interpreter, who had remained a kind of prisoner at large effected his escape and brought the tragic tidings to Astoria.

Such was the fate and such is the melancholy story of the Tonquin. We have been somewhat minute in our details as regards this part of Mr. Astor's enterprise, because we regard the fate of his ship as the most tragic event belonging to the Rocky Mountain fur trade. For a fuller and more accurate account of Mr. Astor's Herculean enterprise, which failed, by his trading post or factory falling into the hands of the English during the late war, we refer the reader to Irving's *Astoria*, a book that is certainly one of the best of the many valuable productions of the popular author, Washington Irving.

After the return of peace, when the trading post at the mouth of the Columbia was surrendered, Mr. Astor sought to renew his enterprise, to start it afresh; but he was not successful in securing the fostering aid of the general government and the factory at Astoria was transferred to Vancouver. The Hudson Bay Company enjoyed a perfect monopoly and had the uninterrupted sway over all the country west of the Rocky Mountains until 1823, when Mr. Ashley made a successful expedition beyond the mountains. In 1826 the Rocky Mountain Fur Company of St. Louis commenced regular expeditions to the borders of the Columbia and Colorado. The American Fur Company then extended their operations. Through all the intermediate country, also, that is on the waters of the Mississippi, Missouri, Yellow Stone, Platte, Arkansas, etc., the various fur companies are carrying on their operations. Each company has a number of men (trappers) in their employment whose services are engaged at a fixed price by the year. There is also another class of men who are called free trappers, from the fact that they are not hired by the year, but while they enjoy the protection of the company, they must sell the peltries they obtain to the company.

In the mountains, these companies have their fixed places for their yearly rendezvous, where the scattered trappers come in from every quarter, bringing their furs, which they may have procured the past trapping season. At these places, their employers or their agents meet them, who come from the states (generally from St. Louis) with their loads of merchandise. It is an annual meeting where the hired trappers receive their pay and the free trappers bring their beavers to trade. The Indians also come in from the country around and are present to trade. Some two months are generally spent by all parties at one of those grand stampadoes, as the skin of the beaver at that time (July and August) is of no value and the trappers have nothing to do. The scene that one of these yearly rendezvous presents is truly one that is *suz generis* and to a person that has witnessed nothing beyond the dull monotony of civilized life, very exciting and strange.

After a brisk trade is kept up for several days, the men are seen resorting to every expedient to pass away their time such as shooting, playing cards, horse racing, wrestling, foot racing, passing from camp to camp, cracking their jokes, telling anecdotes and hair-breadth escapes, dancing and courting. "Courting whom?" the reader may ask. Why, courting the young squaws who assemble there, to accomplish their ends, to wit: by their smiles, charms, and graces, win the hearts of the trappers, who in their view are a superior order of beings. To be a trapper's wife, in the eye of a mountain belle, is the perfection of good luck, the height of her coquettish ambition.

The reader must not be surprised when we use the term coquettish. These dames of nature, like their sex in civilized life, are fond of conquests of this kind and to obtain them, they paint and bedeck their persons, flirt about, smile, look pretty and cast their shy-loving glances on those whose hearts they may desire to make their impressions. And by the way, let me tell you, they often succeed in their love adventures and can apply the language of another, as to their undertaking, and say, *veni, vidi, vici.*

Many of those men engaged in the fur business, indeed a majority of them, have their Indian wives and show to the world that if not in other things, at least, in this particular, they are disposed to revere the authority of that Book, which tells us "to marry, multiply and replenish the earth," and that they are firm believers, at least, in one doctrine of that Book which teaches that "it is not good that man should be alone."

Among the articles of trade at these rendezvous is a due supply of the "Oh be joyful," as the New Englanders call it, alias, alcohol, which is retailed at four dollars a pint. It is diluted with water, so as to bring it to the strength of whiskey. It is taken into the Rocky Mountains in the form of alcohol because it is more portable. It is hardly necessary to say that the excitement at these rendezvous is greatly increased by the use of this artificial stimulant.

The principal points of these yearly meetings of fur trappers are the Green

(Colorado) River valley and Pierre's Hole. Here hundreds and hundreds of hunters, trappers, traders and Indians are assembled from two to three months. Before this season of festivity and idleness comes to a close, the men become impatient and desire again to dash into the wilderness and engage in their exciting employment. Two trappers generally go together.

The outfit of a trapper is seven traps, a rifle (of course), an axe, a hatchet, four pounds of lead and one of powder, several blankets, a knife, an awl and a camp-kettle. He is furnished with two or three horses for his trip. Each trapping party takes some particular stream and region as the field of their operations, to which they repair and where they make the necessary preparations for their stay there.

In the trapping season, these adventurous men are scattered all over the Rocky Mountains along every stream and about every lake or pool of water, setting their traps for their favorite game, and in the midst of danger, eagerly pursuing their favorite avocation. Men who have spent several years in this kind of life seldom relish a civilized life. When they come to the States, they soon become restless and impatient, and again seek the haunts of the wilderness.

The state of things on the waters east of the Rocky Mountains is somewhat different from that in the mountains. On those waters our citizens have their forts regularly and safely constructed and some of them mounted with guns. These forts are constructed in reference to the trade that company expects to carry on with the different tribes. For example, a fort that is intended to reap the profits of a trade with the Crow Indians is situated in some place in their country most likely to enjoy that advantage.

Again, as the various western tribes generally occupy a hostile attitude toward each other, a company trading with a particular tribe must, apparently, at least go with that tribe in their hostile feelings toward a neighboring tribe. The Crows and Black-feet are deadly foes. A company trading with the Crows must unite with them against the Black-feet and the Black-feet will regard said company as hostile to them because they trade with their enemies and will treat them as such. This attitude, which the companies are compelled to assume, or which are rather assigned them, frequently involve them in difficulties that result in the loss of life.

I remember a fact communicated to me by a free trapper, who was with a company forted on the Maria River in the Crow country. The Captain of the fort had as a wife a Crow Indian squaw, who was so remarkably vigilant that nothing could occur without her knowing it. Indeed, she was said to have saved the lives of the men in the fort on various occasions by giving them timely notice of their danger and by her constant watchfulness.

On one occasion she reported a band of Indians in the neighborhood of the fort, whose movements indicated hostile intentions. By the aid of a glass, it was ascertained that they were Black-feet, who were disposed to hover around the fort. As it was in the latter part of the day, an eye was kept upon them until dark. Then, the men of the fort turned out to hunt for them and found them within an old breastwork of logs, where they had intended to camp for the night.

There were nineteen of them and as it was presumed, they were Black-feet. They were easily taken and conveyed to the fort to be disposed of as the company might think proper. When they were taken into the fort, they asked some of the Crows that were in the fort to give them some water. Their request was granted and when they received it, they asked the Crows to drink with them. This the Crows declined, by shaking their heads.

At their request, something to eat was next furnished them. They desired the Crows to eat with them, which was also declined by a shake of the head. They then asked for a pipe, and asked the Crows to join them in smoking it. This was also declined in the same manner. The object of these requests was to learn something about their fate, and when they perceived that the Crows were not disposed to do anything that indicated an amicable spirit, the poor fellows seemed to know the doom that awaited them.

The Crows joined with them in a conversation that lasted all night. The next morning one after another was shot and thrown into the river. The company was not at liberty to pursue any other course as they were in the country of the Crows and trading with them and enjoying their protection.

Such is the character of many transactions that make a part of the history of the fur trade, facts that cannot tend to conciliate the natives generally and prompt them to regard the white man as their friend and benefactor. Notwithstanding occurrences of this kind, which are greatly to be deplored, the inducements held out to great gain by this trade have been the means of thoroughly exploring that vast wilderness between the States and the Pacific. Indeed, it has opened the way to Oregon and California and laid open those vast and fertile countries to invite the thousands that are now emigrating there, and to encourage thousands more to go.

Such, however, has been the vigor with which this business has been prosecuted, that it seems destined to be soon extinguished with the race of fur-bearing animals that are fast vanishing from both sides of the Rocky Mountains.

WAY BILL TO OREGON

An emigrant furnishes the following "way bill" to Oregon:

Miles

From Independence, Missouri, to Blue, at Burnett's trace	520
From Blue to Big Platte	25
Up Platte	25
Up the same	117
Across the North Folk of the same	31
Up the same to Chimney Rock	18
To Scott's Bluffs	20
To Fort Laramie	38
From Fort Laramie to the Big Springs at Black Hills	8
To Keryene, North Fork	30
To the crossing of the same	34
To Sweet water	55
Up Sweet water to the snow on the Rocky Mountains	60
To the main divide of the Rocky Mountains	40
To the waters running to the Pacific Ocean	2
To Little Sandy	14
To Big Sandy	14
To Green River	25
Down the same	12
To Black Fork of Green River	22
To Fort Bridger	35
To Koax River	33
Down the same to the hills that run through the same	57
Down the same to the great Sandustry	38
To Partinith, first waters of the Columbia	25
To Fort Hall, on Snake River	58

To Partinith again	11
To Rock Creek	87
To Salmon Falls	42
To the crossing of Snake River	27
To the Boiling Springs	19
Down the same to Fort Boise	40
To Burnt River	41
Up the same	26
Across to Powder, to the Lamepens	18
To Grand Round	15
To Utilla River, Blue Mount	43
To Dr. Whiteman's	29
To Walla-Walla	25
From Walla-Walla to Dalles	120
From Dalles to Vancouver	100

Whole distance from Independence, Missouri to Vancouver, Oregon is 2,021 miles

THE OREGON TERRITORY

On the east, Oregon skirts eight hundred miles along the Rocky Mountains; on the south, three hundred miles along the Snowy Mountains; on the west, seven hundred miles along the Pacific Ocean; on the north, two hundred and forty miles along the North American possessions of Russia and England. The area of this immense valley contains 360,000 square miles, capable undoubtedly of forming seven states as large as New York, or forty states of the dimensions of Massachusetts.

Some of the islands on the coast are very large, sufficient to form a state by themselves. These are situated north of the parallel of forty-eight. Vancouver's Island, two hundred and sixty miles in length and fifty in breadth, contains 12,000 square miles, an area larger than Massachusetts and Connecticut.

Queen Charlotte's, or Washington Island, one hundred and fifty miles in length and thirty in breadth, contains 4000 square miles. On both of these immense islands, though they lie between the high parallels of forty-eight and fifty-five degrees, the soil is said to be well adapted to agriculture. The straits and circumjacent waters abound in fish of the finest quality. Coal of good quality and other mines of minerals have been found.

Captain Fremont describes this avenue to the Oregon territory as one of easy access and gradual elevation.

> It is situated not far north of the forty-second parallel, which is the boundary between our territory and that of Mexico. The ascent had been so gradual that with all the intimate knowledge possessed by Carson, who had made this country his home for seventeen years, we were obliged to watch very closely to find the place at which we had reached the culminating point. This was between two low hills, rising

on either hand fifty or sixty feet.

When I looked back at them, from the foot of the intermediate slope on the western plain, their summits appeared to be about one hundred and twenty feet above me. From the impression on my mind at the time and subsequently on my return, I should compare the elevation, which we surmounted immediately at the Pass, to the ascent of the Capitol Hill from the avenue at Washington.

The width of the Pass is estimated at about nineteen miles. It has nothing of the gorge-like character and winding ascents of the Allegany passes, nothing resembling the St. Bernard or Simplon passes of the Alps. For one hundred miles the elevation is regular and gradual. It presents the aspect of a sandy plain and the traveler, without being reminded of any change by toilsome ascent, suddenly finds himself on the waters that flow to the Pacific Ocean.

The importance of this Pass is immense. It opens the way into the valley of Oregon and is the only avenue to that country from the interior for a long distance. By observing the map, it will be seen that three great rivers take their rise in the neighborhood of the Pass: the Platte, the Columbia, and the Colorado. The first is a tributary of the Missouri; the second, draining all of Oregon, discharges all its accumulated waters into the Pacific; the third flows southward and empties into the bay of California.

From the South Pass then, as a central point, three great valleys are commanded. It is the key to California. It opens the whole Oregon country from the Rocky Mountains to the Western ocean and it subjects both these great regions to the control of the Mississippi valley.

As the South Pass is in our undisputed territory, its importance will doubtless attract the attention of the government. Fort Laramie, on the Platte River, about three hundred miles from the Pass, is mentioned by Captain Fremont as a suitable point for a national post. It is now merely a station for traders. If the President's recommendation is carried out to construct forts and blockhouses on the route to Oregon, these important points will doubtless be regarded.

A LETTER FROM THE AUTHOR TO A FRIEND IN VIRGINIA

Boonville, Cooper County. Missouri. May 20th 1846.

Dear Sir:

In your last communication, which I had the pleasure of receiving, you state that you are thinking about emigrating from Virginia to Missouri and perhaps to Oregon. If the inducements to engage in such an undertaking were sufficiently great and if you can be satisfied that the descriptions you have had of this country and Oregon were true, you ask of me an honest and candid answer to a number of important questions, which you very correctly say interest everyone who thinks of going to the west.

In answer then, to your letter, allow me to say that I know not what you may have read and what you may have heard about this country and that farther west; but I would state there are two classes of witnesses who bear a testimony pro and con in relation to this country to which I do not attach much truth. The first embraces those who indulge in the most extravagant language as to the advantages of this country and describe on paper a country that is not to be found on the face of the earth. Where such persons are believed, they of course mislead. Many persons receiving these statements as true emigrate to the west and are disappointed and of course dissatisfied.

The second class embraces those who are so dissatisfied with the country that they cannot say a word in its favor. They forward to their friends in the old States very doleful and disheartening accounts of the country and indeed, many such persons return back to the place from which they emigrated. I have known some who incurred all the expense and trouble of coming here and instead of examining the country they became dissatisfied and went immediately back to the old States, giving a miserable account of a country they had never seen. The information, which such persons give of the west, cannot therefore be relied on as correct.

You ask me to account for the mania toward Oregon that prevails in Missouri and you seem to think that it does not say much in favor of our State that so many of our citizens are leaving it to cross the Rocky Mountains. You also inquire about the general character of the people who are emigrating from this country to Oregon.

You will remember that the distance from Independence to the white settlement on the Columbia and its tributaries is about two thousand miles and that it takes the greater part of a summer season to make the trip. You must know that no very small amount of means is essential to procure the necessary outfit. It may therefore be taken for granted that the emigrants from our State, who are seeking a home beyond the Rocky Mountains, belong to the most enterprising, patient and resolute portion of our population and are very far from being the poorest people in the country. They are a class of people that are not easily intimidated by difficulties which they may meet in life and who are in possession of the secret that the way to be able to accomplish an objective is to "believe you can do it, and you *can* do it."

They are rather different from those who have acted the part of pioneers in the western states and whose object, in part at least, seems to have been to avoid the restriction of salutary law and order and "to follow the game," which recedes before a well-organized society. Among the hundreds and hundreds that leave us, there are many who are actuated by the very laudable purpose of carrying the principles of our religion and government to that part of the world and laying the foundation of institutions, of a civil and religious character, that will prove great blessings to all who may settle there, as well as to the native populations.

It is true many are going there without any other specific object than simply to be moving, or to find a country where they will be satisfied, an object, by the way, which they in all probability will never attain. They seem, too, to explain your question why so many are leaving this State. When men have once dissolved the relations that bind them to the country of their nativity and education to seek a location in the west, it may be said with too much truth of the majority of them, that they are unsettled for the remainder of their days.

"Having moved once, they are ever ready to move again," and then the finest country is always ahead. In this city (Boonville) now numbering between three and four thousand inhabitants, I have been told the population has undergone an almost entire change within the last five years. That is, very few of the citizens who were living here five years ago are here now. In the old States, you know, it is very difficult to buy a valuable farm almost at any price, from the fact that the proportion of good land is very small and men do not like to dispossess themselves of comfortable homes.

All over the western states, it may be said to be different. Beautiful and very fertile land abounds in every direction and a pretty, splendid farm seems to be no great *desideratum*, because everyone may have it. In this country too, the majority are disposed to sell for no reason that we can assign except to be going ahead and reaching that Elysium that fills the eye of the unsettled emigrant and enchants him along from country to country until he finds himself on the waters of the Columbia River, or Colorado of the west. These statements may serve to furnish one reason why so many are leaving this country for Oregon. But many are emigrating from Oregon to California, for the same reason they move from this State to Oregon.

As to going to Oregon, my opinion is that if a man cannot do well in this State, where he can get as good land as he can get in Oregon or California and at government price in the bargain ($1.25 per acre), he cannot do better by crossing the Rocky Mountains.

I have read everything that has been written professing to give us a description of Oregon and I have yet to learn in what respect that country has one advantage, which this country does not possess. I have frequently conversed with men who have crossed to the mouth of the Columbia and not only carefully examined all the intervening country, but have remained for several years in Oregon and I have never been able to learn why that country is to be preferred to this.

Yet I believe we should do nothing to discourage emigration to Oregon or California. Great goodwill results from it to the world. It will put that vast territory in the possession of a civilized and Christian people who will apply it to the purpose for which the great Creator of the universe intended it. It is certainly a thing to be desired, that all parts of the face of our earth should be reclaimed from Indian life and be occupied by an enlightened people. The good of the human family requires this and the Christian religion sanctions it.

The more territory there is in the far west to be occupied, the more reduced will be the price of land. This is another good resulting from the great emigration to Oregon. It tends well to keep down the price of land in the western states, a circumstance that greatly favors emigrants to the frontier states, whose means are generally limited, if they have any means at all.

The price of land in this State is said to have been higher twenty years ago than it is now and it is likely to continue low. For if our government should acquire the two California regions, or Upper California only, I do not hesitate to predict, although I am not a prophet nor the son of a prophet, that the *emigration* from the frontier States westward will greatly exceed the *emigration* into those States. This must, of course, keep down the price of land in said States and territories. I am inclined, therefore, to think that land in this State in your and my lifetime will not reach a very high price.

I have said that I did not know, for I never have been able to learn, what advantage Oregon has over this part of the world. Now it is generally conceded that Oregon is not a corn country and this in my opinion is a very great objection to it. As long as I can find a corn country, I do not expect to live in any other. The great variety of useful purposes which this kind of grain answers and answers better than anything else, must make the country that grows it more valuable than those countries that do not grow it.

How would we, Virginians and Kentuckians, do without it? "We must have our *"hog* and *hominy"* and we never would be willing to live in a country where we could not raise it. Such a country I understand Oregon to be. If anyone does not know the advantages of a corn-growing country, let him compare the many uses that this grain has, with the very few purposes to which wheat is applied, and he will at once see that it is much easier to get along without wheat than without corn. Oregon is said to be a fine wheat country and I have no doubt that the climate is better adapted to the growing of that kind of grain than any other, but then you may defend upon it, it is no better, for example, than north Illinois, Iowa, Wisconsin or Missouri.

I hope you will not misunderstand me. I am only comparing Oregon with this country with the view of answering your question. It is a fine country, but in my opinion not superior to this. Nor am I to be understood as aiming to discourage emigration to that country. I would rather encourage it and say nothing that would cast a damper over the feelings of the emigrant and cause him to abandon his purpose.

In answer to your question about the soil of Missouri, I reply that it is as fertile as that of any country. I mean the river bottomland. The prairie (table) land is not so rich and on that account the first settlements were made in the timber, which is pretty much confined to the waterways.

For the last few years, the river lands have not been valued so high from the fact that they are liable to be over-flown once a year. The larger classes of rivers in this state originate in the Rocky Mountains and every spring they are swelled to an enormous size from the melting of the snow in those mountains. This is called the June rise and at that season of the year can do a great deal of injury.

On this account, the earlier settlers of this State, who located themselves on the bottomlands, have generally moved up on the high lands. That is, upon the prairies, their crops are not exposed to the danger of being swept away every spring. You have read the various accounts in the newspapers of the great flood of 1844 in our rivers, which strengthens what I have said.

Another advantage of the prairies is that they are healthier than the bottom, timbered lands. They are higher, and being destitute of timber to interrupt the currents of air, a gentle breeze sweeps constantly over their beautiful surface that tends to keep the atmosphere pure.

If you will select a situation on some elevation in these prairies, on the west side of any pond of water or stream that may be in your vicinity, you may have as good health here as you may enjoy anywhere else. I say the west side, for through the entire summer there generally prevails a southwest wind that will blow away the noxious miasma that arises from the surface of standing stagnant water. No opinion as to a healthy location is more generally entertained in the west than the one just advanced.

You wish to know what kind of crops are the most profitable. That will depend, in part, upon the men who undertake to raise a crop of any kind and convert it into money. Corn, wheat, hemp, and tobacco, are the staples of this State and every man should engage in that kind of farming which he understands. I make this statement because I observe a great many here engage in the raising of tobacco, who from want of experience do not know how to handle such a crop and generally lose their labor.

Many, too, raise large crops of hemp, but as they have no way or means of breaking it, these crops are frequently lost. To raise tobacco and make it a profitable crop, I am certain from what I have seen that a man must "serve his trade at the business" and to raise hemp with profit, a farmer needs several strong hands.

Stock of every kind such as horses, cattle, mules, hogs, etc., are more numerous here than in Virginia, and of the very best blood. Our beautiful prairies, in the grass season, are dotted, everywhere, with bands of the different kinds of stock, in grass up to their bellies. And, it is worthy of notice that the prairie-grass has the property of fattening stock much quicker than any of the varieties of tame grass. However poor an ox may be, if he has strength enough to get out upon the prairie when the tender grass begins to shoot up, he seems immediately to spring up with new life and in a few weeks his naked bones are clothed with flesh.

I observe that many persons, coming even a thousand miles to this State, encumber their trip with stock, furniture, etc., believing that these things cannot be readily (if at all) procured in this country. This is a mistake that creates much trouble and expense. A horse that you can sell in Virginia for sixty dollars, you may get here for thirty. A yoke of cattle that will bring thirty dollars here will bring from fifty to sixty dollars in Virginia. It is only recently that a yoke of oxen in this country would bring even thirty dollars. The Santa Fe traders, however, now use them instead of mules and they buy a great many every spring and this has brought them into demand.

While you ask of me "nothing but truth," you say you "want all of the truth," as to the health of this State. It cannot be denied that this country has been very sickly for the last three or four years, but I am constrained to believe that Missouri will become one of the healthiest of the western states. The face of the country is very undulating and I have yet to see one of those sloughs so common in Ohio, Indiana, and Illinois.

Indeed, if there be any objection to the face of the country, it is too dry. Springs of water are scarce and many are compelled to use cistern-water; that is, rainwater conveyed from the roofs of houses to wells dug to receive it. In a very few hours, this water, which is very free from mineral and noxious properties and of course very pure, becomes very cool. You may think this is a poor substitute for the fine springs in the hills and mountains of Virginia but believe me, my dear sir, when I tell you that the majority of persons, after using it awhile, become very fond of it.

Like all persons who may be thinking and talking about moving to the west, you ask a question about the game in this State. There are no buffalo within the limits of Missouri State, nor any within five hundred miles from the boundary line. There are some elk in the unsettled parts of the State and deer are also plenty in some places. But game of every kind, in a prairie country like this, will vanish much faster and sooner than in timbered countries.

I have no doubt as to the fact that there will be deer in the old States when there will not be one in the limits of our State. Game is scarcer about the boundary line and for some distance into the Indian country than it is in the interior. In consequence of this fact, the tribes about the line often ask permission to come within the limits of our State to hunt. This privilege is granted by the Governor if there is no objection raised by the whites living where the Indians wish to hunt.

It is yearly becoming a question of increasing interest, what is to be the fate of the tribes on our frontier. That which constitutes their main dependence for a living (the game) is fast disappearing and the poor wretches must beg, steal, or starve. The day is not very distant when our government will be compelled to do something to prevent the difficulties and annoyances to which our citizens will be exposed from their juxtaposition to these frontier tribes.

STORIES OF THE
GREAT WEST

INTRODUCTION TO STORIES OF THE GREAT WEST BY HENRY HOWE

Written history is generally too scholastic to interest the masses. Dignified and formal, it deals mainly in great events and of those, imperfectly, because it does not pause to present clear impressions of individuals. It is these [eyewitness accounts] that lend to written fiction its greatest charm and attract the multitude by appearing like truth. Although untrue in the particular combinations, scenes and plots delineated, fiction is drawn from nature, experience and these facts in life, as with chessmen, are only arranged in new, but natural positions.

History includes everything in Nature, Character, Customs and Incidents, both general and individual, that contributes to originate what is peculiar in a People, or what causes either their advancement or decline. So broad is its scope that nothing is too mighty for its grasp, so searching, scarce anything is too minute. Were written history a clear transcript of the valuable in history, it would be more enticing than the most fascinating fiction. But as history is written more like fiction, and fiction written more like history, the latter has a hundred fold its readers.

Herein are narrated not only the great events in the History of the West, but the smaller matters of individual experience, as important to its illustration. Interspersed are descriptions of some of those more striking objects of Nature that elicit wonder, or gratify the love of the grand or the beautiful. Additionally, prominent facts are given in relation to a distant Land, which is lashed by the surf of a far western Ocean, a young Empire rising in golden splendor under the rays of a far western Sun.

For this work no originality can be claimed. Like all compilations, it is the production not of one mind, but of a multitude; the offspring not of one father, but of many. Hence, the work given is superior over an original work. The production of a single mind, however masterly, is pervaded by one style and occasionally sinks into commonplace. But a skillful compilation gives a variety and selecting only the best things places them where they will best appear in comparison or combination. The fashion has been to prefer original works and so it will continue until the public forgets to regard the fields of literature as one grand Coliseum and the actors thereon as merely mental Gladiators.

Compilers are but a humble class, mere Camp followers of the great army of Authors who combat alone for Fame. When they are credited with selecting judiciously, abridging carefully, and combining adroitly, their Lilliputian cups are to the brim. Above this plane of a lower level they have no wings to soar. But on this is a broad field for utility. Such has been our object and if we beguile the hours and brighten the memory of other days in the mind of the aged Pioneer, if we amuse and instruct the young Farmer at his evening's fireside after a hard day's toil, then our measure is filled.

Henry Howe (1855)

THOMAS HIGGINS: THE RANGER'S ADVENTURE

Thomas Higgins was a native Kentuckian, who in the late war enlisted in a company of rangers and was stationed in the summer of 1814 in a blockhouse or station, eight miles south of Greenville in what is now Bond County, Illinois.

On the evening of the 30th of August, a small party of Indians were seen prowling about the station, so Lieutenant Journay with all his men, twelve only in number, sallied forth just before daylight in pursuit of them. They had not proceeded far on the border of the prairie before they were in an ambuscade of seventy or eighty Indians. At the first fire, the lieutenant and three of his men were killed. Six fled to the fort under cover of the smoke, for the morning was sultry and the air being damp, the smoke from the guns hung like a cloud over the scene.

Higgins remained behind to have "one more pull at the enemy" and avenge the death of his companions. He sprang behind a small elm scarcely sufficient to protect his body, when the smoke partly rising discovered to him a number of Indians. He fired upon them and shot down the foremost one.

Concealed by the smoke, Higgins reloaded, mounted his horse, and turned to fly, when a voice, apparently from the grass, hailed him with, "Tom, you won't leave me, will you?" Higgins turned immediately around and seeing a fellow soldier by the name of Burgess, lying on the ground wounded and gasping for breath, replied: "No, I'll not leave you, come along."

"I can't come," said Burgess; "my leg is all smashed to pieces." Higgins dismounted and, taking up his friend, whose ankle had been broken, was about to lift him on his horse when the animal, taking fright, darted off in an instant and left them both behind. "This is too bad," said Higgins, "but don't fear. You hop off using your arms so you'll have three legs and I'll stay behind between you and the Indians and keep them off you. Get into the tallest grass, and crawl as near the ground as possible." Burgess did so and escaped.

The smoke, which had concealed Higgins, now cleared away and he resolved, if possible, to retreat. To follow the track of Burgess was most expedient. It would, however, endanger his friend. He decided, therefore, to venture boldly forward and if discovered, to secure his own safety by the rapidity of his flight.

On leaving a small thicket in which he had sought refuge, he discovered a tall, portly Indian near by and two others in a direction between him and the fort. He paused for a moment and thought if he could separate and fight them singly, his case was not so desperate. He started, therefore, for a little rivulet nearby but found one of his limbs failing him—it had been wounded in the first encounter and until now he had been unaware of the injury.

The largest Indian pressed close upon him and Higgins turned round two or three times in order to fire. The Indian halted and danced about to prevent his taking aim. He saw it was unsafe to fire at random and perceiving two others approaching knew he must be overpowered in a moment, unless he could dispose of the forward Indian first. He resolved, therefore, to halt and receive his fire. The Indian raised his rifle and Higgins, watching his eye, turned suddenly as his finger pressed the trigger and received the ball in his thigh. He fell, but rose immediately and ran.

The foremost Indian, now certain of his prey loaded again and with the other two pressed on. They overtook him. Higgins fell again and as he rose, all three Indians fired and hit him. He now fell and rose a third time and the Indians, throwing away their guns, advanced upon him with spears and knives. As he presented his gun at one or the other, each fell back. At last, the largest Indian, supposing Higgins's gun to be empty from his fire having been thus reserved, advanced boldly to the charge. Higgins fired and the Indian fell.

Higgins now had four bullets in his body, an empty gun in his hand, two Indians unharmed, as yet before him and a whole tribe but a few yards distant. Any other man would have despaired. Not so with him. He had slain the most dangerous of the three, and having little to fear from the others, began to load his rifle. They raised an Indian whoop and rushed to the encounter. A bloody conflict now ensued. The Indians stabbed him in several places. Their spears, however, were but thin poles hastily prepared and bent whenever they struck a rib or a muscle. The wounds they made were not therefore deep, though numerous.

At last one of them threw his tomahawk. It struck Higgins upon the cheek, severed his ear, laid bare his skull to the back of his head and stretched him upon the prairie. The Indians again rushed on, but Higgins, recovering his self-possession, kept them off with his feet and hands. Grasping, at length, one of their spears, an Indian, in attempting to pull it from him, raised Higgins up. Higgins took out his rifle and dashed out the brains of the nearest Indian. In doing so, however, it broke the barrel, leaving a portion only remaining in his hand.

The other Indian, who had heretofore fought with caution, now came on manfully into the battle. His character as a warrior was in jeopardy. Retreating from a man thus wounded and disarmed, or allowing his victim to escape, would have tarnished his fame forever. Uttering a terrific yell, he rushed on and attempted to stab the exhausted ranger, but the latter warded off his blow with one hand and brandished his rifle barrel with the other.

The Indian was, as yet, unharmed and under existing circumstances, he was by far the most powerful man. Higgins's courage, however, was unexhausted and inexhaustible. The Indian, at last, began to retreat from the glare of Higgins's untamed eye to the spot where he dropped his rifle. Higgins knew that if the Indian recovered that, his own case was desperate. Throwing his broken rifle barrel aside and drawing his hunting-knife, he rushed upon his foe.

A desperate strife ensued with deep gashes inflicted on both sides. Higgins, fatigued and exhausted by the loss of blood, was no longer a match for the Indian. The latter succeeded in throwing his adversary from him and went immediately in pursuit of his rifle. Higgins, at the same time, rose and sought for the gun of the other Indian. Both, therefore, bleeding and out of breath, were in search of arms to renew the combat.

The smoke had now passed away and a large number of Indians were in view. Nothing, it would seem, could now save the gallant ranger. There was, however, an eye to pity and an arm to save and that arm was a woman's! The little garrison had witnessed the whole combat. It consisted of about six men and one woman, that woman, however, was a host, a Mrs. Pursley. When she saw Higgins contending single-handed with a whole tribe of Indians, she urged the rangers to attempt his rescue. The rangers objected, as the Indians were ten to one. Mrs. Pursley, therefore, snatched a rifle from her husband's hand and declaring that so fine a fellow as Tom Higgins should not be lost for want of help, mounted a horse and sallied forth to his rescue. The men, unwilling to be outdone by a woman, followed at full gallop, and reached the spot where Higgins fainted and fell before the Indians came up. While the Indian with whom he had been fighting was looking for his rifle, Higgins's friends lifted the wounded ranger up and, throwing him across a horse before one of the party, reached the fort in safety.

Higgins was insensible for several days and his life was preserved only by continual care. His friends extracted two of the balls from his thigh; two, however, yet remained, one of which gave him a good deal of pain. Hearing afterward that a physician had settled within a day's ride of him, Higgins determined to go and see him. The physician asked him fifty dollars for the operation. This Higgins flatly refused, saying it was more than a half-year's pension.

On reaching home, he found the exercise of riding had made the ball discernible, so he requested his wife to hand him his razor. With her assistance, he laid open his thigh until the edge of the razor touched the bullet, then inserting his two thumbs into the gash, "he flirted it out," as he used to say, "without costing him a cent."

The other ball yet remained. It gave him, however, but little pain and he carried it with him to his grave. Higgins died in Fayette County, Illinois, a few years later. He was the most perfect specimen of a frontier man in his day and was once assistant doorkeeper of the House of Representatives in Illinois. The facts above stated are familiar to many to whom Higgins was personally known and there is no doubt of their correctness.

WILD BILL, OR THE MISSISSIPPI ORSON

Wild Bill, or the Mississippi Orson, as he has been called, was captured about the year 1809 in the Mississippi swamp, not far from the site of Pinckneyville. The circumstances that led to his being taken are as follows.

Some persons who had recently settled in the vicinity saw on the margins of the swamps the prints of the bare foot of a young person, and on close examination they soon discovered a naked boy walking with the gait and in the manner of a wild animal, on the shore of one of the lakes that abound in that region.

His object was to catch frogs, a species of hunting at which he seemed very expert. When he had caught them, he devoured them raw. The discoverer attempted to approach him, but as soon as the wild lad saw him, he fled with the usual terror of an untamed creature at the sight of man, toward a lake— into which he plunged, diving and swimming with the ease of an amphibious animal.

These occurrences naturally excited much interest among the settlers and they collected in a body to make a united effort to take him. After hunting for him for some time, they at length discovered him under a Persimmon tree eating the fruit. As soon as he observed his pursuers he fled as before, doubling like a fox and making again for the water.

Excusing themselves by their motive, the hunters adopted their usual expedient for catching animals. They put their dogs on the trail of the strange game. They soon tired him down and brought him to bay. Although they were no metaphysicians to form mental theorems out of the case or their new conquest, they discovered that the two-legged un-feathered creature had the natural instinct of fight, for he had made battle upon dogs and men with the full amount of courage and ferocity that might be expected from his age and physical strength. But, although he fought like any other animal, he was compelled to yield to numbers and was fairly caught and bound.

He was at that time, it is supposed, not far from nine years old, naked and perfectly speechless. His form was slender, well proportioned and capable of extreme agility. His eyes were brilliant, his hair sandy, and his complexion florid, a circumstance that may be accounted for by his having lived almost entirely in the deep shades of the forest. Woodville was the nearest considerable settlement and there he was carried and placed in the care of Mr. Benjamin Rollins and his family for domestication.

In two years after his capture, he had made some progress in learning to converse with others. He was also quite intelligible, although he had a wild look, perfectly indicative of his name. It was more difficult to overcome his appetite for raw flesh than to teach him to speak. The love of the excitement of alcohol seems to be another common appetite of the man of nature, for he soon manifested an unconquerable longing for spirits in any form, especially when rendered sweet. He became intoxicated whenever he had an opportunity.

Whether he discovered the usual developments of the other animal propensities we do not know, but he always remained a wild animal in the fierceness of his temper. When playing with lads of his age, the moment his passions were aroused in any way, his first movement was to strike them with whatever instrument was nearest at hand. After his partial domestication they attempted to put him at work, but he showed an aversion to labor. He was sure to run away, generally making for the town, where his amusement was to mount on horseback, whenever he was allowed the opportunity. Riding was his passion and he would successively mount every horse in the livery stable for the pleasure of riding him to water. In other respects, he was quick and intelligent and his appearance rather agreeable and prepossessing.

The training which he received was either unfavorable to a good mental development or it had originally been denied him by nature, for he became quarrelsome, addicted to drunkenness and not at all a lover of the truth. Consequently, a good deal of doubt and uncertainty must rest upon his account of his early recollections, though they were so often repeated and so nearly in the same form, as to have gained credence with the people among whom he lived.

He stated that he had a dim remembrance of coming down the Mississippi with his father's family in a flatboat, that the boat landed, that his father killed his mother, and that he fled in terror into the swamps, expecting that his father would kill him also. From that time until his capture, he had subsisted on frogs, animals, and berries, living in warm weather among the cane and in cold weather in a hollow tree.

It is extremely unfortunate that so few details of the character and domestication of Wild Bill remain. He died, it is believed, at the age of eighteen or nineteen in the year 1818, after living in the civilized world for about nine years.

LIFE AMONG THE TRAPPERS OF THE ROCKY MOUNTAINS

The trappers of the Rocky Mountains belong to a "genus" more approximating to the Indian than perhaps any other class of man. Their lives are spent in the remote wilderness of the mountains with no other companion than Nature, their habits and character assume a most singular cast of simplicity mingled with ferocity, appearing to take their coloring from the scenes and the objects that surround them. Knowing no want save those of Nature, their sole care is to procure sufficient food to support life and the necessary clothing to protect them from the vigorous climate. This, with the assistance of their trusty rifles, they are generally able to effect, but sometimes at the expense of great peril and hardship. When engaged in their avocation, the natural instinct of primitive man is ever alive to guard against danger and provide food.

Keen observers of nature, they rival the beasts of prey in discovering the haunts and habits of game and in their skill and cunning in capturing it. Constantly exposed to perils of all kinds they become callous to any feeling of danger and destroy human, as well as animal life, with as little scruple and as freely as they expose their own. Of laws, human or divine, they neither know nor care to know. Their wish is their law and to attain it, they do not scruple as to ways and means. Firm friends and bitter enemies, with them it is "a word and blow" and the blow often first.

They may have good qualities, but they are those of the animal, and people fond of giving hard names, call them revengeful, blood-thirsty, drunkards, when the wherewithal is had, gamblers, regardless of the laws, and "White Indians". However, there are exceptions and we have met honest mountain men. Their animal qualities, nevertheless, are undeniable. Strong, active, hardy as bears, daring, expert in the use of weapons, they are just what uncivilized white man might be in a brute state, depending upon his instinct for the support of life.

There is not a hole or a corner of the "Far West" that has not been ransacked by these hardy men. From the Mississippi to the mouth of the Colorado of the West, from the frozen regions of the North to the Gila in Mexico, the beaver trapper has set his traps in every stream. Most of this vast country, but for their daring enterprise would be, even now, a terra incognita to geographers. The mountains and the streams still retain the names assigned to them by the rude hunters and these alone are the hardy pioneers who braved the way for the settlement of the western country.

Trappers are of two kinds, the "hired hand" and the "free trapper." The former is hired for the hunt by the fur companies; the latter, supplied with animals and traps by the company, is paid a certain price for his furs and peltries. There is also the trapper "on his own hook" but this class is very small. He has his own animals and traps, hunts where he chooses and sells his peltries where he pleases.

On starting for a hunt, the trapper fits himself out with the necessary equipment; either from the Indian trading forts or from some of the petty tradera—coureurs des bois—found in the western country. This equipment consists usually of two or three horses or mules (one for saddle, the others for packs) and six traps which are carried in a bag of leather, called a "trap-sack." Supplies such as ammunition, a few pounds of tobacco, dressed deer meat, skins for moccasins, etc. are carried in a wallet of dressed buffalo skin, called a "possible pack." His "possible pack" and "trap-sack" are generally carried on the saddle mule while hunting, the others being packed with the furs. The costume of the trappers is a hunting shirt of dressed buckskin, ornamented with long fringes, and pantaloons of the same material decorated with porcupine quills and long fringes down the outside of the leg. A flexible felt hat and moccasins clothe his extremities. Over his left shoulder and under his right arm hang his powder horn and bullet-pouch, in which he carries his musket balls, flint, steel, and odds and ends of all kinds.

Around the waist is a belt in which is stuck a large butcher-knife in a sheath of buffalo hide, made fast to the belt by a chain or guard of steel, which also supports a little buckskin case containing a whet-stone. A tomahawk is often also added and, of course, a long heavy rifle is part and parcel of his equipment. Around his neck hangs his pipe holder and is generally a *"gage d'amour,"* and a triumph of squaw workmanship, in the shape of a heart garnished with beads and porcupine quills.

Thus provided, and having determined the locality of his trapping ground, he starts to the mountains, sometimes alone, sometimes three or four in company, as soon as the breaking up of ice allows him to commence operations. Arriving on his hunting ground, he follows the creeks and streams, keeping a sharp lookout for "signs." If he sees a prostrate cottonwood tree, he examines it to discover if it be the work of' beaver, whether "thrown" for the purpose of food, or to dam the stream.

The track of the beaver on the land or sand under the bank is also examined and if the sign is fresh, he sets his trap in the run of the animal, hiding it under water and attaching it by a stout chain to a picket driven in the bank, or to a brush or tree. A "float stick" is made fast to the trap by a cord a few feet long, which, if the animal is able to carry away the trap, floats on the water and points out its position. The trap is baited with "medicine," an oily substance obtained from a gland in the scrotum of the beaver, but distinct from the testes. A stick is dipped into this and planted over the trap and the beaver, attracted by the smell and wishing a close inspection, very foolishly puts his leg into the trap and is a "gone beaver."

When a lodge is discovered, the trap is set at the edge of the dam, at the point where the animal passes from deep to shoal water and always underwater. Early in the morning, the hunter always mounts his mule and examines the traps. The captured animals are skinned and the tails, which are a great dainty, carefully packed into camp. The skin is then stretched over a hoop, or framework of osier twigs, and is allowed to dry. The flesh and fatty substance is carefully scraped (grained). When dry, it is folded into a square sheet, the fur turned inward and the bundle containing about ten to twenty skins, lightly pressed and corded, is ready for transportation.

During the hunt, regardless of Indian vicinity, the fearless trapper wanders far and near in search of "sign." His nerves must ever be in a state of tension and his mind ever present at his call. His eagle-eye sweeps around the country and in an instant detects any foreign appearance such as a turned leaf, a blade of glass pressed down, the uneasiness of wild animals, the flight of birds. These are all paragraphs to him written in nature's legible hand and plainest language. All the wits of the subtle Indian are called into play to gain an advantage over the wily woodsman but with the natural instinct of primitive man, the white hunter has the advantage of a civilized mind and thus provided seldom fails to outwit, under equal advantages, the cunning Indian.

Sometimes following on his trail, the Indian watches him set his traps on a shrub-belted stream, and passing up the bed like Bruce of old so that he may leave no track, he lies in wait in the bushes until the hunter comes to examine his carefully set traps. Then, waiting until he approaches his ambush within a few feet, the home-drawn arrow flies, never failing at such close quarters to bring the victim to the ground. For one white scalp, however, that dangles in the smoke of an Indian lodge, a dozen black ones at the end of the hunt ornament the campfire of the rendezvous.

At a certain time, when the hunt is over or they have loaded their pack animals, the trappers proceed to the "rendezvous," the locality of which has been previously agreed upon, and here the traders and agents of the fur companies await them with such an assortment of goods as their hardy customers may require, including generally a fair supply of alcohol. The trappers drop in singly and in small bands, bringing their packs of beaver to this mountain market, not infrequently to the value of a thousand dollars each, the produce of one hunt.

The dissipation of the "rendezvous," however, soon turns the trapper's pocket inside out. The goods bought by the traders, although of the most inferior quality, are sold at enormous prices: coffee twenty and thirty shillings a pint cup, which is the usual measure; tobacco fetches ten and fifteen shillings a plug; alcohol, tram twenty to fifty shillings a pint; gunpowder, sixteen shillings a pint cup; and all other articles at proportionately exorbitant vices.

The beaver is purchased at from two to eight dollars per pound, the Hudson's Bay Company alone buying it by the pluie or "plew," that is the whole skin, giving a certain price for skins, whether of old beaver or "kittens." The rendezvous is one continued scene of drunkenness, gambling, brawling and fighting, so long as the money and credit of the trappers last. Seated Indian fashion around the fires with a blanket spread before them, groups are seen with their decks of cards playing at "eucre," "poker," and "seven up," the regular mountain games.

The stakes are "beaver," which is here current coin, and when the fur is gone their horses, mules, rifles, and shirts, hunting packs and breeches are staked. Daring gamblers make the rounds of the camp, challenging each other to play for the trapper's highest stake, which is his horse, his squaw (if he has one) and as once happened, his scalp. A trapper often squanders the produce of his hunt, amounting to hundreds of dollars, in a couple of hours and supplied on credit with more equipment, leaves the rendezvous for another expedition which has the same result, time after time. One tolerably successful hunt, without the rendezvous activities, would enable him to return to the settlements and civilized life with an ample sum to purchase and stock a farm and enjoy himself in ease and comfort for the remainder of his days.

These annual gatherings are often the scene of bloody duels, for over their cups and cards, no men are more quarrelsome than mountaineers. Rifles at twenty paces settle all differences and as may be imagined, the fall of one or other of the combatants is certain or as sometimes happens, both fall at the word, "Fire!"

A TRAPPER'S ENCOUNTER WITH A GRIZZLY BEAR

The grizzly bear is the fiercest animal of the Rocky Mountains. His great strength and wonderful tenacity of life renders an encounter with him so full of danger that both the Indian and white hunters never attack him unless backed by a strong party. Although like every other wild animal, he usually flees from man, in certain seasons when maddened by either love or hunger, he may charge at the first sight of a foe. Unless killed, a hug at close quarters with a grizzly is anything but a pleasant embrace. His strong hooked claws are capable of stripping the flesh from the bones as easily as a cook peels onions.

Grizzlies attain a weight of nearly one thousand pounds and frequently their bodies are eight and ten feet in length. So gigantic is their strength that they will carry off the body of a buffalo to a considerable distance. Many are the tales of bloody encounters with these animals, which the trappers delight to relate to illustrate the foolhardiness of ever attacking the grizzly bear.

Some years ago, a trapping party was on their way to the mountains, led, we believe, by old Sublette, a well-known "Captain" of the west. Among the band was John Glass, a trapper who had been all his life among the mountains and had seen probably more exciting adventures and has had more wonderful and hair-breadth escapes than any of the rough and hardy fellows who make the far west their home and whose lives are spent in a succession of perils and privations.

On one of the streams running from the "Black Hills," a range of mountains northward of the Platte River, Glass and a companion were one day setting their traps, when on passing through a cherry thicket, which skirted the stream, Glass, who was in advance, spied a large Grizzly bear quietly turning up the turf with his nose, searching for pig-nuts. Glass immediately called his companion and both proceeded cautiously to the skirt of the thicket, and taking steady aim at the animal, discharged their rifles at the same instant, both balls taking effect, but not inflicting a mortal wound. The bear gave a groan of agony, jumped with all four legs from the ground and charged his enemy, snorting with pain and fury.

"Hurrah, Bill," roared out Glass, as he saw the animal rushing toward them, "we'll be made 'meat' of, sure as shootin'!" He then bolted through the thicket followed closely by his companion. The brush was so thick that they could scarcely make their way through, while the weight and strength of the bear carried him through all obstructions and he was soon close upon them.

About a hundred yards from the thicket was a steep bluff. Glass shouted to his companion to make to this bluff as their only chance. They flew across the intervening open and level space like lightning. When nearly across, Glass tripped over a stone and fell. Just as he rose, the bear, rising on his hind feet, confronted him. As the bear closed, Glass, never losing his presence of mind, cried to his companion to close up quickly and he then discharged his pistol full into the body of the animal, at the same moment that the bear, with blood streaming from his nose and mouth, knocked the pistol from his hand with one blow of its paw.

The bear fixed its claws deep into his flesh, and rolled with him to the ground. The hunter, notwithstanding his hopeless situation, struggled manfully, drawing his knife and plunging it several times into the body of the beast, which ferocious with pain, tore with tooth and claw at the body of the wretched man, actually baring the ribs of flesh and exposing the bones. Weak from loss of blood and blinded with the blood which streamed from his lacerated scalp, the knife at length fell from his hand and Glass sank down insensible and apparently dead.

His companion, who up to this moment had watched the conflict, which only lasted but a few seconds, thinking that his turn would come next and not having even presence of mind to load his rifle, fled back to the camp and narrated the miserable fate of poor Glass. The Captain of the band of trappers dispatched the man with a companion back to the spot. On reaching the place, which was red with blood, they found Glass still breathing and the bear dead and stiff, actually lying upon his body.

Poor Glass presented a. horrid spectacle. His flesh was torn in strips from his bones and limbs, and large flaps strewed the ground. His scalp hung bleeding over his face, which was also lacerated in a shocking manner. The bear, besides the three bullets in his body, bore the marks of about twenty gaping wounds in the breast and belly, testifying to the desperate defense of the mountaineer.

Imagining that if not already dead, the poor fellow could not possibly survive more than a few moments, the men collected his arms, stripped him of even his hunting shirt and moccasins, and merely pulling the dead bear off from the body, they returned to their party, reporting that Glass was dead and that they had buried him. In a few days, the gloom which pervaded their trappers' camp at his loss disappeared and the incident, frequently mentioned over the campfire, at length was almost entirely forgotten in the excitement of the hunt and the Indian perils that surrounded them.

Months elapsed, the hunt was over and the trappers were on their way to the trading fort with their packs of beaver. It was nearly sundown and the round adobe bastions of the mud-built fort were just in sight when a horseman was seen slowly approaching them along the banks of the river. When near enough to discern his figure, they saw a lank, cadaverous form, with a face so scarred and disfigured that scarcely a feature was discernible. Approaching the leading horsemen, one of whom happened to be the companion of the defunct Glass in his memorable bear scrape, the stranger in a hollow voice, reining in his horse before them, exclaimed:

"Hurrah, Bill, my boy! You thought I was "gone under" that time, did you? But hand me over my horse and gun, my lad... I ain't dead yet, by a long shot!" What was the astonishment of the whole party and the genuine horror of Bill and his worthy companion in the burial story, to hear the well-known, but now altered, voice of John Glass, who had been killed by a grizzly bear months before and comfortably interred as the two men had reported and all had believed!

There he was, however, and no mistake. All the men crowded around to hear from his lips, how after the lapse of he knew not how long, he gradually recovered and being without arms or even a butcher-knife, he had fed upon the almost putrid carcass of the bear for several days until he had regained sufficient strength to crawl. He then tore off as much of the bear's meat as he could carry in his enfeebled state and crept down the river, suffering excessive torture from his wounds, hunger and cold. He made the best of his way to the fort, some eighty or ninety miles distant, living mainly upon roots and berries. After many, many days, he arrived in a pitiable state, from which he had now recovered and was, to use his own expression, "as slick as a peeled onion."

FREMONT'S EXPEDITIONS

John C. Fremont, originally a lieutenant of the United States Topographical Engineers, made three expeditions to the far west under the authority of the General Government, a fourth being on his own individual account. The object of the First Expedition, made in 1842, was to explore the country between the frontiers of Missouri and the South Pass in the Rocky Mountains, on the line of the Great Platte and Kansas Rivers. His party was almost entirely made up in the vicinity of St. Louis and numbered twenty-eight, including himself. It consisted principally of Creole and Canadian voyagers of French descent familiar with prairie life from having been in the service of the fur companies in the Indian country. The noted Christopher, or Kit, Carson was engaged as guide.

On the 10th of June, the party left Choteau's trading-house near the Missouri River, four hundred miles above St. Louis, the route of their intended explorations. The journey was one of much interest and was occasionally enlivened by buffalo hunts and interviews with the Indians of the plains. On the 10th of July, they reached Vrain's Fort, on the south fork of the Platte River and four days later, Fort Laramie, on Laramie's River.

This latter post belonged to the American Fur Company and was inhabited by a motley collection of traders with their Indian wives and parti-colored children. After passing beyond the "Hot Spring and the Devil's Gates," two narrow and lofty rocky passages in the mountains, on the 8th of August, they came to the South Pass of the Rocky Mountains. On the 15th, Fremont ascended the loftiest peak in this part of the range, which is about one hundred miles north of the southern boundary of Oregon. It is now called "Fremont's Peak" and rises 13,570 feet above the Mexican Gulf and is in the part termed the Wind River Mountains.

"We rode on," says Fremont, in describing the ascent, "until we came almost immediately below the main peak, which I named the 'Snow Peak' as it exhibited more snow to the eye than any of the neighboring summits.

"Here were three small lakes of a green color, each of perhaps a thousand yards diameter, and apparently very deep. We managed to get our mules up to a little bench about a hundred feet above the lakes where there was a patch of good grass and turned them loose to graze. Having divested ourselves of every unnecessary encumbrance, we commenced this time like experienced travelers.

"We did not press ourselves but climbed leisurely, sitting down so soon as we found breath beginning to fail. At intervals, we reached places where a number of springs gushed from the rocks and about eighteen hundred feet above the lakes came to the snow line.

"From this point, our progress was uninterrupted climbing. Here, I put on a pair of light, thin moccasins, as the use of our toes became necessary to a further advance. I availed myself of a sort of a comb of the mountain, which stood against the wall as a buttress and which the wind and solar radiation joined to the steepness of the smooth rock had kept almost entirely free from snow. Up this I made my way rapidly. In a few minutes we reached a point where the buttress was overhanging and there was no other way of surmounting the difficulty than by passing around one side of it, which was the face of a vertical precipice of several hundred feet.

"Putting hands and feet in the crevices between the rock I succeeded in getting over it and when I reached the top, found my companions in a small valley below. Descending to them, we continued climbing and in a short time, reached the crest. I sprang upon the summit and another step would have precipitated me into an immense field below. As soon as I had gratified the first feelings of curiosity, I descended and each man ascended in his turn, for I would only allow one at a time to mount the unstable and precarious slab, which it seemed, a breath would hurl into the abyss below.

"We mounted the barometer in the snow of the summit and fixing a ramrod in a crevice, unfurled the national flag to wave in the breeze where never a flag waved before. A stillness of the most profound and terrible solitude forced itself constantly on the mind as the great features of the place.

"The day was sunny and clear, but a bright shining mist hung over the lower plains, which interfered with our view of the surrounding country. On one side, we overlooked innumerable lakes and streams, the springs of the Colorado of the Gulf of California and on the other side loomed the Wind River Valley, where the heads of the Yellow Stone branch of the Missouri River were located. Far to the north, we could just discover the snowy heads of the Trois

Tetons (a cluster of high, pointed mountains covered with perpetual snow, rising almost perpendicularly 10,000 feet), where were the sources of the Missouri and Columbia Rivers and at the southern extremity of the ridge, the peaks were plainly visible, among which were some of the springs of the Nebraska or Platte River.

"Around us, the whole scene had one main striking feature, which was that of terrible convulsion. Parallel to its length, the ridge was split into chasms and figures; between which rose the thin, lofty walls, terminating with slender minarets and columns. We had accomplished an object of laudable ambition and beyond the letter of our instructions. We had climbed the loftiest peak of the Rocky Mountains and had looked down upon the snow below, standing where human feet had never stood before—we felt the exultation of first explorers."

Soon after, the party set out on their return and on the 17th of October, arrived in St. Louis. Fremont's Second Expedition was made to Oregon and California in the years 1843 and 1844. His corps numbered thirty-nine men, consisting principally of Creoles, Canadian French, and Americans. The party started from the little town of Kansas, on the Missouri frontier, on the 29th of May. Their route was up the valley of the Kansas River to the head of the Arkansas River and to some pass in the mountains, if any could be found at the sources of that river.

In the early part of their journey, trains of emigrant wagons were almost constantly in sight on their way to Oregon. On the 10th of July, they came in full sight of Pike's Peak. It looked grand and luminous, glittering with snow at the distance of forty miles. On the 13th of August, they crossed the Rocky Mountains at the South Pass. This is on the common traveling route of emigration to Oregon and about halfway between the Mississippi River and the Pacific Ocean. On the 6th of September, they ascended an eminence from which they beheld the object of their anxious search, the waters of the Great Salt Lake, "the Inland Sea", stretching in a still solitary grandeur far beyond the limits of their vision.

After the party had visited the lake, they resumed their route to the mouth of the Columbia, where they arrived on the 25th of October at the Nez Pierce Fort, one of the trading establishments of the Hudson Bay Company at the junction of the Walla Walla River with the Columbia River.

On the 4th of November, they came to the termination of their land journey westward, from which point they proceeded down the river in boats to Fort Vancouver on the Columbia, about one hundred miles from its entrance into the Pacific. There, Dr. McLaughlin, the executive officer of the Hudson Bay Company west of the Rocky Mountains, hospitably received them.

They set out on their return on the 25th of November, by a southern route. They passed southeasterly of the Cascade Mountains, to the pass in the Sierra Nevada on whose summit they encamped on the 20th of February 1844. From this point, they proceeded in a southwesterly direction toward San Francisco.

The party suffered severely while on this mountainous range. Nearly the whole journey had been made over ground covered with snow without forage for the cattle. When the cattle starved to death, their famished owners ate the animals. The Indian guides would pilot them for short distances and, pointing with their hands the direction they should take, then desert them. With too good a leader to go in any other direction than that pointed out by duty, too brave men to be discouraged by hundreds of miles of virgin snow, too familiar with death to quail at his embrace, they persevered and murmured not.

But among even these iron-hearted travelers, such were their sufferings that some became deranged and plunged into the icy torrents, or wandered in the forests. Well might Fremont had said "That the times were hard when stout men lost their minds from extremity of suffering, when horses died, and when mules and horses ready to die from starvation, were killed for food."

On 10th of January, Fremont discovered the Pyramid Lake in California, about three hundred and fifty miles westerly from the Great Salt Lake. It is about forty miles long and twenty broad and was named from a huge rock of about six hundred feet in height rising from the water, presenting a close resemblance in form to the great pyramid of Cheops.

It appeared to the party like a gem in the mountains, its dark green waves curling in the breeze. The position and elevation of this lake makes it an object of great geographical interest. It is the nearest lake to the western rim, as the Great Salt Lake is to the eastern rim, of the Great Basin that lies between the Rocky Mountains and the Sierra Nevada and has a length and breadth of about five hundred miles. The Great Basin is thus described by Fremont: "Elevation between four thousand and five thousand feet, surrounded by lofty mountains, contents almost entirely unknown, but believed to be filled with rivers and lakes, which have no communication with the sea-deserts and oases which have never been explored and Indian tribes which no traveler has seen or described."

On the 20th of February, they encamped on the summit of the pass, on the dividing ridge of the Sierra Nevada (Snowy Mountains), which rises several thousand feet higher than even the Rocky Mountains. "On the sixth of March," says Fremont, "we came unexpectedly into a large Indian village where the people looked clean and wore cotton shirts and various other articles of dress. They immediately crowded around us and we had the inexpressible delight to find one who spoke a little indifferent Spanish, but who at first confounded us by saying that there were no whites in the country. But just then, a well-dressed Indian came up and made his salutations in very well-spoken Spanish.

"In answer to our inquiries, he informed us that we were upon the *Rio de los Americanos*, the river of the Americans, and that it joined the Sacramento River about two miles below. Never did a name sound more sweetly! We felt ourselves among our countrymen, for the name of American in these distant parts is applied to the citizens of the United States.

"To our eager inquiries, he replied, I am a vaquero (cowherd) in the service of Captain Sutter and the people in this ranch work for him.' Our evident satisfaction made him communicative and he went on to say that Captain Sutter was a very rich man and always glad to see his country people. We asked for his house. He answered that it was just over the hill before us and offered, if we would wait a moment, to take his horse and conduct us to it. We readily accepted his civil offer.

"In a short distance, we came in sight of the fort and, passing on the way the house of a settler on the opposite ridge (a Mr. Sinclair), we forded the river and in a few miles were met a short distance from the fort by Captain Sutter himself. He gave us a most frank and cordial reception, conducted us immediately to his residence and under his hospitable roof, we had a night of rest, enjoyment and refreshment, which none but ourselves could appreciate."

The route homeward was resumed on the 24th of March. They passed along the valley of the San Joaquin River southward to its headwaters, where there was a pass through the mountains to the east.

When at this point, says Fremont, "our cavalcade made a strange and grotesque appearance (as we traveled) and it was impossible to avoid reflecting upon our position and composition in this remote solitude. Within two degrees of the Pacific Ocean, already far south of the latitude of Monterey and still forced on south by a desert on the one hand, and a mountain range on the other, guided by a civilized Indian, and attended by two wild ones from the Sierra, a Chinook from Columbia and our own mixture of American, French and German (all armed), four or five languages heard at once, more than a hundred horses and mules half wild, American, Spanish and Indian dresses intermingled—such was our composition. Our march was a sort of unusual procession. Scouts ahead and on the flanks, a front and rear division, the pack animals, baggage and horned cattle in the center and the whole stretching a quarter of a mile along our dreary path."

On the 18th of April, Fremont struck the "Spanish Trail," the great object of their search. From the middle of December they had been forced south by mountains and by deserts and now would have to make six degrees of north travel to regain the latitude on which they wished to re-cross the Rocky Mountains. They followed the Spanish trail to New Mexico, four hundred and forty miles, and then struck off in a northern direction toward Utah Lake, the southern limb of the Great Salt Lake, which they reached on the 25th of May, having traveled in eight months an immense circuit of three thousand five hundred miles. They crossed the Rocky Mountains about the middle of June, about one hundred and ninety miles south of the South Pass.

On the 1st of July, they arrived at Bent's Fort and on the 31st of July, again encamped on the Kansas, on the frontiers of Missouri. Fremont was accompanied in this expedition, as previously mentioned, by the celebrated Christopher Carson, commonly called "Kit Carson." Although scarcely thirty winters had passed over Kit, no name was better known in the mountains from Yellow Stone to Spanish Peaks, from the Missouri to the Columbia Rivers. Small in stature, slender limbed, but with muscles of wire, with a fair complexion to look at, Kit, (one would not suppose that the mild looking being before him was noted in Indian fight) had "raised more hair" (scalped) from Redskins than any two men in the western country. Fremont relates a desperate adventure in which Carson and another mountaineer were engaged that illustrates the daring bravery of the mountain men:

"While encamped on the 24th of April, at a spring near the Spanish Trail, we were surprised by the sudden appearance among us of two Mexicans, a man and a boy. The name of the man was Andreas Fuentes and that of the boy (a handsome lad eleven years old) Pablo Hernandez. With a cavalcade of about thirty horses, they had come out from Pueblo de Los Angeles, near the Pacific, had lost half their animals, stolen by Indians, and now sought my camp for aid. Carson and Godey, two of my men, volunteered to pursue the Indians with the Mexican and, well mounted, the three set off on the trail. In the evening Fuentes returned, his horse having failed; but Carson and Godey had continued the pursuit.

"In the afternoon of the next day, a war-whoop was heard, such as Indians make when returning from a victorious enterprise and soon Carson and Godey appeared driving before them a band of horses, recognized by Fuentes to be a part of those they had lost. Two bloody scalps, dangling from the end of

Godey's gun, announced that they had overtaken the Indians as well as the horses. They had continued the pursuit alone after Fuentes left them and toward nightfall entered the mountains into which the trail led. After sunset, the moon gave light and they followed the trail by moonlight until late in the night, when it entered a narrow defile and was difficult to follow. Here they lay from midnight until morning.

"At daylight they resumed the pursuit and at sunrise discovered the horses. Immediately dismounting and tying up their own, they crept cautiously to a rising ground, which intervened from the crest, and they perceived the encampment of four lodges close by. They proceeded quietly and had got within thirty or forty yards of their object when a movement among the horses made the Indians aware of them. Giving the war shout, they instantly charged in the camp, regardless of the numbers of Indians the four lodges might contain.

"The Indians received them with a flight of arrows shot from their long bows, one of which passed through Godey's shirt collar, barely missing the neck. Our men fired their rifles upon a steady aim and rushed in. Two Indians were stretched upon the ground fatally pierced with bullets, the rest fled except a lad who was captured. The scalps of the fallen were instantly stripped off, but in the process, one of them, who had two balls through his body, sprung to his feet, the blood streaming from his skinned head and uttered a hideous howl. The frightful spectacle appalled the stout hearts of our men but they did what humanity required and quickly terminated the agonies of the gory Indian.

"They were now masters of the camp, which was a pretty little recess in the mountain with a fine spring and apparently safe from invasion. Great preparations had been made for feasting a large party, for it was a very proper place for a rendezvous and for the celebration of such orgies as robbers of the desert would delight in.

"Several of the horses had been killed, skinned and cut up, for the Indians living in the mountains and only coming into the plains to rob and murder, make no other use of horses than to eat them. Large earthen vessels were on the fire, boiling and stewing the horse beef and several baskets containing fifty or sixty pairs of moccasins indicated the presence or expectation of a large party. They released the boy, who had given strong evidence of the stoicism or something else of the Indian character by commencing his breakfast upon a horse's head as soon as he found he was not to be killed but only tied as a prisoner.

"Their object accomplished, our men gathered up all the surviving horses, fifteen in number, returned upon their trail and rejoined us at our camp in the afternoon of the same day. They had ridden about one hundred miles in the pursuit and return, and all in thirty hours. The time, place, object and numbers considered, this expedition of Carson and Godey might be considered among the boldest and most interesting, which the annals of western adventure, so full of daring deeds, can present.

"Two men, in an Indian wilderness, pursue day and night an unknown body of Indians into the defiles of an unknown mountain, attack them on sight without counting numbers and defeat them in an instant, and for what? So they could punish them and revenge the wrongs of Mexicans whom they did not know. I repeat, it was Carson and Godey who did this, the former an American, born in Boonslick County, Missouri; the latter a Frenchman, born in St. Louis and both trained to western enterprise from early life."

In the fall of 1845, Fremont started on his third expedition. His object was, if possible, to discover a new route to Oregon, south of the one usually traveled. But his expedition ultimately became diverted from its intended object by the beginning of hostilities between the United States and Mexico and he became an active participant in the conquest of California, where he had arrived in January 1846.

In June of 1847, he commenced his return to the United States across the country by the South Pass, in company with General Kearney and other officers and privates, to the number of about forty. At Fort Leavenworth, on the Missouri frontier, he was arrested by General Kearney, tried and condemned to lose his commission, on account of some alleged breach of military etiquette. The President, however, pronounced his pardon, but Fremont, in June (1848) resigned, maintaining that he had done no wrong, and desired no clemency.

The fourth and last expedition of Fremont was a private enterprise. His objects were multifarious, but he appears to have had in view the discovery of a proper route for the great highway connecting the Mississippi River with the Pacific. The termination of this expedition was disastrous to all concerned, the history of which has been given in two private letters of Fremont.

On the 25th of November 1848, Fremont, with his party, left the Upper Pueblo Fort near the head of the Arkansas River. They had upwards of one hundred and thirty good mules and one hundred and thirty bushels of shelled corn, intended as a support for their animals in the deep snows of the high mountains. The great error of the expedition appears to have been in engaging as a guide an old trapper, well known as "Bill Williams," who had spent some twenty-five years of his life in trapping in various parts of the Rocky Mountains. He proved never to have known, or to have entirely forgotten the country through which they were to pass.

"The 11th of December," says Fremont in his first letter, "we found ourselves at the mouth of the Rio del Norte River canyon, where that river issues from the Sierra San Juan, one of the highest, most rugged, and impracticable of all the Rocky Mountain ranges, inaccessible to trappers and hunters, even in summer. Across the point of this elevated range, our guide conducted us and having great confidence in this man's knowledge, we pressed onward with fatal resolution. Even along the river bottoms, the snow was breast deep for the mules, falling frequently in the valley and almost constantly in the mountains. The cold was extraordinary. At the warmest hours of the most pleasant day the thermometer stood at zero. Judge of the night and the storms!

"We pressed up toward the summit, the snow deepening as we rose and in four or five days of this struggling and climbing, all on foot, we reached the naked ridges which lie above the line of the timbered region and which form the dividing heights between the Atlantic and Pacific Oceans. Along these naked heights it storms all winter and the winds sweep across them with remorseless fury. On our first attempt to cross, we encountered a powder-dry snow driven thick through the air by violent wind and in which objects are visible only a short distance and were driven back, having some ten or twelve men variously frozen, face, hands or feet.

"The guide came near being frozen to death here and dead mules were lying about the campfires. Meantime, it snowed steadily. The next day (December), we renewed the attempt to scale the summit and were more fortunate, or so it seemed. Making mauls and beating down a road or trench through the deep snow, we forced the ascent in spite of the driving powder, crossed the crest, descended a little, and encamped immediately below in the edge of the timbered region.

"The trail showed as if a defeated party had passed; there were by-packs, packsaddles, scattered articles of clothing, and dead mules strewed along. We were encamped about twelve thousand feet above the level of the sea. Westward, the country was buried in snow. The storm continued. All movement was paralyzed. To advance with the expedition was impossible. To get back was impossible. Our fate stood revealed. We were overtaken by sudden and inevitable ruin. The poor animals were to go first. It was instantly apparent that we should lose every one.

"I took my resolution immediately and determined to re-cross the mountain back to the valley of the Rio del Norte River, dragging or packing the baggage by men. With great labor, the baggage was transported across the crest to the headsprings of a little stream leading to the main river. A few days were sufficient to destroy that fine band of mules. They would generally keep huddled together and as they froze, one would be seen to tumble down and disappear under the driving snow. Sometimes they would break off and rush down toward the timber until stopped by the deep snow, where they were soon hidden by the snowfall. The courage of some of the men began to fail."

In this situation, Fremont determined to send a party to New Mexico for provisions and for mules to transport their baggage. King, Brackenridge, Creutzfeldt, and the guide, Williams, were selected for this purpose, with the party being placed under the command of King. Now came on the tedium of waiting for the return of this relief party. Day after day passed and no news was received from them. Snow fell almost incessantly in the mountains. The spirits of the camp grew lower. Life was losing its charms to those who had no reasons beyond themselves to live. Proue laid down in the trail and froze to death in a sunshine day, having with him the means to make a fire, yet he threw his blanket down on the trail, lay down upon it and laid there till he froze to death!

Sixteen days passed away and no tidings from the party sent for relief. Weary with delay and oppressed with anxiety, Fremont decided to go in search of the absent party and for relief in the Mexican settlements. Leaving the camp employed with the baggage under the command of Vincent Haler with injunctions to follow in three days, Fremont set off down the river with Godey, Preuss, and Saunders, a colored servant, leaving in camp provisions only for a few meals.

"On the sixth day after leaving camp," says Fremont, "at about sunset, we discovered a little smoke in a grove of timber off from the river and thinking it might be our express party (King and his men on their return), we went to see. This was the twenty-second day since that party had left us. We found them, three of them, Creutzfeldt, Brackenridge, and Williams, the most miserable objects I had ever beheld. I did not recognize Creutzfeldt's features when Brackenridge brought him up and told me his name. They had been starving. King had starved to death a few days before. His remains were some six or eight miles above, near the river. By the aid of the Indian horses, we carried these three with us down the valley to the Pueblo on the Little Colorado, which we reached the fourth day afterward, having traveled in snow and on foot one hundred and sixty miles. I looked upon the feelings that induced me to set out for the camp as an inspiration. Had I remained there, waiting the return of poor King's party, every man of us must have perished.

"The morning after reaching the Little Colorado Pueblo, horses and supplies not being there, Godey and I rode on to the Rio Hondo and thence to Taos, about twenty-five miles where we found what we needed. The next morning Godey, with four Mexicans, thirty horses or mules and provisions, set out on his return to the relief of Vincent Haler's party."

Fremont waited in much anxiety for the successful return of those left behind, from the 17th of January until February 5th, when Vincent Haler came in. In a subsequent letter, written the next day at Taos, some eighty miles north of Santa Fe, he gives the following account of the terrible calamities that befell those that were left behind.

"You will remember that I left in the camp, twenty-three men when I set off with Godey, Preuss, and my servant in search of King and succor, with directions about the baggage and with occupation sufficient to employ them about it for three or four days, after which they were to follow me down the river. Within that time, I expected relief from King's party, if it came at all. They remained seven days and then started, their scant provisions about exhausted and the dead mules on the western side of the great Sierra, buried under snow.

"Manuel, you will remember Manuel, a Christian Indian, of the Cosumne tribe in the valley of the San Joaquin, gave way to a feeling of despair after they had moved about two miles and begged Vincent Haler, whom I had left in command, to shoot him. Failing to find death in that form, he turned and made his way back to camp, intending to die there. The party moved on and at ten miles Wise gave out, threw away his gun and blanket and at a few hundred yards farther, fell over into the snow and died! Two Indian boys, countrymen of Manuel, were behind. They came upon him, rolled him up in his blanket and buried him in the snow on the bank of the river.

"No other died that day. None died the next. Carver raved during the night, his imagination wholly occupied with images of many things, which he fancied himself to be eating. In the morning, he wandered off and probably soon died. He was not seen again. Sorel on this day, the fourth from camp, lay down to die. They built him a fire and Morin, who was in a dying condition and snow-blind, remained with him. These two probably did not last until the next morning.

"That evening, I think it was, Hubbard killed a deer. They killed here and there, a grouse, but nothing else, the deep snow in the valley having driven off the game. The state of the party became desperate and brought Haler to the determination of breaking it up, in order to prevent them from living upon each other. He told them that he had done all that he could for them, that they had no other hope remaining for them than the expected relief and that the best plan was to scatter and make the best of their way, each as he could, down the river, that for himself, if he was to be eaten, he would at all events be found traveling when he did die. The address had its effect. They accordingly separated.

"With Haler, continued five others: Scott, Hubbard, Martin, Bacon, Roher, and the two Cosumne boys. Roher now became despondent and stopped. Haler reminded him of his family and urged him to try and hold out for their sake. Roused by this appeal to his most tender affections, the unfortunate man moved forward, but feebly and soon began to fall behind. On a further appeal, he promised to follow and to overtake them at evening. Haler, Scott, Hubbard, and Martin now agreed that if any one of them should give out, the others were not to wait for him to die, but to push on and try to save themselves. Soon this mournful covenant had to be kept.

"At night Kerne's party encamped a few hundred yards from Haler's with the intention, according to Taplin, of remaining where they were until the relief should come and in the meantime to live upon those who had died and upon the weaker ones as they should die. With this party were the three brothers Kerne, Chaplin, Cathart, McKie, Andrews, Stepperfeldt, and Taplin.

"Ferguson and Beadle had remained together behind. In the evening, Roher came up and remained in Kerne's party. Haler learned afterward, from some of the party, that Roher and Andrews wandered off the next morning and died. They say they saw their bodies. Haler's party continued on. After a few hours, Hubbard gave out. According to the agreement, he was left to die, but with such comfort as could be given him. They built him a fire and gathered him some wood and then left him, without turning their heads, as Haler says, to look at him as they went off.

"About two miles farther, Scott, you remember him, he used to shoot birds on the frontier, gave out. He was another of the four who had covenanted against waiting for each other. The survivors did for him as they had done for Hubbard and passed on.

"In the afternoon, the two Indian boys went ahead, blessed be these boys, and before nightfall met Godey with the relief. He had gone on with all speed. The boys gave him the news. He fired signal guns to notify his approach. Haler heard the guns, and knew the crack of our rifles and felt that relief had come. This night was the first of hope and joy.

"Early in the morning, with the first gray light, Godey was on the trail and soon met Haler with the wreck of his party slowly advancing. I hear that they all cried together like children, these men of iron nerves and lion hearts when dangers were to be faced or hardships to be conquered! They were all children in this moment of melted hearts. Succor was soon dealt out to these few first met Godey with his relief and accompanied by Haler, who turning back hurriedly followed the back trail in search of the living and the dead scattered in the rear.

"They came to Scott first. He was alive and was saved! They came to Hubbard next. He was dead, but still warm. These were the only ones of Haler's party that had been left. From Kerne's party, next met, they learned the deaths of Andrews and Roher; and a little farther on, met Ferguson, who told them that Beadle had died the night before. All of the living were found and saved, Manuel among them, which looked like a resurrection and reduced the number of the dead to ten, one-third of the whole party, which a few days before were scaling the mountain with me and battling with the elements 12,000 feet in the air.

"How rapid are the changes of life! A few days ago and I was struggling through snow in the Indian wilds of the Upper Del Norte, following the course of the river in more than Russian cold, no food, no blanket to cover me in the long frozen nights, uncertain at what moment of the night we might be roused by the Indian rifle, doubtful, very doubtful, whether I should ever see you or friends again. Now, I am seated by a comfortable fire alone, pursuing my own thoughts, writing to you in the certainty of reaching you, with a French volume of Balzac on the table, a colored print of the landing of Columbus before me, listening in safety to the raging storm without!

"You will wish to know what effect the scenes I have passed through have had upon me. The destruction of my party and the loss of friends are causes of grief; but I have not been injured in body or mind. Both have been strained and severely taxed, but neither hurt. I have seen one or the other and sometimes both give way in strong frames, strong minds, and stout hearts; but as heretofore, I have come out unhurt. I believe that the remembrance of friends sometimes gives us a power of resistance which the desire to save our own lives could never call up."

John C. Fremont

In about a fortnight after writing the foregoing account, Fremont made up a party at Santa Fe and started for California, overland by the old Gila route, where he arrived early in the succeeding spring, his family having preceded him by the Panama route.

The father of John Charles Fremont was an emigrant gentleman from

France, his mother, a lady of Virginia. Fremont was born in South Carolina and at the age of four years, his father died. When seventeen years old, he graduated at Charleston College and thenceforward contributed to the support of his mother and her younger children, first in teaching mathematics and then by civil engineering.

He then was engaged as an assistant to Mr. Nicollet in the survey of the Upper Mississippi and was with him two years in the survey and two years additional in Washington City, in drawing the elaborate map of the expedition. Having received a Lieutenant's commission in the Corps of Topographical Engineers, and thirsting for adventure, he proposed and planned the first expedition to the Rocky Mountains. His powers of endurance in a slender form, his intrepid coolness amid appalling danger, his vast contributions to science and his twenty thousand miles of wilderness explorations, has given to his name a widespread celebrity.

THE HUNTER'S ESCAPE

Those who have not experienced them can have but inaccurate ideas of the terrible storms that at times prevail in the plains and mountains of the Far West, and of the sufferings that they often bring upon the unfortunate emigrants and hunters that come within the region of their influence. A traveler describes one of unusual severity, which he encountered in the winter of 1846 to 1847, near the base of the Rocky Mountains in the vicinity of the Pueblo Fort, on the headwaters of the Arkansas River, and in which, as will be seen in the following narration, he narrowly escaped perishing.

"As we were now within twenty miles of the Pueblo Fort, Morgan, who had enough of it, determined to return and I agreed to go back with the animals to the cache and bring in the meats and packs. I accordingly tied the blanket on a mule's back and, leading the horse, trotted back at once to the grove of cottonwoods, where we before had encamped.

"The sky had been gradually overcast with leaden colored clouds until when near sunset it was one huge inky mass of rolling darkness. The wind had suddenly lulled and an unnatural calm, which so surely heralds a storm in these tempestuous regions, succeeded. The ravens were winging their way toward the shelter of the timber and the coyote or prairie wolf was seen trotting quickly to cover, conscious of the coming storm.

"The black threatening clouds seemed gradually to descend until they kissed the earth and already the distant mountains were hidden to their very bases. A hollow murmuring swept through the bottom, but as yet, not a branch was stirred by the wind and the huge cottonwoods, with their leafless limbs, loomed like a line of ghosts through the heavy gloom.

"Knowing all too well what was coming I turned my animals toward the timber, about two miles distant. With pointed ears and actually trembling with fright, they were as eager as I was to reach the shelter; but before we had traveled a third of the distance, with a deafening roar, the tempest broke upon us. The clouds opened and drove right in our faces a storm of freezing sleet, which froze as it fell. The first squall of wind carried away my cap and the enormous hailstones beating on my unprotected head and face almost stunned me.

"In an instant my hunting shirt was soaked and as instantly, froze hard and my horse was a mass of icicles. Jumping off my mule, for to ride was impossible, I tore off the saddle blanket and covered my head. The animals, blinded with the sleet and their eyes actually coated with ice, turned their tails to the storm, and blown before it made for the open prairie. All my exertions to drive them to the shelter of the prairie were useless. It was impossible to face the hurricane, which now brought with it clouds of driving snow and perfect darkness soon set in. Still the animals kept on and I determined not to leave them, following, or rather being blown after them. My blanket, frozen stiff like a board, required all the strength of my numbed fingers to prevent it from being blown away and although it was no protection against the intense cold, I knew it would, in some degree, shelter me at night from the snow.

"In half an hour the ground was covered with snow on the bare prairie to the depth of two feet and through this I floundered for a long time before the animals stopped. The prairie was as bare as a lake; but one little tuft of greasewood bushes presented itself and here, turning from the storm, they suddenly stopped and remained perfectly still. In vain I again attempted to turn them toward the direction of the timber; huddled together they would not move an inch and exhausted my efforts. Seeing nothing before me, but as I thought certain death, I sank down immediately behind them and covering my head with the blanket crouched like a ball in the snow.

"I would have started myself for the timber, but it was pitchy dark, the wind drove clouds of frozen snow into my face and the animals had so turned about in the prairie, that it was impossible to know the direction to take and although I had a compass with me, my hands were so frozen that I was utterly unable, after repeated attempts, to unscrew the box and consult it. Even had I reached the timber, my situation would scarcely have been improved, for the trees were scattered wide about over a narrow space and consequently afforded but little shelter.

"If I had succeeded in getting firewood, by no means an easy matter at any time, and still more difficult now that the ground was covered with three feet of snow, I was utterly unable to use my flint and steel to procure a light, since my fingers were like pieces of stone and entirely without feeling.

"The wind roared over the prairie that night, the snow drove before it covering me and the poor animals partly and I lay there, feeling the very blood freezing in my veins and my bones petrifying with the icy blasts which seemed to penetrate them. For hours, I remained with my head on my knees and the snow pressing it down like a weight of lead, expecting every instant to drop into a sleep from which I knew it was impossible I should ever awake. Every now and then the mules would groan aloud and fall down upon the snow and then again struggle on their legs. All night long, the piercing howl of wolves was borne upon the wind, which never for an instant abated its violence during the night.

"I will not attempt to describe my feelings. I have passed many nights alone in the wilderness and in a solitary camp have listened to the roaring of the wind and the howling of wolves and felt the rain or snow beating upon me with perfect unconcern; but this night threw all my former experiences into the shade and is marked with the blackest of stories in the memoranda of my journeys.

"Once, late in the night, by keeping my hands buried in the breast of my hunting shirt, I succeeded in restoring sufficient feeling into them to enable me to strike a light. Luckily my pipe, which was made out of a huge piece of cottonwood bark and capable of containing at least twelve ordinary "pipe-fulls", was filled with tobacco to the brim and this, I do believe, kept me alive during the night for I smoked and smoked until the pipe itself caught fire and burned completely to the stem.

"I was just sinking into a dreamy stupor when the mules began to shake themselves and sneeze and snort; which, hailing as a good sign and that they were still alive, I attempted to lift my head and take a view of the weather. When, with great difficulty, I raised my head all appeared as dark as pitch and it did not at first occur to me that I was buried deep in snow; but when I thrust my arm above me, a hole was thus made, through which I saw the stars shining in the sky and the clouds fast clearing away. Making a sudden attempt to straighten my almost petrified back and limbs, I rose, but unable to stand fell forward in the snow, frightening the animals, which immediately ran away.

"When I gained my legs, I found that day was just breaking—a long, gray line of light appearing over the belt of timber on the creek and the clouds gradually rising from the east and allowing the stars to peep from patches of the blue sky. Following the animals as soon as I gained the use of my limbs and taking a last look at the perfect cave from which I had just arisen, I found them in the timber, and singular enough, under the very tree where we had cached our meat. However, I was unable to ascend the tree in my present state and my frost-bitten fingers refused to perform their offices, so I jumped upon my horse and, followed by the mules, galloped back to the Arkansas River which I reached in the evening, half dead with hunger and cold.

"The hunters had given me up for lost, as such a night even the "oldest inhabitants" had never witnessed. My late companion had reached the Arkansas River and was safely housed before it broke, blessing his lucky stars that he had not gone back with me. The next morning he returned and brought in the meat, while I spent two days in nursing my frozen fingers and feet, making up in feasting mountain-fashion for the hardships I had suffered."

THE INDIANS OF THE GREAT PRAIRIE WILDERNESS (AS OF 1855)

There are about one hundred and thirty-five thousand Indians inhabiting the Great Prairie Wilderness of whose social and civil condition, manners and customs, we give a brief account. First, we speak of those who reside in the Indian Territory, six hundred miles north and south, extending along the frontiers of the western states. This immense tract has been purchased from the wild tribes by the United States Government for a permanent abiding-place for the emigrating Indians of the settled part of the Union as a spot where they could be free from those contaminating influences that conspired to their ruin while residing near the settlements of the whites.

It is an admirable location for this purpose; its soil is generally exceedingly fertile with excellent water, fine timber on the streams, mines of iron and lead ore and coal. Thither, for the last forty years, the Government has been inducing the Indians within the jurisdiction of the States to emigrate, until near eighty thousand have moved on to the lands thus assigned them.

Government has been very liberal to them. It purchases the land which the emigrating tribes leave, gives them other land within the new territory, transports them, erects a portion of their dwellings, plows and fences a portion of their fields, furnishes them teachers of agriculture and implements of husbandry, horses, cattle, etc., erects school-houses and supports teachers in them the year round and makes provision for the subsistence of the new emigrants, and uses every effort for the promotion of their moral and physical welfare.

Considering that the ordinary system of government, of Chieftaincies among the tribes, prolific of evil, the United States use all the means in their power to abolish them, making the rulers elective, establishing a form of government in each tribe similar to our State Governments and endeavoring to unite the tribes under a General Government, like that at Washington. Accordingly, a beautiful spot, centrally situated, has been selected on the Osage River, about seven miles square, sixteen miles distant from the Missouri line, as a suitable place for the central government. Any member of those tribes that comes into the confederation may own property in the District and no other.

The Choctaws number about twenty thousand, which includes six hundred Negro slaves and two hundred white men, married to Choctaw women. They reside in the extreme south of the territory, on a tract capable of producing the most abundant crops of corn, flax, hemp, tobacco, cotton, etc. and sustaining a population as dense as that of England. They are improving in comfort and civilization, have fine farms that are well stocked, cotton gins, looms, flouring mills, etc.

They have a written constitution similar to that of the United States, which divides the government into four departments, legislative, executive, judicial and military, together with a National Assembly, which meets annually on the first Monday in October. The Chickasaws, numbering fifty-five hundred, including their slaves, are merged in the Choctaws and are wealthy from the sales of their lands east of the Mississippi to the United States. They have a large fund applicable to various objects of civilization, ten thousand dollars of which is annually applied to education and the Choctaws also have six thousand dollars annually applied to the same object.

The Cherokees, including nine hundred slaves, number twenty-two thousand. They, like the others, own fine farms with lead mines and salt works, where they manufacture one hundred bushels of salt per day and have a form of government similar to the Choctaws. Their dwellings are log homes, with stone chimneys and plank floors, and furnished as well as those of settlers in the new countries and they have good taverns for the accommodation of strangers. Their form of government is similar to the above and their permanent school fund amounts to $200,000. In 1850, they had no less than twenty-two different schools where over a thousand children were taught the common branches, including history. Of these, one hundred and twenty were orphans, who were boarded and clothed at the expense of the Orphans' Fund.

The Creeks number twenty-two thousand five hundred, including three hundred and ninety-three slaves, including sixteen hundred Seminoles. In point of civilization and educational advantages, their situation is similar to the Choctaws and Cherokees, though their form of civil government is less perfect.

The Senecas and Shawnees with them number four hundred and sixty-one, and are, in a measure, civilized, speak good English and live in as much comfort as the others spoken of. The other emigrated tribes are the Pottawatomies; the Iowas; the Weas; the Piankashaws; the Peorias and Kaskaskias; the Ottawas; the Shawnees; the Delawares; the Kickapoos and the Wyandots; the Sacs and Foxes; none of which, with the exception of the two first named, number one thousand souls. They are all, however, more or less civilized and receive the annuities from the general government.

There is scarcely anything the Indian tribes have to encounter so seriously fatal to their improvement as intemperance, of this they are conscious themselves, and most of the emigrant tribes have adopted measures for its prohibition with various degrees of success. Among the Choctaws a law was passed upon this subject that was measurably successful and the spirit, which accomplished its passage, was worthy of the most exalted state of civilization.

It seems that the tribe had generally become sensible of the pernicious influences of strong drink upon their prosperity and had, in vain, attempted various plans for its suppression. At last a council of the headmen of the nation was convened and they passed a law by acclamation, that each and any individual who should henceforth introduce ardent spirits into the nation should be punished with a hundred lashes on his bare back. The council adjourned, but the members soon began to canvass among themselves the pernicious consequences which might result from the protracted use of whisky already in the shops and therefore concluded the quicker it was drank up, the more promptly the evil would be over; so falling to, in less than two hours, Bacchus never mustered a drunker troop than were these same temperance legislators. The consequences of their determination were of lasting importance to them. The law, with some slight improvements, has since been vigorously enforced.

There are about 22,000 Indians of native tribes who reside in the Indian Territory and who receive annuities from the United States. They are the Pawnees, the Sioux, the Quapaws, the Kansas, Otoes, Omahoes, and the Ponsars. The Pawnees number 10,500; the Osages, 5,500; the others are much less in number, and all are in a degraded condition.

These are the native and emigrant Indians within the Indian Territory with their several conditions and circumstances briefly stated. It should be mentioned, however, that one or more of the emigrant tribes have a newspaper among them, and that interspersed throughout them are many devoted missionaries of different denominations, who amid more or less of privation, are laboring with all zeal for the promotion of their temporal and spiritual welfare.

The other Indians in the Great Prairie Wilderness will be briefly noticed under two divisions, those living south and those living north of the Great Platte River. South of the Great Platte are no tribes of note out of New Mexico, except the Comanche, who number about 20,000. They are a warlike tribe and unexcelled as horsemen. Like the Arabs of the desert, they never reside but a few days in a place; but travel north with the buffalo in summer, and when winter comes on, return with them to the plains of Texas.

North of the Great Platte River or Nebraska River are the remains of fifteen or twenty tribes, who average about 800 each. The Sioux and the small pox have thus reduced them. In the upper Mississippi country are the Sioux and Chippewas, both very powerful tribes. Inhabiting the Rocky Mountains and vicinity are the Shoshone or Snakes, the Arapaho, the Crows, and the Blackfoot. The two last named are very warlike. The Blackfoot, in 1828, numbered 15,000 souls, when, having stolen a blanket that year from the American Fur Company's steamboat on the Yellow Stone, one which had belonged to a man who had died of the small-pox on board, the infected article spread the disease among the whole tribe and reduced their number to two-thirds.

In conclusion, we remark that none of the native tribes west of the Mississippi are as brave and warlike as those which inhabited the older states of the Union, as the Wyandots, the Shawnees, the Creeks, the Seminoles, the Cherokees, and the Iroquois. Nor, in general, do they burn their prisoners, or inflict upon them protracted tortures.

They endeavored for a time to bury the dead, but these were soon more numerous than the living. At last, those left alive fled to the mountains, mad with superstition and fear, where the pure air of the elevated vales restored the remainder of the tribe to health. But this infliction, which they believed to be an exhibition of the displeasure of the Great Spirit against them, has in no way humanized their bloodthirsty nature.

A Desperate Boat Fight

In May of 1788 a flatboat loaded with kettles, intended for the manufacture of salt at Bullitt's lick, left Louisville with thirteen persons, twelve armed men and one woman, on board. The boat and cargo were owned by Henry Crist and Solomon Spears and the company consisted of Crist, Spears, Christian Crepps, Thomas Floyd, Joseph Boyce, Evans Moore, an Irishman named Fossett, five others, and a woman, whose name is not preserved. The intention of the party was to descend the Ohio River, which was then very high, to the mouth of Salt River, and then ascend the latter river, the current of which was entirely deadened by backwater from the Ohio, to a place near the licks, called Mud Garrison. This was a temporary fortification, constructed of two rows of slight stockades and the space between filled with mud and gravel from the bank of the river nearby.

The works enclosed a space of about half an acre and stood about midway between Bullitt's lick and the falls of Salt River, where Shepherdsville now stands. These works were then occupied by the families of the salt makers and those who hunted to supply them with food, and acted also as an advanced guard to give notice of the approach of any considerable body of men.

On the 25th of May, the boat entered Salt River and the hands commenced working her up with sweep-oars. There was no current one way or the other, while on the Ohio the great breadth of the river secured them against any sudden attack, but when they came into Salt River, they were within reach of the Indian rifle from either shore. It became necessary, therefore, to send out scouts, to apprise them of any danger ahead.

In the evening of the first day of their ascent of the river, Crist and Floyd went ashore to scout the bank of the river ahead of the boat. Late in the evening, they discovered a fresh trail, but for want of light, they could not make out the number of Indians. They remained out all night, but made no further discoveries. In the morning, as they were returning down the river toward the boat, they heard a number of guns, which they believed to be Indians killing game for breakfast. They hastened back to the boat and communicated what they had heard and seen.

They pulled on up the river until eight o'clock and arrived at a point eight miles below the mouth of the Rolling Fork, where they drew into shore on the north side of the river, now in Bullitt County, intending to land and cook and eat their breakfast. As they drew into shore, they heard the gobbling of turkeys (as they supposed) on the bank where they were going to land and as the boat touched, Fossett and another sprang ashore with their guns in their hands to shoot turkeys.

They were cautioned of their danger, but disregarding the admonition, hastily ascended the bank. Their companions in the boat had barely lost sight of them, when they heard a volley of rifles discharged all at once on the bank immediately above, succeeded by a yell of Indians so terrific as to induce a belief that the woods were filled with Indians. This attack, so sudden and violent, took the boat's company by surprise and they had barely time to seize their rifles and place themselves in a posture of defense when Fossett and his companion came dashing down the bank hotly pursued by a large body of Indians.

Crist stood in the bow of the boat with his rifle in his hand. At the first sight of the enemy, he brought his gun up, but instantly perceived that the object of his aim was a white man and a sudden thought flashed across his mind that the enemy was a company of surveyors that he knew to be then in the woods and that the attack was made in sport, etc. He let his gun down and at the same time, his white foeman sunk out of his sight behind the bank.

The firing had begun in good earnest on both sides. Crist again brought his rifle to his face and as he did so the white man's head was rising over the bank, with his gun also drawn up and presented. Crist got the fire on him and at the crack of his rifle, the white man fell forward dead. Fossett's hunting companion plunged into the water and got in safely at the bow of the boat. Fossett's arm had been broken by the first gunfire on the hill. The boat, owing to the high water, did not touch the land and he got into the river further toward the stern and swam around with his gun in his left hand until he was taken safely into the stern.

So intent were the Indians on the pursuit of their prey that many of them ran to the water's edge, struck and shot at Fossett and his companion while getting into the boat and even seized the boat and attempted to draw it nearer the shore. In this attempt many of the Indians perished Some were shot dead as they approached the boat, others were killed in the river and it required the most stubborn resistance and determined valor to keep them from carrying the boat by assault.

Repulsed in their efforts to board the boat, the Indians withdrew higher up the bank and taking their stations behind trees, commenced a regular and galling fire, which was returned with the spirit of brave men rendered desperate by the certain knowledge that no quarter would be given and that it was an issue of victory or death to every soul on board.

The boat had a log-chain for a cable, and when she was first brought ashore, the chain was thrown round a small tree that stood in the water's edge and the hook run through one of the links. This had been done before the first gunfire was made upon Fossett on shore. The kettles in the boat had been ranked up along the sides, leaving an open gangway through the middle of the boat from bow to stern. Unfortunately, the bow lay to shore, so that the guns of the Indians raked the whole length of the gangway and their fire was constant and destructive.

Spears and several others of the bravest men had already fallen, some killed and others mortally wounded. From the commencement of the battle, many efforts had been made to disengage the boat from the shore, all of which had failed. The hope was that if they could once loose the cable, the boat would drift out of the reach of the enemy's guns; but any attempt to do this by hand would expose the person to certain destruction.

Fossett's right arm was broken and he could no longer handle his rifle. He got a pole and placing himself low down in the bow of the boat, commenced punching at the hook in the chain, but the point of the hook was turned from him, and all his efforts seemed only to drive it farther into the link. He at length discovered where a small limb had been cut from the pole and left a knot about an inch long. This knot, after a number of efforts, he placed against the point of the hook, and jerking the pole suddenly toward him, threw the hook out of the link. The chain fell and the boat drifted slowly out from the bank and by means of an oar worked overhead, the boat was brought into the middle of the river with her side to the shore, which protected them from the fire of the Indians.

The battle had now lasted upward of an hour. The odds against the crew were at least ten to one. The gunfire had been very destructive on both sides and a great many of the Indians had been killed; but if the boat had remained much longer at the shore, it was manifest that there would have been none of the crew left to tell the tale of their disaster.

The survivors had now time to look around upon the havoc that had been made of their little band. Five of their companions lay dead in the gangway: Spears, Floyd, Fossett and Boyce were wounded; Crepps, Crist and Moore remained unhurt. It was evident that Spears' wound was mortal and that he could survive but a few moments. He urged the survivors to run the boat to the opposite side of the river and save themselves by immediate flight and leave him to his fate. Crepps and Crist positively refused, but the boat was gradually nearing the southern shore of the river.

At this time the Indians, numbering forty or fifty, were seen crossing the river above at a few hundred yards' distance, some on logs and some swimming and carrying their rifles over their heads. The escape of the boat was now hopeless as there was a large body of Indians on each side of the river. If the boat had been carried immediately to the opposite side of the river as soon as her cable was loosed, the survivors might have escaped; but to such minds and hearts, the idea of leaving their dying friends to the mercy of the Indian tomahawk was insupportable.

The boat at length touched the southern shore and a hasty preparation was made to bury the wounded in the woods. Floyd, Fossett and Boyce got to land and sought concealment in the thickets. Crepps and Crist turned to their suffering friend, Spears, but death had kindly stepped in and cut short the Indian triumph. The woman now remained. They offered to assist her to shore that she might take her chance of escape in the woods; but the danger of her position and the scenes of blood and death around her had overpowered her senses and no entreaty or remonstrance could prevail her to move. She sat with her face buried in her hands and no effort could make her sensible that there was any hope of escape.

The Indians had gained the south side of the river and were yelling like bloodhounds as they ran down toward the boat, which they now looked upon as their certain prey. Crepps and Crist seized a rifle apiece and ascended the riverbank. At the top of the hill they met the Indians and charged them with a shout. Crepps fired upon them, but Crist in his haste had taken up Fossett's gun, which had gotten wet as he swam with it to the boat on the opposite side, and it misfired.

At this time, Moore passed them and escaped. The Indians, when charged by Crepps and Crist, fell back into a ravine that put into the river immediately above them. Crist and Crepps again commenced their flight. The Indians rallied and rose from the ravine and fired a volley at them as they fled. Crepps received a ball in his left side; a bullet struck Crist's heel and completely crushed the bones of his foot. They parted and met no more. The Indians, intent on plunder, did not pursue them, but rushed into the boat. Crist heard one long, agonizing shriek from the unfortunate woman and the wild shouts of the Indians, as they possessed themselves of the spoils of a costly but barren victory.

Crepps, in the course of the next day, arrived in the neighborhood of Long Lick and being unable to travel farther lay down in the woods to die. Moore alone escaped unhurt and brought in the tidings of the defeat of the boat. The country was at once aroused. Crepps was found and brought in, but died about the time he reached home. Crist described Crepps as a tall, fair-haired, handsome man who was kind, brave and enterprising and who possessed of all those high and striking qualities that gave the heroic stamp to that hardy race of pioneers among whom he had lived and died. He had been the lion of the fight. By exposing himself to the most imminent peril, he inspired his companions with his own contempt of danger.

Crepps and Crist had stood over Fossett and kept the Indians treed while he disengaged the cable and Crepps' coolness during the long, bloody struggle of the day had won the admiration of Crist himself; a more dauntless man had never contended with mortal foe. Crepps left a young wife and one son, then an infant. His wife was pregnant at the time of his death and the posthumous child was a daughter, who is now the wife of the Honorable Charles A. Wickliffe, of Kentucky. Crepps' son died shortly afterwards.

Crist was so disabled by the wound that he could not walk. The bones of his heel were crushed. He crept into a thicket and lay down, and his wound bled profusely. He could not remain there long. His feet were now of no use to him. He bound his moccasins on his knees and commenced his journey. Piece by piece, his hat, hunting-shirt, and vest were consumed to shield his hands against the rugged rocks that lay in his way.

He crawled all day up the river and at night crossed over to the north side upon a log that he rolled down the bank. He concealed himself in a thicket and tried to sleep, but pain, exhaustion and loss of blood had driven sleep from his eyes. His foot and leg were much swollen and inflamed. Guided by the stars, he crept on until, between midnight and day, he came in sight of a campfire and heard the barking of a dog.

A number of Indians rose up from around the fire and he crept softly away from the light. He lay down and remained quiet for some time. When all was still again, he resumed his slow and painful journey. He crawled onto a small branch, and kept on it for some distance upon the rocks, that he might leave no trace behind him. At daylight, he ascended an eminence of considerable height to ascertain, if possible, where he was and how to shape his future course; but all around was wilderness.

He was aiming to reach Bullitt's Lick, now about eight miles distant and his progress was not half a mile an hour. He toiled on all day until night came on, the second night of his painful journey. Since leaving the small branch the night before, he had found no water since the day before the battle and he had not tasted food. Worn down with hunger, want of sleep, acute pain, and raging thirst, he laid himself down to die. But his sufferings were not to end here— guided again by the stars, he struggled on.

Every rag that he could interpose between the rugged stones and his bleeding hands and knee, for he could now use but one, was worn away. The morning came, the morning of the third day, and it brought him but little hope. The indomitable spirit within him disdained to yield and during the day he made what progress he could. As the evening drew on, he became aware that he was in the vicinity of Bullitt's Lick, but he could go no further as nature had made her last effort and he laid himself down and prayed that death would speedily end his sufferings.

When darkness came on, from where he lay, he could see the hundred fires of the furnaces at the licks all glowing and he even fancied he could see the dusky forms of the firemen as they passed to and fro around the pits, but they were more than half a mile off and how was he to reach them? He had not eaten a morsel in four days, he had been drained of almost his last drop of blood, the wounded leg had become so stiff and swollen that for the last two days and nights he had dragged it after him, the flesh was worn from his knee and from the palms of his hands.

Relief was in his sight, but to reach it was impossible. Suddenly, he heard the tramp of a horse's feet approaching him and hope sprang up once more in his breast. The sound came nearer and still more near. A path ran near the place where he lay and a man on horseback approached within a few rods of him. He mustered his remaining strength and hailed the man, but to his utter surprise and dismay, the horseman turned suddenly and galloped off toward the licks. Despair now seized him.

To die alone of hunger and thirst in sight of hundreds and of plenty, seemed to him the last dregs of the bitterest cup that fate could offer to mortal lips. Oh, that he could have fallen by the side of his friend in the proud battle! That he could have met the Indian tomahawk and died in the strength of his manhood and not have been doomed to linger out his life in days and nights of pain and agony and to die by piecemeal in childish despair.

While these thoughts were passing in his mind, the horseman (a Negro) regained the licks and alarmed the people there with the intelligence that the Indians were approaching. On being interrogated, the only account he could give was that some person had called to him in the woods a half-mile off and called him by the wrong name.

It was manifest it was not Indians and forthwith a number of men set out, guided by the Negro, to the place. Crist's hopes again revived when he heard voices and saw lights approaching. They came near and hailed. Crist knew the voice and called to the man by name. This removed all doubt and they approached the spot where he lay.

A sad and mournful sight was before them. A man that had left them but a few days before, in the bloom of youth, health and buoyant spirits, now lay stretched upon the earth, a worn and mangled skeleton, unable to lift a hand to bid them welcome. They bore him home where the ball was extracted; but his recovery was slow and doubtful. It was a year before he was a man again.

The woman in the boat was carried a prisoner to Canada. Ten years afterward, Crist met her again in Kentucky. She had been redeemed by an Indian trader and brought into Wayne's camp on the Maumee and restored to her friends. She informed Crist that the body of Indians which made the attack on the boat numbered over one hundred and twenty, of whom, about thirty were killed in the engagement. Indians, whom Crist met with afterward, and who had been in the battle, confirmed her account. They told Crist that the boat's crew fought more like devils than men and if they had taken one of them prisoner, they would have roasted him alive.

Crist was afterward a member of the Kentucky Legislature and in 1808 was a member of Congress. He died at his residence in Bullitt County in August 1844, aged eighty years.

EXPLORING LANDS OF THE LOUISIANA PURCHASE

Lewis and Clark Expeditions

Just before the transfer of Louisiana to the United States in 1803, President Thomas Jefferson was preparing to have explored what now comprises the northwestern part of our country, of which but little was known. In January 1803, Congress approved of his suggestions and he commissioned Messieurs Merewether Lewis and William Clark to explore the Missouri River and its principal branches to their sources, and then to seek and trace to its termination in the Pacific some stream which might give the most direct and practicable water communication across the continent, for the purposes of commerce.

Other persons were at the same time appointed to examine the Upper Mississippi River and its principal western tributaries below the Missouri River. The exact information about this vast land, to be discovered by these appointed men, was desired as soon as possible. These newly acquired territories from France (that power having previously possessed the country west of the Mississippi) were known under the general name of Louisiana.

Shortly after Lewis had received his instructions, the news of the conclusion of the treaty for the cession of Louisiana reached the United States. In May 1804, the party of Lewis and Clark began the ascent of the Missouri River in boats. Their progress being slow, they did not arrive at the country of the Mandan Indians, sixteen hundred miles from the Mississippi River, near latitude 48 degrees, until the latter part of October.

Remaining in their encampment in the Mandan country until the 7th of April following, Lewis and Clark, with thirty men, commenced their voyage westward up the Missouri River and on about the 1st of May reached the mouth of the principal branch, called by the French traders, the *Roche Jeune*, or Yellow Stone River. They then continued westward on the main stream until on the 13th of June, their navigation being arrested by the Great Falls of the Missouri River.

These falls presented a series of cataracts extending about ten miles in length. At the largest of these cataracts, the whole river rushes over a precipice of rock approximately eighty-seven feet high. Again embarking in canoes on the 19th of July, they passed through the Gates of the Rocky Mountains where the Missouri River, emerging from that chain, runs for six miles in a narrow channel between perpendicular black rocky walls, twelve hundred feet in height. Beyond this, they ascended its largest source, named by Lewis the Jefferson River, near latitude 44 degrees, where the navigation of the Missouri River ends nearly three-thousand miles from its entrance into the Mississippi River.

While the canoes were ascending the Jefferson River, Lewis and Clark, with some of their men, proceeded through the mountains and soon found streams flowing to the west and meeting several parties of Indians belonging to a nation called Shoshone. They were satisfied from the Indian accounts that those streams were the headwaters of the Columbia River.

They then rejoined their men at the head of the Jefferson River, and having cached (concealed in pits) their canoes and goods, procured some Shoshone braves for guides and some horses, the whole party pursued their journey overland. On the 30th of August, the party entered the Rocky Mountains.

Up to this time, their difficulties and privations were comparatively small; but during the three weeks they were passing through the mountains, they underwent every suffering which hunger, cold and fatigue could impose. The mountains were high, the passes through them rugged and in many places covered with snow, and their food consisted of berries, dried fish, and the meat of dogs or horses, all of which the supplies were scanty and precarious.

About four hundred miles by their route from Jefferson River, they reached the Kooskooske River, and on the 7th of October began its descent in canoes that they constructed. In three days, they entered the principal southern branch of the Columbia River, which they named the Lewis River. In seven more days, they reached its junction with its larger northern branch, which was called by them the Clark River.

They were then fairly launched on the Great River of the West, and passing down it through many dangerous rapids, they arrived at the Falls of the

Columbia River on October 31st where it rushes through the lofty chain of mountains nearest the Pacific Ocean. On the 15th of November, they landed on Cape Disappointment, at the mouth of the Columbia, after having passed over about six hundred miles on its waters and reaching a point of more than four thousand miles from the mouth of the Missouri River.

The winter, or rather rainy season, was soon setting in so they built a dwelling in that vicinity which they named Fort Clatsop. Here they remained until March 23rd, 1806. Then they began their return by ascending the Columbia River in their canoes.

Proceeding carefully up the stream, they discovered the Cowelitz River and the Willamette River, the latter now noted for having on its banks the most flourishing settlements in Oregon. At the Columbia Falls, they abandoned their canoes and proceeded on horses to their point of embarkation on the Kooskooske River in the preceding year. From there, they went due eastward, through the Rocky Mountains to the Clark River, which flows for some distance in a northerly direction from its sources before turning southward to join the other branches of the Columbia.

There, on the 3rd of July, in latitude 47 degrees, Lewis and Clark separated to meet again at the mouth of Yellow Stone River. Lewis, with his party, traveled northward some distance down the Clark River and then quitting it, crossed the Rocky Mountains to the headwaters of the Maria River, which empties into the Missouri River just below the Great Falls. Here he met a band of Indians belonging to the numerous and daring race, called the Blackfoot, who inhabit the plains at the base of the mountains and are ever at war with all other tribes. These Indians attempted to seize the rifles of the Americans and Lewis was obliged to kill one of them before they stopped.

The party then hastened to the Falls of the Missouri River and from there floated down to the mouth of the Yellow Stone River, which is scarcely inferior in length, to the main branch of the Missouri River. Meanwhile, the party under Captain Clark rode southward up the Clark River to its sources and after exploring several passes in the mountains, between that and the headwaters of the Yellow Stone River, they embarked on the Yellow Stone River in canoes and descending, joined Lewis and his men at its mouth on the 12th of August. From there, the whole body floated down the Missouri and on the 23rd of September, 1806, arrived in safety at St. Louis after an absence of more than two years, during which they had traveled over nine thousand miles.

The French and Spanish Indian traders, long before this expedition, had explored the Missouri River to the mouth of the Yellow Stone River; but no correct information had been obtained of the river and country. With regard to the country between the Great Falls of the Missouri and those of the Columbia, we have no accounts earlier than those furnished by this exploring expedition. Their journal is still the principal source of information, respecting the geography, natural history, and the original inhabitants of that region.

Politically, the expedition was an announcement to the world of the intentions of the American government to occupy and settle the countries explored, and they thus virtually incurred the obligation to prosecute and fulfill the great ends for which the labors of Lewis and Clark were preparatory.

The Pike Expedition

During the absence of Lewis and Clark, the United States sponsored other explorations in different parts of Louisiana. Lieutenant Z. M. Pike, who was afterward promoted to the rank of General and who fell at York, Upper Canada, in 1813, was sent in 1805 to explore the sources of the Mississippi River. Having set out late in the season, he proceeded to the mouth of the Crow Wing River, where winter having overtaken him, he erected a block-house for the protection of his men and stores, and proceeded in snow-shoes, with a small party, to Leech Lake and other places in that vicinity.

He returned on the opening of navigation in the spring without having fully accomplished the objects of his journey. During his absence, he purchased from the Indians the site where Fort Snelling, the first American establishment in Minnesota, was founded in 1819.

In the year 1806, the United States Government sent him with a party of men on another exploring expedition. In the course of this expedition, he traveled southwestward from the mouth of the Missouri River up the Arkansas River with directions to pass to the sources of that stream, for which those of the Canadian River were then mistaken. However, he passed around the head of the Canadian River and crossed the mountain with an almost incredible degree of peril and suffering. The party then descended upon the Rio del Norte River. Pike's party at that time numbered fifteen.

Believing himself now upon Red River, within the then assumed bounds of the United States, he erected a small fort for his company until the opening of the spring of 1807. This small fort would enable him to continue his descent to Natchitoches. However, he was within the Mexican territory about seventy miles from the northern settlements. His position was soon discovered and a force sent out to take him into Santa Fe, which by a treacherous maneuver was accomplished without opposition.

The Spanish officer assured him that the governor, learning that he had missed his way, had sent animals and an escort to convey his men and baggage to a navigable point on Red River (Rio Colorado), and that his excellency desired very much to see him at Santa Fe, which might be taken on their way. However, as soon as the governor had him in his power, he sent him with his men to the Commandant-General at Chihuahua, where most of the expedition's papers were seized. Pike and his party were then sent under an escort, via San Antonio de Bexar, back to the United States.

The Red and Washita Rivers were at the same time being explored to a considerable distance from the Mississippi, by Messieurs Dunbar, Hunter, and Sibley, whose journals, as well as those of Pike, Lewis, and Clark, were subsequently published and contain many interesting descriptions of those parts of America.

Thus, within three or four years after Louisiana came into the possession of the United States, it ceased to be an unknown region and the principal features of the country drained by the Columbia were discovered and recorded.

Adventures of Colter and Potts

On the arrival of the exploratory party of Lewis and Clark at the headwaters of the Missouri River, Mr. Colter, one of the guides, obtained permission for himself and another hunter by the name of Potts, to remain awhile and hunt for beaver. Aware of the hostility of the Blackfoot Indians, one of whom had been killed by Lewis, they set their traps at night and took them up early in the morning, remaining concealed during the day.

They were examining their traps early one morning in a creek, which they were ascending in a canoe, when they suddenly heard a great noise resembling the trampling of animals. They could not see the source of the noise as the high perpendicular banks on each side of the river impeded their view.

Colter immediately pronounced it to be Indians and advised an instant retreat, but was accused of cowardice by Potts, who insisted the noise was caused by stampeding buffaloes. Colter bowed to Potts' wishes and they proceeded on. In a few minutes afterward, their doubts were removed by the appearance of about five or six hundred Indians on both sides of the creek, who beckoned them to come ashore. As retreat was now impossible, Colter turned the head of the canoe to the shore and at the moment it touched, an Indian seized the rifle belonging to Potts. Colter, who was a remarkably strong man, immediately retook it.

Colter handed the rifle to Potts, who remained in the canoe, and on receiving the rifle Potts pushed the canoe off into the river. He had scarcely quitted the shore when an arrow was shot at him and he cried out, "Colter, I am wounded." Colter chastised him on the folly of attempting to escape and urged him to come ashore. Instead of complying, Potts instantly leveled his rifle at an Indian and shot him dead on the spot.

This conduct, situated as he was, may appear to have been an act of madness, but it was doubtless the effect of sudden, but sound enough reasoning, for if taken alive, he must have expected to have been tortured to death, according to the Indian custom. In this respect, the Indians in this region excelled all others in the ingenuity they displayed in torturing their prisoners. Potts was instantly pierced with arrows so numerous, that to use the language of Colter, "he was made a riddle of."

They now seized Colter, stripped him entirely naked, and began to consult with each other on the manner in which he should be put to death. They were first inclined to set him up as a mark to shoot at, but the Chief interfered and seizing him by the shoulder, asked him if he could run fast. Colter, who had spent some time living with the KeeKatsa, or Grow Indians, had acquired the Blackfoot language and was also well acquainted with Indian customs. He knew that he had now to run for his life with the dreadful odds of five or six hundred Indians against him, and these being armed. He therefore cunningly replied that he was a very bad runner, although in truth he was, considered by the hunters, remarkably swift.

The Chief now commanded the party to remain stationary and led Colter out on the prairie three or four hundred yards and released him, bidding him to save himself if he could. At that instant the war-whoop sounded in the ears of poor Colter, who urged with the hope of preserving life, ran with a speed at which even he was surprised. He proceeded toward Jefferson's Fork, having to traverse a plain six miles in breadth, abounding with the prickly pear, on which he every instant was treading with his naked feet.

He ran nearly halfway across the plain before he ventured to look over his shoulder. He realized that the Indians were very much scattered and that he had gained ground to a considerable distance from the main body; but one Indian, who carried a spear, was much before all the rest and not more than a hundred yards from him.

A faint gleam of hope now cheered the heart of Colter. He derived confidence from the belief that escape was within the bounds of possibility, but that confidence was nearly fatal to him, for he exerted himself to such a degree that the blood gushed from his nostrils and soon almost covered the forepart of his body.

He arrived within a mile of the river when he distinctly heard the appalling sounds of footsteps behind him and every instant expected to feel the spear of his pursuer. Again he turned his head and saw the Indian not twenty yards from him. Determined, if possible, to avoid the expected blow, he suddenly stopped, turned around and spread out his arms.

The Indian, surprised at the suddenness of the action and perhaps at the bloody appearance of Colter also attempted to stop; but exhausted with running, he fell while attempting to throw his spear, which stuck in the ground and broke in his hand. Colter instantly snatched up the pointed part, with which he pinned the Indian to the earth and then continued his flight.

The foremost of the other Indians, on arriving at the place, stopped until others came up to join them and then gave a hideous yell. Every moment of this stop was utilized by Colter, who although fainting and exhausted, succeeded in gaining the skirting of the cottonwood trees on the borders of the Fork River, to which he ran and plunged into the water.

Fortunately for him, a little below this place was an island, against the upper point of which a raft of drift timber had lodged. He dove under the raft and after several efforts, got his head above water among the trunks of trees covered over with smaller wood to the depth of several feet. Scarcely had he secured himself when the Indians arrived on the river, screeching and yelling—as Colter expressed it, "like so many devils."

They were frequently on the raft during the day and were seen through the chinks by Colter, who was congratulating himself on his escape until the idea arose that they might set the raft on fire. In horrible suspense he remained until night, when hearing no more from the Indians, he dived from under the raft and swam instantly down the river to a considerable distance, where he landed and traveled all night. Although happy in having escaped from the Indians, his situation was still dreadful. He was completely naked under a burning sun, the soles of his feet were filled with the thorns of the prickly pear, he was hungry and he had no means of killing game although he saw abundance around him and was at a great distance from the nearest settlement.

Almost any man but an American hunter would have despaired under such circumstances. The fortitude of Colter remained unshaken. After seven days of sore travel, during which he had no other sustenance than the root known by naturalists under the name of psoralea esculenta, he at length arrived in safety at Lisa's Fort on the Big Horn branch of the Roche Jaune, or Yellow Stone River.

A Shoshone Brave's Account of Lewis and Clark

A few years after the expedition by Lewis and Clark, there was residing at Brown's Hole in Oregon, an old Shoshone Indian who was the first of his tribe who saw the cavalcade of Messrs. Lewis and Clark on the head waters of the Missouri River in 1805. He appears to have been galloping from place to place in the office of Sentinel to the Shoshone camp, when he suddenly found himself in the presence of the whites.

Astonishment fixed him to the spot. He had never seen men with faces as pale as ashes, nor had any member of his Indian nation. "The head rose high and round, the top flat—it jutted over the eyes in a thin rim. Their skin was loose and flowing and of many colors." His fears at length overcoming his curiosity, he fled in the direction of the Indian encampment. But being seen by the whites, they pursued and brought him to their camp, exhibited to him the effect of their firearms, loaded him with presents, and let him go.

Having arrived among his own people, he told them he had seen men with faces pale as ashes, who were makers of thunder and lightning, etc. This information astounded the whole tribe. They had lived many years; their ancestors had lived many more and there were many legends that spoke of many wonderful things, but a tale like this they had never before heard. A council was therefore held to consider the matter. The man of strange words was summoned before it and he rehearsed in substance what he had before told to others, but was not believed.

All men were red and therefore he could not have seen men as pale as ashes. The Great Spirit made the thunder and lightning; he therefore, could not have seen any men of any color that could produce it. He had seen nothing, had lied to his Chief and should die.

Upon this, the Indian brave produced some presents, which he had received from the pale men. These being quite as new to them as pale faces were, it was determined that he should have the privilege of leading his judges to the place where he had declared he had seen these strange people. If such people were indeed found there, he should be exculpated; if not, these presents were to be considered as conclusive evidence that he dealt with evil spirits and that he was worthy of death by the arrows of his kinfolks.

The pale men, the "thunder-makers," were found and were witnesses of the poor fellow's story. He was released and has ever since been much honored and loved by his tribe and every white man in the mountains. He is now about eighty years old and poor. But as he resides about Fort David Crockett, he is never permitted to want.

THE GREAT PRAIRIE WILDERNESS

The Great Prairie Wilderness is the vast territory that lies between the States of Louisiana, Arkansas, Missouri, Iowa, and the Upper Mississippi on the east, and the Black Hills and the eastern range of the Rocky and the Cordillera mountains on the west. About a thousand miles of longitude and nearly two thousand miles of latitude make up its region, which equals the combined area of several of the powerful Empires of Europe and that too, of an almost continuous plain. The sublime Prairie Wilderness!

The portion of this vast region, two hundred miles in width, which lies along the coast of Texas and the frontier of Louisiana, Arkansas, Missouri, and that lying within the same distance of the Upper Mississippi in Iowa, possesses a rich, deep alluvial soil, capable of producing the most abundant crops of the grains, vegetables, etc. that grow in such latitudes.

Another portion, lying west of the irregular western line of that just described, five hundred miles in width, extends from the mouth of St. Peters or Minnesota River to the Rio del Norte, and is an almost unbroken plain destitute of trees, save here and there one is scattered at intervals along the banks of the streams. The soil, except the intervals of some of the rivers, is composed of coarse sand and clay, so thin and hard that it is difficult for travelers to penetrate it with the stakes they carry with them to fasten their animals, or spread their tents. Nevertheless, it is covered thickly with an extremely nutritious grass peculiar to this region of country, the blades of which are wiry and about two inches in height.

The remainder of the Great Wilderness, lying three hundred miles in width along the eastern base of the Black Hills and that part of the Rocky Mountains between the Platte and Arkansas Rivers and the Cordilleras Mountains east of the Rio del Norte River, is the arid wasteland usually called the Great

American Desert. Its soil is composed of dark gravel mixed with sand. A small portion of it on the banks of streams is covered with tall prairie and bunch grass; others, with wild wormwood, but even these kinds of vegetation decrease and finally disappear as one approaches the mountains. This scene of desolation is scarcely equaled on the continent when viewed in the dearth of midsummer from the bases of the hills.

Above the prairie, rising in sublime confusion, is mass upon mass of shattered cliffs, through which struggle the dark foliage of stinted shrub cedars, while below the burnt and arid desert spreads far and wide. The solemn silence here is seldom broken by the tread of any other animal than the wolf, or the starved and thirsty horse that bears the traveler across its wastes.

The principal streams that intersect the Great Prairie Wilderness are the Colorado, Brasos, Trinity, Red, Arkansas, Great Platte, and the Missouri. The latter is in many respects a noble stream. In the months of April, May, and June, it is navigable for steamboats to the Great Falls; but the scarcity of water during the remainder of the year, the scarcity of wood and coal along its banks, its rapid current, its winding course, its falling banks, the timber imbedded in its channel, and its constantly shifting sandbars, will ever prevent its being extensively navigated.

Above the mouth of the Little Missouri, and in the tributaries there flowing into it, are said to be many charming and productive valleys separated from each other by secondary rocky ridges sparsely covered with evergreens. High over all, far in the southwest, west, and northwest, tower the Rocky Mountains, where inexhaustible magazines of snow and ice have for ages supplied these valleys with refreshing springs and vast rivers with their tributaries to the seas.

Lewis and Clark on their way to Oregon in 1805 made the passage at the Great Falls of the Missouri, thirteen miles in which the water descended three hundred and fifty-two feet, the greatest pitch being ninety-eight feet. They traveled to the extreme head of its navigation, making the mouth of the Missouri from where they started, a distance of 3,096 miles (four hundred and twenty-nine of which lay among the sublime crags and cliffs of the Rocky Mountains).

The Great Platte, or Nebraska, River has a course by its northern fork of about 1,500 miles and by its southern, somewhat more. During the summer and autumn, it is too shallow to float even a canoe and in winter is bound with ice. But it is of great value as the route of overland emigration to California and Oregon. Loaded wagons pass without serious interruption from the mouth of the Platte River to navigable water on the Columbia River in Oregon and the Bay of San Francisco in California.

The Platte River, therefore, when considered in relation to our trade with the habitable countries in the Western Ocean, assumes an unequaled importance among the streams of the Great Western Wilderness! But for it, it would be impossible for man or beast to travel those arid plains destitute alike of wood, water, and grass, save what of each is found along its course.

The headwaters of the north fork of the river are the only way or opening in the Rocky Mountains at all practicable for a carriage road through them. That route, traversed by Lewis and Clark, is covered with perpetual snow. Near the passage of the south fork of the river is over-high and nearly impassable precipices, and farther south it is, and ever will be, impassable for wheel carriages. But the Great Gap or "the South Pass," nearly in a right line between the mouth of Missouri River and Fort Hall on Clark's River, the point near where the trails to California and Oregon diverge, seems designed by nature as the great gateway between the nations on the Atlantic and Pacific seas.

The Red River has a course of about 1500 miles and derives its name from the color of its waters, which is produced by a rich, "red earth" or marl in its banks, far up in the Prairie Wilderness. So abundant is this marl in the waters that during the spring freshets it leaves a deposit on the overflowed lands of half an inch in thickness.

Three hundred miles from its mouth commences what is called "the Raft," a covering formed by driftwood that conceals the whole river for forty miles and is so thickly covered with the sediment of the stream that vegetation, even trees of a considerable size, are growing upon it. For seven hundred miles above the raft, the river is one series of sandbars, and in summer, the water stands in ponds. As one approaches the mountains, the river becomes contracted within narrow limits over a gravelly bottom and is a swift, clear and abundant stream.

The Trinity, the Brasos, and the Rio Colorado Rivers each have a course of about 1,200 miles, rising in the plains and mountains on the north and northwest of Texas and running south and southeast into the Gulf of Mexico. The Rio Bravo del Norte bounds the Great Prairie Wilderness on the south and southwest. It is nearly 2000 miles long, but it is shallow and for most of its course, it is scarcely navigable at times even for the canoe of the Indian.

The Arkansas River, after the Missouri River, is the most considerable river of the Great Prairie Wilderness. It takes its rise among the mountains, in places passing through charming valleys and again through awful chasms. Its total length is 2,173 miles. In freshets, large and heavy boats can pass from its mouth to where the river escapes from the mountains. In the dry season, its waters are strongly impregnated with salt and sediment.

The trials of a journey across the Great Prairie Wilderness, and from there over the mountains through the western wilderness beyond, can never be detailed in words; to be understood, the hardships must be endured. The desolation of one kind and another which meets the eye everywhere, the sense of vastness associated with dearth and barrenness, one half the time on foot treading on the flinty gravel and the thorns of the prickly pear along the unbroken way, starving and thirsting until the muscles wilt and send preternatural activity into the nervous system, and through the whole animal and mental economy there is a feebleness and irritability altogether indescribable.

THE GREAT EARTHQUAKE OF 1811

This memorable earthquake, after shaking the Mississippi valley to its center, vibrated along the courses of the rivers and villages and passing the Allegheny Mountains, died away along the shores of the Atlantic Ocean. The town of New Madrid in the southern part of Missouri on the west bank of the Mississippi, and the settlement of New Prairie some thirty miles below it, appeared to be near the center of the most violent shocks. The first shocks occurred on the night of the 15th of December and were repeated at intervals for two or three months. A gentleman who resided at New Madrid a few years later, derived from eyewitnesses a full account of these disturbances, which he recorded.

"From the accounts, I infer that the shock of these earthquakes must have equaled in their terrible heaving of the earth anything of the kind that has been recorded. I do not believe that the public has ever yet had any idea of the violence of the concussions. We are accustomed to measure this by the buildings overturned and the mortality that results. Here, the country was thinly settled. The houses, fortunately, were frail and of logs, the most difficult to overturn that could be constructed. Yet, as it was, whole tracks were plunged into the beds of the Mississippi River.

The graveyard at New Madrid with all its sleeping tenants was precipitated into the bed of the stream. Most of the houses were thrown down. Large lakes of many miles in extent were made in an hour. Other lakes were drained. The whole country from the mouth of the Ohio River in one direction and to the St. Francis River in another, including a front of three hundred miles, was convulsed to such a degree as to create lakes and islands, the number of which is not known.

The trees split in the middle, lashed one with another, are still visible over great tracts of country, inclining in every direction and at every angle to the earth and the horizon. The people described the undulations of the earth as resembling waves, increasing in elevation as they advanced and when they had attained a certain fearful height, the earth would burst and vast volumes of water and sand and pit coal would discharge as high as the tops of the trees. I have seen a hundred of these chasms that remained fearfully deep, even in a very tender alluvial soil, after a lapse of seven years.

Whole districts were covered with white sand, so as to become uninhabitable. The water at first covered the whole country, particularly at the Little Prairie River and indeed, it must have been a scene of horror in these deep forests and in the gloom of the darkest night, to wade in the water and fly from these concussions, which were occurring every few hours with a noise equally terrible to beasts and birds as to men.

The birds themselves lost all power and disposition to fly and retreated to the bosoms of men, their fellow sufferers in this general convulsion. A few persons sunk in these chasms and were providentially extricated. A number of people perished, sunk with their boats in the Mississippi River. A bursting of the earth just below the village of New Madrid arrested the mighty Mississippi River in its course and caused a reflux of its waves, by which in a little time, a great number of boats were swept by the ascending current into the mouth of the Bayou, carried out and left upon the dry earth, when the accumulating waters of the river had again cleared their current.

There were a number of severe shocks, but two series of concussions were particularly terrible, far more so than the rest. The shocks were clearly distinguishable into two classes: those in which the motion was horizontal and those in which it was perpendicular. The latter were attended with the explosions, and the terrible mixture of noises that preceded and accompanied the earthquakes in a louder degree, but were by no means so desolating and destructive as the other. Then the houses crumbled, the trees waved together, the ground sunk, while ever vivid flashes of lightning gleaming through the troubled clouds of night, rendered the darkness doubly horrible.

After the severest shocks, a dense black cloud of vapor overshadowed the land, through which no struggling sunbeam found its way to cheer the heart of man. The sulfurous gases that were discharged during the shocks tainted the air with their noxious effluvia, and so impregnated the water of the river for one hundred and fifty miles, as to render it unfit for use.

In the interval of the earthquakes, there was one evening, and that a brilliant and cloudless one, in which the western sky was a continued glare of repeated peals of subterranean thunder, seeming to proceed as the flashes did, from below the horizon. They remark that the night so conspicuous for subterranean thunder was the same period in which the fatal earthquakes at Caracas in South America occurred and they seem to suppose these flashes and that event part of the same scene.

One result from these terrific phenomena was very obvious. The people of this village had been noted for their profligacy and impiety. In the midst of those scenes of terror, all Catholics and Protestants, praying and profane, became of one religion and partook of one feeling. Two hundred people speaking English, French, and Spanish crowded together, their visages pale, the mothers embracing their children as soon as the omen that preceded the earthquakes became visible, as soon as the air became a little obscured, as though a sudden mist arose from the east, all in their different languages and forms; but all deeply in earnest, betook themselves to the voice of prayer. The cattle, much terrified, crowded about the people seeking to demand protection or community of danger.

The general impulse when the shocks began was to run and yet when they were at their severest point of their motion, the people were thrown on the ground at almost every step. A French gentleman told me that in escaping from his house, the largest in the village, he found he had left an infant behind and he attempted to mount up the raised piazza to recover the child and was thrown down a dozen times in succession.

The venerable woman, in whose dwelling we lodged, was extricated from the ruins of her house, having lost everything that appertained to her establishment that could be broken or destroyed. The people at the Little Prairie, who suffered most, had their settlement, which consisted of a hundred families and which was located in a rich and very deep fertile bottom, broken up.

When I passed it and stopped to contemplate the traces of the catastrophe which remained after several years, the crevices where the earth had burst were sufficiently manifest and the whole region was covered with sand to the depth of two or three feet. The surface was red with oxidized pyrites of iron and the sand-blows, as they were called, were abundantly mixed with this kind of earth and with pieces of pit-coal. Only two families remained of the whole settlement. The object seems to have been, in the first paroxysms of alarm, to escape to the hills. The depth of water that soon covered the surface, however, precluded escape so other avenues had to be found.

The people, without exception, were unlettered backwoodsmen, of the class least addicted to reasoning. And yet, it is remarkable how ingeniously and conclusively they reasoned from apprehension sharpened by fear. They observed that the chasms in the earth were in the direction from southwest to northeast and they were of an extent to swallow up men and houses "down deep into the pit." These chasms occurred frequently within intervals of half a mile. Therefore, they felled the tallest trees at right angles to the chasms and stationed themselves upon the felled trees. Meantime, their cattle and their harvests, both there and at New Madrid, principally perished.

The people no longer dared to dwell in houses. They passed that winter and the succeeding one in bark booths and camps, like those of the Indians, of so light a texture as not to expose the inhabitants to danger in case of their being thrown down. Such numbers of laden boats were wrecked above on the Mississippi and the lading driven into the eddy at the mouth of the bayou at the village, which makes the harbor, that the people were amply supplied with provision of every kind. Flour, beef, pork, bacon, butter, cheese, apples, in short, everything that is carried down the river was in such abundance as scarcely to be matters of sale.

Many boats that came safely into the bayou were disposed of by the affrighted owners for a trifle, for the shocks continued daily and the owners deeming the whole country below to be sunk were glad to return to the upper country as fast as possible. In effect, a great many islands were sunk, new ones raised and the bed of the river very much changed in every respect.

After the earthquake had moderated in violence, the country exhibited a melancholy aspect of chasms, of sand covering the earth, of trees thrown down or lying at an angle of forty-five degrees, or split in the middle. The Little Prairie settlement was broken up. The Great Prairie settlement, one of the most flourishing before on the west bank of the Mississippi River, was much diminished. New Madrid dwindled to insignificance and decay; the people trembling in their miserable hovels at the distant and melancholy rumbling of the approaching shocks.

The general government passed an act allowing the inhabitants of the country to locate the same quantity of lands that they possessed here in any part of the territory, where the lands were not yet covered by any claim. These claims passed into the hands of speculators and were never of any substantial benefit to the possessors. When I resided there, this district, formerly so level, rich and beautiful had the most melancholy of all aspects of decay, the tokens of former cultivation and civilization, which were now mementos of desolation and desertion. Large and beautiful orchards left unenclosed, houses deserted, deep chasms in the earth, obvious at frequent intervals. Such was the face of the country, although the people had for years become so accustomed to frequent and small shocks that did no essential injury, that the lands were gradually rising again in value and New Madrid was slowly rebuilding with frail buildings adapted to the apprehensions of the people.

VOYAGE OF THE FIRST STEAMBOAT

The first western steamboat was the New Orleans, a craft of four hundred tons burden, which was built at Pittsburgh in 1811. The origin of this boat and the history of her first voyage is thus given by Latrobe, from which it will be seen that she narrowly escaped being overwhelmed in the great earthquakes that signalized the latter part of that year in the annals of the west.

The complete success attending the experiments in steam navigation made on the Hudson, and the adjoining waters previous to the year 1809, turned the attention of the principal projectors to the idea of its application on the western waters. In the month of April of that year, Mr. Roosevelt of New York, pursuant to an agreement with Chancellor Livingston and Mr. Fulton, visited those rivers with the purpose of forming an opinion whether they would allow steam navigation or not. At this time two boats, the *North River* and the *Clermont* were running on the Hudson River.

Mr. Roosevelt surveyed the rivers from Pittsburgh to New Orleans, and as his report was favorable, it was decided to build a boat at the former town. This was done under his direction and in the course of 1811 the first boat was launched upon the waters of the Ohio River. It was called the *New Orleans*, and was intended to ply between Natchez and New Orleans.

In October, it left Pittsburgh on its experimental voyage. On this occasion, no freight or passengers were taken, the object being merely to bring the boat to her station. Mr. Roosevelt, his young wife and family, Mr. Baker, the engineer, Andrew Jack, the pilot, and six hands with a few domestics, formed her whole burden. There were no wood-yards at that time and constant delays were unavoidable.

When, as related, Mr. Roosevelt had gone down the river to scout it, he had discovered two beds of coal, about one hundred and twenty miles below the

229

rapids of Louisville and now took tools to work them, intending to load the vessel with coal and to employ it as fuel, instead of constantly detaining the boat while wood was procured from the banks.

Late at night, on the fourth day after quitting Pittsburgh, they arrived in safety at Louisville, having been but seventy hours descending upward of seven hundred miles. The novel appearance of the vessel, and the fearful rapidity with which it made its passage over the broad reaches of the river, excited a mixture of terror and surprise among many of the settlers on the banks, whom the rumor of such an invention had never reached. It is said that on the unexpected arrival of the vessel before Louisville, in the course of a fine, still moonlit night, the extraordinary sound, which filled the air of pent-up steam escaping from the valves, produced a general alarm and multitudes in the town rose from their beds to ascertain the cause.

I have heard the general impression among the good Kentuckians was that a comet had fallen into the Ohio; but this does not rest upon the same foundation as the other facts which I lay before you and which I may at once say I had directly from the lips of the parties themselves. The small depth of water in the rapids prevented the boat from pursuing her voyage immediately and during the consequent detention of three weeks in the upper part of the Ohio several trips were successfully made between Louisville and Cincinnati. In time, the waters rose and in the course of the last week in November the voyage was resumed, the depth of the water barely admitting their passage.

When they arrived about five miles above the Yellow Banks, they moved the boat opposite the first vein of coal, which was on the Indiana side and had been purchased in the interim of the State government. They found a large quantity already quarried to their hand and conveyed to the shore by looters who had not found the means to carry it off, and with this they commenced loading the boat. While thus employed, our voyagers were alarmed by the squatters in the neighborhood who inquired if they had not heard strange noises on the river and in the woods in the course of the preceding day and stated that the shores shook, insisting that they had repeatedly felt the earth tremble.

Hitherto, nothing extraordinary had been experienced. The following day, they pursued their monotonous voyage in those vast solitudes. The weather was observed to be oppressively hot, the air misty, still and dull and although the sun was visible like a glowing ball of copper, its rays hardly shed more than a mournful twilight on the surface of the water. Evening drew near and with it some indications of what was passing around them became evident.

As they sat on deck, they heard a rushing sound and a violent splash and saw large portions of the shore tearing away from the land falling into the river. It was, as my informant said, an awful day—so still that you could have hard a pin drop on the deck! They spoke little, for everyone on board was thunderstruck. The comet had disappeared about this time, which circumstance was noticed with awe by the crew.

The second day after leaving the Yellow Banks, the sun was over the forests, the same dim ball of fire and the air was thick, dull and oppressive as before. The portentous signs of this terrible natural convulsion continued and increased. The pilot, alarmed and confused, affirmed that he was lost as he found the channel everywhere altered and where he had hitherto known deep water, there lay numberless trees with their roots upward. The trees were seen waving and nodding to the bank without a wind, but the adventurers had no choice but to continue their route. Toward evening, they found themselves at a loss for a place of shelter. They had usually brought to under the shore, but everywhere they saw the high banks disappearing, overwhelming many a flatboat and raft from which the owners had landed and escaped.

A large island in mid-channel, selected by the pilot as the better alternative, was sought for in vain, having disappeared entirely. Thus, in doubt and terror, they proceeded hour after hour until dark, when they found a small island and moored themselves at its foot. Here they lay, keeping watch on deck during the long winter's night, listening to the sound of the waters which roared and gurgled horribly around them and hearing, from time to time the rushing earth slide from the shore and the commotion as the falling mass of earth and trees was swallowed up by the river.

The lady of the party, a delicate female, who had been confined on board as they lay off Louisville, was frequently awakened from her restless slumber by the jar given to the furniture and loose articles in the cabin, as several times in the course of the night, the shock of the passing earth was communicated from the island to the bow of the vessel.

It was a long night, but morning showed them that they were near the mouth of the Ohio. The shores and channel were now not recognizable, for everything seemed changed. About noon of that day, they reached the small town of New Madrid, on the right bank of the Mississippi River. Here, they found the inhabitants in the greatest distress and consternation, a part of the population had fled in terror to the higher grounds, while others prayed to be taken on board as the earth was opening in fissures on every side and their houses were hourly falling around them.

Proceeding from there, they found the Mississippi unusually swollen, turbid and full of trees, and after many days of great danger, although they felt and perceived no more of the earthquakes, they reached their destination at Natchez at the close of the first week in January 1812 to the astonishment of all, the escape of the boat having been considered an impossibility.

The *Orleans* continued to run between New Orleans and Natchez, making her voyages to average seventeen days, until 1813 or 1814, when she was wrecked near Baton Rouge by striking on a snag. In the course of the few years succeeding the construction of the *Orleans*, several other boats were built and launched upon the western rivers. However, such was their want of success that the public had no faith that steamboat navigation would succeed upon the western waters until the trip of the Washington boat in the spring of 1817, when she went from Louisville to New Orleans and returned in forty-five days.

This boat was of four hundred tons burden and was built at Wheeling under the direction of her Captain, H.M. Shreve. "Her boilers," says Judge Hall in his notes, "were on the upper deck and she was the first boat on that plan, since so generally in use."

KENTUCKY
SHARPSHOOTERS

We have individuals in Kentucky that are considered wonderfully adept in the management of the rifle. Having resided some years in Kentucky and having more than once been a witness of rifle sport, I shall present the results of my observation, leaving the reader to judge how far rifle shooting is understood in that State.

Several individuals who conceive themselves adept in the management of the rifle are often seen to meet for the purpose of displaying their skill and betting a trifling sum, they put up a target, in the center of which, a common sized nail is hammered for about two-thirds its length. The marksman makes choice of what they consider a proper distance and which may be forty paces.

Each man cleans the interior of his tube, which is called "wiping" it, places a ball in the palm of his hand, pouring as much powder from his horn as will cover it. This quantity is supposed to be sufficient for any distance short of a hundred yards.

A shot that comes very close to the nail is considered that of an indifferent marksman; the bending of the nail is of course somewhat better; but nothing less than hitting it right on the head is satisfactory. One out of three shots generally hits the nail and should the shooters amount to half-a-dozen, two nails are frequently needed before each can have a shot.

Those who drive the nail have a further trial among themselves and the two best shots out of these generally settle the affair. All the sportsmen then adjourn to some house and spend an hour or two in friendly conversation, appointing before they part, a day for another trial. This is technically termed, "driving the nail."

"Barking of squirrels" is a delightful sport and in my opinion, requires a greater degree of accuracy than any other. I first witnessed this manner of

233

procuring squirrels while near the town of Frankfort. The performer was the celebrated Daniel Boone. We walked out together and followed the rocky margins of the Kentucky River until we reached a piece of flat land, thickly covered with black walnuts, oaks, and hickories. As the general mast was a good one that year, squirrels were seen gamboling on every tree around us.

My companion, a stout, hale, athletic man, dressed in a homespun hunting shirt, bare-legged and in moccasins, carried a long and heavy rifle which, as he was loading it, he said had proved efficient in all of his former undertakings and which he hoped would not fail on this occasion, as he felt proud to show me his skill.

The gun was wiped, the powder measured, the ball patched with six-hundred-thread linen and a charge was sent home with a hickory rod. We moved not a step from the place, for the squirrels were so thick that it was unnecessary to go after them.

Boone pointed to one of these animals, which had observed us and was crouched on a bank about fifty paces distant and bade me mark well where the ball should hit. He raised his piece gradually until the "bead" or sight of the barrel was brought to a line with the spot he intended to hit. The whip-like report resounded through the woods and along the hills in repeated echoes. Judge my surprise when I perceived that the ball had hit a piece of bark immediately underneath the squirrel and shivered it into splinters, the concussion produced by which, had killed the animal and sent it whirling through the air as if it had been blown up by the explosion of a powder magazine.

Boone kept up his firing and before many hours had elapsed, we had procured as many squirrels as we wished. Since that first interview with the veteran Boone, I have seen many other individuals perform the same feat.

The snuffing of a candle with a ball, I first had an opportunity of seeing near the banks of Green River not far from a large pigeon roost, to which I had previously made a visit. I had heard many reports of guns during the early part of a dark night and knowing them to be those of rifles, I went forward toward the spot to ascertain the cause.

On reaching the place, I was welcomed by a dozen tall, stout men, who told me they were exercising for the purpose of enabling them to shoot at night, the reflected light from the eyes of a deer or wolf by torchlight. A fire was blazing nearby, the smoke of which rose curling among the thick foliage of the trees.

At a distance, which rendered it scarcely distinguishable, stood a burning candle, but which, in reality, was only fifty yards from the spot on which we all stood. One man was within a few yards of it to watch the effect of the shots, as well as to light the candle should it chance to go out, or to replace it should the shot cut it across.

Each marksman shot in his turn. Some never hit either the snuff or the candle and were congratulated with a loud laugh; while others actually snuffed the candle without putting it out and were recompensed for their dexterity with numerous hurrahs. One of them, who was particularly expert, was very fortunate and snuffed the candle three times out of seven, while all the other shots either put out the candle or cut it immediately under the light.

Of all the feats performed by the Kentuckians with the rifle, I might say more than might be expedient on the present occasion. By way of recreation, they often cut off a piece of the bark of a tree, make a target of it, using a little powder wetted with water or saliva for the bulls-eye and shoot into the mark all the balls they have about them, picking them out of the wood again.

THE ADVENTURES OF SIMON KENTON

Simon Kenton, one of the most noted pioneers of the West, was born in Fauquier County, Virginia on April 3, 1755. His father was a native of Ireland and his mother was from Scotland.

In the spring of 1771, three years before Dunmore's war, when he was just sixteen years of age, he had a serious quarrel with a young man, a neighbor by the name of Veach. Simon became desperately enamored with a young lady, who soon after married young Veach. Stung to frenzy by this disappointment and imagining himself exquisitely injured, in the heat of passion he attended the wedding uninvited. As soon as he entered the room, he went forward and intruded between the groom and his bride. The result was that young Veach, as soon as Simon's back was turned, knocked him down, gave him a severe beating and expelled him from the house with black eyes and sore bones.

A few days after this altercation, Simon met Veach alone and anxious to repair his wounded honor had a pitched battle with him. Victory for some time hung on a doubtful balance. Simon at length threw his antagonist to the ground and as quick as thought drew Veach's queue of long hair around a small sapling, and kicked him in his breast and stomach until all resistance ceased.

Veach attempted to rise, but immediately sank back upon the ground and began to vomit blood. As Simon had not intended to kill him, he now raised him up and spoke kindly to him, but Veach made no answer and was apparently lifeless. Erroneously supposing he had murdered him, Simon was overcome with the most poignant and awful guilt and immediately fled to the woods.

Lying concealed by day and traveling by night, he passed over the Alleghenies until he arrived nearly starved at a settlement on Cheat River, where he changed his name to Simon Butler. Soon afterwards, he went to Fort Pitt where he formed a friendship with a man called Simon Girty, a desperate renegade. There Kenton spent his young adulthood with the trappers and hunters of the region.

Simon Kenton served as an active spy for Governor Dunsmore in 1774 during the time of "Dunsmore's War" and had many encounters with the Indian tribes of the region. He served for a time in the capacity of a ranger to detect the approach of the Indians. He became highly distinguished for his courage, skill and stratagem against the natives and their methods of warfare. He had then just arrived at manhood, being nineteen, and was a noble specimen of the hardy, active backwoodsman hunter.

Until Dunmore's war broke out, Kenton employed his time mainly in hunting. Kenton described this as the happiest period of his life. He was in fine health, found plenty of game and fish and he was free from the cares of an ambitious world and the vexations of domestic life. He passed his time in a happy state of ease, indolence and independence that is the glory of a hunter of the forest.

Kenton was over six feet tall, muscular, graceful and of uncommon strength, endurance and agility. His complexion and hair were light, and his soft, grayish blue eyes would light up with a bewitching, fascinating smile. He was frank, generous and confiding to a fault and was more interested in doing a kindness to others than in serving himself. When enraged, his glance was withering. To give a full account of his adventures would fill a volume. A few anecdotes must do.

Kenton, Williams and Stoner

In the spring of 1775, at the age of twenty, Kenton descended the Ohio River to explore Kentucky's famous "cane lands." He and his companion, a man by the name of Williams, landed at the mouth of the Limestone River on the site of Maysville and made a camp a few miles inland. They finished a small clearing where they planted some corn, the first planted north of the Kentucky River. Here, tending their corn with their tomahawks, they remained the undisputed masters of all they could see, until they had the pleasure of eating roasting-ears.

In one of his solitary hunting excursions at this time, Kenton, disguised as an Indian, encountered upon the waters of the Elkhorn River a man named Michael Stoner, a hunter from North Carolina who was also in Indian disguise. A silent contest of Indian strategy for mutual destruction commenced, but not a word was spoken. Each man believed his antagonist was an Indian and therefore sought all the arts of Indian warfare to protect against, and to draw, the enemy's fire.

After mutual efforts and maneuvers ineffectually to draw each other from shelter or to steal fire, Stoner suspected that his antagonist was not an Indian and exclaimed from his place of cover, "For God's sake, if you are a white man, speak!" The spell was broken and they became companions in the solitary wilderness for a few days. It was Stoner who conducted and introduced Kenton to the new settlements of Boonesborough and Harrodsburg. Kenton had, before this, supposed that he and Williams were the first settlers of Kentucky.

After Kenton's encounter with Stoner, he returned to his camp and clearing. The Indians had been there and had plundered it. Nearby, he found the evidence of a fire with human bones near it, which proclaimed too sadly the fate of Williams, the first victim in Kentucky of the war between settlers and Indian tribes. Kenton became a companion of Daniel Boone during this time and with Boone discovered and settled lands of the Kentucky wilderness. Kenton then returned to Harrodsburg.

Kenton and Major Clark

In June 1778, Kenton was the first volunteer from the Kentucky stations to join in Major Clark's hazardous expedition against Illinois. The settlers of the Kentucky region were being attacked and many believed the English forts in the region to be responsible for fostering Indian aggression. Major Clark submitted a plan to the Virginia legislature in 1777 to deal with these forts. He received two sets of instructions: one to defend Kentucky, and the other, on a private level, to attack the British fort at Kaskaskia.

Early in the spring of 1778, Clark's company landed upon Corn Island, at the Falls of the Ohio River, six hundred and seven miles by water below Fort Pitt. Joining them on the island was Simon Kenton, a young man then of twenty-two years and by reputation, one of the boldest pioneers in the region.

With Simon, Clark's company proceeded in boats to the mouth of the Tennessee River and landed upon the site of Paducah. There they met a party of hunters from Kaskaskia and obtained valuable reconnaissance of the British troops and movements. They discovered that Phillip Rocheblave, commander of the garrison at Kaskaskia, and Governor of Fort Gage, was an exceedingly vigilant officer and kept spies continually on alert to discover the approach of Kentuckians. The hunters believed a surprise might be effected on the

Governor and they offered to accompany the expedition as guides.

Their services were accepted and the company continued down the Ohio River until they reached a proper point on the Illinois shore. They concealed their boats and began a march through the wilderness surrounding Kaskaskia, intent on capturing the British fort.

They arrived at the outskirts of the town on the fourth of July, where they remained hidden until dark. When the surprise attack on Kaskaskia occurred, Kenton was the first man to enter Fort Gage and it was he who surprised the Governor in his bed and who compelled him to surrender the garrison. The Governor's wife, who the polite invaders would not disturb, calmly destroyed as many of her husband's papers as she could. Those papers that remained revealed the British plans to incite the Indian tribes in the region against the colonials, justifying Clark's mission against the fort.

It is to Kenton and Clark's credit that the fort was taken at Kaskaskia without any loss of life. Governor Phillip Rocheblave was conducted back to Williamsburg, Virginia and Kenton returned to Boonesborough.

Kenton's Daring Exploits and Captures

One cold evening in March 1778 after a hard day's hunt, Kenton and two companions were resting upon bearskin pallets before a cheerful campfire in the Kanawha region when suddenly the sharp crack of an Indian rifle turned one of them into a lifeless corpse. Within minutes, a party of Indians surrounded them.

Kenton and his surviving companion sprang to their feet and fled with only their lives and their shirts. Thus exposed in the wilderness in winter weather, they were compelled to wander through briers, over rough stones and frozen ground, without fire and without food for six days, until at last they fell in with a party of hunters descending the Ohio and obtained relief. Their legs and bodies had become so lacerated and torn that they were more than two days in traveling the last two miles.

On a separate instance, early one morning in the summer of 1778, Kenton and two companions were just leaving the fort at Boonesborough on a hunting excursion when two men who had gone into a field to drive in some horses were fired upon by five Indians. The men fled, and when within about seventy yards of the fort, an Indian overtook and killed one of them by a blow with his tomahawk. The Indian was beginning to scalp him when Kenton shot him down. He and his companions then drove the remainder of the Indians into the forest.

In the meantime, Daniel Boone, with ten men, came out to their assistance. As they were advancing, Kenton discovered and shot another Indian, just as he was in the act of firing. By the time Boone had come up, they heard a rush of footsteps upon their left and discovered that a number of Indians had gotten between them and the gate. Their peril was extreme. As their only salvation, Boone gave the desperate order to charge through the Indian column, upon which they first discharged their rifles and then, clubbing wildly, they dashed down all Indians who stood in their way.

The attempt was successful; but Boone would have lost his life had it not been for Kenton. An Indian bullet broke the leg of Daniel Boone and he fell. Another Indian sprang forward, uplifted his tomahawk for the fatal blow, but Kenton stepped in and shot him through the body. Kenton then seized Boone from the ground and carried him safely into the fort. Of the fourteen men engaged in this affray, seven were wounded, but none of the wounds were fatal. Boone, after they had gotten to the fort, sent for Kenton and said, "Well, Simon, you have behaved like a man today, indeed, you are a fine fellow!" This simple eulogium from the great man touched the heart of Kenton.

Boonesborough was twice again besieged by the Indians before the close of summer, during which the garrison was depleted of food supplies and would have perished, but for Kenton's skill and fearless daring. In the dead of night at the peril of his own life, Kenton would steal through the camp of the enemy and plunge into the forest far beyond the Indian scouts in search of deer and elk to bring back to the fort. His success in these hunting forays kept the garrison from starving.

The most marked incidents in Kenton's history are the circumstances of his captivity among the Indians. Several anecdotes of those times follow.

In September 1778 Kenton, Montgomery and Clark left forts in Kentucky to steal horses from the Indians. They crossed the Ohio River and traveled cautiously to the Indian village on the area of land near Old Town, at the site of Chillicothe. They caught seven horses and rapidly retreated to the Ohio River, but the wind was blowing almost like a hurricane and made the river so rough that they could not induce their horses to take to the water.

The next day the Indians were in hot pursuit and the men were easily spotted. The hunters happened, at the moment the Indians saw them, to be separated. Kenton, judging the boldest course to be the safest, very deliberately took aim at the foremost Indian. His gun flashed in the pan. He then retreated. The Indians pursued on horseback. In his retreat, he passed through a piece of land where a storm had torn up a great part of the timber. The fallen trees afforded him some advantage of the Indians in the contest, as they were on horseback and he on foot. It was easier for him to maneuver through the debris.

The Indian force divided. Some rode on one side of the fallen timber and some on the other. Just as Kenton emerged from the fallen timber at the foot of a hill, one of the Indians met him on horseback and boldly rode up to him, jumped off his horse, and rushed at him with his tomahawk. Kenton concluded that a gun barrel was as good a defense as a tomahawk, so he drew back his gun to strike the Indian rushing at him.

At that instant, another Indian unperceived by Kenton slipped up behind him and clasped Kenton in his arms. Being now overpowered by numbers, further resistance was useless, and he surrendered. While the Indians were binding Kenton with tugs, Montgomery came in view and fired at the Indians, but missed his mark. Montgomery fled on foot. Some of the Indians pursued, shot at and missed him. A second gunfire was made and Montgomery fell. The Indians soon returned to Kenton, shaking at him Montgomery's bloody scalp. Clark, Kenton's other companion, escaped.

The horrors of his captivity during nine months among the Indians may be briefly enumerated, but they cannot be described. The sufferings of his body may be recounted, but the anguish of his mind, the internal torments of spirit, none but himself could know.

The first regular torture was the awful one of Mazeppa. He was securely bound hand and foot upon the back of an unbroken horse, which plunged furiously through the forest, through thickets, briers, and brush, vainly endeavoring to extricate his unwelcome rider until the animal was completely exhausted. By this time, Kenton had been bruised, lacerated, scratched, and mangled until life itself was nearly extinct, while his sufferings had afforded the most unbounded ecstasies of mirth to his captors. This, however, was only a prelude to subsequent sufferings.

Upon the route to the Indian towns, for the greater security of their prisoner, they would bind him securely with his body extended upon the ground and each foot and hand tied to a stake or sapling to preclude the possibility of escape. A young sapling was laid across his breast, having its extremities well secured to the ground, while a rope secured his neck to another sapling. In this condition, nearly naked and exposed to swarms of gnats and mosquitoes, he was compelled to spend each tedious night upon the cold ground, exposed to the chilling dews of autumn.

On the third day at noon, he was within one mile of old Chillicothe, the present site of Frankfort, where he was detained in confinement until the next day. Toward evening, curiosity had brought hundreds of all sexes and conditions to view the great Kentuckian. Numerous grunts, kicks, blows and stripes, inflicted amid applauding yells, dancing and every demonstration of savage indignation, evinced their satisfaction at his wretched condition.

This, however, was only a prelude to a more energetic mode of torture he would experience the next day, in which the whole village was to be partakers. The torture of a prisoner is a school for the young warrior to stir up his hatred for their white enemies and keep alive the fire of revenge, while it affords sport and mirth to gratify the vindictive rage of bereaved mothers and relatives by participating in the infliction of the agonies, which the prisoner is compelled to suffer.

Running the gauntlet was the torture of the next day when nearly three hundred Indians of both sexes and all ages were assembled for the savage festival.

The ceremony commenced. Kenton, nearly naked, and freed from his bonds, was produced as the victim of the ceremony. The Indians were arranged in two parallel lines, about six feet apart, all armed with sticks, hickory rods, whips, and other means of inflicting pain. Between these lines, for more than half a mile to the village, the wretched prisoner was doomed to run for his life, exposed to such injury as his tormentors could inflict as he passed. If he succeeded in reaching the council house alive, it would prove an asylum to him for the present.

At a given signal, Kenton started in the perilous race. Exerting his utmost strength and activity, he passed swiftly along the line, receiving numerous blows, stripes, buffets, and wounds, until he approached the town, near which he saw an Indian leisurely awaiting his advance with a drawn knife in his hand, intent upon his death.

To avoid him, he instantly broke through the line and made his rapid way toward the council house, pursued by the promiscuous crowd, whooping and yelling like infernal furies at his heels. Entering the town in advance of his pursuers, just as he had saw the council house within his reach, an Indian was leisurely approaching him, with his blanket wrapped around him. This Indian suddenly threw off his blanket and sprung upon Kenton as he advanced.

Exhausted with fatigue and wounds, he was thrown to the ground and in a moment he was beset with crowds, eager to strip him and to inflict upon him each kick or blow that had been avoided by his actions of breaking through the line. At this point, Kenton was beaten, kicked and scourged until he was nearly lifeless, and was left to die.

A few hours afterward, having partially revived, he was supplied with food and water and was allowed to recuperate for a few days until he was able to attend a meeting at the council house and receive the announcement of his final doom. After a violent discussion, the council, by a large majority, determined that he should be made a public sacrifice to the vengeance of the nation and the decision was announced by a burst of savage joy, with yells and shouts, which made the structure ring.

The place of execution was Wappatomica, the present site of Zanesfield in Logan County, Ohio. On the route to this place, Kenton was taken through Pickaway and Mackacheck where he was again compelled to undergo the torture of the gauntlet and was scourged through the line. At this place, smarting under his wounds and bruises, he was detained several days in order that he might recuperate preparatory to his march to Wappatomica.

At length, being carelessly guarded, Kenton decided to try and make his escape from the impending doom. He successfully escaped and had traveled two miles from the place of confinement when he encountered two Indians on horseback. They brutally drove him back to the village. The last ray of hope had now expired and loathing a life of continual suffering, he resigned himself to his fate in despair.

His latest attempt to escape had brought upon him a repetition of savage torture, which had nearly closed his sufferings forever and he verily believed himself a "God-forsaken wretch." Taken to a neighboring creek, he was thrown in and dragged through mud and water, submerged repeatedly, until life was nearly extinct and again left in a dying state. However, the constitutional vigor within him revived and a few days afterward he was taken to Wappatomica for execution.

At Wappatomica he first saw at a British trading post, his old friend Simon Girty, who had become a renegade in all the glory of his Indian life, surrounded by swarms of Indians who had come to view the doomed prisoner and to witness the torture. Girty did not suspect the presence of Simon Kenton at Fort Pitt.

Although well acquainted with Kenton only a few years before, Kenton's present mangled condition and his blackened face left no traces of recognition in Girty's mind. Looking upon him as a doomed victim, beyond the reach of pity or hope, he could view him only as the victim of sacrifice. As soon as Kenton managed to make himself known, the hard heart of Girty at once relented, and sympathizing with Kenton's miserable condition and still more horrid doom, he resolved to make an effort for his release.

Girty's whole personal influence and his eloquence, no less than his intrigue, were put in requisition for the safety of his fallen friend. He portrayed in strong language the policy of preserving the life of the prisoner and the advantages that might be gained for the Indians by holding prisoner one man so intimately acquainted with all the white settlements.

For a time Girty's eloquence prevailed and a respite was granted; but suspicions arose, and Kenton was again summoned before the council. The death of Kenton was again decreed. Again, the influence of Girty prevailed and through finesse he accomplished a further respite, together with a removal of the prisoner to Sandusky.

Here at Sandusky, the council again decreed Kenton's death, and again he was compelled to submit to the terrors of the gauntlet preliminary to his execution. Still Girty did not relax his efforts. Despairing of his own influence with the council, he secured the aid and influence of a man called Logan, "the friend of white men."

Logan interceded with Captain Drouillard, a British officer, and procured through him the offer of a liberal ransom to the vindictive Indians for the life of the prisoner, Kenton. Captain Drouillard met with the council and stressed the great advantages such a prisoner would be to the commandant at Detroit in procuring from Kenton such information as would greatly facilitate his future operations against the rebel American colonies. At the same time, appealing to their avarice, he suggested that the ransom would be proportionate to the value of the prisoner.

Drouillard guaranteed the ransom of one hundred dollars for his delivery, and Kenton was given to him to hold as prisoner for the commandant at Detroit. As soon as Kenton's mind was out of the extreme danger of captivity, his robust constitution and iron frame recovered from the severe treatment they had undergone. Kenton passed the winter and spring at Detroit. Among the prisoners held captive there with him were Captain Nathan Bullit and Jesse Coffer. The men were not confined to any one building, had the liberty of the town, and could stroll about at pleasure.

With these two men, Kenton began to formulate an escape. They had frequent conferences on the subject, but the enterprise was almost too appalling for even these hardy, enterprising pioneers. If they should make this bold push, they would have to travel nearly four hundred miles through the

Indian country where they would be exposed to death by starvation, by flood, by the tomahawk, or to capture, almost at every step. But the longer they brooded over the enterprise, the stronger their resolutions grew to make the attempt.

They could make no movement to procure arms, ammunition, or provisions without exciting suspicion and, should they be once suspected, they would be immediately confined. In this situation, they could only brood over their wished flight in secret and in silence. Kenton was a handsome man, with a dignified and manly deportment, and a soft, pleasing voice, and was, everywhere he went, a favorite among the ladies.

A Mrs. Harvey, the wife of an Indian trader, had treated him with particular respect ever since he came to Detroit and he decided that if he could engage this lady as a confidant, by her assistance and countenance, ways and means could be prepared to aid them in their meditated flight.

Kenton approached Mrs. Harvey on this delicate and interesting subject with as much trepidation and coyness as ever a maiden was approached in a love affair. The great difficulty with Kenton was to get the subject opened with Mrs. Harvey. If she should reject his suit and betray his intentions, all his fond hopes would be at once blasted. However, at length he was convinced he could trust this lady with the scheme of his meditated flight and the part he wished her to act for him.

He watched for an opportunity to have a private interview with Mrs. Harvey and such an opportunity was soon offered. Without disguise or hesitation, in full confidence, he informed her of his intention and requested her aid and secrecy. She appeared at first astonished at his proposal and stated that it was not in her power to afford him any aid. Kenton told her he did not expect or wish her to be at any expense on their account, that the men had a little money for which they had labored and that they wished her to be their agent to purchase such articles as would be necessary for them in their flight. Kenton also explained to her that if the men were go to purchasing, it would create suspicion, but that she could aid them in this way without creating any suspicion and if she would be their friend, they had no doubt they could effect their escape.

This appeal, from such a fine looking man as Kenton, was irresistible. There was something pleasing in being the selected confidant of such a man and the lady, though a little coy at first, surrendered at discretion. After a few conversations, she entered into the escape plans of Kenton with as much earnestness and enthusiasm as if she had been his sister. She began to collect and conceal such articles as might be necessary in the journey, such as powder, lead, moccasins, and dried beef.

These were procured in small quantities and concealed in a hollow tree some distance out of town. Guns were still wanting and it would not do for a lady to trade in them. Mr. Harvey, her husband, had an excellent fowling rifle, if nothing better should be found, that she said should be at their service. They had now everything that they expected to take with them in their flight ready, except for guns.

At length the third day of June 1779 came, and a large concourse of Indians were in the town engaged in a drunken frolic. The Indians had stacked their guns near Mrs. Harvey's house and as soon as it was dark, she went quietly to where the Indians' guns were stacked and selected the three best looking rifles, carried them into her garden, and concealed them in a patch of peas. She next went privately to Kenton's lodging and conveyed to him the intelligence where she had hid the Indians' guns. She told him she would place a ladder at the back of the garden (it was picketed) and that he could come in and pick up the guns.

No time was to be lost, so Kenton conveyed the good news he had from Mrs. Harvey to his companions, who received the tidings in ecstasies of joy. They felt as if they were already home. It was a dark night when Kenton, Bullit and Coffer gathered up their little stash and pushed to Mrs. Harvey's garden. There they found the ladder. Kenton mounted over, drew the ladder over after him, went to the pea-patch and found Mrs. Harvey sitting by the guns. She handed him the rifles, gave him a friendly shake of the hand and bid him a safe journey to his friends and countrymen.

She appeared to Kenton and his comrades as an angel. When a woman engages to do an action, she will risk limb, life, or character to serve those whom she respects or wishes to befriend. How differently the same action might have been viewed by different persons, but to Kenton and his friends, her conduct was viewed as the benevolent action of a good angel. If the part she had played on behalf of Kenton and his companions had been known to the commander at Detroit she would have been looked upon as a traitor who merited the scorn and contempt of all honest citizens. This interaction was the last time that Kenton ever saw or heard of her again.

A few days before Kenton left Detroit, he had a conversation with an Indian trader, a Scotchman by the name of McKenzie, who was well acquainted with the geography of the country and range of the Indians between the lakes and the Ohio and Mississippi Rivers. The Scotchman slyly told Kenton that if he was going to Kentucky and did not wish to meet with the Indians, he should steer more west than the common route and get into Wabash prairies as soon as possible. Kenton did not know what to think of the remarks of the Scotchman. He began to think that perhaps Mrs. Harvey had divulged his secret to this man and that he was pumping Kenton, or possibly that he wished to aid him and this was done by offering friendly advice. As no more was said, Kenton did not pretend to notice what the Scotchman said, but treasured the remarks in his mind.

As soon as Kenton and his companions took leave of their friend and benefactress, Mrs. Harvey, they made their way to the little stash in the hollow tree, bundled it up, and pushed for the woods. They steered a more westerly than direct course to Kentucky. They had no doubt but that every effort would be made to recapture them. Consequently, they were very circumspect and cautious in leaving as little trace as possible by which they might be discovered to a tracking party.

They went on slowly, traveling mostly in the night, steering their course by the cluster called the seven stars, until they reached the prairie country on the Wabash River. In this time, though they had been very sparing of their stock of provisions, most of it was now exhausted and their lives depended on their guns. In these large prairies there was little game and they were now days without enough food and water. They began to wish themselves again with the fleshpots at the prison yard of Detroit.

One day as they were passing down the Wabash River, they were just emerging out of a thicket of brushwood, when an Indian encampment suddenly came in view, not more than one hundred and fifty or two hundred yards ahead of them. No ghastly visit could have set their hair on end sooner. They immediately dodged back into the thicket and concealed themselves until night.

They were now almost exhausted with fatigue and hunger and they could only travel a few miles in a day. They lay still in the thicket consulting with each other on the most proper measures to pursue in this their precarious situation. Bullit and Coffer thought the best plan to save their lives would be voluntarily to surrender themselves to the Indians. The Indians who had taken them had not treated them so roughly as Kenton had been handled. Kenton wished to lie still until night and make as little sign as possible and as soon as it was dark, they would push ahead and trust the event to Providence.

After considerable debate, Kenton's plan was adopted. The next morning, Kenton managed to shoot a deer. They made a fire and went to cooking and never did food taste more delicious. They then pursued their toilsome march and arrived, without further adventure, at the falls of the Ohio River (now Louisville) on the thirty-third day of their escape.

Until the close of the war, Kenton continued an active partisan. From 1784 to 1792, he was in many severe encounters with the Indians and on one occasion with Tecumseh, then a young Chief rapidly rising into prominence. Kenton was with Wayne, in the capacity of Major, in the early part of Wayne's campaign. When the war was over, Kenton settled on his farm, near Maysville, where he possessed extensive lands and was considered one of the wealthiest men in Kentucky. His house was the abode of hospitality and he began to enjoy the comforts of a great old age in peace and competence, but a dark cloud was lowering upon his prospects.

Ignorant of the technicalities of the law, he had failed to render his title secure and like Daniel Boone and Clark before him, he was robbed in successive lawsuits of one piece of land after another until he found in his declining age, himself and his family reduced to poverty and want.

In 1802, beggared by lawsuits over his land and losses, he became landless. Yet he never murmured at the ingratitude that had taken away his holdings. In 1813, Kenton joined the Kentucky troops under Shelby. He was then 58 years old. He fought in the battle of Thames and again, served his country well as a decorated veteran. In 1824, then seventy years old, he journeyed to Frankfort, in tattered garments and upon a miserable horse, to ask the Legislature of Kentucky to release the claims of the state upon some of his mountain lands so that he might have a place to live out the remainder of his days. He was stared at by the young politicians and shunned by the citizens, for none recognized or knew of him. At length, General Thomas Fletcher realized who the poverty-stricken man was. He secured new clothing for Kenton, put the word out about the venerable old hero and entertained Kenton in his home.

Kenton was taken to the Capitol building and seated in the Speaker's chair before the legislature. When it became known who he was, the Capitol building was flooded by scores of people who flocked to listen and see the old hero. Kenton won his victory at last: his lands were released and Congress awarded to him a pension of two hundred and forty dollars a year.

He died in 1836, when he was 81 years old, at the home he built on the headwaters of Mad River, Logan County, Ohio—a home within sight of the place where fifty-eight years before, the Indians were about to put him to death. Simon Kenton had been a member of the Methodist church for over a quarter of a century. The frosts of more than eighty winters had fallen on his head without entirely whitening his locks. At the time of his death, he had passed through more dangers, privations, perils and hairbreadth escapes than any man living or dead.

INDIANS OF CALIFORNIA

California Indians: A Discussion of Features and Culture, 1852

The male and female roles in the California tribes are shown in the lines of their faces. In the man's eye, there is all the fire and vigor of his race expressed, while the head of the woman is equally expressive of the milder characteristics of the other sex. For the Indian women are the patient, laboring and willing slaves of their lord – far more so than can be found in any portion of the white race on the face of the globe. They do all the domestic drudgery, cook, cultivate the few vegetables that are used by the people, do all the household labor, and indeed, carry all the burdens; in short they are the "hewers of wood and the drawers of water."

The male, on the contrary, is "the monarch of all he surveys" and he disdains aught else but smoke, drink (when he can get spirit), hunt, and murder the whites, for their property, and lead an abandoned and reckless life. Such seems to be their nature. As to digging gold, it is difficult to induce them to do it, even by liberal offers of coin and rum, but a few are, indeed, engaged by miners. They look upon the whites as a poor, deluded, drudging, labor-loving, and degraded race of creatures, and never fail to stab them when they can do so in the dark and from behind. They do not possess one chivalric principle that has yet been discovered, and are treacherous and deceitful to the utmost degree.

The Indian "Rancheria" is admirable, a place primitive enough for even the most fastidious. There is probably no Indian settlement of any considerable size in California so well known as the Rancheria on the Feather River, opposite the mouth of the Yuba River. It contained a year ago, a population numbering over two hundred, which has continued gradually to grow less, and very soon the whole tribe are likely to seek a more remote location. The "digger" race is variously described by those who have written on the subject in this country in many ways. In seasons of war, they have been set down as brave and formidable enemies, and by their stratagems and success in escaping the hostile demonstrations directed against them, have given some coloring of truth to this view of their character; indeed, it might reflect upon the military achievements of the past year to draw a different conclusion. By those who judge of the native Indians from observations of their appearance, manners and customs when living in their Rancherias, at peace with the whites, they are seldom esteemed other than meek, spiritless, undefensive, and altogether the most utterly worthless of the Indians of the Americas.

The number of Indians in California is reckoned from twenty thousand, upwards. In the northern part of the State toward the Oregon border, they exhibit evidence of civilization in their way of living, and a knowledge and practice of some of the useful arts, besides being more brave and warlike than elsewhere.

Their food is confined to acorns, game and fish. In the valley of the Sacramento River, they live in holes about five feet deep, roofed over in a conical shape, with a network of wood and bark, covered with earth. Theft is the chief natural vice of the diggers, besides their filthy and slothful habits. In the proximity of the whites they are perfectly docile, sluggish and indifferent, caring for naught but food and water, which they beg or barter for some servile labor.

Had the Indians of the country been treated according to the Spanish policy, the discord and animosity now generated between the races would have been avoided. As it is however, the disposal of the native tribes of the country has become one of the most embarrassing and vexatious questions of the day; the settlement of which threatens no ordinary political and social calamity. But it is of little importance in the discussion of the subject, since it seems to be the design of Providence that they shall gradually die out and vanish from the face of the globe. Why then should we hasten their demise? They have generally gone from State to State in the Union, gradually growing less and less in number, until Indians are becoming, as it were, curiosities and relics of the past, and rarely to be met with except in distant wilds and without the borders of civilization. They have gradually been pressed westward, where the Pacific must at length stay their course, and the waves of its bosom flow over the last of the persecuted and forlorn race. Like prairie dogs and wolves, they seem almost to burrow in the ground; and the low, gypsy-like tents covered with undressed buffalo hides, as seen on the prairies, are the very best habitations that the California Indian enjoys.

Yet some of them have a pride, or a "weakness," if you please to call it so, for some one thing that partially ennobles their general character. Some of them will possess themselves of a colt and rear it to a horse that would astound an eastern horse jockey for its fleetness, docility and training. Another has a passion for a rifle, and he so perfects himself in the use of the instrument he has stolen or purchased from the whites, that he would put a Kentucky sharp shooter to the blush. Another throws the lasso with precision, as scarcely ever to miss his aim, though it is always done from horseback, and when at full speed. In this exercise they are said to far surpass the wild cattle catchers of the plains of South America, who make it their entire occupation thus to obtain hides, horns, etc. for exportation.

We have often thought how novel must all these peculiarities appear to the Yankees—town bred for instance—who leave a comfortable home to dig gold in El Dorado. Once here, comforts, even necessities, soon become scarce and difficult to attain, and life and health are risked every hour. Out of this fiery ordeal of chance some come forth safely, but the larger portion are generally lost to themselves and their friends forever. Year upon year must transpire before California presents any real attractions for the refined and intellectual. It is a child yet: a whining, capricious infant, one of Uncle Sam's youngest, but experience will teach it to become a man; and that it may grow to the full and goodly stature of one is our most earnest and reiterated wish. The eyes of the world generally have been turned to this new acquisition to our regularly represented territory and directed with so much of earnest curiosity to the present important position which it fills, as it regards the Union, that it has been difficult to keep pace in the imagination with its strides of improvement, and people abroad have even looked upon the representations made public, as it regards the growth and increase generally of California, as somewhat fabulous and questionable; but the heavy receipt of the pure metal by every steamer from thence, gotten, no matter at what cost, displays at all events the richness of its mines and placers, and gives the stamp of authenticity and truth to its story.

San Francisco is destined to exert an influence beyond the mere value of the gold that her soil yields. In possessing her harbor we are made strong on the Pacific Ocean, that great field of commerce, where the battles of trade and industry must in future be fought. Bloodless battles, but important ones, nevertheless, and the results will be far more interesting in history than those of the battles fought with destructive weapons.

It will be curious, fifty years hence, to record the story of California's rise and progress in the history of states and colonies. It will look no less fabulous to our descendants than it does now to ourselves; for it is, indeed, little short of an absolute miracle, although the evidence of its wealth and internal resources is brought so distinctly before our eyes.

—Gleason's Pictorial Drawing Room Companion, 1852

BIRDS FOR BREAKFAST

(A True Story of The Settlement of Arkansas)

Westward ho! A party of hunters had brought back marvelous reports of the fertile prairies on the banks of the Red River, and in less than a month— I think it was August, 1820—a long train of Conestoga wagons had crossed the Mississippi, en route for the land of promise. They were under the direction of Squire Frierson, a wealthy old planter who had grown rich by land speculations, and now hoped not only to locate some rich tracts for himself, but to get mortgages on the farms of his associate pioneers. Stalwart sons of toil, they had little idea that they were in reality but serfs, and indulged in high hopes of future prosperity, as they goaded along the sluggish oxen, or kept together the herds that grazed as they journeyed.

The wagons, generally speaking, would rumble over about ten miles in a day, and when the sun began to decline, they were so halted as to form a square, within which the campfires were lighted. The cattle were corralled, supper was prepared, and then groups would gather round the fires to listen to marvelous tales of frontier life. As the fires burned low, the groups would diminish, and soon the watchful guards would have the lights in the tents extinguished, one by one, until the silence of night reigned.

One morning, three young men who had been patrolling through the night, lingered behind the train to cook some fine birds that Hal Harson, the youngest of the trio, had shot at early dawn. His companions, gaunt and weather-bronzed, were veteran hunters, but Hal was a fine-looking fellow, ruddy with health, and having every pioneer attribute. Everyone wondered he should have left a good paternal farm in Tennessee, to be a hireling guard on Frierson's train; yet he was the favorite of the party.

"Now for a breakfast," said Hal as he approached the fire. "Well, bird meat's better 'n deer meat," replied Jim Long, who had just succeeded in resuscitating the fire. "But here comes old Frierson on his pacer, biting the stem

254

of his pipe. He be dogged. What does he want?"

The leader of the train, who now rode up, had that cramped, heartless, cold expression of countenance, peculiar to those who make Mammon their god. In his opinion, men were good or bad according to their means, and he especially disliked poor young men, regarding them as adventurers who sought to deprive capitalists of wealth. Perhaps, too, he feared that someone might woo and wed his niece, whose property had been of such essential service in several speculations.

Left an orphan at an early age, Mary Frierson had been brought up on her uncle's farm, in wild independence. She could shoot, fish and hunt like Diana, yet as she ripened into womanhood, her feelings became chastened. An undefined yearning took possession of her. She became acquainted with Hal Harson, and soon discovered that he loved her, and as the wagon train moved slowly along, it was her delight to have him join the merry group of girls, for she felt that she, of all others, was first in his thoughts. And he, although sensible that there was a great gulf between them, which nothing but a bridge of dollars could span, lived in the intoxication of her presence. To enjoy that, he felt that he could endure any privation, face any difficulty—nay, even bear the insulting manners of her uncle.

"What's this!" exclaimed Frierson in an insolent tone. "Who shot those birds?"

"I did," coolly replied Harson.

"You did, Hal. Well, I was fool enough to think the Injuns would trouble us, and so hired you lazy fellows as a guard. But I didn't buy powder for you to shoot birds with."

"The birds were shot with my own ammunition, purchased at Memphis—look!" And as Harson spoke, he exhibited a small canister of "Dupont" with a leather bag of shot. "I have done my duty, sir," he continued, "and if you think there are Indians around, I ..."

"Humbug!" interrupted Frierson. "You had better look stricter after the cattle."

"Look a here," grumbled Bill Long, one of the young men and a friend of Hal's. "If you think you can put on yer airs here, old hoss, you're a cave-in. We was hired to guard the camp at night; we've stood our guard—Hal, here, more than we two—but we ain't your slaves, no sir-ree. So keep civil, or dry up!"

"What!" exclaimed Frierson, turning purple with rage. "But never mind. In a week you all can travel. But don't be loitering here, or the wagons will get out of sight." Ere Harson could reply, he had turned his horse, plunged in the spurs, and was hastening after the wagon train. Hal gazed after him with flashing eyes and a dark cloud of anger on his forehead, but he did not speak.

"I would like to send a bullet after him," said Long, kicking apart the blazing wood of the fire.

"Never mind, never mind," said Hal Harson. "He's a crusty old fellow; but after all, it wasn't perhaps right to linger behind. So I'll carry along the birds and we'll have them for supper."

"I'm amiable," laconically replied the third member of the party, and they trudged along in silence.

Overtaking the wagon train, the hunters joined a party of young fellows, who were ever ready to listen to their yarns, while Hal Harson bashfully approached a wagon in which the girls of the train were riding, having rolled up the canvas covering either side of the wagon. Prominent in this galaxy of rosy beauty was Mary Frierson, who welcomed Hal with a meaningful smile. Untutored in those arts which refinement has adopted to conceal the wildest passions of the soul, there was, in the glance that beamed from her flashing eye, an assurance of regard which made her lover's breast beat high with hope. But another saw that glance, and Hal was roused from his dream of bliss by the voice of Frierson. "Well, young man, having finished your game breakfast, you are now making morning calls! Go back and mind the cattle, sir. This is no place for you."

Hal trembled and nervously grasped his rifle, but looking towards his insolent employer, he caught the eyes of Mary. Her look was more eloquent than words, mingling entreaty and regret and love. Passing his hand across his forehead, as if to banish the scene, he slowly moved away.

"A pretty guard," growled Frierson, eyeing his niece. "I don't see what business a pennniless fellow like that has hanging about you girls. You ought to know that he is after your money."

Mary Frierson's lip quivered as she spoke angrily to her uncle. "We girls know where our money is, and who tries to keep it."

The old man started in his saddle, and then gave Mary an earnest look, as if to read her thoughts. "You are sharp," he at length said with a faint smile, but it could not mask his vexation, and then making some remark about the road, he passed on to the next wagon.

Night threw her sable mantle over the prairies, and Hal Harson again found himself on guard. At first, the young sentinel felt sad. Affection for Mary Frierson and resentment against her uncle struggled for mastery. But as he paced his round, his spirits rallied. Hal's imagination soon began to revel in lighter scenes. Hark! He heard a rustling. Cocking his rifle, he brought it to his shoulder, but then the familiar tones of her whom he loved echoed through his heart. In a moment, she stood at his side.

"Mary! Miss Frierson!" exclaimed Hal, offering his hand.

"Speak low," replied the excited girl, cordially returning his grasp. Then, with a slight tremor in her tone she said, "I could not sleep, Hal Harson, without thanking you for the manner in which you received my uncle's insulting remark this morning. It stung you to the heart, I saw, but—but..."

"But love for you chained my temper," interrupted Hal. "Hear me, Mary Frierson. You are far my superior, but I can but adore you. Can I hope for a return of my love? Can you share my humble lot? Can you become my wife?"

Mary looked earnestly into the anxious face of her lover, but her heart was too full for utterance. Yet she suffered Hal Harson's stalwart arm to steal around her waist, and when he imprinted a long, deep kiss upon her lips, it was returned—she was his own. Just then the moon shone approvingly forth and sentinel stars brightly witnessed this union of fond hearts.

"You will be mine, then, Mary."

"With all my heart and soul," replied Mary; but at that moment the well-known figure of her uncle approached them, and he shouted, "Mary Frierson, leave that beggar, or..."

A hundred hideous yells interrupted him, and a cloud of arrows whistled through the air, as a large party of Indians dashed into the camp. They passed the lovers, but two sprang from their saddles as they approached Mr. Frierson, who was soon leveled to the ground by the heavy blow of a war-club. In an instant an Indian grasped him by the hair, and drawing his scalping knife, was about to seize his fatal trophy, when a shot from Hal Harson's rifle laid him low. Confusion now reigned. The sharp cracks of the rifles and curses of the whites mingled with the yells of the Indians, and the shrieks of the women and children.

Leaving Mary to attend to her senseless uncle, Hal Harson dashed into the thickest of the fight, and by his bravery soon turned the scale. The warfare was waged with demonical fury, but soon the Indians, uttering a whoop of despair, abandoned the strife, while a loud cheer of victory went up from the whites.

Hal Harson now hastened to the spot where he had left Mary Frierson and her uncle, where he arrived just in time. One of the Indians, mounted on a fine horse, had fled from the scene of contest in that direction, and was in the act of throwing a lasso over the poor girl, who was kneeling by her uncle's side. Just as the rope had tightened, and she was expecting to find herself dragged over the ground, a bullet from Hal's never-failing rifle passed through the Indian's heart and he fell dead. She was safe. Squire Frierson was sensible of the kindness he had received—and hailed Hal Harson as the preserver of his life. He told Hal he might claim Mary as his bride.

They were married on the broad prairies of Arkansas, just as the sun appeared above the eastern horizon. There, surrounded by the stalwart pioneers and their delighted wives and daughters, they took each other for husband and for wife—pledging a mutual vow which angels might have witnessed and Heaven sanctioned, although there was neither priest nor license. The doubt and fear of love was over, and the two, heart-united, looked forward to the future as they did on their pathway—a pleasant journey, to be taken in company. The only ones who appeared at all to regret the happy event were Hal's comrades on guard-duty, and as Squire Frierson was gazing with some pride upon the newly wedded couple, Bill Long came up, bearing the game shot by Hal the previous morning and asked in a malicious tone: "Well, Squire, hadn't you better let him eat for birds for breakfast after all?"

In a few days the party reached their destined abiding place, where a village soon sprang up. The prairies were converted into smiling fields, and when Arkansas was admitted into the Union as a State, the Honorable Mr. Frierson had a seat in the Senate, while Colonel Hal Harson was a prominent member of the House of Representatives. A turnpike road now traverses their original route, leading through towns which are the abodes of intelligence, industry and art. Whenever Colonel and Mrs. Harson journey over it, they stop to revisit the scene of the night attack and when they pass a night at the hotel nearby, kept by Old William Long, Esquire, he always inquires, with a meaningful smile, if they will have "birds for breakfast."

—By Ben Perley Poore, Ballou's Pictorial Drawing-Room Companion, 1855.

FREMONT: THE RIDE OF THE ONE HUNDRED

A late decision of our United States Supreme Court having rendered a tardy act of justice to one who has opened to us an empire, it seemed to me that a personal reminiscence might be acceptable.

In the early part of the year 1847, business called me to Alta, California; having been long a resident on the Pacific coast, and being familiar with the language and customs of the people, I was selected to effect a large contract of hides, for one of our eastern firms, the trade being nearly paralyzed at the time by the war then in progress between our country and Mexico. A handful of noble men were accomplishing deeds which have given them a place in history by the side of Leonidas and his braves. The land called the "Californias" had become to us a desideratum; although their mineral wealth still slumbered, waiting for that enchanter of modern days, Yankee enterprise; their splendid harbors, the contiguity of our possessions in Oregon, and the facilities for trade with China were a sufficient incentive. Commodore Stockton had hurried up from Callao in the frigate Congress, and General Kearney had crossed the plains from the Missouri River, with a force of armed hunters, for the purpose of taking the country and holding it as a gage for a satisfactory treaty.

The native Californians, who had long groaned beneath the imposts of a distant government and venial governors, had themselves invited our overtures; but a few of their leaders, with a deadly hatred towards the Yankees and hope of personal reward from Mexico, were assiduously striving to stir the people up to a revolt; in many cases with too great success. Manuel Castro, a wealthy and influential ranchero, noted for his determined opposition to all change and enmity to the "Gringos," had arranged for an attack on the Pueblo los Angelos, the headquarters of Kearney, held by a small force of marines and volunteers. His agents were in all parts of the country, inflaming the inhabitants and urging them to join him. By some means his plan leaked out.

I was at this time at the ranch of my old friend, General Martinez Vallejo, on the Sonora Creek; my companion was Captain D-, who has since espoused one of our host's daughters. Vallejo was one of the largest landholders in California, owning some sixty square miles, with forty thousand head of cattle and several hundred horses, cattle and horses at that time being a man's available wealth. He had been formerly military governor of the country, and was considered fair spoil by our people, though in justice I must state that he was kindly disposed towards the Americans. The house was a substantial edifice of two stories, surrounded by a corral with a stout gateway; the household consisted of some twenty persons.

We had all retired to rest and were wrapped in slumber, when the loud barking of dogs and helloing of many men aroused us suddenly from our dreams. Expecting an attack of the Bear Party, a band of lawless desperadoes who infested the country all rushed to the courtyard armed as well as the time permitted, and in costumes the most picturesque, as primitiveness is usually considered so. The general, saber in hand, came last; he challenged the intruders with: *"Quien es la?"* (Who is there?)

"Americanos y amigos, abre la puerta," (Americans and friends, open the gate) was the response, a blow accompanying the words that made the door shake again.

The demand was perforce complied with, and a band of some fifty men were presented to our view, mounted and arrayed as trappers and hunters, and armed to the teeth. Foremost among them on a black mustang was a small, sinewy, dark man, evidently their leader, with "an eye like Mars to threaten and command," a countenance expressive of the greatest determination, and a bearing, that, notwithstanding his rough dress, stamped him as one born to command—to lead. This was Fremont.

"I am an officer of the United States," said he. "I am on my way to Los Angelos, I must have horses."

"But..." said Vallejo.

"I said, sir, I must have them; you will be recompensed by my government. I order you, sir, to deliver to my men what horses you may have in corral."

Finding remonstrance would be of no avail with such a man; Vallejo called his vaqueros and gave the requisite directions. In the meanwhile, my friend D-made himself known to Fremont, having met him in Washington.

"I have information of Castro's intention to attack Los Angelos," said Fremont. "I have six days to reach there before the outbreak; for that I need these horses, for I must be in at the death."

"But the distance...six hundred miles," said D-. "The roads...."

"I shall do it," he replied, and turned away to supervise his arrangements.

In half an hour they departed as unceremoniously as they came, taking with them some three hundred horses, and leaving us astounded at this raid, to wonder if we were yet awake, or whether it was all an unsubstantial dream.

"Lost diablos," exclaimed the general, "they have even taken my wife's saddle horse!" so thoroughly had Fremont's lieutenant executed his order.

From Sonora to Yerba Buena, the little hamlet where now stands the queen city of the Pacific, San Francisco, he augmented his stock to the number of fifteen hundred, completely clearing the country; and then commenced one of the most peculiar races for a fight ever probably known. Barely pulling bridle to devour a steak cut from the quarter of a scarce dead bullock; driving before them their spare horses—on, on they went; the roads at all times bad, at this season were horrible; fifty miles being a hard day's journey, even for a Californian.

As their exhausted mounts dropped under them, they tore off the saddles and, placing them on other horses, hurried on, leaving the poor animals to be devoured by coyotes or recover, as chance might bring about. Ever at the head, the last to dismount and the first to leap into the saddle was this mountaineer, this companion of Kit Carson, this pioneer of the empire—Fremont! Rarely speaking but to urge on his men, or to question some passing native, taking the smallest modicum of refreshment, and watching while others snatched a moment's repose, was he—wrapped up in his project and determined to have some of the fight!

Through San Pablo, and Monterey, and Josepha, they dashed like the phantom riders of the Hartz Mountains, startling the inhabitants and making the night watcher cross himself in terror as their band flew on. The River Sacrificios was reached; swollen by the rains it rolled on, a rapid, muddy stream: his men paused.

"Forward! Forward!" cried Fremont and dashed in; the struggle was a fierce one, but his gallant mustang breasted the current and reached the opposite shore in safety. His men came after a time to join him, two brave fellows finding a watery grave and many horses being carried down the stream, but nothing could stop him. The heights adjacent to the Pueblo were in view and a smile was seen on the implacable visage of the leader—'tis the sixth day and the goal is won!

With ninety men on the last of his caravan of horses, he rode like a thunderbolt on the rear of the Mexicans. The day was with Fremont—the little band of stout hearts guarding the presidio were taken by surprise, and not having the advantage of the Mexicans in regards to horses, began to waver. However, with Fremont coming into view, the battle was again enjoined and with shouts of triumph, Fremont and his men rode in to triumph in a rout.

With Fremont was a Wallawallah Chief, the sole remnant of a band that joined Kearney on his journey across the plains. In his war paint, mounted on a bareback mustang, he would ride up at full speed to the enemy, and as a lance was thrust at him, dexterously throw himself on one side of his horse and avoid the blow. He would then grasp the pole, draw up his antagonist and with a stroke of his tomahawk cleave the opponent's skull, ejaculating a grunt of satisfaction. Three did he dispatch in this manner, alone and unassisted; and as, with his face covered in blood and his reeking hatchet uplifted, he rode here and there, all fled before him.

The rout was complete and had not Fremont's men been utterly exhausted, none would have escaped. So ended the Ride of the One Hundred!

I would state that Government, with their usual speed in such matters, passed on appropriation to satisfy General Vallejo and others for their losses—six years later.

This put a virtual end to the war, for though they again made a stand at the San Pascal, headed by Pico, still they were dispirited, and General Kearney with his mounted men defeated them with great loss. The governorship of the country being decided, which had long been a source of trouble between Kearney, Stockton, and Mason, affairs became more settled and the American force, now largely augmented, was placed on such a footing as to soon "crush the head of rank rebellion" and Pico and Castro fled to the lower country, to fight for a time longer against inevitable fate.

—Frederick Stanhope, Ballou's Pictorial Drawing-Room Companion, 1855.

THE LIFE OF PONTIAC

Pontiac was a great chief of the Ottawa tribe, who was respected and feared by frontier settlers during the mid-1700s. History has recorded Pontiac as an angry, warring chief who had an intense hatred of the white man and who was renowned for bloody warfare and aggressive intentions. But as is usually true when all the facts are understood, there were reasons for his hostilities.

The name "Pontiac" first became known to settlers when he was chief of the northwestern portion of the lands of colonial America prior to the Revolutionary War. It was in the autumn of 1760 that Major Rogers first met the great chief. Major Rogers informed Pontiac that the English had taken Canada from the French and then made a treaty of friendship with the nations of Indians that he governed.

Although Pontiac had been an active ally of the French during the French-Indian wars, he had been young and inexperienced. When Major Rogers encountered him to inform him of the new treaty with Britain, Pontiac was a man wise to the ways of negotiation and war.

Pontiac was initially sincere in his approach to the treaty with the British offered to him, but the promises made to his nation were not fulfilled and with the communication continuing to him from French emissaries, he soon grew suspicious of the ultimate intentions of the white man in his territory. He used his great mind and tactical skills with more efficiency against the white man's encroachment than any other chief before or since.

Pontiac confederated all the Indian tribes of the Northwest Territories and directed them to exterminate the white settlers at all cost. His goal was to drive them from the land, from all of their forts and outposts on the Great Lakes, and from the frontier lands that bordered the Ohio River.

Like the other great chief Philip, Pontiac viewed the encroachment of the white settler with jealousy and alarm. He saw in the future the growing possibility that his people would be displaced, destroyed by either war or integration and he was determined to stop the process with any means at his disposal. So adroitly were his plans developed and executed that the commanders of the western forts and outposts had no knowledge that he intended to attack, until the first blows were struck.

During the operations of 1763, Pontiac appointed a commissary and issued bills of credit that were passed among the French inhabitants of the Northwest Territories he defended as his lands. The French General, Montcalm, who came to know Pontiac as a result of the French Indian wars, esteemed Pontiac highly and gave him a uniform which Pontiac wore, even when he was eventually killed.

Early in the summer of 1763, within a fortnight, all of the posts in possession of the English west of Oswego were overthrown and taken by Pontiac, except for the fort at Niagara, Pitt, and Detroit. In the spring of 1764, Colonel Bradstreet with a strong command of soldiers penetrated as far into Pontiac's territory as Detroit. His victory subdued the Indian tribes that had supported Pontiac, and broke the hold Pontiac had over the nations in his command. These tribes sent representatives to ask for pardon and for peace, but still Pontiac refused to bow to defeat.

He went to the country of the Illinois nation. In 1769, a Peoria Indian murdered Pontiac, having been bribed to do so by an English trader for a barrel of rum. Pontiac was murdered at Cahokia, on the east side of the Mississippi, a short distance down river from St. Louis, Missouri.

A great man fell when Pontiac died. He was a warrior who, although feared, was respected for his mind and his military leadership. Some felt at the time that although an enemy, he deserved a better fate.

HOLLOW REVENGE: THE STORY OF THE WILDERNESS BRADY FAMILY

The Brady men were Indian fighters from before the Revolutionary War to the turn of the century. They were renowned frontiersmen and scouts and could always be depended upon to join the ranks of those who were going out into the wilderness to retaliate against Indian aggression.

The warlike exploits of Samuel Brady began in 1775, when he was seventeen years old, and continued throughout most of his life. After fighting as a soldier in the Revolutionary War, he rose to the rank of Captain before he had turned twenty-one years old. After the war, his regiment was detached to the frontier, to guard settlers against Indian hostilities and continued British aggressions.

It was during this period that Samuel lost his father and his younger brother, James, to an Indian attack. The incident made him bitter and created a blind hatred for all tribes and he swore to live only for revenge.

In 1780, nearing the end of the Revolutionary War, General Washington had decided that a region known as Sandusky, which was a hotbed of British and Indian aggression, should be obliterated by military force. Determined that he should know the region prior to beginning a campaign, Washington sent orders to Colonel Broadhead, the commander of the regiment to which Captain Brady belonged, to send out a qualified scout to survey the area, the numbers of enemy, and the positions of their forts. Without hesitation, the man Colonel Broadhead chose for the dangerous mission was Captain Samuel Brady.

Brady selected a few men he felt he could rely on, and dressed as warriors on the warpath they slipped away into the wilderness. It was a desperate mission, but Brady knew how to work the environment. He traveled only by night, carefully concealing his party by day and covering up their tracks. After many days of cautious travel, the small band arrived near the area of Sandusky. Here, the dangers increased when his Chickasaw guides deserted their posts, taking with them the company's provisions.

The situation was now very precarious for they were sure to be discovered and had no stores of ammunition or supplies to fortify their position. Brady reminded his remaining men that they were soldiers, to prime their rifles and to be ready to fight to the death. There was no other alternative, as without provisions they would starve, and if they were captured, they were sure to be tortured. He secreted some of his men in the thick underbrush and then Brady and another soldier forded a shallow river to an island in the middle that was thickly covered in underbrush. They all waited patiently for the day.

Morning found them staring at a celebration of nearly three thousand Indians who had just returned from a successful raid on colonial settlements. They could now count the numbers and locations. When night returned, they decided to head back to report to Colonel Broadband. Brady knew from the celebration witnessed at Sandusky that the Chickasaw guides had not betrayed their presence. The critical goal now was to provide food and shelter for the return trip with only a limited amount of ammunition. Since Brady was the most accomplished frontiersman of the group, the responsibility for food fell on his shoulders. He managed to kill deer and otter in addition to berries and small animals they killed for food.

One day, Brady was tracking a deer when he heard the sound of voices and the neigh of a horse. Seeking cover, he saw a party of Indians come in sight, one of which was on horseback with a white woman behind him and a white child in his arms. The rest of the party were on foot, single file behind the leader, and numbered nine men. Brady decided to wait until the party had passed his hiding spot, then emerge and take down the warrior at the rear of the party. He would steal the gun and ammunition and get away safely.

When the party passed by, Brady was able to see the woman and child clearly. Both had been abused and the child was in the act of being shaken. Brady's plans were immediately altered, but he could not attack outright for lack of ammunition. He had but one shot and a tomahawk.

He quietly stole from his hiding place and moved to a position where they would have to pass him again. When the man on horseback came even with him again, Brady sprang from his hiding place and shot the Indian dead in one shot. In falling, he dragged the woman and child with him. Brady raised his tomahawk, and quickly removed the shot from the dead warrior's ammunition bag. The woman, certain that he was Indian by his dress and appearance would not move, even though he told her to run. He shouted for his men and the other Indians, confused by the ambush, surrendered their weapons to the ground.

Alone, Brady knew it would not take the Indians long to realize that they had him outnumbered. He again explained to the woman that he was a soldier and seizing her, dashed into the forest with the woman and child just as the Indians were beginning to become aware he was alone. The Indians grabbed their muskets and a shower of balls pelted the woods, but did not strike Brady or the woman or child. Although the Indians fired after the trio, they did not attempt to follow them, fearing that an ambush might indeed be waiting. Brady, with his two freed captives, managed to reach Fort McIntosh, an outpost in the wilderness, safely. His men were already there waiting for him. They too were aware of the Indian hunting party, and fearing that Brady may have been captured, had traveled to McIntosh to regroup and wait to hear from him. At first, Brady was angry with them and felt deserted, but he was reminded that they had no ammunition, he was the only one designated to have any, and so he was able to understand their actions.

After leaving the woman and child at the fort, Brady and his men proceeded to Pittsburg, where he was received with honors. There he also found the Chickasaw guides, who having seen the great numbers of Indians present in the Sandusky region, had assumed that all would be lost, and that Brady and his men would be captured and roasted in the enemy's fires.

In another expedition, Brady was sent scouting with some men along the banks of a stream some called Beaver River. Brady had a force of five men. They were following the stream, which had steep banks on either side of thirty feet or more and granite sides, when they spied ahead a party of Indians eating breakfast. Although Brady's men were outnumbered by five to one, he decided that they should attack. They fired and four warriors were killed. Almost immediately, they were fired upon in turn from behind. Two of Brady's men were killed outright. There was nothing left to do but flee.

The men all darted off in different directions, but Brady's escape was cut off by the attack from the rear. He charged the approaching Indians and broke through their ranks by stabbing two of them. Continuing his path, he heard the Indians cheer as they realized he was heading directly to the steep banks of the River with its thirty-foot drops of granite. The River across was twenty-five feet wide and it was impossible for a man to leap from one bank to the other. The Indians felt he was trapped and were ready to approach and claim their victim.

Brady knew the kind of death that awaited him at capture and to die from the drop of the cliff was much quicker and kinder than the fate the Indians had in store for him. But Brady was also a strong man who had spent his entire life in the wilderness. He was quick and he was powerful and as he sped toward the chasm of the River, he strained every muscle for the tremendous leap that would either save him or kill him outright.

When Brady reached the edge of the cliff he sprang without any hesitation and with all his might toward the other bank, striking the opposite ravine with a force that nearly stunned him. He tottered for a moment, landing with an insufficient foothold, then he reached down and grabbed at some bushes, succeeding in drawing himself up on the opposite bank to safety. The Indians were astonished and before they could look about for a means of crossing, Brady had made his escape. Due to their concentration on capturing Brady, the Indians had not given chase to his companions and they were also able to make their escape.

Brady had developed a reputation with the Indian tribes as a man who was a dangerous fighter and enemy. While scouting one day with four companions, Brady came across a recently deserted Indian camp in which a fire was still burning. Nearby was the carcass of a deer, freshly killed and neatly dressed out. From all indications, Brady concluded that they had happened upon a hunting party of no more than six men. He decided that they would follow them and engage them in combat, once they had eaten the kill they left behind.

While sitting around the fire, waiting for the venison steaks, Brady grew uneasy. His intuition was telling him that something was terribly wrong and that they had more than likely been entrapped. The meat could have been poisoned or the Indians had set the camp up on purpose to lure them in.

No sooner had the thought crossed his mind, then the reality of it proved true. He heard the report of fifteen to twenty rifles and his men all were killed. He had escaped the fire and seizing his rifle he dashed for his freedom. But it was not to be.

Brady was surrounded, and accepting his fate he submitted to being bound as a prisoner. He was conveyed back to the village under continual guard and hailed with yells of delight. The man who was their nemesis could now suffer their anger in the fire.

Fearing that his prowess would still allow him to escape, the Indians decided to subject him to the gauntlet before torturing him in the fire. They made the gauntlet severe in order to weaken him. He emerged from the run a mass of bruises, beaten about the head and body. The Indians built the fire and moved him to the stake, but they did not tie him. Instead, they surrounded him so they could attempt to humiliate him by making him fend off their blows.

The etiquette of the stake demands that the victim receive punishment without begging for mercy. Brady was too familiar with Indian culture not to be aware of the Indian viewpoint on the stake and he was determined not to show fear or pain as he knew it would only gratify them that they had caused him to flinch from their blows. He took it all while his brain was formulating a way to escape.

There was a character trait in this that differentiated the Indian brave from the frontiersman: an Indian brave would have considered it cowardice to have considered a way to escape and would have submitted to the torture stoically; a frontiersman like Brady would have considered it cowardice not to look for an escape and never would surrender to torture without actively evaluating a means to escape it. His opportunity was presented in the form of the Chief's wife.

Women and children were allowed to participate in the torture of the stake. They would grab weapons and poke, prod, and club the unfortunate victim. The Chief's wife selected a large club from the weapons pile and with a young child in her arms, dealt Brady a severe blow. His eyes flashed at the prospect of being beaten by a woman who showed no mercy in her eyes. The fact that she carried a child in her arms gave him a means of surprise and escape.

Each member of the circle of Indians that surrounded him had one turn to level a blow at him. As the circle advanced, it came again to the Squaw's turn. She advanced with the child in her arms and her heavy club drawn high to hit him. Brady was unbound, bleeding and bruised but alert. As she drew near, he lunged at her and seized her by the throat. He wrested her child from her arms and cast the child into the hottest portion of the fire. As he had anticipated, the Indians' focus was on saving the child and he dashed through them and into the shelter of the forest. He eluded their pursuit and after several days managed to reach Pittsburg.

Samuel Brady continued as a scout and the legends surrounding his skills continued to grow. His brother James also became an Indian fighter. James was attacked by a group of Indians led by two Indian Chiefs: Bald Eagle, and Corn-Planter, Seneca Indians. They severely wounded him, scalped him and left him for dead. Before he died, he made it to a fort to report the attack and name those who had killed him.

Years later, Samuel Brady, in an attack against the Seneca Indians at a place called Brady's Bend, came across Bald Eagle, the Indian chief who had killed his brother. He shot the Indian chief through the heart and exacted his revenge.

Captain John Brady, father of the two Brady boys, was sent to Seneca territory to exact peace with the Seneca nation. A year after the death of James, on the way to secure provisions for Fort Augusta, he encountered a Seneca warrior who had sworn vengeance against him years before. Captain Brady was ambushed, killed and his scalp taken by the Seneca warrior.

WHEN TWO MAKE ONE

In the fall of 1779, a number of keel-boats under the command of Major Rogers ascended the waters of the Ohio River. At the mouth of a small river called the Licking River, Major Rogers thought he saw three Indians on a sandbar, and a canoe putting out from the Kentucky shore of the river.

Believing that they had not been seen, the white men tied their boats to some trees on the Kentucky side and making a circuit through the woods, completely surrounded the place they thought the Indians would land. But they were mistaken.

As the white men settled in to wait, hundreds of Indians descended on the men with a war whoop, and raising muskets poured a destructive volley into the panic-stricken men. Major Rogers and forty-five of his men were instantly killed. The remaining soldiers attempted to fight their way through the Indian attack and regain their boats, but the effort was futile as the five men left to guard the boats, realizing the circumstances of the attack, cut the last boat loose and made off in the current. The remaining keel-boats were quickly taken by the warriors.

Several men managed to fight their way through the hordes and found shelter in the woods. With night coming on, they traveled safely and ultimately reached Harrodsburg, with several of them severely wounded.

When the men had first burst through the ring of Indians during the battle, they had counted among their number Captain Robert Benham and a soldier named Taylor. Benham fell in the woods after being shot in both thighs with the bones of both legs broken by the impact. The Indians in pursuit of the fleeing men believed him dead and left him as he lay. Once they had passed, he dragged himself to the shelter of a fallen tree with a bushy stand of undergrowth and secreted himself deep within the foliage. The Indians returned to strip the dead, and although he was suffering from shock, thirst and hunger, Benham stayed quietly in his shelter until they were done.

Unable to move his legs, the next day Benham was able to shoot a large raccoon that was descending from a nearby tree. However, he was unable to crawl the short distance to retrieve it. He heard a voice calling in the woods a short distance away and loaded his rifle, lying perfectly quiet, expecting that the Indians had returned upon hearing his gunfire. The voice called again but Benham did not answer. It called a third time, saying, "For God's sake, answer—whoever you are—even if it is an Indian!"

This convinced Benham that the man calling must be one of the Kentuckians and he called out his location. Taylor appeared through the woods and it was immediate evident to Benham that the man had been severely wounded in both his arms. They were dangling useless at his sides. Able to walk but not shoot to capture game, Taylor would have starved just as Benham would have starved if Taylor had not found him. Together, they made a complete man.

Taylor went over to the dead raccoon and kicked it back in Benham's direction. Benham grabbed it, skinned it and cooked it where he lay. The two men filled themselves on the dinner and designed a manner of living that would keep both of them alive.

Benham would load his rifle and kill game that passed by or that was driven by through the efforts of Taylor. Once dead, Taylor would kick the game carcass back to Benham and push the wood needed for fires with his feet. When they needed water, Taylor would take his hat in his mouth and wade into the nearby river, dipping it in until full of water and carrying it back to Benham in this manner. Benham dressed both their wounds.

Living together as one man for several weeks, their wounds healed sufficiently for the two men to begin to move about. They built a rude shelter near the mouth of the Licking River and remained there several more weeks until late November, looking about daily for a boat. On the 27th of November they spied a large flatboat moving slowly down the river toward them. They eagerly began to call to it, but with their strange appearance the men on the boat believed they might be decoys for hostile Indians. They pleaded with the boat, yelling out their story, and stating again and again their need for assistance. Finally, the boat came alongside and with extreme caution, the two men were brought aboard.

Benham and Taylor were conveyed to Louisville where they slowly recovered. Benham required crutches to move about and his movements were limited. He never fully regained the use of his legs, although he was able to eventually gain better mobility. Taylor was severely injured and regained only the partial use of one hand. Benham went on years later to serve through the war against the Northwestern Indians, taking part in the campaigns of Harmer and Wilkinson and serving with "Mad Anthony" Wayne.

THAYENDANEGEA, CAPTAIN JOSEPH BRANT

Thayendanegea, or Captain Joseph Brant, was one of the most renowned warriors of the Six Nations of Indians residing in the state of New York. He was a respected member of the Mohawk tribe. His father was an Onodaga chief, and Thayendanegea, which means "a bundle of sticks, or strength," was born on the banks of the Ohio River in 1742.

His father died shortly thereafter and his mother took the two children, Joseph and a sister, back to the Mohawk Valley. She married a Mohawk warrior, whom the white people called "Barent" and which abbreviated became "Brant."

His sister became the concubine of an English gentleman named Sir William Johnson. Sir William took Joseph and mentored him into Dr. Wheelock's school at Lebanon, in Connecticut, where he was given a white name, "Joseph." It was at Dr. Wheelock's school that Joseph was educated with the purpose of teaching the Christian ministry among his own people.

Sir William employed Joseph as a secretary and agent in public affairs with the Indians, but his missionary labors never extended much beyond the services of an interpreter during this period of his life. He served in this capacity from 1762 to 1765.

When the Revolutionary War approached, Joseph Brant resisted the advice to remain neutral and under the influence of his relationship with Sir William; he took an active part with the British and the Tories. In 1775, he left the Mohawk Valley and went to Canada and from there to England. In England, he became somewhat of a curiosity and celebrity and had free access to the nobility of the time. The Earl of Warwick commissioned the great painter Romney to complete a portrait of Brant. The painting became famous during its time and many copies were made from it.

Throughout the years of the Revolutionary War, from 1775 to 1783, Brant was engaged in predatory attacks on the colonists on the border settlements of New York and Pennsylvania with the Johnsons and the Butlers. Although he held a colonel's commission from the King of England, Brant was generally referred to as Captain Brant.

In 1783, at the conclusion of the war, Brant returned to England to make arrangements for the Mohawk people who had left their ancient country to settle on the Grand River, west of Lake Ontario, in upper Canada. The territory granted them by the government encompassed six miles on either side of the river from its mouth to its source. There, Brant served as head of the Nation until his death.

Joseph Brant was an educated and compassionate man who wanted the best for his people. He translated a part of the New Testament into the Mohawk language and labored during his remaining years after the war for the spiritual and temporal welfare of his people. One of his sons was a British officer on the Niagara frontier during the War of 1812 and a daughter married an English gentleman of Niagara, W.J. Kerr, Esquire, in 1824. Joseph Brant died on the 24th of November in 1807 at the age of sixty-five years.

EYEWITNESS ACCOUNTS: TREATIES, CULTURE & WARS

OBSERVATIONS OF THE AMERICAN INDIANS: A LETTER, 1852

The calm, high-bred dignity of their demeanor, the scientific manner in which they progressively construct the framework of whatever subject they undertake to explain; the sound argument by which they connect as well as support it; and the beautiful wild flowers of eloquence with which, as they proceed, they adorn every moral architecture they are constructing, form altogether an exhibition of grave interest; and yet it is not astonishing to reflect that the orators in councils, whose lips and gums are, while they are speaking, black from the wild berries on which they have been subsisting—who have never heard of education, never seen a town—but who, born in the secluded recesses of an interminable forest, have spent their lives in either following zigzaggedly the game on which they subsist through a labyrinth of trees, or in paddling their canoes across lakes, and among a congregation of such islands as I have described. They hear more distinctly, see farther, smell clearer, can bear more fatigue, can subsist on less food, and have altogether fewer wants than their white brethren; and yet we consider the red Indians of America as "outside barbarians."

—Sir F.B. Head, Gleason's Pictorial Drawing Room Companion, Vol. II, 1852

LETTER RELATED TO INDIAN WARS & SETTLEMENT QUESTIONS

Extract of a letter, dated Wilkes, Georgia, November, 1791
Written by Morrice Kain

I shall now inform you of our Indian affairs. Our commissioners from the best account I can learn, met at the place appointed to cut the line, and the day appointed Colonel M'Gillivary did not come in, neither will the savages be ruled by him; and we learn at the last talk he had with them, they told him that he had sold their lands, and that he received the money, or part thereof, therefore they would not agree to the treaty, and one of the Indians swore that all they had got was a shirt each one, and raised into such a passion, that he threw off his shirt into the fire that was most convenient to him, and from what I am told the rest followed the same example, and so committed the whole to the flames. This conduct exasperated M'Gillivary, which caused him to say they might go to the Devil their own way—and from what I can understand he is gone to reside in the Spanish dominions, a great distance from the Creeks—what the event hereafter may be is not known – however, there is a gentleman of the name of Boles, who hath lately arrived from England, with eight or ten thousand pounds worth of goods, came up St. Mary's River, and is now among the Creeks; he with his insinuating talk is informing them of the great man over the water—bids them hold their lands and not to give up the three frontier counties, to wit, Franklin, Green, and Washington; and from what I can learn they are much taken with his sophistry and some of the friendly Indians hath warned Captain Philips and some more to move off.

Morris Kain

ADDRESS OF
GOVERNOR TELFAIR

New York, December 30, 1792, Extract from the Address of Governor Telfair, to the Legislature of Georgia

"During the two last years, two whites have been killed by the Creek Indians, and two Creek Indians by the whites; although I have every reason to assure you that the Creeks at large are well disposed towards the people of this State, I cannot at this period give you assurances of perfect amity, as late information mentions some threats, of what they term "retaliation" for the last Indians killed—I still flatter myself, that they will not proceed to violence.

"In virtue of a clause of the appropriation Act, passed the 10th December, 1790, in these words, 'The sum of three hundred pounds for running the Indian temporary line,' I appointed three persons who proceeded to the Rock Landing, and after remaining there some time reported that after being at the place fifteen days from the first of October, no commission from the Creeks had appeared, nor was there any prospect of their coming forward; at the same time, they make mention of a Mr. Hetch, whom the Secretary of War, in a communication of July 13th, 1791, thus announces, 'a military officer of the United States is now probably with Mr. M'Gillivary to urge the delivery of the prisoners, and the making of what he terms the boundaries, next October,'—and the said Commissioners state, that Mr. Hetch did on the 9th ultimo, call on them, who being interrogated on the objects of his mission, avoided to give any satisfactory answer and took his departure next morning for Philadelphia. Upon making a serious review of the whole information, I was of opinion it was necessary and expedient to remand the Commissioners, which was accordingly done. The measures taken on the part of the State for the liberation of prisoners and the restoration of property have not as yet had the desired effect.

"The provident appropriation above referred to, and the tenor thereof, removed every difficulty on the part of the executive with respect to the greatest political concern of the republic; I mean, her territorial right; which subject claims some remarks by way of elucidation.

"When the scope and spirit of treaties are contemplated, it cannot be doubted, that the powers of peace and war are wisely delegated by the Federal Constitution and that the several State governments are bound to support and maintain the exercise of these powers, and in the event of war, to execute such military orders as the President of the United States may deem necessary for the common safety; not withstanding, when these powers of the United States are taken into view, together with those vested in the several States; particularly that of repelling sudden invasions; a distinction must obtain between treaties with nations recognized and Indian tribes within the limits of any State. These animadversions lead to a discussion of the 5th article of the treaty held at New York, viz.

'The United States solemnly guarantee to the Creek Nation all their lands within the limits of the United States to the westward and southward of the described boundaries;'

"By this clause, as well as others in the said treaty, it would appear, as if the United States had in contemplation to place the Creek Indians in the same point of view with nations in civilization, and to secure to them the exclusive right of soil (saving only the consent of the United States)—this measure, if once yielded, would doubtless subvert every future claim of this State to her territory; and might it not even extend to an incompatibility with national policy? For when tribes of Indians can be recognized as possessing the full exercise of territorial right, may they not make sale to foreign powers or individuals, and be charged only with having committed a breach of treaty?

"The regulation of commerce with the Indian tribes is one of those powers expressly delegated, and so far as the act to regulate trade with the Indian tribes passed the 22nd of July, 1790, has for its basis, amity and commerce, the State is doubtless bound thereby; although, the government thereof remains uninformed with respect to the appointment of a superintendent to grant licenses 'to any proper persons.' And here it may be proper to observe, that trade and intercourse with Indian tribes have at all times been considered the great ties by which amity and friendship are secured; and that whatever nation may be in possession of their trade, it will consequently have an influence proportioned to the estimation in which the savages hold their supplies. On recurring to the said act, I have to make some comments on the 4th section thereof, which is, 'And be it enacted and declared that no sale of lands made by any Indians or any nation or tribe of Indians, within the United States, shall be valid to any person or persons, or to any State, whether having the right of pre-emption to such lands or not, unless the same shall be made, and duly executed at some public treaty, held under the authority of the United States.'

"This clause is doubtless an extension beyond the line of commerce, and any of the States having the right of pre-emption, either are or ought to be in the full exercise of the extinguishment of Indian claims; and it is incontrovertible that the consent of a State is necessary to establish a right to any part of its territory;—the cession made by the State of North Carolina of the 25th day of February, 1790, and accepted by the United States on the 2nd of April, 1790, is both proof and precedent thereof.

"I trust, gentlemen, that on the act and Treaty now in question, you will enter into a minute discussion of such part or parts of each, as you conceive do militate with retained rights, and make such dispositions and arrangements of unappropriated territory belonging to this State, as may be most conducive to the interest and dignity of the same."

Governor Telfair

ON ALEXANDER M'GILLIVRAY

Statement on the character of Alexander M'Gillivray, Chief of the Creek Indians as it appeared in the Charleston City Gazette, recorded 1792, original date of publication unknown.

"As there are various accounts respecting Mr. M'Gillivray, the famous Chief of the Creek Indians, the following short sketch may be depended on, it being related by one of his old schoolfellows: About the year 1749, Alexander M'Gillivray, then a youth of ten years of age, was sent by his father from the Creek nation to this city and committed to the care of Mr. Farquhar M'Gillivray, a relation of his father, by whom he was placed under the tuition of Mr. George Sheed, who was then, and now is, an eminent English master, having acted in that capacity upwards of forty years in this city; with great reputation.

"He was taught the Latin language by Mr. William Henderson, one of the masters of the free school, and who was lately one of the Critical Reviewers in London. At the age of 17, M'Gillivray was sent to Savannah, and placed in the counting-house of General Elbert—he was afterwards some time in the house of Messr's Alexander Ingles and Co.

"During his apprenticeship, he was so fond of study, that he devoted much more of his time to reading of history than to the acquisition of mercantile knowledge. On this representation being made to his father, he was sent for to the Creek nation; since which, he has been raised to his present exalted station, his countrymen, the Creeks, having chosen him their King; and his Catholic Majesty having, it is said, promoted him to the rank of a Brigadier-General in his service. His letters, which have at different times been made public, plainly evince the strength of his understanding; and his general character, as a man of undaunted courage and unblemished integrity, is very generally agreed on by such as have had the pleasure of his acquaintance."

REPORT ON A BATTLE

Winchester, December 4, 1792, Report On A Battle
The following article appeared in the American Apollo newspaper.

Tuesday afternoon arrived here from Fort Washington, Lieutenant Stevenson, of the Virginia battalion of levies. He was in the unfortunate action with the Indians on the 4th ult. and has favored us with the following particulars, viz. That the number killed on our side amounts to 637, including officers—that Majors Brown, Clark and Gaither, Lieutenant Hopper, Quarter-Masters, Ward, Reynolds and Semple, are not among the slain as formerly stated; but that Ensigns Wilson and Reeves, not mentioned before, lost their lives in the unhappy conflict—that Colonel Gibson's wounds, it is thought, will prove mortal—that Colonel Darke is but slightly wounded—that Captain Darke, a most promising youth, received a musket shot in his face, which fractured a jaw and rendered him speechless, but that he is still alive—that the Kentucky militia, which were to march with General Scott did not go; General St. Clair having signified to that officer, that the Fort had been amply supplied with provisions, and every other requisite from Head-Quarters—that Major Hamtramack, of the 1st United States Regiment is put under arrest for some supposed misconduct of the day of action—that he had information of the defeat, and was detached, but declined giving the necessary succor to the retreat—that the enemy's loss is conjectured to be between one and two hundred—number of our troops engaged 1400—number of the enemy supposed to be between two and three thousand.

Major Hamtramack was tried and honorably acquitted of the charges.

286

LETTER OF LIEUTENANT JEFFERS

Copy of a letter dated 16th of December, 1791, from a Lieutenant Jeffers, at Fort Franklin, in Venango, the Northwestern part of Pennsylvania. By express to the commanding officer at Pittsburgh, or Major I. Irwin, of the militia.

Sir:

I have this moment received authentic accounts from the Cornplanter, that an attack on this garrison will almost immediately take place; for the Indians from below declare that they are determined to reduce this place, shake the Cornplanter by the head, and sweep the river from end to end.

You are most earnestly requested, and if I have any authority, positively ordered, to send me, without loss of time, one subaltern and 30 men as a reinforcement, together with my men who have been left sick at Fort Pitt. Under this convoy, send me provisions to make five months rations for 70 men. This news is not fictitious; nor this letter to be trifled with. I have written to the minister of war; but his orders will come too late.

I am, & c.,
J Jeffers

Polybius, Letter I

Appearing in the Apollo newspaper, 1792, volume I, a series of letters written by Polybius entitled, "Observations on the Western Territory and the Indian War; in a series of letters to a friend."

Letter I

Dear Sir,

To such a friend as you I am neither accustomed nor inclined to give a denial, however inadequate I may be to the task you have assigned me; and shall therefore, without any ceremony, present you with such information as I have had opportunity to collect, respecting the country which is the seat of the present war with the Indians; the means by which it has hitherto been conducted, and the events which have marked its progress; interspersed with such reflections as have arisen in my own mind, or which have been suggested by those who are better acquainted with the subject.

Before the commencement of the late war with Britain, there was a controversy between the government of Virginia and the Indians on its western frontier. As the settlement of Kentucky began about that time, and was carried on during the whole course of the war, the savages continually molested those settlers. Several expeditions were undertaken against the nations which lie N.W. of the Ohio; most of which were attended with success; and after the peace, efforts were made to form treaties with them.

The treaties of fort Stanwix, in 1784, of fort M'Intosh, in 1785, and of the Great Miami, in 1786, are, I conceive, the basis on which our claim to any lands N.W. of the Ohio is founded. The first was made with the Six Nations, the second with the tribes of Wyandot, Delaware, Chippewa, and Ottawa; the third with the Shawanese. These treaties are printed in the first volume of the Laws of the United States. There was also a treaty at Muskingum in 1789, where delegates from the aforesaid nations, together with some from the Munsees, Powtawatamies and Sauks ratified the treaty held at fort M'Intosh. This treaty of Muskingum is not printed with the others, for what reason I know not.

According to these treaties, the boundary line between us and them, is thus described (as stated in the report of Secretary Jefferson to Congress, November 8, 1791, Part II, Volume I). "Beginning at the mouth of the Cayahoga (which falls into the southernmost part of Lake Erie) and running up the river, to the portage, between that and the Tuscarora (or N.E.) branch of the Muskingum; then down the said branch to the forks, at the crossing place above Fort Lawrence; then westwardly toward the portage of the Great Miami, to the fork of that river, next below the old fort, which was taken by the French in 1752; thence due west to the River De la Panse (a branch of the Wabash) and down that river to the Wabash River. So far the line is precisely defined, and the whole country cleared of the claims of those Indians. The tract comprehended within the above described line, the Wabash, the Ohio and the western limits of Pennsylvania, contains about 55,000 square miles. How far on the western side of the Wabash, the southern boundary of the Indians has been defined, we know not. It is only understood in general, that their title to the lower country, between that river and the Illinois, was formerly extinguished by the French, while in their possession."

To obtain a just idea of these limits, it is best to consult a map of the Western Country. Of these, several have been published within a few years past. One by Hutchins, the late geographer of the United States. Another by M'Murray, his assistant, and a third by Osgood Carleton. But if you cannot command either of these large ones, you may get a tolerable idea of the matter, from the map of the northern States, in Morse's Geography. I will therefore suppose that you have with your pencil drawn this line of partition; all to the southward of it, and between it and the Ohio is the land, to which in the present Court language, "the Indian title is *extinguished*," and all to the northward of this line, and between it and the lakes, is the land, which, to use the same style, "is *allotted* to the Indians, for their hunting ground," and residence.

You will observe in the maps three rivers which bear the name of Miami: Two of these, the great and little Miami, are branches of the Ohio, and fall into it on its N.W. side. Another has its head near the head of the Wabash, and runs on a N.E. course into the west end of lake Erie. About the heads of the two rivers, viz. the Wabash and the Miami of the lake (which is sometimes spelt Maumee) are several tribes of Indians, who have not entered into any treaty with the United States; but have always been inclined to hostility with the settlers on the Ohio, especially with the Kentuckians, to whom they have given the name of the long knife. These Indians, of the Wabash and Maumee rivers, appear to have been the direct object of the expeditions, which have been planned and attempted to be carried into execution within the two last years.

But as these tribes are connected with others, to the northward and westward, and have drawn them into their confederacy; it is necessary that we should take a more general view of the several nations in the N.W. quarter of the territory ceded to the United States by Great Britain. This shall be the subject of my next. In the mean time, Adieu.

Polybius

1792 ARTICLE, KNOXVILLE PAPER

Article in a Knoxville paper, November 19, 1792.

About the 10th inst. A company, going through the wilderness to Cumberland, was met on the road by a party of Indians. Upon first fight the men (being seven in number) rode off with the utmost speed and left the women (four in number) who were so terrified that they were unable to proceed. The Indians came up, shook hands with them, and told them they should not be hurt, made a fire for them, and caught a stud horse that one of the company had jumped from, which they tied to a tree. They then went after a small boy who was attempting to make off, and brought him back to the women. Four of the company did not stop until they reached the settlement—the other three returned to the women after some time.

(The above extract is taken from a Gazette, printed at Knoxville, on the Helstein, in the territory of the United States south of the Ohio; and we have the pleasure in hearing that the women, who had been deserted by their fellow travelers, were indebted for this remarkable proof of friendly attention to a hunting party of Cherokees; the nation with whom Governor Blount made a treaty last summer. —Appeared with the article in the *American Apollo* newspaper, edition no. 5, part II, volume I, 1792.)

POLYBIUS, LETTER II

The American Apollo, no.6, Part II, volume I, Observations on the Western Territory and the Indian War; in a series of letters to a friend by Polybius.

Letter II.

Dear Sir,

It has been a very common thing among Americans to speak of the Indians with indignation and contempt. They have been represented as the very dregs and offscouring of mankind, as governed only by the most malignant passions, and deserving no treatment from civilized people, but absolute extermination. This is the language of one class of men among us. Another class have spoken of them with pity, as the offspring of the same common progenitors with ourselves, bearing the image of the deity and capable of being recovered to a rational and refined life: The grand obstacle to which, has been their wandering mode of living, and their total destitution of, and aversion to, the use of letters and writing. That these obstacles exist, and that the attempts to remove them have proved insurmountable, or at least, ineffectual, must be acknowledged. That they either will not endure civilization or that when civilized they are degraded in the esteem of their brethren of the desert, and treated by their brethren as an inferior rank of the human species, cannot be denied. But not withstanding all that has been said against them, I must believe, because there is the most incontestable evidence, that in their natural state, they are possessed of virtues which do honor to human nature. And I as firmly believe that much of the degeneracy which has appeared among them has been excited and provoked by the vices of their civilized brethren.

What I have said is true of the natives in general, but I have more particular reference to the western Indians, whom I consider as a race of men, superior to the tribes once inhabiting our eastern shores, and I believe the eastern Indians themselves considered them in the same light. The name of a Mohawk was always formidable to the natives of our maritime parts.

My idea of these people is not taken from any second-hand writers, but from those who have been personally conversant among them. In a pamphlet printed at Philadelphia in 1784, written by John Filson and certified as authentic by Daniel Boon, Levi Todd and James Harrod, the first and principal settlers of Kentucky, we have the character of the western Indians thus drawn:

"They are not so ignorant as some suppose them, but are a very understanding people, quick of apprehension, sudden in execution, subtle in business, exquisite in invention, and industrious in action. They are of a very gentle and amiable disposition to those they think their friends, but as implacable in their enmity, their revenge being only completed in the entire destruction of their enemies. Among them, all men are equal, personal qualities being most esteemed. No distinction of birth, no rank renders any man capable of doing prejudice to the rights of private persons; and there is no preeminence for merit which begets pride, and which makes others too sensible of their own inferiority. Though there is perhaps less delicacy of sentiment in the Indians than among us, there is, however, abundantly more probity, with infinitely less ceremony or equivocal compliment. Their public conferences show them to be men of genius, and they have in a high degree the talent of natural eloquence."

Captain Jonathan Carver, who visited them in 1766 and 1767 and was intimately conversant among the tribes of Ottagaumie, Chippewa, Winnebago and Saukie, speaks of them in this manner.

"That the Indians are of a cruel, revengeful and inexorable disposition and receive a diabolical pleasure from the tortures they inflict on their prisoners, I readily grant; but let us look on the reverse of this terrifying picture, and we shall see them sociable and humane to those whom they consider as their friends, and even to their adopted enemies, ready to partake with them of the last morsel and to risk their lives in their defense.

"Accustomed from their youth to innumerable hardships, they soon become superior to a sense of danger or the dread of death, and their fortitude, implanted by nature and nurtured by example, by precept, and accident, never experiences a moment's allay.

"In their public characters, as forming part of a community, they possess an attachment for that band to which they belong, unknown to the inhabitants of any other country. They combine as if they were actuated only by *one soul,* against the enemies of their nation, and banish from their minds every consideration opposed to this.

"They consult without unnecessary opposition, or without giving way to the excitements of envy or ambition, on the measures necessary to be pursued for the destruction of those who have drawn on themselves their displeasure. No selfish views ever influence their advice or obstruct their consultation. Nor is it in the power of bribes or threats to diminish the love they bear their country.

The honor of their tribe and the welfare of their nation is the first and most predominant emotion of their hearts; and from hence proceed in great measure all their virtues and their vices. Actuated by this, they brave every danger, endure the most exquisite torments, and expire triumphing in their fortitude, not as a personal qualification but as a national characteristic.

"From thence also flow that insatiable revenge toward those with whom they are at war, and all the consequent horrors that disgrace their name. Their uncultivated mind, being incapable of judging of the propriety of an action in opposition to their passions, which are totally insensible to the control of reason or humanity, they know not how to keep their fury within any bounds, and consequently, that courage and resolution which would otherwise do them honor, degenerates into a savage ferocity."

Such, my friend, is the general character of the Indians who are now in hostility with the United States.

With respect to the numbers of these hostile tribes, I have no other means of ascertaining them than what are given in the abovementioned pamphlet of Filson. He tells us the names of nineteen tribes of Indians N.W. of Ohio, and within the limits of the United States. He estimates the number of each tribe, on an average, at seven hundred, of whom one fourth part are warriors. Carver has given us the names of five other tribes within the same limits. Deduct from the whole the tribes who have actually made treaties with us, exclusive of the six nations, and we may be certain of sixteen hostile tribes containing eleven thousand, two hundred persons, of whom two thousand and eight hundred are warriors.

We may also reckon some tribes northward of the Lakes, and westward of the Mississippi as joined the confederacy. This will augment the number, but to what extent I know not. You may say, perhaps, what are three thousand Indian warriors to the whole military force of the United States? I will answer you in the words of one of their orators in a conference lately held at Newtown in Pennsylvania.

It is said the United States are so powerful, that they could rise and destroy all the Indians at once. But remember, though you may kill some wolves, and frighten away others, yet you cannot destroy them all. The little tomahawk, with which the Indians fight, cost but little; but the Great Hatchet of the United States cost a great deal.

Polybius

It is said that the transportation only of every ton weight, to the Ohio country, costs the United States twenty guineas.

George Washington Requests a Report on Indian Affairs

Letter From President George Washington Requesting a Report on War

United States, January 16, 1792
Sir,

As the circumstances which have engaged the United States in the present Indian war may, some of them, be out of the public recollection, and others, perhaps, be unknown, it may appear advisable that you prepare and publish, from authentic documents, a statement of those circumstances, as well as of the measures which have been taken, from time to time, for the re-establishment of peace and friendship.

When the community are called upon for considerable exertions to relieve a part which is suffering under the hand of an enemy, it is desirable to manifest that due pains have been taken by those instructed with the administration of their affairs, to avoid the evil.

George Washington

Secretary of War Report on Indian Affairs, to 1792

Report of the Secretary at War on the Causes of Hostilities with the Indian Tribes

The Secretary for the Department of War

A Report: The causes of the existing hostilities between the United States and certain tribes of Indians, northwest of the Ohio, stated and explained from official and authentic documents, and published in obedience to the orders of the President of the United States.

A Recurrence to the journals of the United States in Congress assembled, of the early stages of the late war, will evince the public solicitude to preserve peace with the Indian tribes, and to prevent their engaging in a contest in which they were no wise interested.

But although partial treaties or conventions were formed with some of the northern or western tribes, in the years 1775 and 1776, yet those treaties were too feeble to resist the powerful impulses of a contrary nature, arising from a combination of circumstances at that time; and accordingly all the various Indian nations (the Oneidas, Tuscaroras and a few individuals of the Delawares excepted) lying on our frontiers, from Georgia to Canada, armed against us.

It is yet too recent to have been forgotten, that great numbers of inoffensive men, women and children, fell a sacrifice to the barbarous warfare practiced by the Indians, and many others were dragged into a deplorable captivity.

Not withstanding that these aggressions were entirely unprovoked, yet as soon as the war ceased with Great Britain, the United States, instead of indulging any resentment against the Indian nations, sought only how to establish a liberal peace, with all the tribes throughout their limits.

Early measures were accordingly taken for this purpose. A treaty was held, and a peace concluded in 1784, with the hostile part of the northern Indians, or Six Nations, at Fort Stanwix.

In January, 1785, another treaty was formed with part of the western tribes, of Fort M'Intosh, on the Ohio; to wit, with the Wyandots, Delawares, Ottawas and Chippewas.

During the same year, treaties were formed at Hopewell, on the Keowee, with all the powerful tribes of the South, excepting the Creeks to wit, the Cherokees, the Choctaws and Chicasaws. In January 1786, a treaty was formed with the Shawanese, at the confluence of the great Miami with the Ohio.

It was not long before certain turbulent and malignant characters residing among some of the northern and western tribes, which had formed the treaties of Fort Stanwix and Fort M'Intosh excited uneasiness and complaints against those treaties. In consequence of representations upon this subject on the 5th of October, 1787, Congress directed "That a general treaty should be held with the tribes of Indians within the limits of the United States, inhabiting the country northwest of the Ohio, and about Lake Erie, as soon after the first of April next, as conveniently might be, and at such place and at such particular time, as the Governor of the Western territory should appoint, for the purpose of knowing the causes of uneasiness among the said tribes, and hearing their complaints; of regulating trade, and amicably settling all affairs concerning lands and boundaries between them and the United States.

On the 2nd day of July, 1788, Congress appointed "the sum of 20,000 dollars, in addition to 14,000 dollars before appropriated, for defraying the expenses of the treaties which had been ordered, or which might be ordered to be held in the present year, with the several Indian tribes in the northern department, and for extinguishing the Indian claims; the whole of the said 20,000 dollars, together with 6,000 dollars of the said 14,000 dollars to be applied solely to the purpose of extinguishing the Indian claims to the lands they had already ceded to the United States, by obtaining regular conveyance for the same, and for extending a purchase beyond the limits therefore fixed by treaty, but that no part of the said sums should be applied for any purpose other than those above mentioned."

Accordingly, new treaties were held at Fort Harmar, the latter part of the year 1788, and concluded on the 9th day of January, 1789, with a representation of all the Six or Northern nations, the Mohawk's excepted; and with a representation of the following tribes, to wit: The Wyandots, the Delawares, Ottawas, Chippewas, Pattiwatamas, and Sauks. By these treaties, nearly the same boundaries were recognized and established by a principle of purchase, as had been stipulated by the former treaties of Fort Stanwix and Fort M'Intosh.

Thus careful and attentive was the government of the United States to settle a boundary with the Indians on the basis of fair treaty, to obviate the dissatisfaction which had been excited, and to establish its claim to the lands relinquished on the principle of equitable purchase.

It does not appear that the right of the northern and western Indians, who formed the several before mentioned treaties to the lands thereby relinquished to the United States, has been questioned by any other tribes; nor does it appear that the present war has been occasioned by any dispute relative to the boundaries established by the said treaties.

But on the contrary, it appears that the unprovoked aggressions of the Miami and Wabash Indians, upon Kentucky and other parts of the frontiers, together with their associates, a banditti formed of Shawanese and outcast Cherokees, amounting in all, to about one thousand two hundred men, are solely the causes of the war. Hence it is proper that their conduct should be more particularly adverted to.

In the year 1784, when messages were sent to the Wyandots and Delawares, inviting them to meet the commissioners, first at Cayahoga, and afterwards at fort M'Intosh, their neighbors, the Miami Indians, were also included in the said invitation; but did not attend.

In the year 1785, these invitations were repeated; but the messengers upon their arrival at the Miami village, had their horses stolen, were otherwise treated with insolence, and prevented fulfilling their mission.

In the years 1787 and 1788, new endeavors were used to bring those Indians to treaty; they were urged to be present at the treaty appointed to be held at Fort Harmar; but these endeavors proved as fruitless as all the former.

At a council of the tribes, convened in 1788 at the Miami River, the Miami and Wabash Indians were pressed to repair to the treaty with great earnestness by the chiefs of the Wyandots and Delawares; the Wyandot chiefs particularly, presented them with a large belt of wampum, holding one end of it themselves, and offering the other to the hostile Indians, which was refused. The Wyandots then laid it on the shoulders of a principal chief, recommending him to be at peace with the Americans; but without making any answer, he leaned himself and let it fall to the ground; this so displeased the Wyandots that they immediately left the council house.

In the meantime, the frontier settlements were disquieted by frequent depredations and murders, and the complaints of their inhabitants (as might be expected) of the pacific forbearance of the government, were loud, repeated, and distressing—their call for protection incessant—and at length, they appeared determined by their own efforts to endeavor to retaliate the injuries they were continually receiving, and which had become intolerable.

In this state of things, it was indispensable for the government to make some decisive exertion for the peace and security of the frontier.

But notwithstanding the ill success of former experiments, and the invincible spirit of animosity which had appeared in certain tribes and which was of a nature to justify a persuasion that no impression could be made upon them by pacific expedients, it was still deemed advisable to make one more essay.

Accordingly, in April, 1790, Anthony Gamelin, an inhabitant of Post Vincennes, and a man of good character, was dispatched to all tribes and villages of the Wabash River, and to the Indians of the Miami village, with a message, purporting, that the United States were desirous of establishing a general peace with all the neighboring tribes of Indians, and of treating them in all respects with perfect humanity and kindness, and at the same time warning them to abstain from further depredation.

The Indians in some of the villages on the lower part of the Wabash appeared to listen to him, others manifested a different disposition, others confessed their inability to restrain their young warriors, and all referred the messenger to the Indians at the Miami village. At this village, some appeared well disposed, but the chiefs of the Shawanese returned the messages and belts, informing the messenger however, that they would, after consultation, within thirty nights, send an answer to Post Vincennes. The promised answer was never received. While the messenger was at the Miami village, two Negroes were brought in from our settlements as prisoners; and upon his return to L'Anguille, a chief informed him that a party of 70 warriors, from the more distant Indians had arrived, and were gone against the settlements.

In three days after his departure from the Miami village, a prisoner was there burnt to death. Similar cruelties were exercised at the Ouittanon towns, about the same time; and in the course of three months immediately after the last mentioned invitation, upwards of one hundred persons were killed, wounded, and taken prisoners upon the Ohio and in the district of Kentucky.

It is to be remarked, that previously to the last invitation, the people of Kentucky, who in consequence of their injuries were meditating a blow against the hostile Indians (as before intimated) were restrained by the President of the United States from crossing the Ohio until the effect of the friendly overture intended to be made should be known.

It is also to be observed, that the Wyandots and Delawares, after having frequently and fruitlessly endeavored to influence the Miami and Wabash Indians to peace, upon mature conviction, finally declared that force only could effect the object.

As an evidence that the conduct of the hostile Indians has been occasioned by other motives than a claim relative to boundaries, it is to be observed that their depredations have been principally upon the district of Kentucky, and the counties of Virginia, lying along the south side of the Ohio, a country to which they have no claim.

It appears, by respectable evidence, that from the year 1783, until the month of October 1790, the time the United States commenced offensive operations against the said Indians, that on the Ohio and the frontiers on the south side thereof, they killed, wounded and took prisoners about 1500 men, women and children, besides carrying off upwards of 2000 horses and other property to the amount of fifty thousand dollars.

The particulars of the barbarities exercised upon many of the prisoners, of different ages and sexes, although supported by indisputable evidence, are of too shocking a nature to be presented to the public. It is sufficient upon this head to observe, that the tomahawk and the scalping knife have been the mildest instruments of death. In some cases torture by fire, and other execrable means have been used.

But the outrages which were committed upon the frontier inhabitants were not the only injuries that were sustained; repeated attacks upon detachments of troops of the United States, were at different times made. The following, from its peculiar enormity, deserves recital.

In April, 1790, Major Doughty was ordered to the friendly Chickasaws on public business. He performed this duty in a boat, having with him Ensign Sedam and a party of 15 men. While ascending the Tennessee River, he was met by a party of 40 Indians in four canoes, consisting principally of the aforesaid banditti of Shawanese and Cherokees. They approached under a white flag, the well known emblem of peace. They came on board the Major's boat, received his presents, continued with him one hour, and then departed in a most friendly manner. But, they had scarcely cleared his oars, before they poured in a fire upon his crew, which was returned as soon as circumstances would permit, and a most unequal combat was sustained for several hours, when they abandoned their design, but not until they had killed and wounded eleven out of fifteen of the boat's crew. This perfidious conduct in any age would have demanded exemplary punishment.

All overtures of peace failing and the depredations still continuing, an attempt at coercion became indispensable. Accordingly, the expedition under Brigadier General Harmar, in the month of October, 1790, was directed. The event is known.

After this expedition, the Governor of the Western Territory, in order that nothing might be omitted, to effect a peace without further conflict, did on his arrival at Fort Harmar, in December 1790, send through the Wyandots and Delawares conciliatory messages to the Miamis, but still without effect.

The Cornplanter, a war Chief of the Senekas and other Indians of the same tribe, being in Philadelphia in the month of February 1791, were engaged to undertake to impress the hostile Indians with the consequences of their persisting in their hostilities, and also of the justice and moderation of the United States.

In pursuance of this design, Colonel Proctor, on the fourteenth of March, was sent to the Cornplanter to hasten his departure and to accompany him to the Miami village—and messages were sent to the Indians declaratory of the pacific sentiments of the United States, towards them. But both Colonel Proctor and the Cornplanter, although zealously desirous of executing their mission, encountered difficulties of a particular nature, which were insurmountable, and prevented the execution of their order.

Major General St. Clair, in the month of April, sent messages from Fort Harmar to the Delawares, expressive of the pacific designs of the United States, to the Indian tribes.

A treaty was held at the Painted-Post by Colonel Pickering, in June, 1791, with a part of the Six Nations, at which the humane intentions of the General Government towards them particularly, and the Indian tribes in general, were fully explained.

Captain Hendricks, a respectable Indian, residing with the Oneidas, appearing zealously disposed to attempt convincing the hostile Indians of their mistaken conduct, was accordingly sent for that purpose, but was frustrated by unforeseen obstacles in his laudable attempts.

The different measures which have been recited must evince, that notwithstanding the highly culpable conduct of the Indians in question, the government of the United States, uninfluenced by the resentment or any false principles which might arise from a consciousness of superiority, adopted every proper expedient to terminate the Indian hostilities, without having recourse to the last extremity; and after being compelled to resort to it, has still kept steadily in view the re-establishment of peace as its primary and sole object.

Were it necessary to add proof of the pacific and humane disposition of the general government towards the Indian tribes, the treaties with the Creeks, and with the Cherokees might be cited as demonstrative of its moderation and liberality.

The present partial Indian war is a remnant of the late general war continued by a number of separate banditti, who, by the incessant practice of fifteen years, seem to have formed inveterate and incurable habits of enmity against the frontier inhabitants of the United States.

To obtain protection against lawless violence was the main object of the present government. It is, indeed, a main object of all governments. A frontier citizen possesses as strong claims to protection as any other citizen. The frontiers are the vulnerable parts of every country; and the obligation of the government of the United States, to afford the requisite protection; cannot be less sacred in reference to the inhabitants of their Western, than to those of their Atlantic, frontiers.

It will appear from a candid review of this subject, that the General Government could no longer abstain from attempting to punish the hostile Indians.

The ill success of the attempts for this purpose, is entirely unconnected with the justice or policy of the measure. A perseverance in exertions to make the refractory Indians at least sensible, that they cannot continue their enormous outrages with impunity, appears to be as indispensable, in the existing posture of things as it will be advisable, whenever they shall manifest symptoms of a more amicable disposition, to convince them, by decisive proofs, that nothing is so much desired by the United States as to be at liberty to treat them with kindness and beneficence.

H. Knox, Secretary at War
War Department, January 26, 1792
The American Apollo, no.7, Part II, volume I,

POLYBIUS, LETTER III

Observations on the Western Territory and the Indian War; in a series of letters to a friend by Polybius

Letter III.

Dear Sir,

The late publication of the Secretary of War Department, professes to give an account of the causes of the present war, and as it comes from authority, it deserves to be treated with respect; but you will allow me to use the freedom of an American citizen in remarking on some parts of it; and perhaps what I originally intended to say to you on the subject, may be conveyed on the form of remarks in this production as well as in any form whatever.

After mentioning the treaties held with the Indians in the years 1784, 1785, and 1786, the Secretary tells us that "certain turbulent and malignant characters, residing among some of the northern and western tribes, excited complaints and uneasiness *against those treaties*." In a subsequent paragraph he says, that "the government of the United States had been careful and attentive to obviate the dissatisfaction which had been excited, and to establish its claim to the lands relinquished, on the principle of *equitable* purchase," and this purchase was made with 26,000 dollars. Afterward he says, "it does not appear that the present war has been occasioned by any dispute relatively to the *boundaries* established by the said treaties." On those passages I would remark:

1. That I have no doubt the Congress and their commissioners, who framed those treaties, acted honorably and uprightly according to their ideas of propriety.

2. There are certain difficulties attending purchases made of the Indians, which have frequently occurred on other similar occasions; such as these. To

know when a tribe is fully and fairly represented at a treaty. Whether that tribe has an exclusive right to the tract of country which they assume to cede. To make an adequate compensation for the land purchased, and to know whether that compensation be equitably divided among those who have a right to it. Whether any of these difficulties exist in regard to these treaties, may be a proper subject of inquiry.

3. Supposing none of them to exist, yet there is one principle on which these treaties were grounded, on our part, which may, with the greatest probability, be supposed to have "excited dissatisfaction" among the Indians, and which no purchase money may have been able to remove. This principle is that of SOVEREIGNTY. If you will look into the treaties of Stanwix, M'Intosh and Miami, you will see the prominent features of it.

In that of 1784, with the Six Nations, the word itself does not actually appear, but you will find the language to be "The United States *give* peace to the Six Nations and receive them into their protection." In that of 1785, with the Wyandots, &c. the language rises a little higher; "The Indians *acknowledge* themselves and their *tribes* to be under the protection of the United States, and *of no other* SOVEREIGN, whatsoever." In the next treaty, made in 1786, with the Shawanese, the language rises into the superlative degree, they "*acknowledge* the United States to be the *sole* and *absolute* SOVEREIGN of *all the territory* ceded to them by a treat of peace made between them and the king of Great Britain."

In conformity to this idea, the lands beyond a certain boundary are said to be "*allotted* to the Indians for hunting ground," and certain tracts within the said hunting ground are "*reserved* to the United States," for forts and trading places; and the Indians are made to "relinquish all title or *pretence* of title," to the lands on this side of the boundary.

From the language used in these treaties does it not appear, that the commissioners of the United States supposed themselves to represent the sole and absolute SOVEREIGNS, of the whole territory comprehended between the Atlantic, the Mississippi and the Lakes; that when they gave peace to the Indians, they had a right to *reserve* what lands they pleased to themselves, and *allot* what lands they pleased to the Indians?

Now, however fond we may be of the idea of SOVEREIGNTY over the tribes, and over the lands of the Indians, and however just a title to it we may suppose is derived to us from the treaty of peace made with the king of Great Britain, yet we must remember that the Indians themselves treat this idea with contempt; and consider themselves as absolute proprietors of the country, and as an independent people; and if absolute propriety and independence are the soul and essence of sovereignty; I know not what is.

These nations which have not entered into such treaties with us must, according to their own ideas of independence, despise those who have. And can we wonder that they refuse our invitations to treat of peace, and that the Miami warrior should "drop the belt off his shoulder," as Mr. Knox tells us, when such a proposal was made? Since they know that in figuring a treaty with us they must acknowledge our sovereignty and relinquish their own independence by accepting of our protection? Though we may affect to call those characters "turbulent and malignant" who have excited complaints against these treaties, yet they may possibly be revered among them, as the *Sons of Liberty* were once among us, though at the same time they were loaded with as harsh and opprobrious epithets by the friends of the British usurpation.

A gentleman of a respectable character, who is intimately acquainted with the Indians of the six nations, told me, not long since, that the western tribes reason on the subject in the same manner that Pym and Hamden reasoned against the ship money in the time of Charles I, and that we reasoned against the claims of Britain to draw our money away by taxes. "What (say they)— do you think that the King of England by making a line in the air with his finger can give away our land to whom he pleases? No, our forefathers came out of this earth many hundred years before the king of England's subjects ever set foot upon it. If you want land we will give it you. We always gave it when you asked; and there is enough for us and for you; but you have already more than you can cultivate. It is not the *value* of the land that we contend for, but the *principle* on which you claim it; if we admit that, we give up our right to the whole." Ought we not to respect the Indians for holding sentiments so similar with our own?

I will conclude this letter with an extract from a work of Governor Pownal, entitled, "the Administration of the Colonies." It is the sentiment of an honest man well acquainted with the much injured savages of America and may with as great propriety be addressed to us as it was to the British government at the time when it was written.

"To do justice to our faith and honor, by treating the Indians according to the real *spirit* of our alliance with them; to do justice to them in their lands; to give up that idle, useless claim of *dominion* over them, are points absolutely necessary to be adopted into our politics; unless we have seriously taken the resolution to force our way by war. Until these points are adopted, we shall never have peace. And it deserves mature deliberation how we engage to settle America by war."

While these poor tribes of hunters remain, it will be our own fault if they do not remain in harmony with us. They are continually wearing away, and as they diminish or retire, they cede their lands to us in peace; which we thus in time, as fast as we can really want them, may possess in right and justice, untainted with the impeachment of having gained them by murder.

Adieu,
Polybius

The notion which the Indians have imbibed respecting the origin of the human race is that they grew out of the soil like trees, and that in a course of time, they were loosened from the earth, and acquired a power of motion on its surface.

POLYBIUS, LETTER IV

The American Apollo, no.7, Part II, volume I,
Observations on the Western Territory and the Indian War; in a series of letters to a friend by Polybius

Letter IV

Dear Sir,

It has been given out by the writers of paragraphs in some of the public papers, that the opposers of offensive measures against the Indians are enemies of the federal government. Perhaps it may be true in some instances; but I know for certain, that some of the firmest and most respectable friends of government, are of this sentiment; and I believe it will appear in the end, that they have more wisdom than the advocates of the sanguinary and exterminating plan.

I was in company the other evening where some gentlemen were discoursing on this subject with that freedom and harmony which ever characterize the friends of science and truth, and I will here give you what I can recollect of their conversation.

The most fatal enemy to barbarism is civilization. It is the parent of population; the guardian of the mother, and the infant, and the patron of those arts by which we procure the means of living for a large number of people in a small territory. It enlarges our views, and leads to those important inquiries which exercise all the powers of the human mind. It dispels the clouds of ignorance by which the uncivilized mind is encircled and opens the page in which we may read the dignity of human nature.

When the civilized Europeans gained footing on the American shores, they laid a foundation to secure, by the most righteous means, all the territory they can ever want. Their mode of life was calculated to counteract the vices of the natives. Civilized and uncivilized people cannot live in the same neighborhood. The former are employed in removing as fast as possible that natural growth from the lands, which is absolutely necessary for the food and range of those animals, on which the latter principally depend for food. They are thus driven from their former haunts to seek further for shelter. But they do not find an asylum; for they soon discover that the forests are incapable of giving them ample support. Their number of consequence is diminished.

That many of the tribes of Indians have become extinct since our first settlement in this country is a fact too well established to need proof. Others, reduced by famine, war and disease, have become so inconsiderable, that they have been absorbed in the neighboring tribes and their former names are forgotten.

As we have extended our possessions and increased our cultivation, we have rendered the country in their vicinity of no importance to the natives. For the game essential to their life and happiness retires from the neighborhood of a peopled and cultivated territory. As often as this is discovered by an improvident race, the lands so abandoned have been easily obtained from them, and soon become peopled.

In proportion as their limits have been circumscribed, their numbers have necessarily decreased; for the number of inhabitants must always be governed by the means of subsistence. This is an easy and natural mode of extending our limits. There have been instances of attempting it, in a different way, but carnage and desolation have been the consequence, and *this must always be the case when we attempt to enlarge our borders faster than they are enlarged by the natural retirement of the savages; in consequence of the advantages resulting from civilization.*

It is a truth well established, that each tribe contains as great a number as can be supported within the limits assigned to it. For this reason, no tribe can be driven from its own territory without immediate injury to itself, or to others. That the several tribes are thus full, and that to obtain a supply of food is a laborious and discouraging task to them, may be evinced by this circumstance, that it is common with the women to use various arts to prevent as much as possible the increase in their families.

If it appear that the natives, in a natural course of things, have always retired as fast as we are able to fill up the chasms, must it not excite our surprise, that an attempt, hazardous in itself, injurious to others, and problematical in its issue, should be made to precipitate an event, which in the nature of things, *must* take place?

The ideas entertained by our forefathers that the Deity was interposing in their favor by "casting out the *heathen* before them," seems to have gained too general a reception. It is true of bodies of men as well as of individuals, that when they consider themselves the peculiar favorites of heaven, they become vain and conceited; much happier could it be if they would clothe themselves with justice, mercy and humility.

The idea that the savages are not to be trusted; and that they ought to be exterminated by fire and sword, is too horrid to be entertained in a civilized mind. Though there is the highest probability that they will retire before the light of science and truth, and make way for its becoming universal; yet to hasten this by unrighteous measures, would be as improper as it would be to remove by violence, the present generation of mankind, because God in his providence will certainly remove them and make way for another.

Such was the substance of the conversation as far as it respected the moral and philosophical sides of the question. On the political side it was observed that the consequence of prosecuting the plan of "punishing the Indians," as Mr. Knox is pleased to call the offensive operations, would be the slaughter of a much greater number of our citizens, a long and distressing war, an accumulation of debt which all the lands acquired would never be able to discharge; an increase of half pay officers, and invalid pensioners, a more widely extended frontier to be defended, and a continual drain of men from agricultural and mechanical employments to form a standing army. In fine, that instead of punishing the Indians, we should punish ourselves, and instead of a war against them, we should make a war against the Treasury of the United States.

Adieu,
Polybius

1792 DEBATE OVER BILL FOR DEFENSE OF THE FRONTIERS

Congress of the United States, House of Representatives
Excerpt of a Published Debate Over a Bill for the Defense of the Frontiers
January 29, 1792

In Committee of the whole, on the bill providing for the defense of the frontiers; the question under consideration – a motion to strike out the second section of the bill, which contemplates the raising of three additional regiments of infantry, and a squadron of light dragoons, amounting in all to three thousand and forty men, exclusive of commissioned officers.

In favor of the motion and against the proposed augmentation of the military establishment, it was urged,

"That the Indian war in which the United States are at present involved, was in its origin, as unjustly undertaken, as it has since been unwisely and unsuccessfully conducted; that depredations had been committed by the whites, as well as by the Indians; and the whites were most probably the aggressors, as they frequently made encroachments on the Indian lands, wherein the Indians showed no inclination to obtain possession of our territory; or even to make temporary invasions, until urged to it by a sense of their wrongs.

"A proof of this un-encroaching disposition on their part plainly appeared in their conduct, after the victory they lately obtained over our troops; for when flushed with success, they might have swept the country before them and penetrated as far as Pittsburgh, they contented themselves with the advantage they had gained over their invaders, and did not attempt to invade our territories in return, although there was no where at hand a sufficient force to check their advance.

"The mode of treating the Indians in general, was reprobated as unwise and impolitic; the Indians are with difficulty to be reduced by the sword, but may easily by justice and moderation; and although their cruelties are alleged as reasons for a different conduct, and the sufferings of the white people particularly deplored, these narratives {it was said} are at best but ex-parté evidence: We hear nothing of the sufferings of the Indians. But if Cornplanter's speech were read, it would set the matter in a very different point of view, and furnish a complete answer to all the charges of their accusers.

"Peace (it was said) may be obtained from the Indian tribes at a much less expense, than would be necessary for the support of the war; to persevere in hostilities would be wasting the public money to a very bad purpose indeed; for supposing our arms crowned with victory, what the advantages we may expect to reap from our success; we can only gain possession of their lands, a possession, that must long continue unproductive of the smallest benefit, as we already possess land sufficient, more in fact, than we will be able to cultivate for a whole century to come.

Instead of being ambitious to extend our boundaries, it would answer a much better national purpose rather to check the roving disposition of the frontier settlers, and prevent them from too suddenly extending themselves to the western waters; if kept closer together and more nearly connected with the old settlements, they would be more useful to the community at large, and would not so frequently involve us in unnecessary and expensive wars with the Indians. But, if permitted to rove at pleasure, they will keep the nation embroiled in perpetual warfare, as long as the Indians have a single acre of ground to rest upon.

"If the citizens of the United States were recalled within their proper boundaries, there they might, for years to come, cultivate the soil in peace, neither invaded, nor invading. As the country progresses in population, and our limits are found too narrow, it will then be soon enough to contemplate a gradual extension of our frontiers – but in the mean time, it is an idle profusion of blood and treasure, to carry war beyond our present line of forts. It is only exposing our arms to disgrace, betraying our own weakness, and lessening the public confidence in the general government, to send forth armies to be butchered in the forests, while we suffer the British to retain those posts within our territory.

"As long as Britain is suffered to retain those posts, we can never hope to succeed against the Indians! Nor ought we to trace our late misfortune to any other source than her still holding them in her possession. Were they in our hands, the Indians could not carry on their operations against forts that they obtain their supplies of arms and ammunition, with which they can be at all times, plentifully furnished, as long as things continue on their present footing."

LETTER FROM A GENTLEMAN IN PHILADELPHIA

The military bill has had a long discussion in the Senate; when the question on raising the three additional regiments of regular troops was taken, the Senate divided, 13 against, and 12 in favor of raising them. But when the bill was further pursued, one of the 13 was induced to change his vote and two other members attended by which means the 12 were increased to 15, and I suppose the bill will be carried through, nearly as it came from the other House.

On the subject of the Indian war, Mr. Strong has given his idea very fully; reprobating the plan proposed, as being inconsistent both with justice and sound policy. He exerted himself more than usual, with good sense and argument:

"Whether the frontiers of Pennsylvania shall enjoy peace—or be deluged with blood this approaching summer, will, in considerable degree depend upon the final resolutions of the six Indian nations, for neutrality, peace or war! When the fate of two successive campaigns is taken into view, with the influence of the western Indians on their councils, flushed with victory and plunder, and the weak, defenseless state, in some measure of the frontiers, and the presumption that no considerable army can but savage hostilities? At all events, the situation of the inhabitants, hope and fear; whose lives and property are immediately exposed, should their determinations be hostile, is truly pitiable, and claims the vigilant attention of the government."

Friday, March 23, 1792, *American Apollo*

The plan of military operations on the Frontiers will probably cost the United States upwards of a million dollars for the present year. Notwithstanding this enormous expense to the States, the pay of the private soldiers in the new Regiments will be but three dollars per month, that is, one half as much as the members of Congress have for one day's sitting, or for 20 miles travel. [*O Tempora! O Mores!*]

STATEMENT OF THE COUNCIL OF SIX NATIONS, 1792

Received by Major Call, November 6, 1791

The White Bird King came over, attended by a Chief Warrior of the Cussaras, called the "Mole," and "George the Warrior," from the same towns. The White Bird King began and delivered a talk from the Chief of the Cussaras, called the "Big Little Man," which amounted to this; that they were for nothing but peace and quietness, and wished to take the white people all by the hand, and to keep a white path from here to the nation; that if a white man was killed above here, as was reported, they knew nothing of it; that the Coweras, to whom the debt was due, had not yet sent out a party to take satisfaction.

The Chief, called the Mole, delivered a letter from Bowles, called by Mole the Lying Captain, directed to the commissioners of the United States, for settling the boundary line, and etc., which was read, after which the White Bird King presented Mr. Ellicot with a white wig, which the Mole had brought down as a token of friendship, and to be sent to Congress; he also requested something white in return, to carry to the nation, to show that the path was white.

By Order of the Chiefs in Council Met: Usachees, October 20, 1791

"Gentlemen:
Feeling with deepest concern, the hostilities and bloodshed which have been produced by the difference subsisting between us and the United States,

in all parts of our borders; we now offer our endeavors in behalf of the four nations towards terminating the present war and adjusting such terms of reconciliation as may decide forever the matters now in dispute.

You well know that the cause of discontent with us has ever been the limits and borders of our country. Without entering into the particulars of this dispute as it relates to the various parts of the invisible line between us and the white people, we only beg you to consider whether on an inspection of the map of this country and the history of the two last centuries, it does not appear that of the two people, it is the Indians, and not the white people, who have the most reason to complain of straitened limits.

We have retreated from the plain to the woods, from thence to the mountains, but no limits established by nature or by compact, have stayed the ambition, or satisfied the advance of your people. But there is a time when political disorders have their end, as you yourself have experienced, and we look forward to.

It is the solemn determination of all our Chiefs, in council met, to adhere to an order fairly agreed upon; but such agreement must be national acts, that have the concurrence of the legislative council of the nation, and not a clandestine bargain with an unconnected individual, as this present pretended convention with Alexander M'Gillivray has been; such transactions originate in fraud, and always lead to animosities and bloodshed.

You should be reminded that when his Britannick Majesty had possessions in the Carolinas, Georgia and the Floridas, he never claimed any sovereignty over these nations; but we continued during all that time, spread over this country, and were considered the lawful owners of all the land not sold by us to the British subjects.

We therefore conceive, and you well know, that no sovereignty was ceded to you at the peace of 1783, except over such land as was purchased by his Majesty's subjects by solemn treaty; and that we are now, as we always have been, an independent and free people. Knowing this, and knowing our ability to maintain our independence, we view, with astonishment, the steps taken by the United States to rob us of our land.

We therefore conceive, and you well know, that no sovereignty was ceded to you at the peace of 1783, except over such land as was purchased by his Majesty's subjects by solemn treaty; and that we are now, as we always have been, an independent and free people. Knowing this, and knowing our ability to maintain our independence, we view, with astonishment, the steps taken by the United States to rob us of our land.

We have before us an act passed by the legislative body of the state of Georgia, at Augusta, dated the 20th December, 1789, entitled "an act for disposing of certain vacant lands or territory within this state." We actually see our whole country laid into distress, without considering us to have any claim or right whatever to the country which nature has bestowed upon us, and of which oppression or prejudice alone can attempt to rob us. We also see that numbers of men have solemnly engaged themselves and are now forming plans, to get possession of our lands; this we see in a publication of this year, extracted from the minutes of the companies at Charleston, dated the 14th of January, and finally adjusted and agreed upon the 5th of April, and we at this time see a military force brought within the borders of our country, who pretend to treat with us about a border to be observed in future between us.

Gentlemen—we do not understand your present proceedings; but as it is our wish to put an end to further bloodshed, we propose therefore that you should appoint one or more persons, duly authorized by the Congress of the United States, to treat with the Chiefs in council me at the Usachees, where all public business will be transacted as soon as my be: But should your intentions be dishonest, know that we will still have warriors sufficient to stain your land with blood, and that it is our solemn determination to sell our lives with out country.

But peace is best for all men; we therefore desire you to consider well the business now in hand, and let us know your determination as soon as possible.

By Order Of The Supreme Council,

General William A. Bowles, Director of Affairs, Creek Nation."

A REPORT FROM KENTUCKY

New York, February 22, 1792. *American Apollo* No. 9, Part II, Vol. 1

The Pittsburgh paper of February 4, mentions that by the arrival of a gentleman at that place immediately from Kentucky, the following intelligence was received:

"That just before he left the falls of Ohio, an express had passed along on his way to Fort Washington, with dispatches from the commandant at Post Vincennes for the Governor, the purport of which was, that he had sent a Frenchman and an Indian across the country to the Miami towns with some dispatches, in hopes of finding our army there; that on their arrival they found the towns deserted except by a few women; that for fear of being discovered they buried their dispatches, and they proceeded to meet our army, but had not gone more than five or six miles before they met a party of 30 Indians returning with their share of the plunder, one of them had 127 scalps strung on a pole, the rest were heavily loaded with different articles, and they had three pack-horses loaded with kegs of wine, etc.

"The Indians immediately accused them of being spies, but on making inquiry and examining them very minutely, believed them friends, they were then obliged to return with them to the towns and the Indians gave them a full account of the battle, (which agrees with the account heretofore published) except that only 1200 Indians were in the engagement and that these were Miamis and Indians from the lakes, that 600 arrived the day after the battle, and 300 were out hunting to supply the rest, which was their whole force; that a dispute arose about dividing the plunder between them and the lake Indians, the latter wishing to have that of the smallest bulk and easiest carriage, as they had a great way to go, but the former refused.

"This greatly enraged the lake Indians who began to use the tomahawk, but did not do much damage; however, they went off very much dissatisfied, determined never again to come to the assistance of the Miamis, let the consequences be what they would; and that only 50 Indians were killed.

"After giving them this information they were permitted to proceed homewards with a promise of sending them a trader (which was the business the Frenchman said they were upon) as they had as much plunder as would amply do for them all winter.

"We are also informed that an expedition consisting of 500 men, on horseback, was to go from Kentucky the beginning of January, against the Miami towns and from the enterprising spirit of the Kentuckians we flatter ourselves those towns are laid in ashes before now. There is no doubt but this expedition has taken place, as our informant had the information from a person that may be depended on."

GENERAL SCOTT'S EXPEDITION

Indian Defeat. From the Powtowmack *GUARDIAN*, printed at Shepherd's Town, of the 7th inst. *American Apollo*, No. 9, Part II, Vol. I., 1792.

Last Saturday evening came to this town, a young man from Cat-Fish, which he left about two weeks ago, and who gave us the following pleasing, interesting, and important intelligence, viz. That two days before he left Cat-Fish, two men arrived there from Licking, who informed that they had been out with a body of 1300 volunteers on horseback from Kentucky under General Scott; that they left Licking on the expedition a few days before Christmas; that General Scott dispatched three spies in advance, who, when they arrived about 13 miles beyond the spot where General St. Clair was defeated, discovered a large body of Indians, diverting and enjoying themselves with the plunder they had taken, riding the bullocks, dancing &c. and appeared to be mostly drunk. That on this information being given to General Scott, who with the main body, were a few miles in the rear, he divided them into three divisions, advanced and fell on the enemy by surprise. That the contest was short but victorious on the side of the volunteers, seven hundred of the enemy being killed on the spot, all the cannon and stores in their possession retaken, and the remainder of the savage body put to flight; that General Scott having lost but six men, returned to Licking in triumph with most of the cattle, stores &c. leaving the cannon at Fort Jefferson – That General Scott had previously gone our with 400 men but finding his number insufficient was returning but met a body of 900 volunteers, who upon joining him he immediately proceeded in prosecuting his original design, which fortunately proved successful.

Our informant further adds that he saw a Kentucky newspaper of the

8th of January, at Morgan Town, brought by Major Ried, containing the account of General Scott's expedition, which corresponded with that given by the two men at Cat-Fish, and that General Scott brought in near 700 scalps.

LETTER FROM POST VINCENNES

Philadelphia, March 14, *American Apollo*, 1792, No. 13, Part II., Volume I.

Extract of a letter from a gentleman, dated Post-Vincennes, January 4th, 1792, to his friend in Montgomery county, Pennsylvania:

When we entered the Ouabache river it was full of floating ice. Major Hamtramack, with whom I came, had about 50 men; we had 170 miles to ascend the river in this situation and we had but ten days provision. About 200 Pyankeshaw Indians, who had heard of the defeat of the army, and that their prisoners were hanged at Fort Washington, fell in with us: we happened fortunately to have two Indians with us who had been up to Fort Washington to see their friends, who were taken by General Scott and General Wilkinson; these two informed their brethren, that their prisoners had not been hanged, as has been told them, but were well treated, this pleased them. But still we apprehended they might wish to take some prisoners, which they could offer in exchange for their wives and children, and there were *three* or *four* of them to *one* of us. To account for it, I cannot, but the fact is, they were very kind to us, gave us plenty of fresh meat, and all the assistance they could in coming up. God grant they may always continue in this disposition...

WESTERN DISCOVERIES

American Apollo, No. 27, Part II, Vol. I

It is incredible what pains are taken at this day, by more European nations than one, to send enterprising travelers to explore the interior regions of America. Among these, the British take the lead; and forgetting the narrow insular limits that nature has assigned them, and the various checks they have experienced in the road to universal empire, on this continent, they are still projecting a tributary government, in the pathless forests of interior America.

A Mr. Stuart, said to be in the employ of the British court, has not long since returned from four years' travels through the hitherto unexplored regions to the westward. Taking his course west southwesterly from the posts on the lakes, he penetrated to the head of the Missouri, and from thence due west to within bout five hundred miles of the shores of the Pacific ocean. Nothing prevented his reaching the coast but an inveterate war which had for some years been carried on with all the implacability of savage revenge, between the interior Indians, and those towards the sea coast parts.

So great, however, was the ardor of the enterprising Mr. Stuart to obtain his object (the exploring the continent from sea to sea) that he joined the interior Indians, in several battles against the shore Indians, all which coming short of his object, the procuring a peace, after some stay, he returned nearly by the route he had pursued going out.

Our information adds, that beyond the Missouri, Mr. Stuart me with many powerful nations of Indians, in general, hospitable and courteous. The Indian nations he visited westward appeared to be a polished civilized people, having regularly built towns and being in a state of society not far removed from the European, and only wanting the use of iron and steel to be perfectly so. They are always clad in skins, cut in an elegant manner, and in many respects preferable to the garments in use among the whites.

Adjacent to these nations is a vast range of mountains, which may be called the Allegany of the western parts of America, and serves as a barrier against the too frequent incursions of the coast Indians, who entertain a moral antipathy to the nations and tribes inhabiting the country eastward beyond the mountains.

ACCOUNT OF INDIANS OF MARTHA'S VINEYARDS

An account of the Traditions and Customs of the Indians of Martha's Vineyards as communicated to Benjamin Bassett, Esquire of Chilmark, by Thomas Cooper, a half-blooded Indian, of Gay Head, aged at the time, sixty years, and which, he says he obtained of his grandmother, who, to use his expression, was a stout girl, when the English came to the island. Published in *Massachusetts Historical Collections*, Volume I, 1792.

"The first Indian who came to the Vineyard, was brought thither with his dog on a cake of ice. When he came to Gay Head, he found a very large man, whose name was Moshup. He had a wife and five children, four sons and one daughter; and lived in the den. He used to catch whales, and then pluck up trees, and make a fire and roast them. The coals of the trees and the bones of the whales are now to be seen.

"After he was tired of staying here, he told his children to go and play ball on a beach that joined Norman's Land to Gay Head. He then made a mark with his toe across the beach at each end, and so deep that the water followed, and cut away the beach; so that his children were in fear of drowning. They took their sister up and held her out of the water. He told them to act as if they were going to kill whales; and they were all turned into killers {a fish so called}. The sister was dressed in large stripes. He gave them a strict charge always to be kind to her. His wife mourned the loss of her children so exceedingly, that he threw her away. She fell upon Seconet, near the rocks, where she lived some time, exacting contribution of all who passed by water. After a while, she was changed into stone. The entire shape remained for many years. But after the English came, some of them broke off the arms, head, etc. But the most of the body remains to this day. Moshup went away, nobody knows whither. He had no conversation with the Indians, but was kind to them, by sending whales, etc. ashore to them to eat. But after they grew thick around him, he left them.

"Whenever the Indians worshipped, they always sang and danced and then begged of the sun and moon, as they thought most likely to hear them, to send them the desired favor; most generally rain or fair weather, or freedom from their enemies or sickness.

"Before the English came among the Indians, there were two disorders of which they most generally died, viz. the consumption and the yellow fever. The latter they could always *lay* in the following manner. After it had raged and swept off a number, those who were well met to *lay* it. The rich, that is such as had a canoe, skins, axes, etc., brought them. They took their seat in a circle; and all the poor sat around, without. The richest then proposed to begin to lay the sickness; and having in his hand something in shape resembling his canoe, skin, or whatever his riches were, he threw it up in the air; and whoever of the poor without could take it, the property it was intended to resemble became forever transferred to him or her.

"After the rich had thus given away all their moveable property to the poor, they looked out the handsomest and most sprightly young man in the assembly, and put him into an entire new wigwam, built of every thing new for that purpose. They then formed in two files at a small distance from each other. One standing in the space at each end, put fire to the bottom of the wigwam on all parts, and fell to singing and dancing. Presently, the youth would leap out of the flames, and fall down to appearance, dead. Him they committed to the care of five virgins, prepared for that purpose, to restore life again. The term required for this would be uncertain, from six to forty eight hours, during which time the dance must be kept up. When he was restored, he would tell, that he had been carried in a large thing high up in the air, where he came to a great company of white people, with whom he had interceded hard to have the distemper layed; and generally after much persuasion, would obtain a promise, or answer of peace, which never failed of laying the distemper."

CONFLICT AT WRENTHAM

Account of the Surprise and Defeat of a Body of Indians, near Wrentham in a Letter from Mr. Mann, written to the Massachusetts Historical Society and recorded in the year 1806.

Gentlemen,

I shall make no apology, for this communication relative to a fact, which has escaped the notice of the historian; but which is, nevertheless as well authenticated, as most transactions are, which are recorded upon the pages of history. The adroit military action alluded to, was considered by the first settlers of Wrentham as of the utmost consequence to them, and, by reason of its importance, deserves to be preserved in perpetuity. The exploit I have repeatedly heard related, by different persons, after the following manner.

A man, by the name of Rocket, being in search after a strayed horse in the woods, about three miles north east from that part of the town where the meeting-house of the first parish stands, discovered a train of Indians, forty-two in number, towards the close of day, directing their course westward. From their warlike appearance Rocket was suspicious, that they had it in contemplation to make an attack upon the inhabitants the following morning, at a time, when the men were scattered, at their labor upon their lands, this mode of assault, by surprise, being usual with the aborigines. Rocket undiscovered followed the trail, until about the setting of the sun; when they halted, evidently with a design to lodge for the night.

The spot chosen was well situated to secure them from a discovery. Rocket watched their movements, until they had laid themselves down to rest; when, with speed, he returned to the settlement and notified the inhabitants with his discovery. They being collected, a consultation was held; whereupon the women, the infirm, and children, being secured in the fortified houses, it was agreed to attack the Indians early the next morning before they should leave their encampment.

The strength of the little army collected consisted of thirteen. At their head was a Captain Ware. Rocket was their guide. This intrepid band arrived upon the ground, before daylight; and were posted within a short musket shot from the encamped Indians with orders to reserve their fire, until the Indians should arise from their lodgings.

Between the appearance of day and sunrise the Indians rose nearly at the same time; when upon the signal given a full discharge was made; which, with the sudden unexpected attack, together with the slaughter made, put the Indians into the greatest consternation; so that, in their confusion, attempting to effect their escape in a direction opposite to that, from which the attack was made, several were so maimed by leaping down a precipice from ten to twenty feet among rocks, that they became an easy sacrifice.

Some of the fugitives were overtaken and slain. And, it is related, that two of them being closely pursued in order to elude their followers buried their bodies, all except their heads, in the waters of Mill-brook, the most southerly branch of Charles River; about one mile from the first scene of action, where they were killed. It is probable that these were likewise injured by their precipitation from the rock. It is added that one Woodcock discharged his long musket, called in those days a buccaneer, at a single fugitive Indian at the distance of eighty rods and broke his thigh bone and afterwards dispatched him.

(Note in 1806 from the Historical Society editor regarding this letter to the readers: "The custom of putting to death wounded Indians, during the Indian wars, is not agreeable to our modern ideas of humanity; but when it is recollected that the inhabitants had not the means to convey them off, the apparent barbarity is more reconciled to our feelings.")

After the action, there were numbered of the Indians killed upon the fields of battle, and by the fall from the rock, twenty, some say twenty-four; of the inhabitants, not one. From the best information, this transaction took place about the commencement of Philip's war, whether the same year or the year after, I have not been able to ascertain. It is certain that the inhabitants removed from their settlements twice during the Indian wars, down to Dedham, as a place of security; and once after the town was incorporated, when most of the houses were burnt by the Indians. Mr. Bean in his century sermon, preached in the year 1774, says they were all burnt but two.

The circumstances of the above action, although transmitted down traditionally, are correctly related, even at this distant period, by several now living. This is not strange when it is known, that the principal part of the present inhabitants are directly descended from those very men, who were engaged. All who pretend to be acquainted with the facts agree in those things material respecting them.

The names of the two persons mentioned as principals, viz. Ware and Rocket, are found upon the ancient records of this town, annexed to a written instrument, engaging themselves and fourteen others to return to Wrentham, after being absent four years, in consequence of the Indian wars. The name of Woodcock is not found among the first settlers of Wrentham; but it is historically known, that a settlement had been made by one Woodcock, about five miles south from Wrentham, previous to that at Wrentham. This settlement was known by the name of Woodcock's garrison; and was during the wars, a place of rendezvous for the detachments from Massachusetts and Plymouth colonies.

(Editor's note in 1806: "This garrison was pulled down in 1806, and a relic of it is deposited in the Museum of the Historical Society. On the spot where it stood, Mr. Hatch has erected a large and elegant house for an Inn. It stands on the great road between Boston and Providence, an cannot fail to attract the attention of the traveler. The Sign of the Inn is King Philip. On the one side, that famous aboriginal prince appears alone, armed with his bow and arrows; on the other, he appears armed with a gun, and on the background are wigwams and appropriate Indian imagery. We were told by the landlord, that the sign was painted by an English artist and cost him one hundred dollars. Regretting its exposure to the winds and tempests, we recommended that it be placed within the portico of the Inn.")

It is not improbable that upon apprehension of danger, Woodcock might repair to this settlement as a place of more security. There is an intelligible man, eighty-seven years of age, Deacon Thomas Mann, now living who when a youth was acquainted with Rocket (who lived to a great age) and perfectly remembers that on the account of the aforementioned deed he received during his life an annual pension from the general court.

A granddaughter of Captain Ware, by the name of Clap, who is also living and aged ninety-four years, well recollects to have heard the story related, when quite young, as a transaction in which her aged grandfather bore a conspicuous part; whether she heard the circumstances of the action direct from her grandparent she at this distant period does not remember. The truth of it, however, she doubts not.

Mrs. Clap still possesses a strength of understanding to an astonishing degree. The energies of her mind and the powers of recollection seem not to be impaired; ancient impressions, as well as those of more recent date, are fresh in her memory. Within a few years, she has recovered her sight, which had been almost lost; so as to be able at this time to thread the smallest needle.

There are now men living who well recollect to have seen the bones in abundance of the unburied Indians left upon the spot where the action happened. Some few have been found since my remembrance. The large flat rock where the Indians were encamped when attacked has to this day been known by the name of Indian Rock. This rock is situated within the bounds of Franklin, three miles northwest from the center of Wrentham. The highest part of the precipice near the middle is about twenty feet perpendicular; it gradually slopes from thence to the extremity of the two wings, where it is ten feet in height. It faces southerly with an arched front, forming a curved line, fourteen rods in length whose chord is twelve rods. We may rise the rock, from the north, northeast, and northwest gradually, where the assailants were posted.

It has been a matter of question with some, that a transaction of such consequence to the original adventurers of Wrentham should not have been noted by primitive historians of New England, when events of smaller importance have by them been minutely detailed. Their silence concerning the above enterprise has led to a suspicion, that the whole is a forged tale, destitute of any foundation.

But when it is considered that the early war achievements, which have been recorded, were most, if not all, executed under the direction of the government and were actions, in part, committed to writing by the very officers who were sharers in them; we shall no longer be surprised that a deed transacted in the first instance without the knowledge of authority; an expedition executed upon the spur of the moment by a few frontier settlers for their own security, should be overlooked among a multiplicity of events which succeeded each other in quick succession; and many of which, on account of display of courage and enterprise, excited both gratitude and astonishment.

Should the gentlemen members of the Historical Society bestow as much credit upon the story as I have, they may not pass it over without some notice; but if they should suppose that this fragment is not accompanied with authenticity sufficient to claim their attention, they will consign it to oblivion.

From their very humble servant,
James Mann
Wrentham, Aug. 22, 1806

EARLY RECORDS OF INDIAN POPULATIONS

An Account of Early Records of the Indian Populations Surrounding the Vicinity of Natick, From the Papers of the Late Thaddeus Mason, Esquire, of Cambridge, and Presented By His Eldest Daughter to the Historical Society.

In 1651, an Indian town was formed at Natick.

In 1660, an Indian church was embodied there.

In 1670, there were two teachers, John and Anthony, and between 40 and 50 communicants.

On June 16, 1749, the following census of Indian numbers in the vicinity of Natick was taken and recorded as follows:

The following 42 Indians named belong to the south side of the Charles River by Dedham:

Name of family and members	Total
Deacon Ephraim, wife and her 3 children	5
Isaac Ephraim	6
Jacob Chalcom, wife and 3 children	11
Jeremy Comacho, wife and one child	14
Joseph Comacho, wife and one child	17
Daniel Thomas, wife and one child	20
Elizabeth, Ann and Uncle Brooks	23
Abram Speen, wife and one child	26
Widow Comocho	27
Judith Ephraim and 2 children	30
Prince Nyar and wife	32
5 children of Samuel Abram	37

Widow of said Samuel Abram and one child	39
Widow of Hezekiah Comacho and 2 children	42

The following 64 Indians are located south of Sawpit Hill on Peegun Plain and nearer now to meeting than said hill is, unless there be a mistake in Sol. Womsquon.

Peter Brand, wife and 2 children	4
Peter Ephraim, wife and 4 children	10
John Ephraim, wife and 3 children	15
Thomas Awonsamug, jun. Wife and one child	18
Widow Rumnemarsh and Zipporah Peegun	20
3 children of Solomon Thomas	23
2 Widow Sooducks, Widow Tray and Thomas Scoggin	27
Benjamin, Jonas, Hannah and Mary Tray	31
Joseph Sinee, wife and 3 children	36
William Thomas and 2 children	39
Mary George	40
Nat Hill, wife and 7 children	49
Widow Womsquon, and 4 children	54
Solomon Womsquon, wife and 3 children	59
Jonas Obscow	60
Widow Pitimee, Ruth and Ruth's 2 children	64

Fifteen Indians are within two miles and an half of our meeting house.

Thomas Peegun, wife and 3 children	5
Josiah Sooduck and wife	7
Widow Tom and one child and Sarah Francis	10
5 Pogenits	15

These 16 Indians live west, or own land – most of them west of Sawpit Hill, and it is to be noted that Deacon Ephraim's wife's 4 children, which by mistake are said to be 3, own land west of said hill, so doth Samuel Lawrance and it may be Mary Peegun.

Nathaniel Coochuck, wife and child	3
Josiah Speen, wife, child and grandchild	7
Moses Speen and child	9
Widow Speen	10
Betty Babesuck and her niece Rhoda	12

Patience Pequassis	13
Zachary, son of Hannah Speen	14
Daniel Speen	15
Samuel Speen	16

Additional Indian families in the Natick area

Ester Thomas and child	2
Thomas Awonsamug, wife and 3 children	7
Sarah, Rumnemarsh	9
Samuel Lawrance, Thomas and Hannah Waban	11
Widow Mary Peegun and 5 children	17
Oliver Sooduck, Job Speen's child	19
Bethia Cole	20
Mary, daughter of Sarah Womsquon	21
Joseph and Joshua Brook	23
Hannah Peetimee's child	24
Esther Sooduck	25
Elizabeth Wages	26

The most of the last 26 usually resided on the southeast of Peegun Plain, and so are accommodated as the meeting house now stands. The total numbers of Indians as tallied in this count is 166.

Having carefully considered the within list, and being well acquainted with Natick, we hereby signify that we are well assured it may be depended on as a true one, except that perhaps we have not thought of every one, and we hope some may be alive who have been soldiers or at sea, not here named.

JOSEPH EPHRAIM
JACOB CHALCOM
JOHN EPHRAIM
DANIEL THOMAS
June 16, 1749

In 1753, in Natick 25 families, beside several individuals.

In 1763, 37 Indians only; but in this return, probably the wandering Indians were not included.

In 1797, the Reverend Mr. Badger, of Natick, estimated the number of "clear-blooded" Indians then in this place and belonging to it, to be "near twenty." The number of church members was then "reduced to twenty three."

WILLIAM MARSHE'S JOURNAL OF THE 1744 TREATY WITH THE SIX NATIONS

William Marshe's Journal of the Treaty Held With the Six Nations by the Commissioners of Maryland, and Other Provinces, at Lancaster, in Pennsylvania, June, 1744.

Saturday, June the 16th, 1744

This day the Honorable Edmund Jenings, and the Honorable Philip Thomas, Esqrs. of the council of state in Maryland, having heretofore been appointed (by a special power from his Excellency Thomas Bladen, Esquire Governor, under his hand, and the seal of that province) commissioners for treating with the Six Nations of Indians, on behalf of the province, concerning some lands claimed by them, and to renew all former treaties betwixt the Six Nations and this government, agreed to proceed on their embassy.

I was required by them to stay at Annapolis, and receive the bills of exchange (to defray our expenses) from Mr. Ross, clerk of the council; and after receiving the bills on Sunday, p.m., I went to Mr. Thomas's, where I lodged that night.

Sunday, 17th

Mr. Commissioner Jenings went over Chesapeake Bay, as also did Mr. Benedict Calvert, who accompanied him to the treaty.

Monday, June 18th, 1744.

Breakfasted at Mr. Thomas's about 8 o'clock this morning, and soon after set out with him, and the Reverend Mr. Craddock (who accompanied us in quality of chaplain to the Maryland commissioners) for Patapscoe. Arrived at James Moore's ordinary, at the head of Severn River, about one o'clock, where we dined; but such a dinner was prepared for us, as never was either seen or cooked in the highlands of Scotland, or the isles of Orkney. It consisted of six eggs fried with six pieces of bacon, with some clammy pone or Indian bread. But as hunger knows little of cleanliness, and withal very impatient, we fell to, and soon devoured the victuals. Our liquor was sorry rum mixed with water and sugar, which bears the heathenish name of "bumbo." Of this we drank about a pint, to keep down the nauseous eggs and bacon.

Mon. p.m. Paid for our slovenly dinner and liquor, and pursued our journey to Mrs. Hughes's, at Patapscoe River (over which she keeps a ferry) to whose house we came about 3 o'clock. Here we refreshed ourselves with some good coffee and toast and butter, which was served to us in a neat and handsome manner: we likewise drank a bottle of generous wine; then paid our reckoning and went over the river to Whetstone-Point, and from thence proceeded to William Rogers's ordinary in Baltimore town, being three miles distant from Mrs. Hughes's.

Monday evening, in Baltimore County. I left Mr. Thomas and the Rev. Parson at the ordinary, and went to Mr. Robert North's where I supped with some blithe company; and from thence returned to Rogers's. Mr. Bourdillon, minister of this parish, visited his brother of the cloth, and staid with us till near 11 o'clock this night. It was with this gentleman and his wife that I came into Maryland on the 1st of January, 1737. She is niece to Sir Theodore Janssen, Baronet. When Mr. Bourdillon had bidden us *bon soir*, we retired to rest our wearied limbs, having rode 44 long miles this hot day.

Tuesday Morning, June 19th, 1744

Rose about 5 o'clock and ordered breakfast to be got presently; which was done. Drank tea, and then mounted our horses to reach Edward Day's, who keeps the ferry on this side Joppa. Came to his house about 11 o'clock, baited ourselves and horses, and then passed over Gun-Powder River in his ferry-boat to Joppa Town.

At Joppa. Rested at Mr. Brown's, who keeps a brick ordinary. Here we dined on a boiled ham, and some chickens fried with bacon. Drank good wine and small beer, and rendered ourselves fit to encounter the fatigue of riding twenty-five miles further in this sultry weather.

Here I waited on the Reverend Hugh Deane, who is parson of this parish, to deliver him a packet of letters, &c. I received from Dr. Lyon, at Baltimore town. He read to me some of the news, mentioned in his European letters, concerning the queen of Hungary, the king of Prussia, and the Lord knows how many other potentates; but as I was neither politician, nor courtier, I gave but little attention to it. I understood Mr. D. had his intelligence from his wife's brother, who had some place in the government at home, or is in dependence of favors from some *great man*: God help him!

After dinner, about 3 in the afternoon, we took the route to Mr. Benjamin Chew's in Cecil county, whose house is distant from Joppa twenty-six miles. Betwixt six and seven of the clock in the evening, we reached Susquehannah lower ferry; we tarried some small time, and sent our horses over it in a boat by themselves. From hence we went to the eastern side of Susquehannah, and then rode to Mr. Chew's about a mile and a half distance from the river.

At this house we supped very heartily, for which our priest returned thanks. After supper we had a good deal of chat on various subjects; and then, very willingly retired to bed.

Wednesday morning, June 20th, 1744

We breakfasted at Mr. Chew's, and then set out (with him) for Nottingham township, which place we reached about a quarter of an hour after ten this morning. We put our horses at Thomas Hughes's who keeps here an ordinary. He was an honest, facetious, and sober Quaker, a man of good plain sense and character.

Here we proposed to dine, and bespoke a dinner accordingly, which was prepared for us about two o'clock. Here we were shaved by our friend and companion Mr. Chew, for no barber could be got in the whole neighborhood.

I thought it a little odd our friend (who was a justice of the peace in his county) should officiate as our tonsor; but as we could get no other, he, purely out of good nature, did the office of one.

This township is a large body of land, consisting of between 30 and 40,000 acres. It lies in Chester County, within the Province of Pennsylvania. It is chiefly settled by Quaker farmers who strive to imitate those in our mother country in everything. There have been great disputes between the present Lord Baltimore, proprietor of Maryland, and Messrs. Penns, proprietors of Pennsylvania, concerning this place; the first averring it to lie within the bounds of his province; and the others, that it is contained within theirs.

The inhabitants (being Quakers) are desirous of living under the Penns' government, by reason of the small taxes they are burdened with; and more especially as in that, they are not obliged to pay anything to the priests of the steeple-houses; whereas in Maryland, by a law made anno 1704, every male, white and black, and also black women, above the age of 16, and under the age of 60, are obliged to pay 40 lbs. of tobacco per poll to the incumbent of their respective parishes. This is a most iniquitous tax and is a most grievous burden to those who have many white men servants and a great many slaves, which a great number of people have in Maryland.

The difference between the proprietors of the two provinces is likely to be ended by the Lord Chancellor, before whom a suit is depending, brought by the Penns against Lord Baltimore, for not standing to, or fulfilling some agreement relating to the bounds of both provinces, wherein the Quakers had been too sly for his Lordship, whereby their several titles may be drawn in question.

Weds. p.m. There was a great disputation betwixt the Hon. Mr. Thomas, and one Gatchell, an Inhabitant of this place, concerning carnal weapons. The latter being one of the followers of George Fox, strenuously insisted that it was not lawful to use any offensive weapon whatever. As this is the common cant of that set of people, it is in vain to think of arguing them out of it, though founded on no reason.

In this government subsists a quarrel betwixt the Governor of it, and the Quaker members of the house of assembly, occasioned by the latter's not consenting to a militia law, which they will not grant for the defense of the province. Who has the most reason on their side, I know not; but I really cannot blame the Quakers for not consenting to such a law, unless the power of putting it into execution should be lodged in the house of assembly, and such officers to be appointed by them.

At six this evening, the Hon. Edmund Jenings, Esq., Col. Thomas Colvill, and Col. Robert King (being the other honorable commissioner for Maryland) with Mr. Calvert, arrived here from Col. Colvill's in Cecil county. We all lodged at Mr. Hughes's and agreed to set out for Lancaster early in the morning and to go thither over the Barrens.

Expenses at Mr. Hughes's paid in silver currency to the value of £2-17-2, Pennsylvania currency.

Thursday morning, June 21, 1744.

Breakfasted before five; then prepared ourselves for riding. Set out from hence with the commissioners, Mr. Calvert, Mr. Gatchel, and our landlord, who undertook to be our guide to Lancaster town. We were joined on the road by some Quakers, who accompanied us to our designed stage.

At eleven o'clock, we arrived at one Sheppard's Mill, having rode twenty miles from Nottingham. Here we all baited, and refreshed ourselves with some good neat's tongue, cold ham, and Madeira wine. We eat our repast under a tree, upon a long plank, close to which was a trough and in that our horses were fed. We rested at this place about an hour and an half, and then pursued our journey to Lancaster.

From hence we had a good road, the land being less hilly and stony than that we had rode over in the morning. Here are several large and fine farms, settled by the Germans. They sow all kinds of grain, and have very plentiful harvests. Their houses are chiefly built with stone, and generally seated near some brook or stream of water. They have very large meadows, which produce a great deal of hay, and feed therewith variety of cattle, &c.

Thursday, p.m. Arrived at Lancaster town about two o'clock, and put our horses at Peter Worrall's, who here keeps an Inn. Here I bespoke a dinner for our commissioners and the Maryland gentlemen, which was soon got ready, to our great comfort. Procured a room and two beds in Worrall's house for our chaplain and myself.

Neither the governor of Pennsylvania nor the Virginia commissioners were arrived at the time when we did; but about six in the evening they came hither attended by several Virginia gentlemen and some from the city of Philadelphia.

Here we were informed that the Indians would not arrive till tomorrow, they marching very slow, occasioned by their having a great many small children and old men.

Messrs. Calvert, Craddock and myself went into and viewed the court-house of this town. It is a pretty large brick building, two stories high. The ground room, where the justices of this county hold their court, is very spacious. There is a handsome bench, and railed in, where they sit, and a chair in the midst of it, which is filled by the judge. Below this bench, is a large table, of half oval form; round this, and under their Worships sit the county clerk, and the several attorneys of the court, who here as well as in most other courts of the plantations, plead as counselors. There are particular seats and places allotted to the sheriff, crier, &c.

Fronting the justices' bench, and on each side of it, are several long steps or stairs, raised each above the other, like the steps leading into the north door of St. Paul's. On these steps, stand the several auditors and spectators, when a court is held here. It was on these, that the Indians chiefs sat, when they treated with the several governments. This court-house is capable to contain above 800 persons without incommoding each other.

When we had surveyed this room, we went up stairs, into one overhead. This is a good room, and has a large chimney. In this the justices sit in the month of February, for the convenience of the fire. Adjoining to this room is a smaller one, where the juries are kept to agree on their verdict.

On the top of the court-house is a kind of cupola. We ascended a ladder, and got into it. From hence we had a complete view of the whole town, and the country several miles round and likewise of part of Susquehannah River, at twelve miles distance.

This town has not been begun to be built above sixteen years. It is conveniently laid out into sundry streets and one main street in the midst of which stands the court-house and market. Through this runs the road to the back country, on Susquehannah. There are several cross streets on each side of the main street, which are indifferently well built, as to quantity of houses.

The inhabitants are chiefly High-Dutch, Scotch-Irish, some few English families, and unbelieving Israelites who deal very considerably in this place.

The spirit of cleanliness has not as yet in the least trouble the major part of the inhabitants; for in general they are very great sluts and slovens. When they clean their houses which by the by is very seldom, they are unwilling to remove the filth far from themselves for they place it close to their doors which in the summer time, breeds an innumerable quantity of bugs, fleas and vermin.

The religions here which prevail are hardly to be numbered. Here are Dutch Calvinists, who have a church built with square logs and their interspaces filled with clay. In this, is a small organ, good for little, and worse played on by the organist.

The sect of Luther have a church likewise. This is more spacious than that of the Calvinists, being built of stone, and is much larger than the other. The minister of this church is a gentleman of good character, and by his true pastoral conduct keeps his congregation in good order. The ministers of these Dutch churches are allowed no stipend for preaching, but are paid at the will of their hearers. This is a great tie upon them to do their duty and makes them more diligent than our clergy are. Happy people! In this, we may envy them.

A clergyman of the church of England sometimes officiates in the court-house, there being no church here built by those of that persuasion. There are great numbers of Irish Presbyterians and several Jews, as I hinted before, with diverse others, that neither themselves, nor anyone else, can tell what sect they follow or imitate.

The houses for the most part are built and covered with wood except some few, which are built of brick and stone. They are generally low, seldom exceeding two stories. All the owners of lots and houses here pay a ground rent, greater or less, according to the grant of them by James Hamilton, Esquire, who is the proprietor of the town.

There are hills which environ Lancaster, as likewise some thick woods, which in the summer, render it very hot, especially in the afternoon. The soil is then dry and very sandy, which when a fresh wind blows, almost choke the inhabitants.

The water here is very bad, occasioned by their springs and even wells, being stored with lime-stones. This gave me a looseness and palled my appetite; but soon left me, after I refrained from drinking the water by itself. They have a good market in this town, well filled with provisions of all kinds and prodigiously cheap.

Our commissioners and company supped at Worrall's, and passed away an hour or two very agreeably; after which I retired to bed but had not long reposed myself when I was most fiercely attacked by the neighboring Dutch fleas and bugs which were ready to devour both me and the minister. However, after killing great quantities of my nimble enemies, I got about two hours of sleep.

Mr. Calvert was more inhumanly used by them than myself, as was likewise Mr. Craddock. On the next night, Mr. Calvert left our lodgings and laid in the court-house chamber, among the young gentlemen from Virginia, who there had beds made on the floor for that purpose.

Friday, June 22nd, 1744

Rose betwixt 4 and 5. Breakfasted with Mr. Commissioner Thomas, Colonels Colvill and King, at Worrall's. The Indian Chiefs not being yet come, we had no business to do.

The honorable the commissioners of Virginia gave our commissioners, and the several Maryland gentlemen, an invitation to dine with them in the court-house which we did betwixt one and two. During our dinner, the deputies of the Six Nations with their followers and attendants, to the number of 252, arrived in town. Several of their squaws, or wives, with some small children rode on horseback, which is very unusual with them. They brought their firearms and bows and arrows, as well as tomahawks. A great concourse of people followed them. They marched in very good order, with *Cannasateego*, one of the Onandago chiefs at their head; who, when he came near to the court-house wherein we were dining, sung in the Indian language a song inviting us to a renewal of all treaties heretofore made, an that now to be made.

Mr. Weiser, the interpreter, who is highly esteemed by the Indians, and is one of their council of state (though a German by birth) conducted them to some vacant lots in the back part of the town where sundry poles and boards were placed. Of these, and some boughs of trees from the woods, the Indians made wigwams, or cabins, wherein they resided during the treaty. They will not on any occasion whatsoever dwell, or even stay, in houses built by white people.

They placed their cabins according to the rank each nation of them holds in their grand council. The Onondagoes nation was placed on the right hand and upper end; then the others, according to their several dignities.

After dining and drinking the loyal healths, all the younger gentlemen of Virginia, Maryland, and Pennsylvania went with Mr. Conrad Weiser to the Indian camp, where they had erected their several cabins. We viewed them all and heartily welcomed *Cannasateego* and *Tachanuntie* (alias the Black Prince) two chiefs of the Onondagoes to town. They shaked us by the hands and seemed very well pleased with us. I gave them some snuff for which they returned me thanks in their language.

The first of these sachems (or chiefs) was a tall, well-made man; had a very full chest, and brawny limbs. He had a manly countenance, mixed with a good-natured smile. He was about 60 years of age; very active, strong, and had a surprising liveliness in his speech, which I observed in the discourse betwixt him, Mr. Weiser, and some of the sachems.

Tachanuntie, another sachem, or chief of the same nation, was a tall thin man; old, and not so well featured as Cannasateego: I believe he may be near the same age with him. He is one of the greatest warriors that ever the Five Nations produced, and has been a great war-captain for many years past.

He is also called the Black Prince, because as I was informed, he was either begotten on an Indian woman by a negro, or by an Indian chief on some negro woman; but by which of the two, I could not be well assured.

The Governor of Canada (whom these Indians call Onantio) will not treat with any of the Six Nations of Indians, unless *Tachanuntie* is personally present, he having a great sway in all the Indian councils.

Our interpreter, Mr. Weiser, desired us whilst we were here not to talk much of the Indians nor laugh at their dress or make any remarks on their behavior. If we did, it would be very much resented by them, and might cause some differences to arise betwixt the white people and them. Besides, most of them understood English, though they will not speak it when they are in treaty.

The Indians, in general, were poorly dressed, having old match-coats and those being ragged. Few, or not shirts were worn and those they had as black as the Scotchman made the Jamaicans when he wrote in his letter they were as black as an [ink] blot.

When they had rested some little space of time, several of them began to paint themselves with diverse sorts of colors, which rendered them frightful. Some of the others rubbed bear's grease on their faces and then laid upon that a white paint. When we had made a sufficient survey of them and their cabins, we went to the court-house, where the Indians were expected to meet the Governor of Pennsylvania, the Honorable George Thomas, Esquire and to be by him congratulated on their arrival at this town.

Friday, p.m. Between 5 and 6 o'clock, Mr. Weiser accompanied the several Indian chiefs from their camp up to the court-house, which they entered and seated themselves after their own manner. Soon after, his honor, the Governor, the honorable commissioners of Virginia, the honorable the commissioners of Maryland, and the young gentlemen from the three governments, went into the court-house to the Indians. There the Governor, and all the commissioners, severally welcomed the Indians to Lancaster and shaked hands with the sachems.

Then his Honor seated himself in the chair on the bench, the Virginia commissioners placed themselves, to wit, the Hon. Col. Thomas Lee, and Col. William Beverly, on his right hand, and our honorable commissioners on his left. William Peters, Esquire, secretary of Pennsylvania, sat in the middle of the table, under the Governor, and Mr. William Black, secretary to the commissioners of Maryland, on his left hand.

The Governor desired the interpreter to tell the Indians, "He was very glad to see them here, and should not trouble them with business this day, but desired they would rest themselves, after their great journey." This, Mr. Weiser interpreted to them whereat they seemed well enough pleased and made the Governor a suitable answer.

When this was done, a good quantity of punch, wine, and pipes and tobacco were given to the sachems and the Governor and all the commissioners drank to them, whom they pledged. When they had smoked some small time and each drank a glass or two of wine and punch, they retired to their cabins.

Our landlord showed me the book, wherein he keeps the account of the expenses of ours and the Virginia commissioners and which was ordered to be produced every morning to me, to know exactly the amount of each day's expenses.

Saturday, June 23rd, 1744 at Lancaster

This day I was seized with a lax and small fever, occasioned by drinking the water of this town.

After breakfast, the Governor, the honorable the commissioners, and several other gentlemen, went to the Dunker's nunnery about twelve miles from hence. They returned hither about six in the evening.

All this day the Indians staid in their wigwams; and it is usual for them to rest two days after their journey, before they treat, or do business with the English. After supper this evening I went with Mr. President Logan's son and diverse other young gentlemen, to the Indians' camp, they being then dancing one of their lighter war dances.

They performed it after this manner: thirty or forty of the younger men formed themselves into a ring, a fire being lighted (notwithstanding the excessive heat) and burning clear in the midst of them. Near this, sat three elderly Indians, who beat a drum to the time of the others' dancing. Then, the dancers hopped round the ring, after a frantic fashion, not unlike the priests of the Bacchus in old times, and repeated, sundry times, these sounds, Yohoh! Bugh! Soon after this, the major part of this dancers {or rather hoppers} set up a horrid shriek or halloo!

They continued dancing and hopping, after this manner, several hours and rested very seldom. Once, whilst I staid with them, they did rest themselves; immediately thereupon, the three old men began to sing an Indian song the tune of which was not disagreeable to the white bystanders. Upon this, the young warriors renewed their terrible shriek and halloo and formed themselves into a ring, environing the three old ones and danced as before.

Mr. Calvert, myself, and some others slipped through the dancers and stood near the fire and when the drum-beaters ceased their noise, we shaked them by the hand. Here we presented some clean pipes to them, which were very acceptable, most of the Indians being great smokers of Tobacco.

A Conestogoe or Susquehannah Indian stood without the circle and importuned the white bystanders to give money to the young children, which was done. Whilst this diversion happened, some High-Dutch, belonging to the town brought their guns with them to the camp; which being perceived by the Conestogoe, he informed us it would be very displeasing to the Indians who would resent it, though brother thither with ever so innocent an intent; therefore desired us to tell the Germans to withdraw and leave their muskets out of their sight, otherwise some bad consequence might ensue. We complied with his request and made the Germans retire.

From the camp I went to Worrall's and sat up till eleven o'clock; to whose house I heard the Indian drum and the warriors repeating their terrible noise and dancing; and at this sport of theirs, they continued till near one in the morning.

These young men are surprisingly agile, strong, and straight limbed. They shoot both with the gun and bow and arrow most dexterously. They likewise throw their tomahawk (or little hatchet) with great certainty at an indifferent large object for twenty or thirty yards distance. This weapon they use against their enemies when they have spent their powder and ball and destroy many of them with it.

The Chiefs, who were deputed to treat with the English by their different nations were very sober men, which is rare for an Indian to be so, if he can get liquor. They behaved very well during our stay amongst them, and sundry times refused drinking in a moderate way. Whenever they renew old treaties of friendship, or make any bargain about lands they sell to the English, they take great care to abstain from intoxicating drink for fear of being over-reached; but when they have finished their business, then some of them will drink without measure.

Sunday, June 24th, 1744

Mr. Commissioner Jenings ordered me to copy the speech to be made by him, in the name of the governor of Maryland to the Indians in the court-house tomorrow morning. This and transcribing some copies of it busied me so much that I could not go to the court-house where divine service, according to the church of England, was performed by my fellow-traveler, the Reverend Mr. Craddock, to a numerous audience, this day. He also preached a very good sermon, which met the approbation of the several gentlemen present.

His Honor the Governor invited Mr. Craddock to dine with him, which he did and received a hearty welcome. Betwixt 1 and 2, our honorable commissioners and those of Virginia dined in the court-house, and the gentlemen of both their governments; after which, the office of the day was again performed by another minister of the established church. He gave us an excellent sermon, and expatiated very feelingly on the too prevalent vices of the age. He used plain language and thereby fitted his discourse for all capacities by which all might truly edify, if they had any grace or good disposition thereto.

In the evening, walked to the Indian camp, where they were dancing in the manner described last night, only the number of dancers was augmented, they having taken in several small boys, to make a larger ring. Betwixt 8 and 9 this night, supped with my brother secretary, Mr. Black, in his lodgings at Mr. George Sanderson's. We had pleasant company, good wine, and lime punch. From hence I went to Worrall's where in my room three very impudent Indian traders had taken possession of my bed and caused another to be there made; but after some disputes, our landlord made these scoundrels quit their beds and leave the parson and myself in quiet possession.

These traders for the most part are as wild as some of the most savage Indians amongst whom they trade for skins, fur, &c. for sundry kinds of European goods, and strong liquors. They go back in the country, above 300 miles from the white inhabitants; here they live with the Indian hunters till they have disposed of their cargoes; and then, on horses, carry their skins, &c. to Philadelphia, where they are bought by the merchants there and from thence exported to London.

It is a very beneficial trade, though hazardous to their persons and lives; for the weather is so excessively cold where they trade, which is near the lakes of Canada, and their cabins so poorly made to defend themselves from the bitter winters that they often perish; and on the other hand, they are liable to the insults and savage fury of the drunken Indians by selling to them rum and other spirituous liquors. The government, as yet, have not provided a law prohibiting the selling such liquors, although it has been pressed by his Honor, who is but too sensible of the ill effects produced by the Indian traders carrying so much to barter with the hunters of the Six Nations.

I rested well, after dispossessing these intruding guests; but this happened by my giving orders to my landlord's servants this morning to wash our room with cold water and take my bed from its bedstead and lay it on the floor and by this means the bugs and fleas were defeated of their prey.

Monday morning, 25th of June, 1744

At 10 o'clock the Indian sachems met the Governor, the honorable commissioners of Virginia, and those of this province, when his Honor made them a speech to which Cannasateego returned an answer in behalf of all the others present. The Indians staid in the court-house about two hours; and were regaled with some bumbo and sangree. The honorable commissioners from

Virginia and Maryland dined in the court-house as did the gentlemen of both governments; we had two tables and a great variety of victuals; our company being about thirty in number.

In the court-house on Monday, p.m.

The Governor and all the honorable commissioners resumed their several seats here and then the chiefs came in and took their places. Edmund Jenings, Esquire, as first commissioner for Maryland made a speech to the Six Nations which was interpreted to them by Mr. Weiser. Whilst Mr. Jenings delivered his speech, he gave the interpreter a string and two belts of wampum which were by him presented to the sachem Cannasateego; and the Indians thereupon gave the cry of approbation; by this we were sure the speech was well approved by the Indians. This cry is usually made on presenting wampum to the Indians in a treaty, and is performed thus: The grand chief and speaker amongst them pronounces the word, *jo-bab!* with a loud voice, singly; then all the others join in this sound, *woh!* dwelling some little while upon it and keeping exact time with each other and immediately with a sharp noise and force, utter this sound, *wugh!*

This is performed in great order and with the utmost ceremony and decorum; and with the Indians is like our English huzza!

Monday evening in the court-house chamber.

I supped with the Governor, the honorable commissioners and the gentlemen of Philadelphia who attended his Honor to this town. We had an elegant entertainment and after supper the Governor was extremely merry, and thereby set an example of agreeable mirth, which ran through the whole company. During this merriment, two Germans happened to pass by the court-house with a harp and fiddle and played some tunes under the window of our room. Upon that, they were ordered to come upstairs where the Governor required them to divert us, which they did, but not with the harmony of their music (for that was very uncouth and displeasing to us, who had heard some of the best bands in England) but by playing a tune of some sort to a young Indian who danced a jig with Mr. Andrew Hamilton in a most surprising manner. At nine o'clock, the Governor and commissioners left us and then the younger persons raised their jollity by dancing in the Indian dress and after their manner.

Tuesday, 26th of June

Copied fair the proceedings of yesterday with the Indians as also Governor Thomas's speech to them, which were transmitted to his Excellency Thomas

Bladen, Esquire, Governor of Maryland, by Mr. Commissioner Jenings.

We dined in the court-house and soon after I received orders from the above commissioner to acquaint all the Maryland gentlemen, "that they should desist going into the court-house this afternoon, during our treaty with the Six Nations." Pursuant to which order, I informed the gentlemen of our commissioners' pleasure, at which the first were much disgusted as were the Virginia gentlemen who had the same commands laid on them by the secretary of their commissioners.

Five o'clock. p.m. His Honor the Governor of Pennsylvania and the honorable the commissioners of Virginia and Maryland, met the Indian chiefs in the court-house when Cannasateego answered our speech of yesterday and presented a string and two belts of wampum: which being done, the further execution of the treaty was adjourned until the next day.

By order of our commissioners, and at the request of Mr. Weiser, the interpreter, I bought half a gross of tobacco pipes to be presented to the Indians at their camp, which was accordingly done and they seemed well pleased with the gift, such pipes being scarce with them.

Wednesday 27th of June

After breakfast, viewed Mr. Worrall's book of our expenses, which we settled; and the whole amount thereof from the 20th instant to this day was £46-0-5, Pennsylvania currency. – N.B. Mr Worrall's account for the negroes' expenses was not included in the above sum.

This day our commissioners wrote a letter to our Governor giving him an account of their transactions with the Indians, which I fairly copied by their order.

p.m. 5 o'clock. The Governor and all the honorable commissioners again met and treated with the Six Nations in the court-house when Tachanuntie, the famous Black Prince (mentioned before) answered the speech made yesterday by the Hon. Col. Lee, one of the Virginia commissioners; and in token that it was well received and approved by the chiefs, Tachanuntie presented one string and two belts of wampum to his Majesty's commissioners of Virginia. Then Mr. Commissioner Jenings desired the interpreter to ask the Indians if they would be ready for a conference tomorrow morning in the court-house chamber with the commissioners of Maryland; which he did, and the Indians answered that they would meet for that purpose, as desired.

At 8 o'clock this evening I went with three of our honorable commissioners to a ball in the court-house chamber; to which his Honor, the governor of

Pennsylvania, the commissioners of Virginia and Maryland, and the gentlemen of the several colonies with sundry inhabitants of this town, were invited.

James Hamilton, Esquire, the proprietor of Lancaster, made the ball and opened it by dancing two minuets with two of the ladies here, which last danced wilder time than any Indians. Our music and musicians were the same as described last Monday evening.

The females (I dare not call them ladies, for that would be a profanation of the name) were in general very disagreeable. The dancers consisted of Germans and Scotch-Irish; but there were some Jewesses, who had not long since come from New York that made a tolerable appearance being well dressed and of an agreeable behavior.

There was a large and elegant supper prepared in the court-house chamber, of which the Governor, some of the honorable commissioners and the female dancers first eat: then the other gentlemen in order, and afterwards the younger gentlemen. The dances were concluded about 12 o'clock; but myself, with several others of the younger sort, staid till after one in the morning.

Thursday, 28th June, 1744, a.m.

At 9 this morning, the commissioners of Maryland and the Six Nations met in the court-house chamber according to the agreement of yesterday.

Here we opened the several bales and boxes of goods to be presented the Indians, they having been bought at Philadelphia and sent hither for that end. Before the chiefs viewed and handled the several goods, Mr. Commissioner Jenings made them a speech in the name of the Governor of Maryland, with which, after it was interpreted to them by Mr. Weiser, they seemed well pleased.

The chiefs turned over and narrowly inspected the goods, and asked the prices of them; which being told them, they seemed somewhat dissatisfied; and desired to go down into the court-house to consult among themselves (which is their usual method if it concerns any matter of importance, as this was, for they must give a particular account of their whole negotiation to their several tribes, when they return) with their interpreter. They did so and after some time came up again, and agreed with our commissioners to release their claim and right to any lands now held by the inhabitants of Maryland and for which the said Indians were not heretofore satisfied in consideration of the following goods, viz:

| 4 pieces of strouds, at £7 | £28 00 |
| 2 pieces ditto, £5 | 10 00 |

200 shirts	63 12 0
3 pieces half thicks	11 00
3 ditto duffle blankets, at £7	21 00
1 ditto, ditto,	6 10 0
47 guns, at £1-6-0,	61 2 0
1 lb. Vermilion	0 18 0
Carried over	£202 2 0
Brought over,	£202 2 0
1000 flints,	0 18 0
4 doz. Jews-harps	0 14 0
1 doz. Boxes	0 1 0
1 cwt. 2 qrs. 0 lb. Bar lead	3 0 0
2 qrs. Shot	1 0 0
2 half barrels gun-powder	13 0 0
Pennsylvania money	£220 15 0

The above quantity of goods were accordingly given the Indians, as agreed on by both parties; after which our commissioners ordered me to go to Mr. Worrall and desire him to send some punch for the sachems, which was accordingly done; and after they had severally drank health to the commissioners and the compliment returned by the latter, the Indians retired to their wigwams and the honorable commissioners went to their lodgings about 12 o'clock.

Post Meridiem. The commissioners of Virginia had a private treaty with the chiefs in the court-house, when Col. Lee made them a speech. In the evening, about 7 o'clock, I accompanied my friend, Col. Nathan Rigbie to the Indian cabins, where having collected several of their papooses (or little children) together, he slung a handful of English half-pennies amongst them for which they scrambled heartily and with the utmost earnestness.

This pleased the elder sort very much and they esteem it a great mark of friendship if the white people make presents to their children or treat them with any particular notice. I gave the papooses some small beads, which were kindly received. The young men this night again danced a war dance, as described on Saturday last; at which were present a great number of white people. When the colonel and myself had taken a view of the Onondagoes' Cahugas' and Senecas' cabins, he went from me to the ring of dancers and then I went to a cabin where I heard the celebrated Mrs. Montour, a French lady, (but now, by having lived so long among the Six Nations, is become almost an Indian) had her residence.

When I approached the wigwam, I saluted her in French and asked her whether she was not born in Canada? Of what parents? And whether she had not lived a long time with the Indians? She answered me in the same language very civilly and after some compliments were passed betwixt us, told me in a polite manner that she "was born in Canada, whereof her father (who was a French gentleman) had been Governor; under whose administration the then Five Nations of Indians had made war against the French, and the Hurons in that government (whom we term the French Indians from espousing their part against the English and living in Canada) and that in the war she was taken by some of the Five Nations warriors, being then about ten years of age; and by them was carried away into their country, where she was inhabited and brought up in the same manner as their children. That when she grew up to years of maturity, she was married to a famous war captain of those nations who was in great esteem for the glory he procured in the wars he carried on against the Catawbas, a great nation of Indians to the southwest of Virginia, by whom she had several children; but about fifteen years ago, he was killed in a battle with them; since which, she has not been married. That she had little or no remembrance of the place of her birth, nor indeed of her parents, it being near fifty years since she was ravished from them by the Indians."

She has been a handsome woman, genteel and of polite address, notwithstanding her residence has been so long among the Indians; though formerly she was wont to accompany the several chiefs who used to renew treaties of friendship with the proprietor and governor of Pennsylvania, at Philadelphia, the metropolis of that province; and being a white woman, was there very much caressed by the gentlewomen of that city, with whom she used to stay for some time.

She retains her native language by conversing with the Frenchmen who trade for fur, skins, &c. among the six nations; and our language she learned at Philadelphia as likewise of our traders, who go back into the Indians' country. In her cabin were two of her daughters, by the war-captain, who were both married to persons of the same station, and were then gone to war with the Catawbas before mentioned.

One of these young women had a son about five years old, who I think, was one of the finest featured and limbed children mine eyes ever saw and was not so tawny, or greased, as the other Indian children were; but on the contrary, his cheeks were ruddy, mixed with a delicate white, had eyes and hair of an hazel color and was neatly dressed in a green ban-jan, and his other garments were suitable.

Madame Montour has but one son, who for his prowess and martial exploits, was lately made a captain, and a member of the Indian council and is now gone to war against the Catawbas, with her son-in-law.

She is in great esteem with the best sort of white people and by them always treated with abundance of civility; and whenever she went to Philadelphia (which formerly she did pretty often) the ladies of that city always invited her to their houses, entertained her well, and made her several presents.

From this cabin, when I had taken leave of Mrs. Montour and her daughters, I returned to the dancers who were continuing their mirth; and afterwards returned to my lodgings.

Friday, June the 29th, 1744, a.m.

Our commissioners and the Six Nations had a private conference in the court-house chamber, when they jointly proceeded to settle the bounds and quantity of land the latter were to release to Lord Baltimore, in Maryland; but the Indians, not very well apprehending our commissioners, in their demand respecting the bounds of the lands to be released, occasioned a great delay in the finishing of that business; however, it was wholly settled in the afternoon, upon Mr. Weiser's conference with the Governor of Pennsylvania, his Majesty's commissioners of Virginia and those of Maryland and also with the Indians in council where he debated the matter more fully and explained our commissioners' demands in so clear a manner that they came to such an amicable determination as proved agreeable to each party.

We again presented the sachems, here with bumbo punch, with which they drank prosperity and success to their Father, the great King over the waters and to the healths of our commissioners.

This day we dined at our landlord Worrall's and it was agreed by the commissioners of Maryland to invite all the Six Nations' chiefs, to dine with them, in company with the Governor and Virginia commissioners, tomorrow in the court-house; against which time orders were given to prepare a large and elegant entertainment.

In the evening I went with Col. Rigbie and other gentlemen to visit one Mr. Adams, a German doctor who we understood, had got an organ; but it was with the greatest importunity he would favor us in playing a tune, telling us that unless he himself was possessed with a strong desire to play, he could oblige nobody; yet, seeing we were so very importunate, he at last complied and strummed over three or four High-Dutch psalm tunes, to which he sang the words in the most enthusiastic raptures.

For my part, what with the horrid noise he made on the organ, and his horse-voice, I never suffered so great an anticipation of pleasure in hearing music, or at least a musical instrument, in my whole life. When he had finished his rapturous fit of noise, he acquainted us that he had been a consummate rake in his more youthful days; but soon after he married, turned himself into a sober and religious life and praised his Maker several hours in a day by playing on and singing to his organ. He seemed to us to be a perfect enthusiast; and upon inquiry among his neighbors, he has borne that character ever since he took to himself a wife. Being very much tired with his cant and noise, we at last took our leaves of him though not before inviting him to drink a glass of wine with us at our lodgings; but he desired to be excused accepting our invitation, at which we were not displeased since we might have expected his visit would have proved very troublesome.

Saturday, 30th June, 1744, a.m.

Mr. Commissioner Jenings having this morning drawn a deed of release from the chiefs of the Six Nations for the lands they claim in Maryland, to the use of Lord Baltimore, sent for me to engross it, which I so did, pursuant to his order about nine o'clock.

At ten, his Majesty's commissioners had a conference with the Indians in the court-house chamber, to which no other persons than themselves were admitted.

One o'clock, p.m. The twenty-four chiefs of the Six Nations by invitation of yesterday from the honorable commissioners of Maryland dined with them in the court-house; when were present, at other tables, his Honor the Governor of Pennsylvania, the honorable commissioners of Virginia, and a great many gentlemen of the three colonies. There were a large number of the inhabitants of Lancaster likewise present to see the Indians dine.

We had five tables, great variety of dishes and served up in very good order. The sachems sat at two separate tables. At the head of one, the famous orator, Cannasateego sat and the others were placed according to their rank. As the Indians are not accustomed to eat in the same manner as the English, or other polite nations do, we who were secretaries on this affair, with Mr. Thomas Cookson, prothonotary of Lancaster county,

William Logan, Esq., son of President Logan, and Mr. Nathaniel Rigbie of Baltimore county, in Maryland, carved the meat for them, served them with cider and wine, mixed with water and regulated the economy of the two tables.

The chiefs seemed prodigiously pleased with their feast, for they fed lustily, drank heartily and were very greasy before they finished their dinner, for the bye, they made no use of their forks. The interpreter, Mr. Weiser, stood betwixt the table, where the governor sat and that, at which the sachems were placed, who by order of his Honor, was desired to inform the Indians he drank their healths, which he did; whereupon they gave the usual cry of approbation, and returned the compliment, by drinking health to his Honor and the several commissioners.

After dinner, the interpreter informed the Governor and commissioners, "that as the Lord Proprietary and Governor of Maryland was not known to the Indians by any particular name, they had agreed in council to take the first opportunity of a large company to present him with one: And, as this with them was a matter of great consequence, and attended with abundance of form, the several nations had drawn lots for the performance of the ceremony; and the lot falling on the C hûga nation, they had chosen Gâchrâd don, one of their chiefs, to be their speaker and he desired leave to begin; which being given, he on an elevated part of the court-house, with all the dignity of a warrior, the gesture of an orator, and in a very graceful posture, spoke as follows: 'As the Governor of Maryland has invited us here, to treat about our lands, and brighten the chain of friendship, the united Six Nations think themselves so much obliged to him that we have come to a resolution, in council, to give the great man, who is proprietor of Maryland a particular name, by which we may hereafter correspond with him: And as it hath fallen to the Cahugaes' lot in council to consider of a proper name for that chief man, we have agreed to give him the name of 'Tôc ry-hô-gôn' denoting Precedency, Excellency, or living in the middle, or honorable place, between Asseriogoa and our brother Onas, by whom our treaties may be better carried on."

And then, addressing himself to his Honor the Governor of Pennsylvania, the honorable the commissioners of Virginia and Maryland, and to the gentlemen then present, he added: "As there is a company of great men now assembled, we take this opportunity to publish this matter, that it may be known Tocary-ho-gon is our friend, and that we are ready to honor him and that by such name he may be always called and known among us; and we hope, he will ever act towards us, according to the excellence of the name we have now given him and enjoy a long and happy life."

When the speech was ended, all the other chiefs expressed their assent and great satisfaction at what was said to our commissioners, insomuch that they sent forth five several cries of approbation.

Gachradodon having finished his complimentary oration, Mr. Commissioner Jenings, in the name of the other commissioners, and on behalf of Lord Baltimore, spoke in reply to the sachem: "That his Lordship was much obliged to the six nations for distinguishing him by the name of Tocaryhogon, esteeming it a mark of kindness and honor; that his Lordship would entertain the most unfeigned friendship for them and that the government of Maryland would ever be ready and desirous to render them its best offices, conducive to their tranquility and undisturbed safety" which Mr. Weiser, by command, interpreted to the Indians and at the same time was ordered to acquaint them that the governor and the commissioners were then preparing to drink his Majesty's health; all which was done, and the chiefs expressed sincere joy by their cry of approbation and drank the same in bumpers of Madeira wine. The governor, commissioners, and indeed all the persons present, except the Indians, gave three several huzzas, after the English manner, on drinking the King's health; which a good deal surprised them, they having never before heard the like noise.

Upon ending the ceremony of drinking healths, the governor and commissioners retired some little time; but within an hour, the comimssioners of Virginia and Maryland entered the court-house, and afterwards went up into the chamber, as likewise the several chiefs, Mr. Weiser, and a great many of the young gentlemen. Here, by order of our commissioners, I produced the engrossed release for the lands, with the seals fixed.

We were obliged to put about the glass pretty briskly; and then Mr. Weiser interpreted the contents of it to the sachems, who, conferring amongst themselves about the execution of it, the major part of them seemed very inclinable to sign and deliver it; but upon Shukelemy, an Oneydoe chief's remonstrance, some of the others, with himself, refused for that day executing it; which refusal of Shukelemy we imputed and that not without reason, to some sinister and under-hand means, made use of by the Pennsylvanians to induce the sachems not to give up their right to the lands by deed, without having a larger consideration given them by the province of Maryland than what was specified in the release.

Shukelemy, who before we had esteemed as one of fastest friends, put us under deep surprise and confusion by his unfair behavior; yet we, in some measure, extricated ourselves out of them by the honest Cannasateego's and the other sachems, to the number of sixteen, delivering the deed after the forms customary with the English, to which there were a great many gentlemen signed their names as witnesses. Weiser assured the commissioners that he, with Cannasteego and some other chiefs, would so effectually represent the unfair dealilng of Shukelemy and his partisans in council, that he did not doubt to induce him and them totally to finish this business on Monday next, maugre all the insinuation and misrepresentations agitated by the enemies of Maryland; and indeed Mr. Interpreter proved successful, as is evident in the transactions of Monday, and may be seen in the printed treaty.

Monday, July the 2nd, 1744, a.m.

The honorable commissioners of Maryland, with Mr. Weiser, met at the house of George Sanderson, in this town, when the several chiefs, who had not signed the deed of release, and renunciation of their claim to lands in Maryland, did now cheerfully, and without any hesitation, execute the same, in the presence of the commissioners and Mr. Weiser; which latter they caused to sign and deliver it on behalf of a nation not present, both with his Indian name of Tarachiawagon, and that of Weiser.

Thus we happily effected the purchase of the lands in Maryland, by the dexterous management of the interpreter, notwithstanding the storm on Saturday, that threatened to blast our measures; and hereby gained not only some hundred thousand acres of land to Lord Baltimore, who had no good right to them before this release, but an undisturbed and quiet enjoyment of them to the several possessors, who in fact, had bought of that Lord's agent.

The names of the chiefs who signed and delivered the deed were: Cannasteego, Tacanoontia, Johnuhat, Caxhayion, Toruchdadon, Netokanyhak, and Rotierawuchto, sachems of the Onondago nation.

Saguchsonyunt, Gachradodon, Hutasalyakon, Rowanhohiso, Osochquah, and Seyenties, sachems of the Cahugaes.

Swadamy (alias Shukelemy), Onichnaxqua, Onochkallydawy (alias Watsatuha), Tohashwanrarorows, Arughhocththaw, and Tiorhaasery, sachems of the Oneydoes.

Sidowax, Attiusgu, Tuwaiadachquha, sachems of the Tuscaroroes.

Tanasanegos, and Tanachiuntus, chiefs of the Senikers, or Senecaes.

This deed was delivered by Mr. Commissioner Jenings, on his return to Annapolis, to his clerk, Mr. Richard Burdus, who recorded it among the land records, in the provincial court office of Maryland, in libro. E.I. fo. 8, 9, 10, 11.

This morning the Governor met the Indians on business and Cannasteego answered his Honor's speech made to the Indians on Thursday last, relating to the murder of John Armstrong, and his two men, Indian traders. The chief said, "That the Indians were from the bottom of their hearts, very sorry such a misfortune had happened; but hoped their brother Onas would dry up his tears, and wipe his eyes: That they would send the two Delawares down to Philadelphia who were suspected to be, and charged as accessories to the murder, though they really believed them guiltless for they assured the Governor, that on the trial of the Indian in Philadelphia jail committed for perpetrating Armstrong's and his men's murder, it would appear that he was the sole person who did the horrid deed: however, to comply with the Governor's request, they would send the Delawares (but not as prisoners) to be examined and tried; and if they were found guilty to suffer the as the English law prescribes; but if innocent, to then to return them safe to the Six Nations." His Honor, in return, said, "That great care should be taken to do the Delawares all the justice in the world: and if, upon a fair trial, they should be acquitted, he would send them in safety to their own homes."

The Indians gave the Governor four strings of wampum and he, in return, presented them with three strings. But for a more particular account of Armstrong and his men's murder, see the treaty at large.

In the afternoon, the honorable commissioners of Virginia had a conference with the Indians in the court-house chamber, when a deed in the nature of ours, releasing their claim to a large quantity of land, lying in that colony was produced by Mr. Weiser to the sachems for execution, which was signed and delivered by them in the presence of diverse gentlemen of the three colonies, who were witnesses to the same.

Wine and sangree was presented to the chiefs, who drank to the continuation of the friendship betwixt them, and his Majesty's subjects in Virginia. After the deed was executed, Cannasateego, commanded the young Indian men then present to entertain the Governor and commissioners in the evening with a particular dance, according to the custom of their nations; which was complied with about 8 o'clock.

Before they performed the dance, I went to their camp, where I saw the young warriors paint themselves in a frightful manner and on their heads place a great quantity of feathers. They took arrows and tomahawks in their hands and then unanimously ran out of their camp, hallooing and shrieking {which was terrible to us, being strangers} up the street to Mr. Cookson's where the

Governor was: and there they made a ring, a person placed in it, and danced round him to a horrid noise made by the enclosed person and the others.

In this manner, they continued some time flourishing their weapons and striving to destroy him in the ring. When they had acted thus about seven or eight minutes, then their captain ran before them, very swift, to another place about twenty or thirty yards distance from Mr. Cookson's and there acted the same over again. This was a representation of the Indians besieging a fort of their enemies (who have no cannon) the person in the midst of the circle representing the fort besieged, and the Indians encircling him, the besiegers. And, as it sometimes happens, that they are beaten from a fort when besieging it, so their running away as described above was the manner of their retreat.

As soon as the Indians recovered their fatigue, they renewed the attack of the supposed fort. When they had finished the siege and the Governor and commissioners had treated them with sangree, they immediately retired to their wigwams.

Tuesday, 3rd July, 1744.

At 11 o'clock this morning, the Governor and all the honorable commissioners had a meeting with the Six Nations in the court-house when his Honor made a speech to them, as did the commissioners of Virginia and Maryland; and each party presented strings and belts of wampum, on receipt of which, the Indians gave the usual cry of approbation, and in a stronger and more cheerful tone than heretofore. They were served with plenty of rum at the conclusion of the speeches and drank it with good *goût*.

Wednesday, 4th July, 1744.

The Indian chiefs assembled in the court-house and the Governor and commissioners met them there, when the speeches made yesterday by the latter gentlemen were answered by the Indian orators. After this, the chiefs made a present of a large bundle of deer-skins to his Honor, the commissioners of Virginia, and to those of Maryland, which were kindly accepted. The Governor, commissioners of Virginia, and the white bystanders, gave three loud huzzas, and thereby put an end to the treaty in regard to them.

In the Afternoon. Court-house.

The Shawanese nation of Indians, who compose the sixth body amongst these Indians in the year 1742, came down to Maryland on the eastern shore of that province to a nation of our friendly Indians and tributary to the Six Nations, called the Nanticokes, from inhabiting near a river of that name. And, by their artifices, persuaded them to rise upon the English to recover all the lands that had been formerly theirs, but now possessed by the English under Lord Baltimore, at the same time promising the Nanticokes all the assistance in the power of them, the Shawanese, though they were in perfect friendship with us by the treaty made during the administration of the Honorable Charles Calvert, Esquire, who giving ear, but too unwarily, to the Shawanese, did intend to have put in practice the wicked scheme of destroying the white inhabitants of that shore; but their machinations were opportunely discovered by one of the Nanticoke chiefs a day or two before they were to have perpetrated the intended murders of the English.

Upon this, the militia of the counties were raised, who after a great and close search, took 68 Nanticoke chiefs prisoners with old Panquash, their emperor and they were brought to Annapolis in sloops and there examined and confined, but afterwards set at liberty. As these actions of the Shawanese (who indeed are the most dishonest and treacherous of all the other Six Nations and for that reason hated by them) were contrary to the treaties then subsisting betwixt us and them as a part of the Six Nations, the commissioners took an opportunity in a private conference with them this afternoon, "to ask them the reason of the Shawanese's procedure and whether they had any countenance from other nations? And, also desired the chiefs, then present, to search this business fully and reprimand the criminal Shawanese who were more blamable than the deluded Nanticokes."

The Six Nations, by their orator, said "that they were heartily sorry for what the Shawanese had done but on their return to Onondago, they would make a strict inquiry of the whole affair and if they found them so culpable as we alleged they were, then they would severely reprimand them for their treacherous behavior, contrary to the faith of treaties." When this answer was finished, our commissioners shook the several chiefs by the hand, and took their leaves of them, presenting Gachradodon with a fine laced hat.

This Gachradodon is a very celebrated warrior, and one of the Cahuga chiefs, about forty years of age, tall, straight limbed and a graceful person, but not so fat as Cannasateego. His action, when he spoke, was certainly the most graceful as well as bold that any person ever saw without the buffoonery of the French, or over-solemn deportment of the haughty Spaniards. When he made the complimentary speech on the occasion of giving Lord Baltimore the name of Tocaryhogan, he was complimented by the Governor, who said "that he would have made a good figure in the forum of old Rome." And Mr. Commissioner Jenings declared, "that he had never seen so just an action in any of the most celebrated orators he had heard speak."

Thursday, 5th July, 1744

This morning Mr. Peters, secretary to the Governor, Mr. Black, secretary to the honorable commissioners of Virginia and myself, examined the whole treaty and finished all matters any way relating to it. At 12, Colonels Colvill and King, with the Virginia commissioners, settled our accounts with Mr. Worrall. Here we dined and immediately afterwards mounted our horses and went form this filthy town to our kind, facetious landord's, Mr. Hughes, at Nottingham township, by the Gap-Road, so called from a space or gap being open in the ridge of blue mountains which extend a great way to the south-westward of Virginia and north-eastward of Pennsylvania.

I was so fatigued with my journey, which was forty-four miles, and the weather was so sultry, withal, having no good accommodations on the road, that several of us were seized with a fever. Lay at Mr. Hughes's, where good care was taken of me by my kind host.

Friday, 6th of July, 1744

Breakfasted at Mr. Hughes's; and about eight in the morning set our for Mr. Benjamin Chew's in Cecil county, after having taken leave of the honorable commissioners of Virginia and the several young gentlemen of that colony, with the latter of whom I had contracted a friendship and received many civilities from them. My horse tired in my journey to Mr. Chew's, though it was but ten miles. Here I rested this day and night, my fever continuing, and my horse still remaining lame.

Saturday, 7th of July, 1744

Went from Mr. Chew's about six this morning: crossed the lower ferry of Susquehannah: baited at Mr. Treadway's ordinary and arrived at Joppa about 11 o'clock. Ferried from thence over Gunpowder River to Mr. Day's, where I dined. From hence proceeded to Baltimore town, where I rested at the Reverend Mr. Benedict Bourdillon's; staid and drank tea with him and his lady, and then went over Potapscoe River to Mrs. Hughes's ordinary, where I lodged this night.

Sunday, 8th July, 1744

After breakfast, about six this morning, went from hence to Annapolis, with Mr. William Dallam, and arrived there at ten o'clock.

The end of my Journal.

WILLIAM MARSHE,
Secretary to the Hon. Commis. Of Maryland

LETTER OF STEPHEN BADGER

Historical and Characteristic Traits of the American Indians in General, and Those of Natick in Particular; in a Letter From the Reverend Stephen Badger of Natick, to the Corresponding Secretary of the Scots Commissioners, Addressing Their May 14th Query on the Numbers, Customs, Habits and Causes of Decline in the Natick Indians.

Reverend Sir,

Your letter of the 20th of May has been received. Had the queries contained in it been proposed to me at an earlier part of my residence in this place, I should have been much better able to give a satisfactory answer to some of them, than I am at so late a period, it being now the forty-fifth year of my stated ministry here. I have not any printed materials from which I can collect any information on the subject of your letter and have no other manuscripts than the church records which originated with my immediate predecessor and which have been continued by myself to the present time.

As also [at my disposal] the records of the town and the records of the original proprietors of the soil, all of whom were Indians, but neither of these records contain any certain and conclusive documents relating to their number or state at any particular period. Neither from the number of those of them that have been baptized, including adults, minors and infants; nor from the bills of mortality that have been recorded, can any accurate account be derived as they are all imperfect and deficient and some of them very irregular and as none of them were designed to give any enumeration of them, or any direct and general information concerning them.

Although I have scarcely any turn for historical researches and inquiries, yet since my connection with the Indians commenced, I have not been without some degree of curiosity relating to them. This, in times past, when they were more numerous and when there were a considerable number of aged persons living, both among the English and Indians, led me to make some inquiries and observations concerning them, as occasions were offered; but as I had not any expectations or even apprehensions that they would be of any use to others, and did not think of committing any of them to writing, the unretentiveness of my memory, in addition to the many scenes of difficulty which I have had to pass through, both before, and especially since, the commencement of the political revolutions of our country, in a great measure prevent my recollection of many of them. Such, however, as I can call to mind and such observations as I may at this time make, and such of the causes of their past and present state, as can be rationally investigated and assigned by me, and which may have any tendency to elucidate the subject of your letter, shall be freely communicated to you.

That the number of Indians in this place, as well as others, especially where the white people have been either intermixed with them or have settled in their vicinity, has been diminished from time to time, and is now greatly lessened, is well known and cannot be disputed. This diminution, I apprehend, is not to be considered as originating in or confined to, any single cause but as arising from a concurrence and co-operation of several. Which of them has been the most predominant one, I shall leave to others to determine.

That it is wholly, or chiefly, the effect of a limited and less refined civilization, of regular industry, and of Christianity, either simply or separately, or collectively considered, I think cannot rationally be admitted because the most obvious and direct tendency of each of these, more especially of the two last, is to promote health and morals and consequently, to bring on that longevity of which Indians generally fall short. Other causes therefore are to be sought for by which to account for this strange and melancholy effect.

It may not therefore be improper to observe, that while the white people in America, either by descent or by emigration from the different nations of Europe, have increased in population and been otherwise prospered, even at those times in which they had great difficulties to encounter and overcome, the Indians, at the same time, and when under every advantage and excitement that are supposed to arise from regular habits of industry, melioration of manners, an associated state somewhat similar to that of Europeans and from the means of religion, have notwithstanding, dwindled, become wretched and in some places are almost extinct.

But it is to be considered that the white people under the just mentioned circumstances, instead of having to alter, and even to set aside that mode of life, and that regular and stated course of industry to which they had been early accustomed had only, (and that without any difficulty), to continue and make additional improvements in them. And also, that instead of having to give up those religious principles and forsaking those religious rites, customs and practices, to the belief and habits of which they had been very early, very gradually, and imperceptibly introduced, influence and examples of their progenitors, had been more and more established and confirmed in them. The Indians, instead of all this, have been called upon and have had it pressed upon them by the inculcation of the arts of civilization (which perhaps have been too much refined, at least at first, for nature in its rude and unpolished state) by a regular and uniform attention to the practice of industry, and especially by the enforcement of the self-denying principles and precepts of Christianity and the future and distant prospects which it held up to them.

By all these united, I say, they have been urged to an almost total change of their old customs and manners to substitute others in their stead, some of which are directly opposite to their ancient usages; to put a greater force upon nature than they could easily and at once give in to; to oppose and give up what they had always before been habituated to, and had had a veneration for; and even to set aside those superstitious rites, in the zealous performance of which, what religion they had, exclusive of the religion or law of nature, very much consisted, and of which they were not a little fond and tenacious. These things, so far as they embraced and conformed to them, have had a corresponding tendency and effect and have been not a little unfavorable to their health and constitution, and of course, had a tendency to shorten their lives.

It may not be improper further to observe that where the principles of the gospel, the habits of industry, and a regular mode of life, have had to counteract and to combat the principles and habits of indolence and laziness, roughness and ferocity of manners, and an irregular and improvident disposition and practice, the struggle, which has consequently not a little unfavorable, especially at first, to natural constitution, to health and long life.

It is also to be observed and considered that there is a wide and important difference between the Indian natives of America and the emigrants from Europe and those that have been descended from them, with regard to religion in other respects. When Christianity was first promulgated by the divine mission of its author, and by those that were commissioned and sent by him for the same purpose, both before and after his resurrection; the principles and doctrines, the institutions and precepts which were taught and enjoined by them, in addition to the reasonableness of them, and to the fulfillment of ancient prophecy, were authenticated and supported by a series of miraculous operations and events. A record of these has been handed down to succeeding ages, through several periods of the Christian church; by which, most of the nations of Europe and that nation, in particular, from which the inhabitants of the United States principally originated, have preserved and continued in the possession of it. They were generally instructed in its principles from their infancy, unopposed by the principles, influence and examples of those who had not embraced it, or whose principles were different from it; the knowledge and belief of it grew up with them; they received it as a revelation from heaven; the public worship and institutions of it were established and statedly attended upon; and it had the sanction not only of civil government, but of parental authority and example; so that an early prepossession in favor of its belief generally took place among them.

This is very far from having been the case with the original natives of this land. Christianity was proposed to them after the principles and habits of superstition and idolatry were established and even deeply rooted in their minds. They had no tradition, either oral or written, from their ancestors to found a belief of it upon and as those miraculous operations and effects, by means of which it gained credit, and was established at first, had ceased, it could not rationally have been expected that it should obtain such a cordial and easy credit and reception with them as it had done in those parts of the world which were the theatre of its first appearance and promulgation.

If I mistake not, it has been the opinion of a writer of no inferior character, both for literature and critical knowledge and inquiry, that as the continent of America, for unknown ages, had been detached form the other quarters of the globe, if there ever was a territorial connection and communication between them previous to the time of its discovery by Columbus; whenever Christianity, in its simplicity and efficacy, shall take place in the regions of America and among the aboriginal natives of it and its doctrines and institutions shall be received and adopted, unadulterated by human schemes and systems of theology and unenforced by ecclesiastical domination, some more extraordinary means than have yet been made use of, even those that are miraculous will be necessary; and accordingly that such will be employed by divine providence, in order to its being embraced by them.

Be this as it may, it is evident beyond contradiction, that the success of the missions among them has been very small; and that where there have been strong and promising appearances of the genuine influence and effects of it, they have been far from durable; and they have generally, and in a great measure, returned to their old customs and habits of indolence and improvidence, of intemperance and irreligion.

This has unquestionably been the case with individuals, and I believe in a great measure so with respect to whole tribes of them. There are other causes to which the effects, expressed and implied in the society's queries, may be attributed, without having recourse to those of civilization of manners, industry in business, and the principles, institutions, and precepts of Christianity, especially the two last; the obvious tendency of which is most certainly, altogether the reverse of what has been intimated and stated to the society, from whatever quarter, and from whatever even respectable authority it may have had its rise; for though these effects may be and undoubtedly have been the frequent, if not the constant concomitants of those measures that have been made use of to Christianize the Indians; yet it is very unlogical and inconclusive to infer that they have been derived from, and produced by them, especially when such as have been intimated above, and others that may be mentioned, may be assigned as the much more probable, if not the certain sources of them; for, to proceed, to whatever cause it may be assigned, it is evident, that they are generally considered by white people, and placed as if by common consent, in an inferior and degraded situation and treated accordingly.

Of this, they themselves seem to be not a little sensible. This sinks and cramps their spirits and prevents those manly exertions, which an equal rank with others has a tendency to call forth. If they have landed property as has generally been the case and are intermixed with white people; or if these last are settled near their borders, to say the least, they have been under temptations to encourage their Indian neighbors in idleness, intemperance and needless expenses and thereby do involve them in debt for the sake of preparing the way for the sale and purchase of their lands, which it is probable, under such circumstances, have generally been sold at a very low rate, in order to have their debts discharged; and the game, undoubtedly from the same motives, may have been continued and repeated, by which they have been impoverished and disheartened.

Whether this has been the case in this place or not, it cannot be denied, that near a hundred years ago, they were the exclusive proprietors of this plantation, which I suppose then contained about eight or nine thousand acres; but at this time, the remnant of them, I conjecture, and not without reason, are not owners of half so many hundreds, and I believe not so much as that.

At the beginning of the present century, they were in a state of civil society and were embodied into a military corps. They made choice of town officers, and some of them were invested with military titles and though it does not appear that they had either civil or military commissions, yet they had the countenance and support of the chief magistrate and of other persons of rank and influence. They then held up their heads, considered themselves of some importance, and were for some time stimulated to continue both in the profession of the Christian religion, which they had embraced, and in some measure to conform to the manners of their English neighbors, but their examples of irregularities and excesses had {it is to be apprehended} too great and even a predominant effect upon them.

This, in conjunction with that strange propensity in their constitutions to excess, brought them into some degree of disrepute. Their military parades were too often followed with drinking frolics until at length they were discontinued. And, as the English were, from time to time, gaining settlements among them by the purchase of their lands, they were joined with them by votes of the propriety in the administration of their prudential affairs and at one of their meetings they made choice of one of their number, in conjunction with one of the English settlers, to read the psalm in public. After this, some English from neighboring towns, some of whom through indolence and excess had neglected the cultivation of their own farms and were necessitated to sell, purchased small tracts of the Indians and became settlers and by degrees, obtained possession of more.

The Indians were dispirited and adopted some of the vicious manners of which they had too many examples before their eyes. They became indolent and remiss in their attention to the improvement of their lands to which they had before been encouraged, and in some degree lost their credit. Their civil and military privileges were gradually lessened and finally and exclusively transferred to the English inhabitants, who were become more numerous, and some of whom, it is to be apprehended, took every advantage of them that they could, under color of legal authority and without incurring its censure, to dishearten and depress them.

Under these circumstances, those habits which have a direct tendency to beget and promote bad morals, to injure health and to shorten life, were undoubtedly freely indulged, and the effects were answerable to this, in conjunction with other causes.

Indians are also strangely disposed and addicted to wander from place to place and to make excursions into various parts of the country and sometimes at no small distance from their proper homes, without anything on hand for their support in their perambulations. For this, they depend, with anxious concern, upon the charity and compassion of others. Some of them, after an absence of near twenty years, have returned to their native home.

The most trifling and uninteresting causes have been assigned by some of them for their traveling thirty, forty, fifty miles and more and this sometimes in the most unfavorable seasons of the year and in very bad weather. They have not infrequently taken infant and other children with them in their journeys, which they generally perform very leisurely. Many times they take shelter in barns, and in some old, impaired, and uninhabited buildings and sometimes they sleep on the ground, in the open air, without sufficient covering.

While in this vagrant state, they scarcely ever have any regular meals and hardly any that has been recently prepared for the stated repast of the families into the houses of which they seem to think they have some kind of right to enter, as their forefathers were the original proprietors and possessors of the land.

They are generally not very well furnished with clothing. Most of what they have, they beg, or purchase, with a little temporary labor by the way and what they thus procure is not very comfortable or durable. A cup of such drink as it is known they are not a little fond of is more easily handed to them and with less expense of time and trouble to those who give it than a meal of victuals – and by which they sooner get rid of them. Therefore, the latter is not so often offered to them as the former and though a first draught, under some circumstances may be proper, especially when thirsty, wet and weary; yet their unhappiness is that it leads to a second and to a third and so on as they pass from house to house, until some of them are quite overcharged. This I scarce ever known to have been the case when they have been at home and had access to food as they wanted it and when they have been employed in such business as usually takes up their time in their own houses.

This wandering and irregular practice, especially when applicable to the females, not only exposes their virtue and their morals, but it is a great injury to their own health and to that of their children that accompany them and lays a foundation for consumptive sickness which has generally (exclusive of accidental causes) been the means of their death. To these causes, may be added their males engaging in military service to which they have been very easily enticed.

During several of the first years of my ministry and residence among them, I joined more Indians in marriage and baptized more of them than of the English inhabitants, after which, military expeditions at different periods and in different directions were set on foot and in the several wars that took place between 1754 and 1760, many of them engaged in service; not a small number died while in it; others returned home and brought contagious sickness with them; it spread very fast and carried off some whole families. This was in 1759. In the space of about three months, more than twenty of them died, all of the same disorder, which was a putrid fever; it carried them off in a few days.

But two of those to whom the disorder was communicated recovered; they were both young women. Though their English neighbors were not backward in affording such assistance as the Indians stood in need of, at this time of general calamity, yet but one of them received the infection and to that person it proved mortal. There was a time of sickness and of great mortality in this place and in several neighboring towns a few years before, when but one Indian inhabitant sickened and died of the same fever that proved fatal to many others.

These facts seem to prove that there is a dissimilarity between the natural constitutions of the English and Indians. In what that difference consists, it may be difficult to decide; or if the events just now mentioned, originated from accidental causes it may be difficult to determine what those causes were. Perhaps, these different effects may proceed from different modes of living, as to diet, habitations, and general habits and conduct, or they may be derived from some only, or from all these causes united.

The general disposition and manners of Indians are so distinguishingly characteristic that a very worthy Indian of good understanding, who was a deacon of the church in this place and an ornament to the Christian society for many years and who from the first of his making a Christian profession to the end of his life, was an example of seriousness and temperance, of a regular conversation, and a constant, grave and devout attendant on the public institutions of religion. Upon being asked how it was to be accounted for—that those Indians when youths and were put into English families chiefly in other towns for education, who had free access to such liquors as are the produce of the country, and intoxicating when taken to excess, but who refrained from partaking of them, and were regular and steady in their attention to business— yet soon after they had the command of themselves and of their time and had associated with those who were of the same complexion, became Indians in the reproachful sense of the word, were idle, indolent, and intemperate, and became habituated to all the excesses of those who had not been favored with such advantages, made this laconic reply, "Ducks will be ducks, notwithstanding they are hatched by the hen."

And I myself have thought that by the peculiarity of their natural constitution, in whatever it consists, and by whatever it is discriminated form that of others, they are addicted to, and actually contract such habits of indolence and excess as that they cannot, without the greatest efforts, which they seem not much disposed to make, give up if ever they be entirely rid of them. They seem to be like some plants that thrive best in the shade; if the overgrowth is cut off, they wither and decay, and by degrees are finally rooted out.

To what has been observed, with reference not only to the diminution of Indians in general but to the success of the gospel among them in this place may be added one that I suppose is peculiar to those in this and that is, the unhappy disagreement and contention between the English inhabitants about the placing of the meeting-house, which began in the latter part of my predecessor's time, has at times been revived ever since, and now rages with no small degree of violence among them.

There is no doubt to be made that the disaffected to its present situation have endeavored to warp their minds, not only with respect to the meeting-house, but to alienate them from those who have been employed as missionaries and to discourage their attendance on public worship, which was supported on their account by some charitable funds in England before and has been part of the time since the American revolution; remittances from which have ceased for several years.

Out of these there were yearly donations of blankets and books. These had a tendency to keep them together in a more compact and associated state; but by the circumstances of the times in which we live and by that looseness and licentiousness of manners that are now prevalent and the general indifference about the important matters of religion, and the public institutions of it, that are everywhere visible to the most superficial observer, and of the spirit and influence of which Indians participate their full share; but few of the remnant of them attend public worship; and none are remarkable for the genuine influence of the principles and prospects of that religion which is from above; and it is a poor consolation, when suggested, that the spirit of the gospel, and an attention to its precepts, prevail as much among them, in proportion, as among their English neighbors.

My immediate predecessor observes, in a note, that after the most diligent inquiry, he could find no record of anything referring to a former church in this place; but by Mr. Hutchinson's history it appears that a Christian church was founded here about 150 years ago in consequence of the labors of the renowned Mr. Eliot, of what number it consisted it is not said. *The number of church members is now reduced to two or three.*

It is difficult to ascertain the complete number of those that are now here, or that belong to this place as they are so frequently shifting their place of residence and are intermarried with blacks and some with whites and the various shades between these, and those that are descended from them, make it almost to come to any determination about them. I suppose there are near twenty clear blooded, that are now in this place, and that belong to it.

I find no mention made of any missionaries before the time of my immediate predecessor; but there is an incidental mention of John Nesorummin, an Indian, in the records of the proprietors, who made him a grant of a tract of land, on his living and dying in the ministry of this place. Between twenty and thirty years ago, his son Isaac came and made a claim to his father's land; it could not be ascertained where it lay; and some of the elderly Indians at that time, declared upon their own knowledge, that he left Natick and never returned.

Not any among us retain the knowledge of the language of their progenitors, so as to speak it. One aged woman, a church member of good character, daughter of the good deacon mentioned before, has told me she could understand it when spoken by others; but of this she has not lately had a trial. Upon looking over the record of the propriety, I could not find when it commenced, as the book is very old, in some places defaced, and some pages missing. The entries in the first part are written by Indians, and in the Indian language; other parts in broken English, by an Indian scribe; some of the dates are in a transposed state and some pages are written when the book was inverted; after which, an English clerk was chosen and continued in that office.

By a vote of the propriety, a piece of land was assigned to the English inhabitants to be made use of as burying ground for their dead. This is enclosed by a stone fence. There are two burying places appropriated for the use of Indians, both of which are without any enclosure; they carefully confine themselves to the improvement of these; while blacks, that are unconnected with them, invariably deposit their dead in the burying ground of the white people.

This is far from being the only instance of their being kept detached and separate from the whites. This disconnection is extended much farther and to matters of much greater magnitude. There has not been, so far as my information reaches, any civil coalition between them by any act of incorporating authority; and where any voluntary association has taken place, it has been of short duration. The same may be said as to any religious connection.

Immediately previous to my settling in this place, a church was gathered which consisted partly of English and partly of Indian members; and though some additions were soon after made of Indian professors, yet, from the causes that have already been mentioned, a decrease gradually took place, and has been continuing to the present time. From their being everywhere kept a separate and distinct people, notwithstanding the means that have been employed to form a union between them and different nations, especially in a religious view, one is apt to conjecture that they are the descendants of ancient Jews, though we cannot form a conjecture by what extraordinary methods they obtained a passage to the American continent and settlements, such as they were in the several parts of it. Their case, with the circumstances attending their situation, is truly deplorable, and, contrasted with our own, is adapted in a higher degree to excite gratitude to heaven for the unaccountable and unmerited distinction.

But my limits admonish me of a conclusion. You, Sir, and others, will accept my feeble efforts to comply with the request of your letter. Whatever is redundant or deficient, unadapted or improper, candor will impute, in addition to what has been already exhibited, to the imbecility of my advanced age, being now in the 72nd year of my life; proper reflections upon which will be left to my own mind, and those that relate to Indians to the reflections of others.

And with the most respectful salutations, I write myself your friend and brother.

STEPHEN BADGER

February, 1797

BIBLIOGRAPHY

Ballou's Pictorial Drawing-Room Companion, M.M. Ballou Publisher, Boston, Volume VIII, 1855.

Collections of the Massachusetts Historical Society For The Year 1792, Volume 1, Apollo Press, By Belknap And Hall, Boston, 1792.

Collections of the Massachusetts Historical Society For The Year 1798, Volume 5 of the first series, reprinted John Eliot, No. 5, Court Street, Boston, 1816.

Collections of the Massachusetts Historical Society For The Year 1800, Volume 7 of the first series, reprinted Charles C. Little and James Brown, Boston, 1826.

Coyner, David H., *Tales Of The Lost Trappers*, Hurst and Company Publishers, New York, 1847

Gleason's Pictorial Drawing-Room Companion, F.Gleason Publisher, Boston, Volume II, 1852.

Howe, Henry, *The Great West*, Volumes I and II, E. Morgan and Company Publisher, Cincinnati, 1855.

Lossing, Benson, *Eminent Americans*, Mason Brothers, New York, 1857.

Lossing, Benson, *Pictorial Guide To The Revolution*, Volume II, Harper and Brothers Publishers, New York, 1859.

Triplett, Colonel Frank, *Conquering The Wilderness*, N.D. Thompson and Company, New York, 1883.

Printed in the United Kingdom
by Lightning Source UK Ltd.
131721UK00001B/340/A